THE
COMING COLLAPSE
OF CHINA

THE
COMING COLLAPSE
OF CHINA

Gordon G. Chang

RANDOM HOUSE

NEW YORK

RANDOM HOUSE and colophon are registered trademarks of Random House, Inc.

Library of Congress Cataloging-in-Publication Data

Chang, Gordon G.
The coming collapse of China / Gordon G. Chang.
p.   cm.
Includes index.
ISBN 0-375-50477-X
1. China—Economic conditions—1976–   2. China—Social conditions—1976–
3. China—Politics and government—1976–   I. Title.
HC427.92.C3375   2001
951—dc21   00-054782

Random House website address: www.atrandom.com

Printed in the United States of America on acid-free paper

2 4 6 8 9 7 5 3

First Edition

For the boy who left China in search of a better life—
my father

Revolution is impossible until it is inevitable.

—LEON TROTSKY

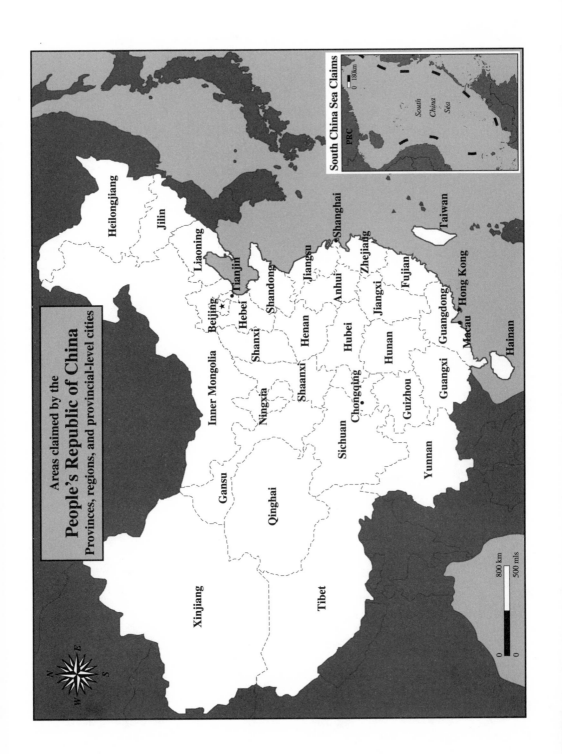

Areas claimed by the
People's Republic of China
Provinces, regions, and provincial-level cities

South China Sea Claims

PRC

South
China
Sea

0   180km

Heilongjiang

Jilin

Liaoning

Xinjiang

Gansu

Qinghai

Tibet

Inner Mongolia

Ningxia

Shaanxi

Shanxi

Beijing

Hebei

Tianjin

Shandong

Henan

Jiangsu

Shanghai

Anhui

Hubei

Zhejiang

Chongqing

Sichuan

Hunan

Jiangxi

Fujian

Taiwan

Guizhou

Guangxi

Guangdong

Hong Kong

Macau

Yunnan

Hainan

N
E
W
S

800 km
500 mls

0
0

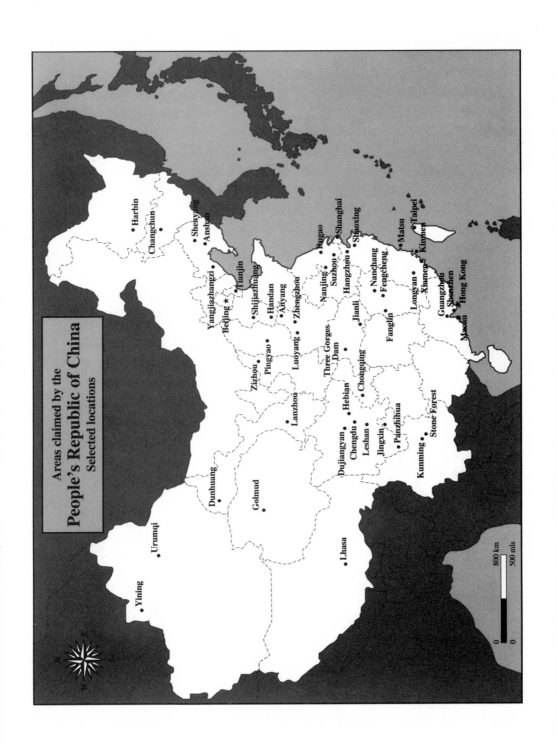

Areas claimed by the
People's Republic of China
Selected locations

CONTENTS

FOREWORD

The Final Chapter

A single spark can start a prairie fire.
—MAO ZEDONG

"SEEK TRUTH FROM FACTS," said former Chinese leader Deng Xiao-ping, who used that Maoist slogan to attack the foundations of Mao Zedong's China. Today some see the facts as pointing to a glorious future for the world's most populous country. Extrapolate current trends, we are told, and in 2010 China will have the world's largest economy.

It is easy to make the case, based on the facts, that China will dominate first Asia and then the rest of the world in some not-too-distant future. Multiply the world's largest population by extraordinarily high rates of economic growth and you get a giant of awesome proportions. Think of the United States, only three times larger and more powerful. To get a glimpse of what is possible in the future, just look at how far China has come since 1978, when Deng Xiaoping began to junk Mao's legacy.

The fear, sometimes overtly stated but under the surface if not, is that China will one day push its neighbors out of the areas it claims and America back across the Pacific. The outrage over the supposed Chinese theft of nuclear secrets from Los Alamos is as much a reflection of

America's apprehension as of its indignation. Today China is the only nation that is targeting the United States with nuclear weapons.

Historical inevitability seems to be on the side of Beijing. China was the "world's sole superpower" for fifteen hundred years after the Roman Empire fell. Chinese art, culture, science, trade, and exploration flourished. Next, European society triumphed and then the United States. What could be more appropriate than China starting the new millennium as the world's leading nation as the torch is returned to its rightful owner?

Foreigners, for various reasons and in many ways, have been fascinated, even blinded, by China, so it has been difficult for them to see the facts. Many have been dazzled by its potential, a theme that binds together most perceptions of China. Others see in China only danger, a threat magnified by the breath of its geography and the mass of its people.

The truth is that China has all the makings of a great nation, one that can fulfill the destiny it sees for itself. And China does not suffer from small vision: President Jiang Zemin is pursuing "Big Country" diplomacy, which seeks recognition of China as an equal to the United States and the European Union on the world stage. It should come as no surprise that Jiang, as a part of these efforts, is pushing China into the World Trade Organization.

On paper, China looks powerful and dynamic even today, less than twenty-five years after Deng Xiaoping began to open his country to the outside world. In reality, however, the Middle Kingdom, as it once called itself, is a paper dragon. Peer beneath the surface, and there is a weak China, one that is in long-term decline and even on the verge of collapse. The symptoms of decay are to be seen everywhere.

The fanaticism that carried Mao from one campaign to another, from the Great Leap Forward to the Cultural Revolution, burned out and left the Chinese empty. Today that spirit has been rekindled as millions follow the teachings of an exile who promises hope. The Communist Party looks at Li Hongzhi and his Falun Gong spiritual movement and sees the images of Mao's peasant army of the late 1940s sweeping across the plains. No wonder China's leading political organization acts as if it were fighting for its survival.

The Communist Party has a destiny, and that is to lead the Chinese people for all time. There has never been any tolerance for other voices, and there is none today. Thus China's leaders could do only one thing when the Falun Gong, without warning, surrounded the Party's leadership compound in Beijing in April 1999. The Party banned that group and drove it underground. But the Falun Gong is fighting back; its members have lost their fear.

Cultists, activists, splittists, and others: China is fighting them all. Beijing "strikes hard" against these elements but so far has been able only to muzzle sentiment, not extinguish it. Dissidents may retreat. Their ideas, however, do not.

There are other threats. Resentment against the corruption of Party officials and lawless government smolders and is infinitely harder to handle than protesters. The price the Party has paid for its monopoly on power is the loss of community with the people of the People's Republic. The Party, as a result, is fundamentally unpopular, surviving only by withdrawing from the lives of the masses.

Then there are the armies of the unemployed roaming China, the single most immediate threat to the continued existence of the Party and the government it dominates. At any one time, the unemployed and underemployed exceed the combined populations of France, Germany, and the United Kingdom. When will they speak?

True, the Communist Party thinks about corruption and resentment and unemployment, but it is unwilling to undertake structural reform. The Party rejects most change of consequence and so does not deal with the fundamental sources of instability. In its fight against its enemies, from the Tibetans to the Taiwanese, the political leadership seeks stability above all else. In seeking stability, the Party is preventing the change that could save the People's Republic.

And change is needed because the symptoms of economic decline are all too evident. State-owned enterprises, or SOEs, the product of Stalinist notions of economic development and Maoist ideas on social planning, are uneconomic. The state-owned banks are hopelessly insolvent, as a group the weakest in the world. Deflation has gripped China for more than three years. Mountains of obsolete inventory scar balance sheets. Foreign investment stagnates. Corruption eats away at the fabric of the economy, and foreign currency flees the country.

If these were simply economic issues, Beijing's technocrats could find answers. Unfortunately, any solutions must first meet the test of ideological correctness. Communist Party theologians have argued, seemingly endlessly, about correct socialist remedies. Deng's contribution to the development of socialist theory was not to let theory get in the way of development. "'Do not debate!' is one of my inventions," said the late Chinese leader. His heirs take a different approach.

As time passes, the underlying problems fester. Economic dislocations become social ones, with dark political overtones. At some point there will be no solution. Then the economy, and the government, will collapse. We are not far from that time.

Can China's leaders prevent the economic tragedy that is unfolding? The central government is now doing the only thing it can: keeping the economy going through fiscal stimulus on a massive scale. How to pay for all of this? China's budget deficit has mushroomed in the last few years. Add the bad and nonperforming loans of the state-owned banks to the official national debt, and China's financial status looks precarious.

How much time does China have? No one knows for sure, but China cannot continue to spend at the current pace for much longer. Beijing has about five years to put things right. No government, not even China's, can defy the laws of gravity forever.

Time is in extremely limited supply now that China is on the verge of joining the World Trade Organization. In order to become a member, China has agreed to open its markets. U.S. Trade Representative Charlene Barshefsky says that the changes to be unleashed by WTO accession will be "profoundly important." That is understating the case: accession will shake China to its foundations.

Commentators assume that Jiang favored WTO membership because he wanted to further reform. It's more likely that he thought that by doing something truly dramatic, he would find a place in history beside Mao and Deng. So now we need to know if China's economy can survive the competition that WTO membership will bring. Are the Chinese leaders being misled by their own reports of improving SOE profitability? Do they really believe that their insolvent and backward banks can compete with modern financial institutions? This would not be the first time that Beijing has been trapped by exaggerated notions of its own accomplishments. In the catastrophic Great Leap Forward tens of millions of peasants died because Mao deluded himself by believing glowing, and completely falsified, reports of crop production. The world can only hope that Jiang Zemin has not made a similar miscalculation. His insistence on maintaining orthodox and gradualist policies and at the same time accepting the shock therapy of WTO membership does not provide much basis for optimism.

Foreign businesses have put so much hope and effort into China's WTO accession. Behind all the lofty talk of the benefits of world trade is anticipation. They know that on a more level playing field they will prevail. Color them eager. And color an unprepared China endangered.

At present, the Party and the central government are able to control 1.3 billion people. Virtually every day unpaid workers, resentful peasants, and other disaffected elements of society take to the streets, but the mechanisms put into place over the past five decades are still able to maintain social order. One day, the central government will not be able to fight all those who challenge it; there simply will be too many. When that time comes, the consequences will be severe. Virulent protests will spin out of control and meet the full fury of the state. No government can withstand the will of all of its people.

The challenges facing China's current crop of leaders are more difficult than the ones that Deng confronted. Deng had time; Jiang does not. Deng's party stood supreme and for the most part unchallenged. Jiang's is diminished by two decades of reform and a decade of withdrawal. Deng chose to fight only one enemy at a time. Jiang has decided to battle them all, both real and imagined, from those who seek to divide his country to those who merely want to pray in peace. He also wants to be a world leader, a role he does not have time to play.

In 1992, when economic reform efforts flagged, Deng Xiaoping made his famous Southern Tour. By the sheer weight of his personality and vision, he turned China around. Only a few years later, there is no one in Beijing who can, or would, do the same. His successor, Jiang Zemin, also urges the populace to seek truth, though with much less conviction. Today China's political leadership, not liking the facts it sees, blinds itself to the urgency of the problems it faces. Worse, there is little agreement as to what to do about them. As a result, progress is measured at the speed of molasses. In the past, China could muddle along. Now, however, its WTO agreements have put a specific timetable on structural reform. Unfortunately, the central government is not ready to fulfill the commitments Jiang has made so easily. The consequence of failure will be the end of Chinese institutions as they now exist.

Today China is only halfway to somewhere with no consensus as to the future. It is suffering from the pain of a transition partially completed, yet at the same time it does not enjoy most of the benefits of modernization. Liberalization will help China, but a slowly reforming society stagnates. The center has given up enough control to let destructive forces loose, but not enough to complete the job of transformation. China is drifting, unwilling to go forward as fast as it must and unable to turn back.

Remarkable progress has been made since December 1978, when Deng Xiaoping pushed aside Mao's chosen successor, the hapless Hua Guofeng. The issue, however, is not whether China is doing the right things these days. Look at the country, and you will find evidence of solutions that, with time and political will, could work. If China had, say, thirty years, everything might come out right. But whether China is on the right road is not the matter at hand.

When historians write the final chapter on the People's Republic, they will say that there wasn't enough time. Jiang Zemin's cautious—sometimes glacial—approach to reform is not suited to the severe problems that are plaguing China or, for that matter, a world where the pace of change is accelerating. Although the collapse of the Soviet Union has highlighted the deficiencies of moving too fast, Beijing is erring by progressing too slowly. Misery can hit from either direction.

Mao said that it takes only one spark to start a prairie fire. The next spark could cause the conflagration that history will remember. Now it's only a matter of time.

Shanghai
March 2001

ACKNOWLEDGMENTS

Robert Elegant isn't—at least he wasn't on the day I met him in April 2000. The author of all things Chinese was sporting his light tan bush jacket, but there's no wild game in the Hilton, at least of the four-legged variety. He was in Shanghai to research his latest book, a "biography" of China's grandest city. No, he wasn't elegant, but he was perceptive about the leadership of the country he had introduced to so many readers around the world. "They'll forgive you for anything except for being right," he said, referring to China's leaders. Perhaps he was speaking from experience.

The regime will also not forgive you for being critical. Senior Communist Party leaders are a sensitive lot these days. And because they're also unforgiving, I must mention that only seven people knew the theme of this book when they helped me. The innocent helpers include Julian Baum, Laura Burt, Paul Cavey, Leslie Chang (the *Wall Street Journal* reporter, not my sister of the same name), Matt Eaton, Jonathan Fenby, Don and Rosanna Hall, Tion Kwa, Bernice Lee, Karby Leggett, Steven McCormack, Joe McDonald, Matt Miller, Rachel Morarjee, Trish Saywell, Henny Sender, Mike Shelley, Evan Stewart, Chris Tibbs, Jing Ulrich, Alysha Webb, and Peter Wonacott. I want to especially thank Sed Crest, editor of *China Law & Practice,* who granted permission to use portions of my articles that previously appeared in his publication, and Jerry Cohen, who pushed me into the noble profession of writing.

The innocent also include about a dozen Chinese citizens living in China. To thank them by name might end up causing them harm. When the prediction in this book comes true, I will acknowledge their assistance. To them goes my heartfelt appreciation. My research assistant, one of the unnamed dozen, found the sources of many quotations from Chinese leaders, past and present, and he remarked to his mother, "Mao Zedong and Deng Xiaoping said a lot of things that contradict each other." To foreigners, that is not news, but to some Chinese, raised in Mainland schools, it is. "You can't say these things outside the home," his mother, showing the fear that the regime instills, cautioned him. Now you can see why writing this book became a passion: the Chinese have a right to know their past—as well as their future.

Now for the guilty, those who knew the theme of this book beforehand. They are Susanna Porter, Rosalie Siegel, Janet Wygal, Lynn Anderson, Matt Thornton, Denise Lager, and my wife, Lydia. First comes the staff of the Porter School; that is, the Susanna Porter School for Nonfiction. Thank you, Susanna, Janet, Matt, and Lynn, for many things, especially for your patience.

And thank you, Rosalie and Denise. Rosalie Siegel's office in lovely Pennington, New Jersey, is piled high with unsolicited proposals sent by aspiring authors—so high that on some days she and Denise can play hide-and-seek among the stacks. I thank both for giving me so much help. And I again give offerings to the gods for guiding Rosalie and Denise toward reading my proposal instead of somebody else's.

Then there is my wonderful wife. This book could have been written without her, but not by me. She worked tirelessly and with good humor. She was relentless, pushing me to do my best. Most important, she did not complain when I wanted to leave my day job to write this book. That said, any mistakes in these pages are hers.

Finally, my daughter, who thinks it's cool that I wrote this book, has lost more than one vacation with her father recently. Maybe this should be an apology, but I will frame it as an acknowledgment instead. Thanks, Winnie, for being so understanding. Oh, almost forgot: that goes for my wife as well.

THE
COMING COLLAPSE
OF CHINA

I

The Dinner Party

The Revolution Has Grown Old

[A] revolution is not a dinner party, or writing an essay, or painting a picture, or doing embroidery; it cannot be so refined, so leisurely and gentle, so temperate, kind, courteous, restrained and magnanimous. A revolution is an insurrection, an act of violence by which one class overthrows another.

——MAO ZEDONG

THEY WILL MOVE Mao Zedong's body soon; it lies on hallowed ground. When the Communist Party of China falls, when the third Chinese revolution succeeds, they will move him from Tiananmen Square, the center of Beijing and the heart of China. So much history has occurred in Tiananmen, and so much more has yet to happen. The People's Republic was proclaimed there, and there, inevitably, its end will be announced. And when it falls, the people will take Mao's body from the square to mark a new beginning.

"We should die fighting," said Mao. The Party, born of conflict, knows no other way. It will not politely leave when the people demand it; they will have to take back their government by force. Revolution is not a dinner party, Mao informed us, and it's not gentle, temperate, or kind. It's an insurrection and an act of violence. And China's history has set the pattern. Dynasties appear strong, even toward their end. Chinese rulers resist to the last moment, even when it is clear that change must occur. It seems that peaceful evolution is not yet part of this people's story. The Chinese have endured so much during the past century. If all were fair, this century, the one that has just begun, should be kinder to them. It won't work out that way, however. "We should die fighting," Mao said, and that's just what is going to happen. Their suffering is not over yet.

So the Communist Party has shown the world that only force will be able to move it. The people are supposed to be intimidated by this colossal display of obstinacy, and, at least for the moment, many are. But they just wait in silence and let their resentments fester. The Party knows how to suppress, but it no longer has the power to lead. It has forgotten what once made it great.

"The Revolution has become a dinner party," says Maggie Farley, who has taken Mao Zedong's quip on revolution and stood it on its head. Her one short sentence summarizes the history of the People's Republic.

Both Mao and Farley are correct. Indeed, if Mao could see what has become of his China, he would agree with Farley, a journalist and former resident of Shanghai. Mao, unprompted, might even say the same thing himself. He would, no doubt, utter Farley's words as a condemnation of the current state of affairs or perhaps as one of his many calls to action. No, revolution is not a dinner party, but there is little that is revolutionary in present-day China. Farley conveys the image of a mass movement institutionalized, something that Mao, who promoted the concept of "continuous revolution," sought to prevent.

Today the people no longer want Mao's revolution or the party that administers it. And so the People's Republic is going to fall, just like its predecessors. History shows that the Chinese people, once aroused, will not be denied. The Ming and the Qing, the last two imperial dynasties, and Chiang Kai-shek's Kuomintang, the Nationalists, all fell quickly.

For the Qing, it was over almost as soon as it began. The Chinese, disgusted by their oppressive and inept rulers, demanded change. Some sought constitutional restraints on imperial power and others wanted revolution, but all knew that the current system had failed China. At the end it took just an incident—and almost any would have sufficed—to trigger rapid collapse. An accidental explosion in October 1911 ended in the abdication, four months later, of Puyi, the six-year-old emperor. With him went a dynasty of more than two hundred years and imperial rule of two thousand. Sun Yat-sen's Revolutionary Alliance stood triumphant; China, for the first time in its history, had a republican form of government. And for the first time in many decades there was hope.

China's troubles had not ended, however. Turmoil followed the first days of Sun's Republic of China. Disorder resulted in national weakness, which triggered yet another wave of idealism and activism. The Communist Party of China was founded in 1921 in those crosscurrents, and during that time of turbulence the Communists thrived. They espoused the hope of Chinese nationalism and struck a responsive chord in both city and countryside.

Sun Yat-sen died in 1925, but by then new leaders had already taken his place. Chiang Kai-shek, a general who married a sister of Sun's widow, succeeded in uniting most of China under Kuomintang rule in the late 1920s. The Kuomintang, the renamed Revolutionary Alliance, and the Communist Party were born of a common Leninist model and throughout their histories have been allies and enemies, creating a confusing tale from the 1920s through the 1940s. They struggled together as allies to unite China and drive out their common enemy, the Japanese, but they also could not help but fight one another. The Kuomintang's campaign against the Communists, the story of brother against brother, resulted in bitter struggle. At one point, the Communist army faced extinction. Beginning in October 1934 from inland Jiangxi Province, Mao Zedong's force of 80,000 started a 6,000-mile retreat that took slightly more than a year. When the legendary Long March was over, the army was reduced to a tenth of its original size, but it survived to fight again. Further conflict was inevitable: two Leninist parties could not inhabit the same space.

During the Second World War, China, briefly united under Chiang Kai-shek, was split into pieces controlled by the Kuomintang, the Japanese, the Communists, the Tibetans, and the Muslims. Chiang's Kuomintang had failed; the Chinese fear of disunity had come to pass. Chiang could not hold China together, so he did not succeed in leading its people.

When the end came for the Kuomintang, it came quickly. Chiang Kai-shek had large forces, but Mao had something more important. The ragtag Communist army swept out of the countryside after the Second World War to surround the cities and prevail. The people had had enough of

Kuomintang corruption, brutality, and incompetence. In 1949, Chiang's forces simply disintegrated, falling to the Communists as fast as the Ming Dynasty had to the Qings three centuries earlier. His capital of Nanjing surrendered without resistance. Chiang could only retreat to Taiwan.

"We the 475 million Chinese people have now stood up and the future of our nation is infinitely bright," proclaimed Mao Zedong. On October 1, 1949, he would declare the founding of his republic from the Gate of Heavenly Peace, the main entrance to the Forbidden City of the Ming and Qing emperors. And he would make the old imperial capital of Beijing the Communist seat of power. With the exception of Taiwan, Mao would unify China within a year. Decades of internal strife and disunity would come to an end. With the exception of the tiny enclaves of Hong Kong and Macau, foreigners had been removed from Chinese soil. A chapter of humiliation, a period spanning hundreds of years, had closed. Chinese revolutionaries had prevailed for the second time in the twentieth century, but now they would remake the country as they saw fit. It was morning again in China.

"A clean sheet of paper has no blotches," wrote Mao, "and so the newest and most beautiful words can be written on it, the newest and most beautiful pictures can be painted on it." China was war-torn, exhausted, and hungry. It was what Mao later would call "poor and blank." To him, that was a virtue. He could build New China as he saw fit. He had the power, and the people, poor and blank, were eager to follow. His radical transformation of Chinese society began in the countryside with land reform. Redistribution built initial support for the new regime. Collectivization, more radical in scope, would follow.

For a time private industry survived. Despite mass campaigns designed to make them compliant, patriotic "national capitalists" continued to operate their own businesses alongside the government's enterprises, which had been confiscated from foreigners and departed followers of Chiang Kai-shek. At first the private sector contributed about 40 percent of China's industrial production. Mao either thought that China needed a transitory stage of capitalism before socialism could develop or felt that he could not do everything at once. In any event, China's mixed economy, part public and part private, seemed to work well in the initial years.

Mao, however, changed course. In 1953, China both inaugurated the

First Five-Year Plan, which called for rapid industrialization along Stalinist concepts, and formally announced the "transition to socialism." State-owned enterprises, soon to embody China's industrial might, were formed. Nationalization at the end of 1955 ended most private ownership of industrial assets.

The push to Stalinize industry was not controversial at the time. Deng Xiaoping, who later won praise for experimenting with capitalist techniques, was a supporter of this radical step to Stalinism. National pride, not to mention considerations of self-sufficiency, overcame Communist Party cadres' misgivings about following a Soviet model of industrialization. Moreover, initial economic success, aided by contributions from China's neighbor to the north, ensured continued support of the idea within the Party.

In order to create and maintain state enterprises, the People's Republic developed a modern bureaucracy, the largest China had ever known and one of the world's largest up to that time. Of course, state-owned enterprises, or SOEs, did not operate according to market forces; they moved according to decisions made by economic planners, who organized themselves into bureaus and ministries that grew in both size and number. Mao wanted rapid industrialization, and he wanted a centrally planned economy. Yet he could not stand the bureaucratic and professional elites that came into existence to sustain these goals.

Mao's irreconcilable ambitions led to the concept of "permanent revolution," which was later transformed into "continuous revolution." These theoretical notions then resulted in the excesses for which he is remembered: the Hundred Flowers movement, the ensuing antirightist campaign, the Great Leap Forward, and the mother of all Chinese upheavals, the Great Proletarian Cultural Revolution. Although different in nature, all these events, one following the other in quick succession beginning in 1957, were the result of Mao's desire to continually cleanse the Party and central government of the bureaucrats and others needed to run the centralized society and economy he had envisioned in the early 1950s.

These campaigns forever scarred China and the party that conceived them. The Great Leap Forward, for instance, was intended to produce a thousand years of Communist happiness. More to the point, Mao, the Great Helmsman, promised in 1958 that China would catch up to the

West in fifteen years. Mao's utopian mass campaign to decentralize industrialization to backyard furnaces and collectivize agriculture into communes ended in the deaths of tens of millions of people. The effort devastated agricultural production, but falsified statistics showed bountiful harvests and those claims led to tragedy. Millions starved while granaries were full with crops of past years. Bodies literally littered the fields, but few were willing to tell Party leaders that the people were suffering from their ill-conceived policies. Steps to alleviate the greatest famine in history could not be taken as the Party, founded on revolutionary fervor and optimism, could do anything but admit its own failure.

As a result, the glorious Communist Party brought the People's Republic almost to the brink of collapse. By 1961, even senior Party cadres recognized that they had no choice but to abandon the Great Leap. China then reemphasized large-scale industrialization. State-owned enterprises, as a concept, could not help but look good in comparison to the Great Leap's utopian ideal of decentralized communal development, which had caused such unimaginable suffering to the Chinese peasantry.

Then there was the Cultural Revolution. Mao launched that bizarre campaign in 1966 in yet another attempt to revitalize society, this time by destroying all that was old: customs, habits, culture, and thinking. Millions of youths roamed the country in one of the most abnormal periods of history. State-sponsored chaos destroyed the institutions of society and scarred generations of Chinese. The People's Liberation Army eventually restored order in the country after clashing with youthful Red Guards, and by 1969 the campaign was declared over. A revision of official history, undertaken to support the political aims of later leaders, now recounts that the Cultural Revolution lasted until 1976, when members of the infamous Gang of Four, which included Mao's wife, were arrested. China emerged from an era of struggle and began the arduous task of rebuilding.

China's economy had been shattered by the Cultural Revolution. Moreover, during the last years of Mao's rule it became evident that the development model he had copied from the Soviets was unsuitable. It was not so much that China's industry was technologically deficient; it was more that the nature of the system, with its large central planning apparatus and its overriding emphasis on output, was grossly inefficient. The process of reform tentatively started just at the end of Mao's reign.

Zhou Enlai, his premier, announced the now-famous Four Modernizations (of agriculture, industry, defense, and science and technology) in January 1975. With Mao's death in September 1976, the way was cleared for innovation that hadn't been possible during his rule. First Hua Guofeng, Mao's chosen (but politically inept) successor, and then Deng Xiaoping began to roll back the more utopian and unrealistic aspects of Mao's achievements.

Deng's name became synonymous with change as a refreshing burst of experimentation followed his successful grab for control of the Party. Almost everything was remade, whether or not it was covered by one of the designated modernizations. During these heady times even unorthodox methods were tried. The Party of Public Assets, a literal translation of the name of the Chinese Communist Party, experimented with privatization, a dreaded term in today's China. Stock of state-owned enterprises was first issued in the middle of the 1980s, mostly to employees. Then equity markets opened in Shanghai and Shenzhen. People were again free to get rich. That, Deng claimed, was "glorious." "Poverty is not socialism," he reminded Party theoreticians. Deng could accept the notion that some would achieve wealth before others, however unpalatable that was to those who demanded egalitarianism before all else. After all, Mao was no longer able to complain.

In the extraordinary era from 1978 through the middle of the 1990s, China had the fastest-growing economy in the world, perhaps the fastest in world history. Most people benefited, and a few, by speculating in the volatile stock markets or starting their own businesses (or both), became wealthy. Enrichment of the few, however, was not the point of the exercise. In the eyes of Party cadres, it was an undesirable but inevitable consequence of reform.

Reform, however, was taken only so far. State-owned enterprises proved remarkably resistant to change. SOEs, inspired by Stalin and designed by Mao, were not only the provider of goods to the state, they were also the primary deliverer of social services to the people. In a completely self-contained society, such enterprises could prosper. In an increasingly interconnected world, they are uncompetitive and have no place at all. Today, at the beginning of the Tenth Five-Year Plan, China's planners still do not know how to help them. SOEs are the greatest economic problem facing the People's Republic.

Years ago, Beijing made a serious problem worse by postponing real reform. Instead of trying to restructure Chinese industry, the government decided to buy time. China forced its state-owned banks to lend to the state-owned enterprises. A seemingly endless stream of free liquidity kept these enterprises alive but ultimately made the banks sick—very sick. No one knows the extent of the damage that Beijing has inflicted on its financial system. This much, however, is clear: instead of one critical problem, China now has two.

As Beijing dithers, the state sector is bleeding workers. Rural poverty forces people off the land and into the cities, where they simply add to the throngs looking for a livelihood. People are losing their jobs as China makes the transition from a "command" economy to a semi–market economy and from an agricultural society to an urban one. At the same time, the economy has slowed from the unsustainably high growth of the early 1990s, leaving serious economic dislocations in its wake. There is no comprehensive "safety net" for Chinese workers, and the listless economy these days cannot absorb all of those who have been thrown out of work. Thus unemployment and its cousin underemployment threaten stability. Those victimized by change hold the Party accountable.

The biggest victim of reform, however, is the Party itself. Reform has meant that the Party has removed itself from the lives of the people and given them choice. The Maoist mechanisms of social control have been loosened. A totalitarian state has become merely an authoritarian one. The drifting Party has lost first its meaning for the populace and then its vibrancy. For many, it no longer provides. Today it may talk about itself being the "vanguard production force," but few listen. They know that the economic miracle that foreigners are talking about is nothing more than the state letting the Chinese be Chinese. The government hasn't created anything; it has just gotten out of the way.

As the Communist Party stumbles into the future, the past is being lost. And the people are losing something too. The patriotism that supported the Party is being replaced by selfishness. Soong Qingling, the wife of Sun Yat-sen and one of the first vice chairmen of the People's Republic, would be appalled. "To help China is to help yourselves," she said. Deng correctly reversed that proposition. He realized, after seeing decades of Maoist campaigns, that idealism mostly resulted in misery.

China would be helped only as ordinary citizens went about bettering their own lot, and Deng's reforms made it possible for them to do that.

"Reform," Deng explained, "is China's second revolution." "Revolution" may be somewhat of a strong term for what did, in fact, happen, but there is no denying that the China he passed to Jiang Zemin, his chosen successor, in 1994, the year of his last public appearance, was hardly recognizable as the one he had taken from Hua Guofeng at the end of 1978.

Except in one area. The Fifth Modernization, say dissidents in China, is democracy. There was a brief moment when that concept could have succeeded. Sun Yat-sen, the founder and first president of the Republic of China, believed that eventually the Chinese people should govern themselves. He was not around long enough for the concept to take hold, however. In 1912, on the republic's second day in power, Sun relinquished his position to the military leader who had arranged the abdication of the Qings. The second president did not share any of Sun's democratic notions and eventually had himself proclaimed emperor after subverting new institutions of self-governance. That proved unpopular with just about everyone. China began to disintegrate: provinces declared themselves independent, and warlords rose to power. Democracy did not have time to take root. The Chinese were not yet ready to govern themselves—or at least those with power were not ready to allow it.

Representative government made no progress in the following decades. Chiang Kai-shek was no democrat. Mao talked about "democratic centralism" and "people's democratic dictatorship," but those concepts bore no resemblance to democracy. He spoke of "the people," but the poet in him was just using words. There was no place in New China for new forms of government. Power would be concentrated in the hands of one party, and power in that organization would be concentrated in the hands of a few. The Communist Party had a destiny, and that was to rule.

While he ruled, Deng Xiaoping predicted that China would have national elections in fifty years. That proved, however, to be just idle chatter. Deng was prepared to make only the smallest concessions toward mass participation in the political process. China's leading political organization had no intention of permitting real reform. Perhaps the memories of the turbulence of the years following the fall of the Qings was still too strong. In any event, change was glacial and not enough for some Chinese who wanted more.

The tumult of the Beijing Spring of 1989, capping demonstrations stretching back for more than a decade, could have led the way toward democratization, but calls for self-governance were premature. Said one 1989 protester, Han Dongfeng, "I didn't really know what democracy was, and I just adopted [the] word." In any event, Deng Xiaoping was not prepared to relent to the Tiananmen Square protesters, whatever their concept of democracy was. There would be no challenges to Party rule. The People's Liberation Army hunted the people in the streets of Beijing during the evening of June 3 and in the early hours of June 4 of that year. Ordinary Beijing residents fought bare-handed against tanks and armored vehicles as the vicious Twenty-seventh Army made its way to Tiananmen Square to eject the students and their allies. By dawn perhaps two thousand people were dead. The exact toll will never be known. It was state-sanctioned murder. And after it was over, the world was appalled.

Although that night is now years old, the Chinese still mourn. Nonetheless, the Party's leadership refuses to look back with anything but disdain for what Deng called the "dregs of society," China's own common citizens who dared to protest. "Apologize to your people," say the people of the world. The Party is adamant: it will not. Nor has it even come to terms with what it did. "At that time, I was the chief of general staff, and I can tell you in a responsible and serious manner that not a single person lost his life in Tiananmen Square," said Defense Minister Chi Haotian during an official visit to Washington in late 1996.

Perhaps the leadership in Beijing is still too close to the events of that night in the square to face the truth. Perhaps Jiang Zemin remembers that he was unexpectedly elevated to the Party's highest post at that time to restore order and orthodoxy. Yet there is more. Having admitted that Mao made "serious mistakes," the Party cannot say the same of his successor, Deng. That would set a pattern and suggest that it's the system that is at fault, the system that Defense Minister Chi and all the others still inhabit. And there is one more reason: the program of the Party today was set by Deng, so criticism of him would strike too close to home.

Deng's pragmatic ideas, designed to keep the Party in power after Tiananmen, accelerated change and further reduced meddling in people's lives. As a result, the vices of old China returned: trafficking in human beings, for instance. "I forgot how to laugh or cry," says Jin Yi, who was sold into marriage when she was twelve for the equivalent of a few hundred U.S. dollars. "Each time I did, his family would beat me." While Beijing loosened Maoist controls, other evils, such as corruption, gambling, drugs, concubinage, and prostitution, reappeared and now threaten society.

For both good and bad, Deng Xiaoping remade China, and on balance it is a far better country for all that he did. Today, however, the nation must carry on with tasks that he left unfinished. China has a modern veneer now, but the essence of Mao's system remains. That Deng did not change. Senior cadres still have the power to demand, and they still do not understand why they should not use it. And like Chi Haotian, they create their own truth rather than seek it. His Tiananmen Square lie, breathtaking in its boldness, reveals more than just the contempt of the Chinese leadership for the rest of us. It says that China's current leaders have not left their Maoist universe, where they control the reality they want others to see. Beijing's senior cadres will not, and cannot, change the nature of the Party or the government it leads. Unless that happens, however, there is only so much more progress that will occur in China.

The limits of Mao's system have just about been reached. Party cadres say they want the benefits of the Internet, but they also want to be able to censor it. They say they want to be a technological leader of this century, but they restrict innovation. They say they want a modern society, but they cannot relinquish their hold. Those who rule from Beijing want the benefits of change, but they do not want change itself. That's the fundamental contradiction of today's China: progress will soon be blocked by the confines originally set by Mao and enforced by his successors.

So there is little realism in the upper reaches of Beijing today, mostly doctrinaire answers. Today's leaders, for instance, carry on with Deng Xiaoping's program as if conditions had not changed since his passing from the scene. Even as they push the country forward economically, they are trying to freeze the process of political development. Wang Dan, a student leader in the euphoric days of Tiananmen, subsequently remarked, "Political reform must go hand in hand with economic reform. If that contradiction gets bigger and bigger, one day it will explode." That could happen someday, but if activist Wang is looking for something that will explode before then, he should focus on corruption, both in the government and, worse, in the Party itself. Resentment over the looting of the country by its keepers is widespread. Corruption is at a zenith, and the people have noticed. The Party can only ask its cadres not to steal. Sometimes it metes out punishment, but it cannot attack the root cause of the problem: the fact that the power of the Party's cadres is unchecked. Taking away power would require fundamental change. And Jiang Zemin is by no means ready for that. Instead, he stops government activity for months so that the Party's cadres can learn more about Marxist theory. That is surely not the answer for China in the twenty-first century. Mao, however, would heartily approve. "You must put politics in command," he commanded. Jiang has obeyed. And the Chinese people will, once again, pay the price.

The Chinese have suffered as much in the last century as any other people. They at least have stability now, but that may be all their current government is willing to give them. The Party remembers China's days of national weakness and disintegration and is not prepared to take any risks for a more lasting political system. It remembers the Cultural Revolution and has become obsessed with stability and order. And the Party mistakes today's absence of conflict for consent. There is a difference. Repression can work, but only for so long. It holds no good outcomes for the Chinese state, at least over the long term. The Party's faltering campaign against the resistant Falun Gong proves that it knows only how to censor, imprison, and suppress. It can no longer inspire or even teach. Its tactics are counterproductive, creating the very thing that it is most worried about: a determined opposition.

Senior cadres resort to repression because they are really concerned about only one thing. "All these leaders care about is staying in power," says a middle-aged investment banker with a sleek ponytail and a black silk Mao-style jacket. "They're not the same." To her, the successors to the charismatic Mao Zedong just don't measure up. She's right, of course, but she's not a fair judge. Her father is considered one of the "immortals," one of a select few men who fought alongside Mao and with him built New China. Yet even in her bias, she perceives clearly that today's China is not what her father or Mao had in mind. They would disapprove of what they would now see, but one thing would trouble them above all else. The leaders of their party, the Communist Party of China, are still powerful, still dominating the country they lead, but they have lost their way.

If the People's Republic is to survive for more than a few years, it needs a leader, someone on the order of Deng Xiaoping, perhaps, with that combination of vision and realism and the political skills to match. Jiang Zemin is not such a person, and there is no one on the horizon who is. If a real leader from the Party does not step forth soon, the Chinese people will find their own. And then China will once again be racked by struggle. Han Dongfeng, the Tiananmen Square protester, knows something about struggle. This labor leader was imprisoned in the days after the suppression of the demonstrations in 1989. In jail he began to hit his head against the wall in anger and shout, "Those who can hear me just remember what I am saying. I will never be Chinese in my next life. Don't be Chinese. It is too horrible to be Chinese, too sad."

There are plenty of Chinese this evening, but nothing is horrible and no one is sad. If anything, some are a bit too merry. The crowd, numbering in the hundreds, is boisterous as free-flowing liquor enlivens the revelers on the rooftop terrace of Shanghai's historic Peace Hotel. The city around them is sparkling, floodlit in clashing colors against a pitch black sky, and the Huangpu River just below is bustling with commerce even at this late hour. On the roof this perfect evening the wealthy and the famous mingle with Shanghainese on the make; pride, arrogance, and envy all on display. Personalities in black tie chat with gentlemen in long gray robes, and women in floor-length gowns mix with friends in tight-fitting *qi pao* split almost to the waist. Guests have traveled across China and halfway around the world to be on display this evening in the radiant city that is Shanghai.

But now the guests take their seats and the table chatter slowly dies. They look at the figure standing before them this Saturday evening in October 1999, just days after the fiftieth anniversary of the People's Republic. The ornate ballroom at the top of the Peace Hotel is finally quiet. The tall American woman is particularly striking; she's in her finest revolutionary red. Her gown, covered in hundreds of Mao buttons of red and gold, is a fashion statement, however, not a political one, because she's here to have fun. She takes a look around the room before starting. "The Revolution has become a dinner party," says Maggie Farley, and the crowd cheers.

Yes, the revolution has become a dinner party. The People's Republic today is not gentle, temperate, or kind, but it is not revolutionary either. The country and the party that leads it are now both old in their ways. The zeal that carried Mao from near defeat to total victory has been spent, lost in all the campaigns and programs that have gone wrong. Here, in the city where the Chinese Communist Party was born, there is nothing that is revolutionary.

Nothing, that is, except the opponents of the current regime. They are weak today, but that will change. The Chinese now want something different, as they did at the end of the Qing Dynasty and at the fall of the Kuomintang. The people are no longer poor and blank. They know what they want.

The Chinese will take what they want one day, and that day will be soon. The truth is that Party cadres will have only themselves to blame when that time comes. They have, over more than five decades, failed. Their republic is corrupt, repressive, and brutal. Its sheet of paper is no longer unblemished. China, for all its recent progress, is still poor. Chinese history has a pattern: governments like the current one fall. In the spring of 1989, Wang Ruoshui, then deputy editor in chief of *People's Daily,* the Party's flagship newspaper, marched with students and workers in the streets of Beijing.

> We walked to Tiananmen, where it was a sea of people. I remembered how I had joined the demonstrations in the late 1940s, but that was under the rule of the Nationalists. The slogan we shouted back then was "We want freedom and democracy." I thought, "My goodness, after so many years we've gone full circle, and now we're back shouting the same slogan."

The Nationalists of Chiang Kai-shek fell because Wang Ruoshui wanted freedom and democracy and was willing to take to the streets. Their successor will fall too. Karl Marx himself said, "History repeats itself." And when it does, they will move Mao Zedong's body from Tiananmen Square and the Chinese people will have their way.

2

Lake of Gasoline

The Discontent of the People Is Explosive

> Without anybody organizing a demonstration, the passersby had turned into demonstrators who filled the main square in Prague.
>
> —VÁCLAV HAVEL

IN A FEW HOURS it will be midnight, and the Year of the Golden Dragon, the luckiest in the sixty-year cycle of the lunar calendar, will begin in Tiananmen Square, the center of Beijing. It is February 4, 2000, and China is bidding farewell to the Year of the Rabbit. The majestic Gate of Heavenly Peace, the entrance to the Forbidden City in Beijing, is outlined in white lights, giving a cheery glow to the festivities below. Crowds are celebrating in the heart of China.

Tourists are not the only ones in Tiananmen Square this evening. Falun Gong practitioners, both young and old, brave the frigid air. Like many days during the last nine months, they are gathering in the square to ask the state for freedom to practice their beliefs. This night is no different, except that they are all bundled in warm clothing now. Groups of practitioners congregate around the flagpole in the center of the square and unfurl banners. It is not long before police spot them and intervene, hustling dozens of the protesters toward large blue-and-white vans parked nearby. The state is especially well prepared on this special night.

There is a group of practitioners by a van, and officers are shoving them into its side door. A woman is pulled down by her hair, but she recovers by holding on to one of her tormentors, a plainclothesman dressed entirely in black. The young have no problem stepping up into the vehicle, but an old man in a green army jacket appears overwhelmed. He is spun around and shoved in the back by the officer in black. The old man crumples, his arms flailing as he hits the ground. The man in black spits and then kicks the old man in the kidneys while he is lying on the pavement. A plainclothes officer in a white coat, approaching this van, roughly pulls the old man up by the collar and drags him toward it.

More than a hundred Falun Gong practitioners were arrested that night in Beijing, and about two thousand others are believed to have been detained across China in the first week of the Year of the Golden Dragon. They included two soldiers, in uniform, who were practicing their Falun Gong exercises in Tiananmen Square.

Arrests have not worked: Falun Gong protests continue. Once again blood stains the pavement of Tiananmen as security forces beat and gag devotees in the square. Children are incarcerated clinging to their mothers. Scores of practitioners have died in detention, and tens of thousands have been held in labor camps and "transformation" centers. Wang Yao-qing, now a spokesman for the sect, was kept in solitary confinement, force-fed, and beaten for months. The state's tactics, however, are failing: repression has only made the faith—and resistance—of devotees stronger. Wang's jailers tried to force her to renounce her beliefs, but she would not. Those who recant to escape detention go back to the square to be arrested again.

And some go there to die. "One man sat on the ground, doused himself in gasoline, and set himself on fire," reported CNN's Rebecca MacKinnon. "Four women walked along, their bodies aflame, holding their hands up in a classic Falun Gong meditation pose." Exactly one year after the old man in the army jacket was beaten, Falun Gong practitioners try to take their lives in the square. Security forces were able to save four of the protesters. The fifth, one of the women, died on the last day of the Year of the Dragon.

The first sign of the end is defiance. When the people dare to oppose a regime, when they sacrifice themselves to the state, the final act has probably begun. Today many groups challenge Beijing's apparent might.

The Falun Gong is but one. Religious adherents, democracy advocates, and "splittists," those seeking their own homeland, are confronting the regime. The tragedy is that none of these people had to be enemies of the state. It is the state that has made them so.

As one century turned into the next, China was battling all these groups and, in the process, becoming distracted. As some of these conflicts escalate and others spiral out of control, the state is not dealing with the real challenges it is facing, the dislocations caused by decades of economic mismanagement. Workers and the unemployed take to the streets daily, often in the thousands, and it is they who pose the greatest threat to the People's Republic. The leaders in Beijing should be focusing on them instead of fighting the Falun Gong.

FORCE FIGHTS FAITH

China's leaders were stunned. There was no warning on April 25, 1999, for China's security forces. More than ten thousand adherents of the Falun Gong, founded by Li Hongzhi, surrounded Zhongnanhai, the Communist Party's leadership compound in central Beijing. In silent protest the faithful petitioned the central government for nothing more than tolerance.

China's leaders had never seen anything like it. And at least at first, they were as confused as the old man in the army jacket in Tiananmen Square. Premier Zhu Rongji, China's most popular national official, talked to the protesters who formed that wall of determination. On that day he reportedly made a promise: the Falun Gong would not be banned. Jiang Zemin, enraged by the protest around Zhongnanhai, took a different view. In July 1999, the state proclaimed the Falun Gong an illegal cult. China then asked Interpol to arrest Li Hongzhi, believed by the faithful to be the reincarnation of God but known by all to be living in New York. Interpol declined to detain the Supreme Being.

Falun Gong adherents fought back, staging protest after protest in Tiananmen Square, almost as if they thought that they could win their homeland by occupying its most hallowed ground. They sacrificed themselves to security forces, which were unmoved. The full weight of the state was brought to bear against an organization composed mostly of the elderly and the powerless.

It was inevitable that the state would battle the sect. The truth is that the Communist Party simply cannot tolerate another mass organization, no matter how benign. And the Falun Gong committed another sin: it would not submit. The Party is comfortable only when dealing with those organizations it can control. Consequently, it tolerates a "patriotic" Catholic Church, which is not permitted to acknowledge the authority of the pope in Rome. Catholics who do must pray on their own.

And when they do they are amorphous, as is now the Falun Gong. Driven underground, Li Hongzhi's followers are far more dangerous to the authorities and infinitely harder to suppress. They are formless, nowhere and everywhere at the same time. The Party, an institution if there ever was one, cannot understand organizations that do not have a formal structure. Because it cannot deal with what it cannot see, Falun Gong devotees, like many Catholics, are now beyond the Party's control. Master Li, as Li Hongzhi is known to his followers, it is claimed, can make himself invisible. Falun Gong practitioners have also mastered that trick: the state can only detain them when they present themselves for arrest.

And so the battle continues. The Falun Gong remains defiant, the Party adamant. This struggle will not end soon. The Falun Gong takes on darker overtones as thousands are arrested and jailed. The Party breeds resentment and, as the protesters in Tiananmen show us, defiance as well. And the rebellion spreads. Disgruntled Chinese citizens, especially the newly unemployed, join the sect as a "symbol of protest." We watch the modern Chinese state in puzzlement, and we disapprove.

And so would Mao Zedong. He would understand the Falun Gong's guerrilla campaign and be appalled at how his successors could forget all that he taught the world on tactics and statecraft. Today the state jails protesters who publicly protest, and the Falun Gong quickly reshapes itself for the next challenge. There is an endless stream of old men in army jackets who offer themselves up to detention. Imprisoning the faithful won't make a difference, argues Li Hongzhi, in New York. "The government can punish people's bodies, but they cannot change their hearts," he says. Maybe that's why the Chinese police state has not been able to prevail against the Falun Gong.

In Mao Zedong's Great Leap Forward, that most absurd of economic development campaigns, millions died from starvation: perhaps 30 million, although some say more. It might have been the worst famine in history, but the populace, for all its suffering, stood by the Party and its leader. Today, when the Chinese people are enjoying relative prosperity, the nation is plagued by social disorder. In other countries it would be explained as a crisis of rising expectations, but in China there are other reasons as well. For one thing, the Party's voice no longer commands now that its ideology has lost its vigor. China's leading political organization may retain its ideals, but it simply sounds unconvincing and, worse, insincere as it continues to depart from socialism. Li Hongzhi preaches ideas that are even zanier than those of the Party, but at least he appears genuine when he claims to be the incarnation of the supreme divinity. Li might be delusional, but he is persuasive. And he fills the vacuum left by that other slightly off-balance leader, Mao Zedong.

There is another reason, more important than the first, why the Chinese state is showing the signs of wear: the Party no longer knows what its flock is thinking. It did not use to have this problem. Mao was, among other things, a meddler of the worst sort, and social control, exercised through work and neighborhood units, affected virtually all aspects of daily living. After the Tiananmen Square massacre, Deng Xiaoping, China's leader at the time, realized that the Party had to withdraw further from the day-to-day lives of the people if it was to survive in the aftermath of tragedy. Today the Chinese may not be "free," yet they enjoy considerable latitude in their lives. But the dozen years of withdrawal have left the Party largely isolated from the masses. As a result, the Party, especially for a people's movement, is surprisingly inept in influencing China's people. It did not create the Falun Gong, but it is giving it a profile and status that it did not have and could not possibly have developed for itself. Sima Nan, a winner of China's Hero of Atheism Award and an opponent of the sect, says that the government's tactics are counterproductive in the long run. "The result is that people say, 'This Li Hongzhi must really have something, otherwise why would the government talk about him every day?' "

In its weakened condition the Party sometimes fails to understand the country it leads, and when that happens, things go awry. In 1999, an American diplomat in Beijing remarked that the illegal China Democracy

Party, founded the year before, was probably outnumbered by the security forces dedicated to its elimination. As a result, that party was doomed. While public security officers mercilessly hunted democracy advocates, they failed to see the growth of the Falun Gong—and the forces that had propelled its rise.

Religion is certainly rising in China, but you often have to look hard for it. After all, on Xinle Road in the center of Shanghai the Party chased the clergy from the church and replaced them with money changers. There are five onion-shaped domes on the church's roof, one larger than the other four, indicating the Russian Orthodox influence. And the two massive bronze doors are now open to await the faithful. Inside there are a hundred or so souls in a crowded and smoky room waiting for some kind of salvation, but it is not the type that God provides.

There is a plaque at the front of this impressive edifice saying MU-NICIPAL PRESERVED BUILDING. The structure, once the Cathedral of the Holy Mother of God, has been saved. The religion, however, has not been. Instead of parishioners, the people here are stock speculators, for this is an office of Guotai Junan Securities in Shanghai, China's new financial center. In China all things serve the state, and in Shanghai that means that even houses of God are reserved for the worship of money. The Party believes in materialism, and Guotai's customers are certainly materialistic.

From the scene on Xinle Road it looks as if religion were on the way out in China, where the Party hopes that you will get rich and encourages you to enjoy atheism. If the present trends continue, however, Guotai may have to make way for a church because it is religion, not stock trading, that is sweeping China. There may be fewer than 5 million active share traders today. The government encourages investment in the market and discourages attendance at religious services, but the Chinese cannot get enough of religion these days. There are, according to the government, more than 100 million religious followers, but the true number is undoubtedly far higher than the state implies. And it is believed that believers are multiplying faster than stock traders. That's almost inevitable in a rapidly aging country, as people who must contemplate their own mortality tend to start thinking about an afterlife.

"Many people in China are facing a crisis of faith," admits Fu Qing-yuan, director of the Research Institute of Marxism-Leninism at the Chinese Academy of Social Sciences and China's ideologist in chief. "But I still believe that the majority of the Chinese people believe in dialectical materialism." Now you know how far out of touch the Party is—and why some exiled grain clerk in New York named Li is so popular in China.

Master Li has mixed a powerful brew since he first started the Falun Gong in 1992 in Changchun, a grimy provincial capital northeast of Beijing. He fused elements of traditional Chinese thought, such as Buddhism and Taoism, with general moral principles and philosophy (truthfulness, benevolence, and forbearance) and *qi gong,* an ancient art designed to channel energy through the body. He teaches that devotees develop both an orb in the abdomen that absorbs energy and a "third eye" in the head for communing with the universe and expects that they will eventually attain "perfect happiness." He has topped all that off by discovering a new supreme being in the universe: himself. Guess which religion is more popular: the one that promises a life after this one or the one that decrees that there is none?

Li Hongzhi, in addition to being the reincarnation of the supreme deity, has been blessed with a good sense of timing. China is at present the world's biggest growth area for religion. There are about a dozen reasons why religion, in many different forms, is thriving in China, but they boil down to the need for comfort in a world of turbulent and seemingly never-ending change. The point is that the Party has lost the power to control what the Chinese people believe. It has even lost the power to command the thoughts of its own cadres: hundreds of thousands of them fervently practice Falun Gong.

Falun Gong practitioners can't help talking about their faith. It is the first month of 2000, and China is still in the grip of cold weather that has paralyzed the capital and other parts of the nation. A group of actors shooting a television commercial in Suzhou, at the famous Humble Administrator's Garden, are warming themselves in a minibus after a particularly difficult day on location in freezing temperatures. Someone asks one of the extras if he is still cold. "Yes, but that's okay because I practice Falun Gong," says the handsome young man, speaking to no one, and everyone, on the bus, people he had just met for the first time the day before. "I only feel a bit cool." He betrays no concern that he has just openly admitted to strangers a crime deemed to be serious by the Communist Party and the massive security apparatus of the modern Chinese state.

And no one else in this group seems to care that they have just witnessed an act of defiance.

The Falun Gong's defiance is everywhere in China these days, even in the state's own prisons. "China has achieved a great victory in taking decisive action in the struggle against Falun Gong," said the hapless Li Peng, chairman of the National People's Congress, as he gave his report to the annual session of that body in March 2000. Falun Gong protesters, despite elaborate security precautions, had managed to stage protests outside the Great Hall of the People while the Congress met. Seventy of those arrested, held in a detoxification center in Beijing, were refusing food. Their colleagues smuggled out photos showing the hunger strikers doing their Falun Gong meditation exercises while in detention.

They worship in detention, and they worship anywhere else they can. A church is any place where people gather to pray, and in China there are thousands that have sprung up to take the place of the magnificent structure on Xinle Road. A small room in a Beijing apartment, as dreary as the millions of others in the capital, is one of the Lord's homes in China. There are ten or so men closely huddled around a table studying the scriptures. Saint Peter's it's not, but the faith of its members burns strong nonetheless. These men know persecution; some of them were arrested on the first day of 2000 when their "objective discussion on [G]od and the soul" was broken up by authorities. "They treated us brutally," says Xu Yonghai. "They dragged me around on the ground and held me without food or water for twenty-four hours." That didn't do the regime much good. Xu got to tell his story to the world on CNN.

The state, for all its resources, is losing its crusade against religion, and that's a problem because the stakes for Beijing are high. Party leaders do not want a highly disciplined, single-minded organization marching on Beijing. In China's imperial past, organized religious cults with weird beliefs became political and wreaked havoc on those who got in their way, but the Falun Gong had the look and feel of a peaceful organization. Retired folks, by and large, do not have enough energy to bring down governments—unless, of course, they are provoked. Now, after Beijing's campaign of suppression, they are. Yet the Party is not content to persecute only the Falun Gong but is now turning its eyes on other qi gong sects, even though they are more benign and even though it is not clear what it can possibly achieve.

Today the Falun Gong is just an abnormally large cult. Tomorrow anything can happen. The Falun Gong episode highlights yet again the weakening grip of the apparently mighty Communist Party. It may command the world's largest standing army and an arsenal of nuclear weaponry, but it is helpless against the elderly and infirm. If the Party cannot effectively deal with the Falun Gong, what hope does it have with other foes? And there are plenty of others.

MISERY REINCARNATED

Unlike Falun Gong practitioners, Uighurs, Muslims in China's northwest, and Tibetans want no part of the People's Republic. They are, after all, Chinese only in the sense that they have been incorporated into a country called "China." They see that peoples at the fringes of the Russian empire were able to win their freedom a decade ago, and they are determined to do the same. If the Falun Gong story is light comedy, the tales of the Tibetans and Uighurs are dark tragedies. History and ethnicity mix with religion in an explosive concoction as these peoples battle the dominant Han Chinese for their freedom. This is war that has been fought in various ways and on many fields. And over a very long time.

It is the Lunar New Year celebrations in Dharmsala, India. Tibetan monks, looking like Polynesian kings in their red robes and yellow curved headdresses, throw an effigy of death into a burning straw hut to kill the evil of the year just passed. In moments, the white stick figure with the long fangs and grotesque eyes is consumed. If only dispatching the Han Chinese could be so easy for such a gentle folk.

The Han have periodically invaded Tibet throughout the unhappy history of the two peoples. Chung-rag Dorje, a Buddhist lama who lived in Tibet in the eighth century, discovered sacred texts that warned of an invasion "when the metal bird flies and horses roll on wheels," now believed to be a prediction of China's invasion of Tibet in 1950. China called that particular incursion "liberation." Replied Tibet: "Liberation from whom and what?"

Now, those texts having proven to be so prophetic, Chung-rag Dorje is back. He has been reincarnated in the form of Hollywood action star and "celebrity Buddhist" Steven Seagal, at least according to some believers. This highly controversial reincarnation has not been accepted by many Tibetans and thus mirrors another saga of a succession of a Buddhist leader. The other one, like most about China, began centuries ago. Tibetans believe that when high lamas die, their reincarnations can be found through omens and such. The first Dalai Lama was born in 1391, and, in one form or another, he has been going strong ever since. Today's version is the fourteenth incarnation, an exile who irritates Beijing by rallying international support for his Buddhist homeland. There are, of course, nameless Tibetan and Han officials whom Beijing has installed in the Tibet Autonomous Region and Qinghai Province (where many Tibetans are also found). The Dalai Lama, however, is the Tibetans' leader of choice.

So who chooses the Dalai Lama? That job traditionally went to Tibet's second most important spiritual leader, the Panchen Lama. Six years after the tenth of that line died in 1989, a six-year-old boy, Gedhun Choekyi Nyima, was identified as the eleventh in 1995. Unfortunately for him, he lived in Tibet. Authorities took him and his parents away and identified another six-year-old as the true Panchen Lama in the hope that they could groom and use him for their own ends. Gedhun Choekyi Nyima has not been seen in public since then. Presumably "the youngest political prisoner in the world," as he has been called by Tibetan dissidents, is still alive. In September and October 2000, European diplomats were shown, from a distance, two pictures of the boy, who is said to be living with his parents in northern Tibet, but that is merely one of a number of contradictory explanations that the Chinese have given from time to time. Although Beijing can hold him for as long as it wants, it has not yet been able to convince the Tibetans to embrace its own candidate as the true Panchen Lama, who now has the same problems of acceptance as Steven Seagal.

There is also a tall, gawky teenager who is number three on Tibet's list of reincarnated leaders, the Karmapa. Both the Dalai Lama and Beijing agreed that Ugyen Trinley Dorje was number 17, but that was a mistake on the government's part. While most people in the world were celebrating the arrival of 2000, the Karmapa was on the run. By jeep, horseback, foot, helicopter, train, and taxi, the Karmapa escaped his monastery in Tibet and made his way to the Dalai Lama's government in exile in Dharmsala. The Karmapa's flight was a shock to the Party and a glaring example of its inability to control the situation in Tibet. Beijing got its revenge in the only way it could: officials detained the Karmapa's parents, simple yak herders, and then whisked them out of Tibet. Presumably they're alive as well, but in any event, their plight highlights the harshness of Chinese rule. And the kidnaping is surely an indication of the exasperation of the Han rulers.

Beijing's leaders can abduct all the young boys and yak herders they want, but that's not going to do them much good. Breaking centuries of tradition, the Dalai Lama announced that his successor will be democratically elected, thereby depriving the young Panchen Lama of the task of selecting the Tibetans' most important spiritual leader. The move will help unify the Tibetan exiles in India, where two important Tibetan lamas now reside. In 1959, after an unsuccessful uprising, the fourteenth Dalai Lama fled there, not the first time that a Dalai Lama had done that in Tibet's unhappy history with China. The colony of 150,000 Tibetans in India is the West's favorite group of refugees, an inspiration to those who root for underdogs. As such, they serve as a reminder to the world of Chinese repression in a modern age and form a base of opposition beyond Beijing's control.

The present Dalai Lama, no matter how beloved abroad, is not beyond criticism at home. Many Tibetans want complete independence for their homeland, not the autonomy he now seeks, and think that his Mahatma Gandhi–esque policy of nonviolence is senseless. They favor more dramatic activities to counter Beijing's ruthless suppression of the Tibetan people. There have been periodic uprisings in Tibetan lands against the People's Republic and there is an ongoing low-level campaign of violence, but the Chinese remain entrenched. Beijing could solve its problems in Tibet tomorrow by granting some measure of self-rule because the Dalai Lama favors this option and is willing to talk. China, however, is intent on exercising complete control and has no intention of beginning discussions with him. Now it is clear that the People's Republic will not take the easy path, so the struggle will continue.

Clearly the Dalai Lama has been effective winning sympathy in capitals around the world. But who will push the Chinese out? In his first public address since escaping to India, the Karmapa, before a Lunar New Year's crowd in Dharmsala, said, "The most important tenet of Tibetan

Buddhist teaching is compassion, but to try to practice this one has to be free." Is he saying that Tibetans must free themselves before they can practice compassion? Young and obviously courageous, he seems ready to take on the People's Republic. Beijing's unseemly efforts to control the selection of the next Dalai Lama by abducting the Panchen Lama will be fruitless if the Karmapa seizes the moment. He has already captured the imagination of his people by fleeing his homeland and looks set to carry on the struggle.

With the Karmapa's departure, none of the three most important Tibetan religious leaders remains in Tibet. One day, all three will return. In the meantime, young Tibetans wait like a coiled snake. There are always protests of one sort or another, some involving just one or two monks. Tibetans are patient. After all, they have been struggling with the Chinese for centuries. Sometimes they have been free, sometimes they have not. Now that they are not, they are planning the next phase of the campaign so that one day all can practice compassion in their homeland.

The Xinjiang Uygur Autonomous Region is anything but autonomous. That's because it is home to the rebellious Uighurs, and Beijing is determined to hold on to their land as well. Xinjiang does not flow with Tibetan compassion; it's more like a battlefield. The Uighurs, like the Tibetans, had their own state once. The East Turkestan Republic, proclaimed in 1944 when the Chinese were preoccupied by the Japanese, did not last long, however. The People's Liberation Army, in the same year it invaded Tibet, went on to crush the Uighurs. The Uighurs have not forgotten, and violence flairs in Xinjiang almost daily.

Graeme Allen knew none of this history when he agreed in 1994 to work at the Holiday Inn in Urumqi, the remote capital of desolate Xinjiang. Previously a resident of Bangkok, he accepted the job even before he knew where Urumqi was. After he signed on, the plump Irishman thought he should check out where he would be going. He couldn't locate it on a map, so he bought a Lonely Planet guide and cringed when he read the description of the various peoples, who didn't seem to be on good terms with one another. The place didn't sound so great either: drab and filled with concrete-block architecture of the type favored during the early days of the People's Republic. Urumqi claims to be, of all the cities in the world, the farthest from an ocean, he learned.

If Allen knew anything, it was hotel marketing, and he wanted to create a promotional film for Urumqi's finest hotel. Making that was one of the first tasks upon arrival. The shooting was taking the better part of the day, and by now it was getting on in the afternoon. The film crew had been almost everywhere when Allen realized that they had not yet filmed the Chinese restaurant, an important part of any hotel in China. "Chinese restaurant is a bit of a problem," his assistant explained. "It's closed."

"Closed? What do you mean it's closed? It's not closed." Allen would know if one of the main concessions had been shuttered, even temporarily.

"Well, I've [got] a problem with the cameraman. He doesn't want to go into the Chinese restaurant."

"Why?" asked Allen, who was learning more by the minute in this alien land.

"Terrible smell" was the reason.

"What are you talking about?" Allen had not smelled anything out of the ordinary in the Chinese restaurant when he had been there last.

"Terrible smell of pork and lard."

"What about the Western restaurant?" Allen asked.

"Oh no, no problem."

"There's just as much pork and lard [there]," Allen said. They'd already been filming in that restaurant earlier in the day, and he had noticed no hesitation on the part of the Uighur cameraman.

"Not the same" was the only reply.

Relations between the Uighurs and the Chinese have always been bad, but in the last few years they've gotten even worse, especially since early 1997, when fighting flared in Yining, the capital of the short-lived East Turkestan Republic. Details are sketchy because the central government cordoned off Xinjiang from the rest of the world, but it appears that unrest—and subsequent executions—left several hundred dead, perhaps more. Incidents continue to this day as the Muslims battle China's garrisons of security forces. "There is not a day something is not happening in Xinjiang," says Erkin Alptekin, an exiled Uighur leader. Young Uighurs are desperate, and in their hopelessness they are striking out. There isn't a movement to speak of, but formless resistance is hard to suppress, especially when Chinese soldiers sell young terrorists all the weapons and explosives they need. "There's a fire burning in Xinjiang, and the Chinese can't extinguish it."

Why is there so much violence now? Like the Tibetans, Uighurs have experienced Chinese rule for centuries. Both were fortunate in being far from China's capital. The program of relocation of Hans to Xinjiang by the People's Republic, however, will, if it has not already, result in the Uighurs' becoming a minority in their own homeland. That's part of the same policy that is now diluting the Tibetans in theirs. "The two communities live totally apart," says Allen of the Hans and Uighurs in Xinjiang. There they can't even agree on the time of day, he notes. Officially, all of China is on Beijing's time. Ask a Uighur in Xinjiang, however, and it is two hours earlier. And ask him if he can really smell the stink of pork and lard in Chinese restaurants. The answer will be yes until he has his own homeland.

That won't be anytime soon if it's up to the central government. Beijing's economic planners are going about their work to ensure Han rule. It takes a lot of effort to subjugate a people—more if you try many at a time, Beijing's latest project. It has its own slogan, "Remake the West," a sure sign that it's central government policy. Hardly a day passes without the official media's praising the leadership of the Party's ruling Politburo for having the foresight for embarking on the "West" campaign.

"History repeats itself," said Karl Marx, and so do central government programs to develop the western regions of the People's Republic. In the 1950s, prisoners and demobilized soldiers built the infrastructure needed to tie the recently reannexed Tibetan and Uighur homelands tightly into the Motherland. The biggest campaign was the Third Line, which in the mid-1960s saw the relocation of industry into the interior to safeguard it from foreign attack. The concept, credited to Mao Zedong, had a devastating effect on the country's economy.

At the beginning of the twenty-first century, just when the People's Republic has conclusively proven that centralized planning does not work, Beijing's cadres are at it again. The Remake the West campaign is another enormous exercise in public spending and preferential policies of special incentives. The "West," in reality the central and western portions of the country, need infrastructure, but much of it will prove to be uneconomic if the country's record in the past is any guide to the future.

To its credit, Beijing wants to narrow the income gap between the quickly growing coastal areas and the interior portion of the country.

The differential now looks as if it might threaten stability or at least create an even sharper divide in the nation. Yet suppression of minorities is another motive. For years crude force failed to win anything but temporary peace, but now economic development holds out the process of long-term success. Relentless modernization, and the flow of Han Chinese that goes with it, will further dilute the Tibetans and Uighurs and their fragile cultures. Although development projects bring benefits, they are still unpopular in affected areas. The Tibetans are by no means a modern people, and the same can more or less be said of the Uighurs. Beijing, however, will bring them into the new millennium whether they want to come or not.

The prospect of even more Han settlers on Tibetan land disturbs the Dalai Lama. Lhasa, the capital of Tibet, is being transformed into a modern city as a dominant culture systematically tries to destroy a weaker, though resilient, one. In the last two decades Tibet has had the look and feel of an occupied nation, and China cannot afford to waste its precious resources on conquering small minorities, especially when they are resistant. China is sapping its own vitality when it forces its healthy business enterprises on the coast to invest in the West to further political, and not economic, ends. The same applies when it makes its major banks lend there when there is little prospect of repayment.

So will the Dalai Lama return to Tibet someday? Everyone seems to ask him that question. He always replies with some form of yes. What he does not do is point out that he can live forever. Because he reincarnates every so often, it's a sure thing that one of his versions will make it back. But will it be the fourteenth, the one who carries the hopes of his people today?

Now there is a standoff of sorts, and many think that time will favor the Han over the ethnic minorities. According to this view, relentless economic development will swamp the Tibetans and the Uighurs as well as China's other minorities. These peoples do not want assimilation, as centuries have shown, and they have outlasted the Han up to now as Chinese rulers have come and gone. Today pressure is building in the rest of the People's Republic as others resist the state, but for different reasons. The current campaign against the minorities can work only as long as the government in Beijing remains in place. His Holiness, number 14, will probably see his homeland again, and if not he, then the seventeenth Karmapa for sure. "Totalitarian systems are never forever," the Dalai Lama says.

A SENSE OF ITS OWN MORTALITY

The obsession is on display for all the world to see—all the world that's brave enough to endure the bitter cold, that is. The Jumbo, the world-famous floating restaurant, is within sight of Hong Kong's Supreme Court Building. In real life, they were on opposite ends of an island, separated by a chain of mountain peaks. But this is February 1997 at the ice festival in the city of Harbin, and geography has been compressed so that the attractions of the British colony can be taken in at one glance. The theme is Hong Kong, and the buildings are only elaborate facades of ice in the frozen capital of northeast Heilongjiang Province.

Crowds across China, including those at the ice festival, are celebrating the impending return of Hong Kong. Few events in this vast country can occur without a mention of "reunification." A clock, marking the seconds to the moment when June 30 becomes July 1, is embedded in ice. There is a larger clock in Beijing, in Tiananmen Square, where politics require a public showing. But here, in the subfreezing temperatures of this sooty industrial town, people stand in front of the clock and smile. The joy of Hong Kong's return is real. Two years later, the theme at the ice festival is the reunification of Macau, the last European colony in Asia, and there is yet another clock running in Tiananmen.

What makes Mao popular, even to this day, is his excising the foreign powers that had cut up China for hundreds of years. Nationalism is good politics in the People's Republic, and the Party, ever keen to bolster its position, continually whips up the public and especially the young.

Including the young women at Citibank. Taiwanese pilots sit in their cockpits in the midday sun on alert, ready to scramble within moments. It is early August 1999, and the Mainland's Central Military Commission, chaired by President Jiang Zemin, has just given the "shoot first" order to frontline fighters from the regional commands in Guangzhou and Nanjing. Mainland fighters deliberately enter Taiwanese airspace as tensions rise in the Strait of Taiwan following President Lee Teng-hui's controversial remarks stating that the People's Republic and Taiwan are two separate states. Rumors circulating in American commercial and investment banks in Hong Kong say that Mainland and Taiwanese pilots are already engaged in aerial combat, and Asia's markets shudder. In Shanghai the local staff of Citibank's corporate finance unit, mostly women in their early twenties, cheer what they think are the beginnings of hostilities. They have time for patriotism: China's economy is trending downward, and they have little to do at their desks at America's greatest commercial bank.

Hong Kong and Macau were easy pickings for the People's Republic. Taiwan, on the other hand, is a different story. You don't need to know Mandarin, the country's national tongue, to understand what the Chinese general is saying. His words are meaningless anyway. The message is in the eyes, fierce and belligerent, black and bright. His hand, finger pointed, jabs the air in a forceful thrust. The hard-line three-star General Zhang Wannian of the People's Liberation Army is clearly angry, but on television screens around the world he looks like a buffoon. Everyone knows that China cannot invade Taiwan, at least not successfully by conventional means. In the first decade of the twenty-first century, the Taiwanese are fully able to defend themselves.

Beijing, if it could get its way, would make Taiwan a part of the Motherland. It would also incorporate the islands in the South China Sea extending almost to the shorelines of the Philippines, Malaysia, Brunei, and Vietnam. The island claims, based on explorations that go back before the birth of Christ, are ludicrous, especially because China withdrew from the seas and destroyed its fleet in the middle of the fifteenth century. The claims to Taiwan are not much stronger. The Qing Dynasty ceded Taiwan "in perpetuity" to Japan in the Treaty of Shimonoseki in 1895, and the Kuomintang took over in 1945 at the end of the Second World War. The People's Republic has never, in fact, ruled the island.

After losing to Mao Zedong, the Kuomintang, under Generalissimo Chiang Kai-shek, retreated to Taiwan in 1949 to claim the island as the consolation prize in the civil war. Chiang's rule in the early days was repressive and brutal, just like that of his rival, Mao Zedong. That was not especially surprising because the vanquished Kuomintang and the victo-rious Communist parties were both built on the same model, developed by someone called Lenin.

A funny thing happened on the way to the millennium, however. In the 1990s, the ruling Kuomintang chose democracy. On the Mainland, political dissidents spend time in jail. On Taiwan, they run for president. Chen Shui-bian, the standard-bearer of the opposition Democratic Pro-gressive Party in the 2000 election, was jailed in 1986 for libeling a Kuomintang politician. In 1985, his wife was crippled for life in a myste-rious accident that many blame on Kuomintang thugs. Fewer than four-teen years after his party was formed, Chen beamed as more than two hundred thousand supporters in the streets of Taipei celebrated his vic-tory on election night. His first months as president would be difficult as the Kuomintang and others schemed, but the election, in March 2000, was a historic moment.

History does repeat itself, but must it do so so frequently? In Beijing, Mainland leaders just must hate it when it happens. Once again, they tried to influence Taiwan but produced just the opposite of what they in-tended. What are they thinking in China's capital? It can't be a cultural problem; they're both Chinese. How in the world can Communist cadres dream of ruling Taiwan when they don't understand the first thing about its people? First they tried crude force. In 1996, the PLA conducted live-fire missile tests off Taiwan's waters just before the island's first direct presidential elections in an attempt to persuade the voters not to choose Lee Teng-hui, whom Beijing branded a splittist. America responded by sending aircraft carriers, and the voters responded with a landslide for Lee, who became the first Chinese head of state to be chosen in a demo-cratic election in the five thousand years of that country's history. Then, in 2000, Beijing hurled ultimatums, "paper missiles," over the Strait of Taiwan to prevent the election of Chen Shui-bian, who was propelled to an unexpected victory. The election was truly historic: for the first time in Chinese history there was a democratic transfer of government. The Mainland, in the form of Premier Zhu Rongji, could only explain lamely that the election had been "a joke."

It had not. The voice of the unidentified young woman on the gigan-tic screen is hoarse, but the message is clear. "The people of Taiwan have spoken!" she says at the victory rally in Taipei on the night of the election.

The street looks like Times Square on New Year's Eve except that there are seemingly millions of banners and pennants and the noise is even more deafening. Chen, the only major candidate to be born in Taiwan, represents a real break with the past, which for the last five decades has been ruled by a Kuomintang that kept its Mainland orientation. The people did speak, and they spoke as much to affirm their Taiwanese identity as to defy Mainlanders, Communist and otherwise.

Taiwan is forging a new outlook based on its own culture and history, and, as Beijing fears, it is making its own way in the world. Chiang Kai-shek's Kuomintang suppressed local culture when it took control of Taiwan in 1945. Today all things Taiwanese are cool on the island, and the selections of Lee and Chen, neither from a Mainland family, as president are just a hint of things to come. People at the margins of the Chinese empire want their own lives. For Beijing, the particularly chilling aspect of these elections is that, unlike the Tibetans or Uighurs, the Taiwanese are Chinese.

It did not have to be this way. The Tibetans and Uighurs could probably have worked out some accommodation if Beijing had been willing to allow them real autonomy. After all, they have spent most of the last two centuries under the Chinese tent. China's Communists are great meddlers, however, and they're squarely to blame for much of the unrest the country now faces. Clearly those living in Taiwan were content with the ambiguous status quo. The Mainland and Taiwan had, as a practical matter, already worked out an accommodation.

They had even ritualized military conflict. Ho Ping Hsien, a freshly minted second lieutenant in Taiwan's army, could see that. Ho, a small man with a raspy voice and an enormous smile, had easy duty in 1973, being responsible for just a few soldiers. He would travel the island of Matsu by vehicle or by foot, inspecting his charges in their forward positions. He was just one of the trip wires in the Cold War. If hostilities erupted, he had virtually no hope of surviving. Matsu is only three miles from the Mainland's Fujian Province, so close that Mainland loudspeakers blared propaganda across the water for years. Yet Ho could see that there would be no chance of war during his tour of duty because the Mainland and Taiwan had obviously come to an agreement. On the odd-numbered days of the month, Matsu would shell Fujian for a couple of hours. On the other days, Ho and his troops would head to their concrete bunkers and pass the two hours from seven to nine in the evening eating and gambling while Mainland gunners fired on his positions. There they were safe from the Mainland's shells, which either exploded or divided into four parts and littered the ground with fliers (which were collected by an elite army unit, the specially trained political squad). The conflict, if it could be called that, was contained.

Ho left the army and is now a finance specialist, but he remains a student of history. "Mao made a big mistake changing the name of the country and the flag," he says. If the founder of the People's Republic had not done so in 1949 as an assertion of his triumph, Taiwan today would appear to be merely another province of the Mainland, whose government enjoys diplomatic recognition as the only China by most of the world. Beijing probably would be happy that *its* flag was flying in Taipei and that officials there proclaimed themselves to be part of a government with the same name. In the world of appearances, so important to the Communist Party, there would have been no problem.

The people of Taiwan care little about whether its government is recognized as "China," and for the most part they do not seek independence (Chen Shui-bian had to drop the talk of independence in order to get elected). But they are being pushed out of the orbit of Beijing by Beijing itself. The dire threats of war periodically issued from the Mainland are convincing more and more of the Taiwanese that they must have their own identity. Because of Mao, the Mainland and Taiwan fly different flags, and now, because of his successors, the Taiwanese are beginning to realize they need to have their own country, too.

The truth—no surprise—is that none of the main political groupings on Taiwan wants to become part of a brutal, undemocratic, and economically failing nation. Taiwan has already been there, and it does not want to go back. The People's Republic is, of course, improving, but Taiwan, a more advanced society, is progressing too, and at a much faster pace than the Mainland. Why should it join a crumbling empire? Nonetheless, the Taiwanese are, or maybe were, content to pretend that nothing had changed since 1949. Threats of war haven't worked for China. So why does Beijing keep making them? Doesn't the Mainland have any other problems to deal with?

So the Taiwanese, like all of the other perceived enemies of Beijing, are distracting the attention of the People's Republic. These days, most of the Mainland's foreign policy is directed toward the great cause of "re-unification." Taiwan is an obsession, one that creates a hideous spectacle of a large dictatorship trying to intimidate a small democracy. This is not worthy of a great nation, and China is diminishing itself in foreign capitals, and in living rooms, around the world.

What will happen when Jiang Zemin, who has escalated the rhetoric on Taiwan since the return of Macau in 1999, fails to deliver? Taiwan is supposed to cap his résumé. Will he risk hostilities to ensure a place in history? "I think it's very dangerous to underestimate the willingness of the Chinese leadership to march over a cliff over this issue of sovereignty," says Patrick Tyler, who from 1993 to 1997 served as the Beijing bureau chief for *The New York Times*. The old saying in defense planning is that one must judge an adversary's capabilities, rather than its intentions. On the Taiwan question, one must judge China's intentions, not just its capabilities, in figuring the risk of war. The Mainland, for internal political reasons, is perfectly capable of launching a war it cannot win by conventional means.

Jiang Zemin mortgaged much of his freedom of action on Taiwan to the leadership of the People's Liberation Army to obtain its support in cementing his political standing. The PLA, which is supposed to report to the Party's top leadership and not the other way around, has now taken the initiative in diplomacy as far as Taiwan is concerned. It had effectively ousted China's Foreign Ministry, which in 1996 did not support any show of force against Taiwan, from a policy-making role. It was the PLA's Zhang Wannian, the finger-wagging general, and Defense Minister Chi Haotian who set the hard line that China is now famous for.

In March 1996, PLA generals were humiliated by America's use of its carrier force in waters surrounding Taiwan, a reminder of Western gunboat diplomacy. Today, these guys want some measure of redemption, and they just might take China to the brink to get it. The ominous aspect of the situation is that Jiang's control over the military is weakening because of its anger over Taiwan. In 2000, just after the Taiwan election, the PLA, on its own, once again threatened nuclear war with the United States.

If Mao were alive, he would be lecturing Comrade Zemin. It is the Party, not the PLA, that should be establishing state policy. In fact, the PLA is the world's largest private army. Its generals do not report to the state; they are responsible only to the Communist Party. Yet when it comes to Taiwan, the Party, in reality, is not calling the shots. And when Jiang Zemin passes from the scene in a few years, his successor, whoever he may be, will be even more beholden to the "great wall of steel," as Deng Xiaoping called China's military.

All this has had an insidious effect on the People's Republic: it has increasingly devoted scarce resources to the modernization of the PLA, money that can better be spent elsewhere. Mao's poorly equipped peasant army beat Chiang Kai-shek's vastly superior force in 1949, showing that spirit could prevail over steel. But the PLA now believes that it must have steel to win back Taiwan. The once proud PLA realizes that it is short of everything that it takes to win a modern war. Jiang, never missing an opportunity to shore up his support in the PLA, champions technology on the battlefield—and money for the military's modernization. The growth in China's military budget is accelerating. The official figures show a 12.7 percent increase in 2000 and a 17.7 percent rise in 2001, both numbers in excess of the economy's rates of growth for those years. The real increase in the military budget is not known outside Zhongnanhai, however, because China hides most of its defense outlays. Whatever vast sum China is spending, is this what it should be doing with its money?

No, it's not, but China's Communist Party has lost its sense of proportion about Taiwan and it wants to have a military option. It is not only the growing independence of the island that agitates the Party's top leadership. And it is not only the fear of democracy spreading from Taiwan to the Mainland. There is something else: now, more than ever, the Party must be feeling a sense of its own mortality. It knows that at one time it was as vital as the Falun Gong, but now it is no longer. It has witnessed the fall of the Kuomintang and dreads its own fate. It too is an aging machine that has lost its grip on a society it once dominated.

The Communist Party rants and raves about the island's splittists, but it looks increasingly friendless in the world, where Taiwan's fledgling democracy is attracting international support. The Kuomintang lost the war for the Mainland and, belatedly, in 1991, had the good sense to recognize it. The Communist Party is losing the battle for Taiwan, but unfortunately, it has yet to come to terms with that fact. And having failed to do so, its increasingly desperate maneuverings carry a danger. As the

Party embraced modernization of the economy, it had to jettison much of what it stood for, at least in substance. It is now clinging to nationalism as a basis of its legitimacy and, having raised that flag, has raised the stakes on Taiwan.

Mao Zedong once told Henry Kissinger that China could wait a hundred years for reunification with Taiwan. Today Mao's successors do not think they have that much time. The danger is that Beijing's leaders, through their increasingly intemperate behavior, will box themselves in so that they will have no choice but to start a war they cannot win by conventional means. On the day after the March 2000 election, Beijing moved in that direction, shutting the door to compromise by declaring that it would talk only to Taiwanese who first agreed to the "one China" principle. In other words, the Mainland demanded capitulation before negotiation. So you won't see Zhu Tao again. The soldier who raised the Chinese flag in the ceremony marking the return of Macau in 1999 had also performed that task in Hong Kong two and a half years earlier. Taiwan is in no mood to have Zhu Tao—or Zhu Rongji—come over for another flag raising.

Sure, China can conquer Taiwan by force, but, given its present capabilities, the PLA will have to employ its nuclear arsenal to triumph. War of any type with Taiwan is sure to claim the Mainland as one of its victims. Destruction of your neighbor is destruction of yourself, says the Dalai Lama, and he is right: a conflict would set back China's economy by years if not longer. It would be much worse than the hiatus after the Tiananmen Square massacre, when foreign investors literally fled from China. Shut off from the world except for its ally North Korea, the People's Republic will have to endure isolation in an interconnected world.

But neither is peace an appetizing scenario for the Mainland. By now the world has seen that Beijing is not able to get its way on Taiwan. What happens when China's populace, whipped up by the Party's formidable propaganda machine, realizes that Taiwan has left the fold for good? Twice, in 1996 and 2000, China threatened war in the harshest tones possible. Twice it has backed down. Can the government in Beijing retreat in front of its own people a third time and still survive? Humiliated again, the Chinese will do what they have done throughout the last two centuries when their government has failed to defend the Motherland: they will turn against their leaders, quietly at first and then more vocally. "If the Communist Party doesn't respond, I will go to Tiananmen Square and kill myself to prod the nation into action and erase this national shame," said one firebrand in a Mainland Internet chat room.

It didn't have to be this way. Even as China is beset by so many other problems, it must deal with another. The Party's leaders could have let the status quo continue, which is what people on the island wanted after all. Instead they have created, yet again, more work for themselves and have had to postpone urgent domestic initiatives to focus on Taiwan.

As 1999 became 2000 in the United States, the Dalai Lama in his gentle manner told us that we are all one, or at least should be, as he was interviewed by the hard-charging Larry King. It is perhaps the perfect message for the end of an era. "I think the now modern time, I think, world become smaller and smaller so under this circumstances I believe that concept of 'we' and 'they' as something independent completely separate, you see, that concept I think is wrong so whole world is just like one entity." Not everyone is so broad-minded, however; Chen Shui-bian, for instance. "Taiwan stands up," he said in his inaugural address, harking back to a similar speech fifty years before. Yes, Taiwan is standing up. And so will the other enemies of the state, all in their time.

WHEN FEAR BECOMES RAGE

"For many of us, China represents all that is wrong with globalisation," says Sandra Smits. "Why should Americans be forced to buy goods made with the blood of innocent Chinese? Have you heard about what is going on in Tibet?" This comment, from a protester in Seattle during the World Trade Organization meeting in late 1999, sums up the thoughts of many people around the world about China. While economists and industrialists focus on the concept of comparative advantage, others, such as Ms. Smits, remind us that China is not just a trading partner. The streets of Seattle were filled with extremists, but Smits's sentiments resonate with many, including those who do not participate in public protests.

It would take an essay, perhaps a book, to analyze Smits's highly charged comment. The point, however, is that China, alone among the world's countries, elicits such an emotional response. "Who's talking about the . . . suppression of the demonstrations in Mexico City in 1968? No one." Robert Kapp, president of the U.S.-China Business Council, has a point. There is, he observes, something "symbolically powerful" about China.

Kapp is right, but he misses a larger issue: the regime has only itself to blame when people around the world single out China. From the high plateau of Tibet to the streets of Beijing, the country has presented an image of itself that the world abhors. When senior cadres need to deal with critical economic problems, they prefer instead to tighten their faces in front of the cameras and demand we believe that the gentle Dalai Lama is a threat to world order. Who can blame Sandra Smits for getting a bit emotional? China needs all the help it can get these days, but even governments eager to do business there cannot fully embrace the modern Chinese state.

Yet not all the foreign governments in the world can save Mao's republic from its own people. When the final chapter of the People's Republic is written, the incident in industrial Panzhihua in southwestern Sichuan Province will be forgotten. Under other circumstances, it could have been the spark that triggered collapse. There was no warning at the traffic police station on October 8, 1999. Liu Huawei, a businessman from another province, sought refuge there from three robbers who were pursuing him. The duty officer pushed Liu out, however, and the businessman was severely beaten by the thugs. Angry citizens surrounded the duty officer, and by the evening the crowd had grown to two thousand. The authorities responded by sending in about five hundred armed policemen, who fired tear gas into the protesters' ranks. People threw rocks and bricks back at the police and set fire to three of their vehicles. The unrest continued until the following morning.

In a country where a person from the next town is treated as a foreigner, this protest for someone from another province was an extraordinary reminder just how unstable the People's Republic is. The anger that so easily flared to riot disappeared as quickly. But the resentment remains in Panzhihua and tens of thousands of other cities, towns, and villages. Almost every day there is a protest of one sort or another in the People's Republic, but the state maintains a facade of calm. From a big city on the coast or the capital in Beijing, little seems out of place in this vast country. We hear central government figures continually talk about "stability" and think them obsessive, but the truth is that they have every reason to be concerned about the security of the state. There are Panzhihuas all over China.

And there is a boldness in the people these days, something last seen during the Beijing Spring of 1989, the prelude to the Tiananmen Square massacre. The ferocity of the regime's response to dissent in the square muted protest for a time as activists were jailed or exiled. Slowly, however, the signs of discontent have once again emerged. Today anger and defiance are almost everywhere. "What is the use of working hard? The Communist Party exploits us anyway," said a taxi driver in Guangzhou over a dispatch frequency. The driver's comment was heard all over that prosperous city and illustrates the people's new brazenness.

Perhaps many are no longer afraid because they have so little to lose. "I'm not scared," said Xu Xiaoying in September 2000, when she was told that a "ground patrol" official was coming her way. "My country is not taking care of me anymore." Xu, who had lost her job at a failing state-owned enterprise making construction machinery parts, has now been caught for the second day in a row selling bottled water in her city's most famous attraction, a third-century B.C. irrigation and river control project. Vendors like her are not permitted close to the tourists who come to Dujiangyan in Sichuan Province. Yet she is not afraid, whatever may happen to her this time. Yesterday the city confiscated the few bottles of water that she was selling from the small basket of her rickety bicycle. She does not know what the approaching official will do to her today, but she doesn't care. Xu is openly defiant when Chen Jishou, the young ground patrol officer, arrives. In his native Sichuanese dialect the harsh man commands her not to speak in Mandarin so that the tourists nearby will not understand their conversation. "I want to speak in Mandarin," the woman replies. "I want the foreigners to know."

The discontent that poses the greatest security threat of them all is not religious, ethnic, or regional; it is economic. Reform has left tens of millions of people without jobs, unfortunates like Xu Xiaoying who are suffering from structural change. At any one time, somewhere between 70 to 130 million migrants are roaming China for work. Total all the unemployed and underemployed, and the number undoubtedly exceeds 200 million. And the number is growing as Beijing's senseless campaign against other *qi gong* "cults" continues. Its persecution of the Zhong Gong, for example, has resulted in one hundred thousand additional unemployed as businesses owned by that group are shuttered by an anxious state.

While Beijing fusses over imagined enemies, labor protests occur across China as workers go for years without pay and as simple industrial disputes spiral out of control. In the workers' paradise effective labor unions are not permitted, so there are virtually no mechanisms to channel grievances through. When workers are unhappy, they just simmer—and then sometimes take to the streets. When they do, the regime must often use brute force, which is effective only in the short run. Those who are defeated by the state nurse their resentment. Today the aggrieved just smolder; they have yet to organize themselves nationally as Falun Gong devotees have done. When workers learn the tactics of that cult, the day they march in unison, they will become a potent political force.

Yet it is not only the unemployed who pose a threat. China's new economy has so many other victims. On the day before the Falun Gong laid siege to Zhongnanhai, there was another march to the Communist Party's leadership compound. The Xinguoda Futures Brokerage Company had been sealed by public security officers after the company's officials absconded with the money of more than four thousand investors, who were now seeking reimbursement from the state. On that day in April 1999, the regime was lucky: the crowd left Zhongnanhai peacefully after a cadre accepted a petition. Those who showed up the following day, the followers of Li Hongzhi, would not be satisfied so easily. The state is fighting them to this day.

Cultists, Christians, Tibetans, Muslims, and Taiwanese: How many can China fight at once? And for how long? When Communist regimes fall, they fall quickly. As Václav Havel, the Czech dissident turned statesmen, said, totalitarian societies always appear strong. "It looks like everyone is loyal and the regime will be here for centuries, that nothing will ever change, and it's easy to believe that." At some moment, though, the facade cracks, and soon it is all over. "Without anybody organizing a demonstration, the passersby had turned into demonstrators who filled the main square in Prague," the Czech president wrote about events in his capital, but he could have been describing what happened in Panzhihua—or what eventually occurred in Moscow. In 1992, former American President Richard Nixon recalled that "in the debate that I had with Khrushchev in 1959, the so-called Kitchen Debate, he said to me, jabbing his finger into my chest, 'Your grandchildren will live under communism,' and I responded 'Your grandchildren will live in freedom.' At that time I was sure he was wrong, but, I must admit, I wasn't sure I was right, but now these last three years, particularly the developments in 1991, have proved I was right because his grandchildren do live in freedom."

And so do the people of Eastern Europe. In 1989, the Soviet satellite regimes could not resist. They fell when fears turned to hope. In China the government will fall when fear becomes rage. The revolution will not be velvet. There will be blood because the Chinese Communist Party, born of struggle, will not yield with grace. Or maybe it will happen when apathy becomes hope. Today many are standing behind the current leaders because they think the next set might be worse. "The only reason I still support the regime is that anybody who overthrows it would use their same methods," says Dai Qing, an author. So today the Chinese tolerate the government, but, shown something better, the people will follow.

Somewhere in that country today there is a person who will end the Chinese state as it now exists. He or she will dare to give a voice to thoughts that for most are unspoken or only half formed. Angry, shrewd, or just desperate, that person, by the force of personality or ideas, will lead the Chinese people to something better. China is a lake of gasoline, and that individual, in some small town or large city, will have only to throw a match.

3

Industrial Theme Parks

State-Owned Enterprises Are Dying

The U.S. had Chrysler. China has lots of Chryslers.
—EDWARD STEINFELD

THE NORTHBOUND BUS barely stops as it drops off passengers on the main road of the provincial city, near one of its two central intersections. The motorized pedicabs get there first, and the others, powered by their drivers, crowd in behind as they struggle with the broken pavement. About five of them, kicking up dust, swarm over two travelers from the south, and all ask the same thing: "Do you want a ride?" They angle themselves as close as possible to the potential fares and don't take no for an answer, at least not for a minute or two. As some fall away, others come with the same refrain. The second wave of drivers is more insistent; most of them are women with complexions red from exposure to the cold. They all look worn, even though some of them are barely in their thirties.

This is poor Rugao in rich Jiangsu Province on the Yellow Sea. In the center of tiny family farms, this former boom city is now suffering from unemployment as state-owned enterprises fail one by one. "They're all *xiagang* workers," an old man in his sixties says, referring to the pedicab drivers who have been furloughed from SOEs. They are essentially unemployed; most will never be called back to their jobs. The old man is no longer working and has little money to spare even for a ride, so he walks, but he suggests that the out-of-town visitors hire one of the drivers to navigate Rugao's unmarked backstreets. Rugao, after sweet years, is now poor. There are almost no taxis in the city; the *xiagang* workers in the pedicabs now control its roads.

"Do you want a ride?" asks one who pedals past. It is a phrase one hears all over China these days. That's because SOEs are sick and China's state workforce is in jeopardy. Now that the Communist Party has relinquished day-to-day control over people's lives, it is hard to count all those who are out of work. The rate of urban unemployment in 2000 was 3.1 percent, the same as it was in the three previous years, at least according to official statistics. The real rate is probably six times that or more. In any event, unemployment is bound to increase because central government statistics tell us that more than 30 percent of SOE employees are idle, and accession to the World Trade Organization will aggravate the situation as heightened competition forces ailing SOEs to close.

When workers lose their jobs, they march. They used to demonstrate in the tens and hundreds. Now they protest in the thousands and tens of thousands. Twenty thousand workers, along with several thousand family members, rioted in coastal Liaoning Province in February 2000 upon the closure of the Yangjiazhangzi mine. Order was restored only after People's Liberation Army units were rushed to this rust belt town 250 miles northeast of Beijing. The world was not supposed to know of the Yangjiazhangzi incident; the news was suppressed. Yet we hear of protests weekly, and they occur more frequently than that.

At the core of China's problems is its economy, and at the core of its economic problems are the state-owned enterprises. They are the backbone of China's industrial might, by far the largest business enterprises and the largest employers there. And they are in trouble. Ideology and politics combine to prevent reform of China's industrial might. Despite their serious condition, these enterprises, year in and year out, have proven to be remarkably resistant to change. No wonder Beijing has compared reforming them to "storming heavily fortified positions."

SOEs have been called "one of the world's biggest and best collections of obsolete factories and equipment." That statement, however, understates the gravity of the situation. Today, after more than two decades of attempted reform, SOEs are creating some of the greatest problems facing the People's Republic: they waste valuable resources, distort policy, endanger the banking system, and cause misery for workers.

RESISTANT TO CHANGE

The sparrows are making a comeback. Branded one of the four "evils" in Mao Zedong's China (along with those other criminals of the animal kingdom, rats, mosquitoes, and flies), the birds had been hunted mercilessly to protect harvests during the Great Leap Forward of the 1950s. Today, however, Chinese authorities better appreciate the little creature's contribution to agriculture and have officially rehabilitated it.

Another endangered species, state-owned enterprises, may not be so fortunate. Sparrows faced extinction in China because they were hunted excessively. SOEs, on the other hand, are endangered because they were excessively protected. With little incentive to improve, these leviathans of China's industrial landscape have not evolved much as times have changed.

Maoist China developed the concept of the SOE not only as the provider of employment but also as the primary deliverer of social services. This "iron rice bowl" system distorted the aims of the SOEs, making them both economic actors and governmentlike social service organizations. The bargain for workers was simple: low wages in return for lifetime employment and comprehensive social services (housing, medical care, schooling, the works). SOEs were little communities, company towns in effect. For more than twenty-three years, from the adoption of the First Five-Year Plan until Mao's death, China simply acted as if the theory of comparative advantage (the concept that one can maximize economic performance by concentrating on what one does best) did not exist. As a result of ignoring basic principles, Beijing has had to live with the consequences of creating hundreds of thousands of industrial theme parks.

The outside world knows China Petrochemical Corporation, better known as "Sinopec," as an integrated oil company based in the southern and eastern parts of China. In fact, this giant runs factories making products such as toothpaste and tissue paper for its refinery employees, who work and live in largely self-sufficient communities. And giant it is. Sinopec is listed by *Fortune* as the world's largest employer and, until recently, the only firm with more than a million workers. But by excluding some types of firms, *Fortune*'s criteria do not catch even larger Chinese employers. For example, Sinopec's major competitor, China National Petroleum Corporation (CNPC), has a workforce of about a million and a half.

In a country hermetically sealed from the outside world and dominated by utopian concepts of industrial organization, SOEs, which resemble isolated communes with too many workers, could survive. In any other type of society, however, this model is simply not viable. In preparation for eventual offerings of stock to foreign investors, both Sinopec and CNPC reorganized so that their "noncore" assets, such as the toothpaste and toilet paper factories, were separated from the subsidiaries whose shares were listed publicly. Mao's model of economic development is not salable today, if it ever was. At least the division of CNPC and Sinopec permits the new listed companies to concentrate on finding, refining, and selling petroleum. But what will happen to the enterprises left with the unwanted assets?

SOEs are also resistant to change because they are run for the benefit of the state or, more precisely, as extensions of the state. Even today, after efforts to separate one from the other, the line dividing the government and its commercial enterprises is, at best, blurred. The Golden Summit (Group) Joint-Stock Company, Ltd., shows how, in practice, the boundary sometimes does not even exist.

Golden Summit, a cement maker based in Leshan in Sichuan Province, was formed in 1988, when an existing state enterprise was restructured into a shareholding company. According to its former chairman, Bai Dehua, the purpose of the restructuring was to "separate ourselves from government as much as possible." To that end Golden Summit listed shares on the Shanghai Stock Exchange in 1993. A substantial block, more than 41 percent, of Golden Summit's shares is held by stock market investors, but this fact has little influence on management. Golden Summit's nine-person board is controlled by Leshan's Party and government officials. So when they want something, Gu Song, Golden Summit's current general manager and deputy Party secretary of Leshan, cannot say no.

And Leshan is not shy about asking. The city forced Golden Summit to take over Dadu River Steel in late 1997, when that company, also state-owned, could not pay rioting workers. That was after Golden Summit was required, by a ministry in Beijing, to absorb three cement factories in faraway Shandong Province. Other forced acquisitions included a mineral water plant and another cement company (because it was in the hometown of a senior official). When Bai was also a vice mayor of Leshan, Golden Summit was considered the town's golden goose. So other Leshan officials imposed excessive financial and other demands on his company during that period. Bai, however, resigned his municipal position early to reduce their opportunity to abuse the company.

"The government manages the national economy by economic, legal and necessary administrative means, but it does not directly interfere in the production and management of enterprises." That's the Party speaking of the world it wants to create. In the meantime, however, Golden Summit is the reality. Until the state builds that ideal world, "mothers-in-law," a general term for meddling officials, will distort the commercial activities of the enterprises it owns.

The line between the state and its commercial enterprises, as blurred as it remains, is relatively distinct compared with the line between the Party and the state. Not surprisingly, the Party, whose actions are often indistinct from those of the government, has retained its control over SOE management even after more than two decades of change unleashed by Deng Xiaoping. As much as he believed in reform, he saw it merely as a means of preserving the Party. If anything, President Jiang Zemin feels even more strongly about Party control.

When Party doctrine is aligned with sound economic management (and that does happen from time to time, especially now that the Party is seeking to reform SOEs without privatization), change can occur rapidly— or at least as rapidly as any change occurs in China. On the other hand, change in the face of Party opposition either cannot take place at all or happens only after prolonged struggle and compromise.

For all the change that has occurred in post-Mao China, it still is not possible to draw distinct lines separating the Party, the state, and SOEs.

Need proof? Bai Dehua, Golden Summit's former chairman, was appointed by both Leshan's Party Committee and the city's State Asset Management Bureau. Who did this man report to? And what were their priorities? As long as Party organs have a large say in the selection of personnel, SOE managers are more likely to comply with Party policies than either the laws of the marketplace or the demands of modern management.

SOEs are the primary provider of social services, they are run as extensions of the state, and they are the target of Party meddling. There is yet another reason, more important than the rest, why SOEs are resistant to change. These enterprises, especially the larger ones, exist in a system in which they cannot fail. Therefore, they cannot, as a practical matter, succeed. The single most important mistake that Beijing has made is the failure to let SOEs fail. Today, even after more than two decades of attempts at reform, some enterprises prefer to remain unprofitable to continue to receive government benefits not available to healthy enterprises.

SOE managers know that Party cadres cannot let important enterprises collapse. It is not just that the Party needs their economic output or employment of labor. The Party depends on these enterprises for its survival because of what they are. SOEs are the "public assets" that give the legitimacy to the "Party of Public Assets," the literal name of China's leading political organization. China did not develop the concept of moral hazard; it just enshrined it as permanent policy.

For the most part, Communist Party leaders know better than anyone else that SOEs, with few exceptions, are not viable. After all, they are currently holding the world's largest garage sale by selling off much of Chinese industry. They cannot, however, admit that they are privatizing. That would be doctrinal error, which is sin in a system—socialism—that depends on theory to explain its inevitable triumph. Cao Siyuan, China's most entertaining political thinker, has a simple solution to this otherwise insoluble problem: change the name of the Party. Until that happens, however, Party members will continue to show the world that, at least from the standpoint of doctrine, they are emperors, or more precisely cadres, without clothes.

In the meantime, China's leaders, in a theoretical quandary, continue to misallocate precious resources year after year. In the early years, misallocation was not a significant problem. Mao's spoils of war were a devastated country that had, from the fall of the Qing Dynasty in 1912, endured continuous unrest and civil war and then invasion and brutal occupation. By 1949, when Mao's peasant army entered Beijing, the country was in ruins. When SOEs became the instruments of rapid industrialization, increasing production was the only issue. SOE managers were judged on whether they met output quotas imposed from the center and whether they increased the value of productive (industrial) assets. At least from a theoretical point of view, factory managers had a simple task: produce, and then produce more.

After more than two decades of growth and cascading foreign investment, China produces too much of most manufactured goods. Yet the old system and thinking continue. These days, yearly overproduction accounts for perhaps two to three percentage points of growth of gross domestic product. Overproduction, however, carries a real cost. It is uneconomic, even irrational. Nonetheless, the central government encourages it to create employment. Subsidies keep the grossly inefficient system going. At the same time, Beijing is alive to the problems and seeks change.

Now SOEs are supposed to behave like rational economic actors. The idea is that they are no longer factories; they are, at least in theory, modern businesses (and therefore economically self-sufficient). The problem is that they are not able to stand on their own. The central government has a solution, but it is ironic—and a bit tragic—that the cure is spreading the cancer.

As a means of moving to a more modern economy, Beijing is replacing direct subsidies with loans from state-owned commercial banks. Now SOEs are gobbling up about 70 percent of domestic lending. The theory is that the SOEs will pay those loans back just as any other modern business would. In one sense, there is a certain wisdom in this thinking. Replacing subsidies with loans should instill a sense of financial responsibility in SOE managers. Central government subsidies are grants while loans, no matter how generous the terms, are meant to be paid back. The concept is that, over time, the SOEs will be weaned from direct government support.

That is how reform is supposed to progress. It is not working out that way, however; Beijing's policy of substituting loans for grants is failing.

Large SOEs have evidently perceived, quite correctly as it turns out, that they do not need to pay back the banks. Loans from the state-owned banks to the state-owned enterprises have, in fact, been replaced by new ones when the old ones mature. Sometimes interest is paid to the banks and sometimes not, but for the bigger enterprises the loans are always rolled over. Thus they have begun to look to SOE managers like the old grants. Most SOEs, if they repay at all, do so only when they are forced to and when there are no other options.

The predicament of the banks is illustrated by Anshan Iron & Steel, China's first steel company (and until recently the country's largest such firm). Angang, as it is known, is a good example of a sick SOE: 1950s Soviet technology at work, half a million retirees and laid-off employees to support, and billions of renminbi to be paid back. The good news for the banks is that Angang is too big to fail. Central government leaders, including President Jiang Zemin and Premier Zhu Rongji, periodically troop up to Anshan, in the heart of China's northeast rust belt, to show their support for Angang's costly modernization efforts.

The message is not lost on the banks lending to Angang. "How can we stop supporting these large state enterprises?" asked one banker about Angang and other SOEs. "If we did, they would go under, and so would we." State-owned banks have no choice but to continue to lend. In fact, Angang is one of the biggest beneficiaries of increased state bank lending to SOEs even though it was also the biggest beneficiary of Beijing's debt cancellation plan: Angang was relieved of ¥6.9 billion (US$825.8 million) of indebtedness. The official media tell the world how well Angang is doing these days, but the reality is that this enterprise is seeking even more money from the banks.

As the Angang story indicates, the central government is shifting the state-owned enterprise problem to the state-owned banks. Beijing evidently had the right idea, at least in broad outline, and was utterly practical in its thinking. A complete change in outlook, even under the best of circumstances, would not occur quickly for SOE managers (or, for that matter, central planners and Party leaders). Gradualism, therefore, was made policy. The result of this approach, however sound on paper, is proving disastrous in practice, as now the banks as well as the state enterprises are sick. At least under the old system, the central government paid subsidies and bore the financial consequences of maintaining the state enterprise system. Now those consequences are being transferred to the banks, which are being rendered insolvent as a result. Although the banks are state-owned too, they nonetheless have depositors, who now share the risk for the failure of SOEs: if state enterprises do not pay back their loans, the state banks cannot pay back their depositors. Banking is built on confidence, and these financial institutions are now at risk. Once ordinary depositors learn that the banks are insolvent, anything can happen.

In the meantime, the seemingly endless flow of liquidity, akin to an iron lung for the SOEs, means that real reform can be, and is being, postponed. Today, more than a quarter century after Zhou Enlai's announcement of the Four Modernizations, Communist Party leaders are still debating how to reform state enterprises. Worse, they have yet to learn from their mistakes; even today, central government officials were calling for even more loans for SOEs. Sometimes reform moves forward and sometimes it moves back, but state enterprises are, as ever, resistant to change.

THE PRESENT

Don't cry for them, China, they're doing quite well. SOEs are striding toward the future, making big profits while restructuring. If you worry about them, don't bother, for modern Chinese enterprises are thriving. As *People's Daily* tells us, China has already harvested "rich fruit in SOE reform and development."

You can see the fruit for yourself. It's in the figures—the government's figures, that is. Official sources proclaim that SOEs on the whole turn profits for the state. That profit for 1998 was announced to be ¥49 billion (approximately US$5.9 billion). In 1999, profits increased by about 77.7 percent, and in 2000 they grew by an eye-popping 140 percent. Progress was predictable because Zhu Rongji, when he became China's fifth premier in March 1998, promised to turn around loss-making SOEs in three years. By imposing a tight deadline, the newly installed premier put pressure on SOE managers to produce good numbers—which is exactly what they began doing. These days, there are plenty of reported profits, regardless of actual performance. Relying on all the sunny news, the premier declared that he had achieved his goal before the end of the three-year period.

Deception starts at the top. The central government's own figures are crafted to be misleading. The 1998 profit figure of ¥49 billion, for example, does not take into account government subsidies of ¥150 billion (US$18.1 billion). To those who know basic arithmetic (and this subject really should be taught at the Central Party School for cadres), these figures demonstrate that SOEs actually produced a loss of ¥101 billion (US$12.2 billion). Profit figures for subsequent years are even less illuminating. When we look behind the figures for 2000 we see that half the profits were due solely to an increase in world oil prices, which permitted state companies to charge more for China's crude, and a quarter of the profits resulted from direct government subsidies, such as rebates of value added tax and the relief of the SOEs' debt to the tune of about ¥1.3 trillion (US$157.0 billion). State officials deny that the SOEs heavily rely on state support to produce profits, but they're not fooling anybody.

And then there is outright fabrication. A study released by the Ministry of Finance in 1999 found that 89 percent of state enterprises surveyed had "cooked" their profit-and-loss statements. A follow-up audit released in December 2000 showed 99 percent of SOEs misstated their financial results. Fakery is the only explanation of how they can show profits when all the other economic signs are pointing in the opposite direction. The 1999 profits of China's publicly listed firms, virtually all of which are SOEs, were down from the previous year's, and a record number lost money. Unsold inventories swelled in 1999 and 2000, a sure sign of trouble, and the amount of idle equipment, now valued at more than US$60 billion, appears to be increasing. As one observer said, the reports of improving state-sector profitability are simply "preposterous."

Look a bit deeper, and the structural problems become apparent. The official statistics for 1999 showed that SOEs produced around 28 percent of China's output with about 53 percent of its industrial fixed assets and 41 percent of the urban workforce. This disproportionality screams inefficiency and makes it clear that real reform is needed now. A system such as this is unsustainable. And the situation is getting worse. "There has been no fundamental improvement in state-sector efficiency," says one economist in Beijing. "In fact, there's actually been a further falloff."

One does not get a sense of urgency from high officials, however. Zhu Rongji can brag about the profits that state enterprises generate, but he cannot change the reality that they remain dependent on central government support. Sure, he can pump up enterprises with massive injections of cash, yet any steroid eventually wears off. What happens then? We can hope that the premier knows what he will do next, but neither he nor his colleagues give us hope. Senior leaders have deserted the pursuit of the truth as they create their own facts. They are armed with all the statistics the central government can produce, but the numbers measure a world that has no relevance to the one that matters.

In the world that matters, the real cost to China is not the direct losses of the SOEs, the subsidies, or even the "loans" from China's state banks. The most pernicious cost, and the one that is hidden from view when SOE profitability is discussed, is the maintenance of an inefficient system in order to keep state enterprises afloat. They are the intended beneficiaries of China's high tariff walls, the "buy local" policies, and the cumbersome investment approval processes, to name just a few examples. The SOEs' worst crime is not that they are uneconomic in their present form or that they take away scarce resources from the vibrant private sector (both of which are true). Their principal offense is that the system built to save them makes it difficult for China to advance with the rest of the world. Statistics, both official and otherwise, cannot begin to measure how the country is suffering to keep this system in place.

Consider all these factors, and it becomes clear that SOEs are simply uneconomic. Local cadres can falsify their statistics and Beijing's leaders can pretend not to notice, but none of them can prevent the future. It is not profitability that counts but competitiveness. When China joins the World Trade Organization, state enterprises will face foreign businesses fighting for a share of China's markets. Forced to compete on their own on a truly level playing field, not many SOEs will see the second decade of the new millennium.

Unless, of course, there is meaningful reform. The Party, borrowing words that bring back the wrong memories, terms the "industrialization and modernization" of China "a great historical leap forward." Although this unfortunate phrase conveys a sense of forward motion, official Party reports about enterprise reform are remarkably similar from year to year. The details change, but the story stays the same. The rousing exhortations for more rigorous management and harder work sound distressingly familiar. As Jiang Zemin himself said in 1999, China has had more than twenty years of experience in SOE reform.

So the debate goes around in circles as proposals for reform are reproposed. Cao Siyuan, the political thinker, advocates complete privatization of all "cardiac patients," his term for SOEs. He would have the state sell all of its ownership interests in China's industry, something Beijing assures us will never happen. Senior leaders cannot accept the notion that China's economy can be reformed by ending the SOE system altogether. Then there is partial privatization as a means of reforming particular SOEs (by introducing the largely alien concept of management responsibility to shareholders). The state is, in fact, selling small blocks of stock to private investors, although this is not called "privatization" in China.

Proponents of increased competition and bankruptcy believe that without winter there can be no spring. Their solutions promise quick reform, but at the cost of pain, mainly in the form of unemployment resulting from a significant number of failures. Both old-guard elements in the Party and Ayn Rand capitalists can find much to like here (the former because private ownership is not a necessary element of this plan, the latter because this approach rewards failure in the marketplace with death). Nonetheless, advocates of competition and bankruptcy are not making as much headway as they should. Beijing has an industrial policy to make enterprises bigger by stifling competition, and for the most part this means that only the central government can determine which enterprises will go out of existence. Because worker unrest frightens leaders, relatively few enterprises are allowed to fail.

Tinkering, another option for reform, is fashionable because it is in line with the current attitude of the Party on all things controversial: gradualism, the acceptable face of denial. In the absence of tackling difficult issues head-on, tinkering not only has become an art form in China but has also been elevated to the realm of official policy.

What will SOE reform look like as China evolves? At least in the short run, tinkering will prevail as delay has become the order of the day, even in the face of accession to the World Trade Organization. The central government implements change, but the pace is determined by the complex interplay between China's socialist orthodoxy and its practical approach to reform. The overall result is slow change. Recent history helps us understand why underachieving is so popular when it comes to enterprise reform.

The parade in Beijing on National Day 1999, celebrating fifty years of the People's Republic, featured a float bearing a large portrait of Jiang Zemin during his finest moment to date: delivering his report to the Fifteenth Party Congress in 1997. At that gathering the Party took a momentous step forward by recognizing that the state could not save all state-owned enterprises. Therefore, it decided to "grasp the large, release the small" (it seems that every major Party policy must have its own slogan). In short, the Party declared that it would keep only the larger enterprises in the state-owned stable, about 1,000 of them (out of approximately 110,000 in total at that time). This was leadership at its best, as the Party was finally able to take a decisive step.

Privatization, though it was not termed as such, was not the only medicine prescribed by the Fifteenth Party Congress. Provincial and lower-level officials, however, recognized an opportunity when it presented itself and read no further. They immediately began a massive sell-off of smaller businesses—sometimes to themselves and their associates and most often with their own benefit in mind. They were even able to effectively write off the debts to the state banks in the process, conveniently forgetting to inform those creditors of what they had done. Stories of abuse are already the stuff of legend. The state suffered financial losses, and the Party's reputation was further blackened. If that wasn't bad enough, members of the proletariat were sometimes forced into the ranks of the capitalists as workers were coerced into buying shares in their employers. In the cases where they weren't, the new owners laid them off, often casting them adrift in a workers' state without sufficient workers' benefits. Newly privatized firms also had little stomach for paying off old bank loans (those that were not improperly written off) or back taxes.

Ten years from now, economists will look back and judge one of the greatest sales in history as a success because, despite the excesses in the methods of privatization, the process of renewal began for tens of thousands of enterprises. Moreover, the end result was inevitable. For one thing, the state could not afford to support all its children—the cost would simply have been too high. Even after the binge sale, it was estimated that Beijing would need US$241 billion to US$301 billion to upgrade all of its present enterprises. The state cannot bear even that amount.

From Beijing's point of view, however, what followed the Fifteenth Party Congress was a debacle. The central government lost little time: by July of the following year, it ordered a slowdown in sales through the time-honored tactic of centrally issued fiat. The result is today's stagnation. The combination of an overcentralized bureaucracy that has lost sight of what must be done and a stalemated political party that has generally lost its way is producing reform at slow speed.

Repairing state enterprises should be a relatively fast process. The general propositions of reform are easy to state: SOEs suffer from too much politics and too much theory. Remove them both, and there will be technical fixes that will work. Run them for profit, and they will be profitable. Most people, even most people in leadership circles in Beijing, know this. Yet sometimes it appears that the Party will need generations to implement the simple solutions that are obvious once the general propositions are uttered. Why?

Apart from the lesson that Beijing received at the feet of local officials about the power of self-interest and greed, many factors are slowing the Party's response to the SOE situation. First, to the conservative elements of the Party, the apparently swift collapse of the Soviet Union and its satellites dramatized the dangers of moving too quickly. It is difficult to pinpoint the effect of the historic events in Moscow on Chinese views of change, in large part because progressive Party elements saw in these same events the need to hasten reform. Nonetheless, the Soviet example solidified the thinking and stiffened the resistance of the old guard, thereby affecting the pace of change for years to come.

Second, Deng Xiaoping's gradual disappearance from public view—his last public appearance was in February 1994 in Shanghai—ushered in a period of stagnation. From that time until his death in February 1997, and to a lesser extent afterward, the pace of progress in regard to efforts to modernize the larger SOEs has slowed. His chosen successor, Jiang Zemin, could undertake no controversial moves until Deng in fact died, and only then once he had consolidated power. Like Deng before him and especially Mao before Deng, Jiang likes to put himself above the fray, only stepping in to broker compromises among feuding Party luminaries. This leadership style, perfect for solidifying power, is less than ideal when it comes to taking hard but necessary steps. Now that Jiang has elbowed Zhu Rongji out of the way to become China's leading light on SOE reform, his leadership will be tested.

The absence of strong leadership is especially missed in times like these. When reform was stalling in the early 1990s, it was Deng who went on his now-famous Southern Tour during January and February 1992. Single-handedly, Deng made rapid economic growth and modernization official Party dogma (at least at the time). With no strong leader in the capital after 1994, it is understandable that the least controversial solution has become the most easily adopted. There is now no consensus for fundamental change of SOEs that remained in the state's stable after the sell-off in 1997–98. Jiang took a bold step in allowing the sale of smaller SOEs then, but since that time he seems to have lost his nerve. It now appears that only a person of Deng's strong will and personal following can push important reforms forward.

Third, China can restructure SOEs only as long as its economy grows fast enough to absorb the workers released by ailing state enterprises. With Deng Xiaoping in charge, China, growing faster than any other country in the world at that time, was catching up. Today this is not the case, as the announced growth rates mask economic decline. According to official statistics, gross domestic product grew by 7.1 percent in 1999, less than 1997's increase of 8.8 percent and 1998's 7.8 percent rise. Growth in 2000 was announced to be 8.0 percent, but the turnaround was more apparent than real and most predict another downturn in GDP growth. Deng Xiaoping once said, "Slow growth isn't socialism," but that is exactly what is happening in today's China.

Fourth, "state enterprise reform has no clear winners over the short term." So China is stuck in the middle of the stream. Going forward (and maybe even back) would be better than where it is today. There can be no progress without further reform, but further reform is not politically feasible because of the perceived social costs (and the consequent threats to maintenance of the Party's position). The turmoil and pain resulting from unprecedented growth and reform are unpopular, and, without knowing more about the future, few want to take further risks. Twenty years ago, everyone knew that China would have to change. Mao's vision was patently unsustainable. Now, however, many have something to lose and those who have suffered do not want to suffer more. Jiang Zemin correctly perceives that change is not popular, however much it is necessary.

And there is one more reason, perhaps more important than all the others combined, for zealousness in the cause of delay. The Party has yet to make the admission that it is the problem, not, as it so often proclaims, the solution. It is not hard to see why centrally directed development dominates Jiang Zemin's thinking. If for no other reason, the process creates a role for the Party in society. It takes tens of millions of cadres to run the vast business enterprises that span the country—and the bureaucracies that oversee them. So Jiang continues to insist that the Party actively intervene to guide important state enterprises and the reform process.

And actively work to maintain stability. Accordingly, the Party has now adopted, at least with the one thousand or so larger SOEs, a conservative agenda, suspiciously resembling maintenance of the status quo, largely to address concerns about stability. Maintaining the current situation, however, means that the larger SOEs have little chance of achieving viability.

Until the Party leadership feels that the country is stable, not much more can be hoped for. Tinkering, although not termed as such, is a major theme of Jiang Zemin's program. Specifics on how to reform the SOEs that are to remain on state life support are scarce. "We should ensure that we advance as appropriate, retreat as necessary, and do things as one sees fit," he tells us. This is either a call for pragmatism (unlikely, given his fondness for theoretical orthodoxy) or an admission that the Chinese leaders, even at this late stage, do not know what to do. Jiang Zemin may instruct cadres across the country to read his words and follow them to the letter, but apart from working harder still, they may have a hard time divining what the Party really wants. Policy in this area is, after all, the compromise product of diametrically opposing views inside the world's leading Communist organization.

Tinkering gives the Party time to figure out the next step. The communiqué issued after a Party meeting in 1999 uses all the obligatory phrases to convey urgency and then essentially postpones the Party's self-imposed deadline for SOE reform to 2010. Healing state-owned enterprises was pushed over the horizon.

The Party these days has two initiatives. The first goes under the heading "modern enterprise system." This bland phrase is code for dramatic restructuring: a range of reforms including the severing of governmental social service functions (housing, schooling, and so on) from the SOEs. Unfortunately, political will has been lacking since 1993, when reforms were enunciated by the Party, so SOEs will have to continue carrying these burdens for the indefinite future.

The Party's second objective is the delicate and critically important task of removing itself from SOE management at the same time that it is asserting its leading role in SOE reform. How, exactly, will the Party accomplish this feat? This is, after all, not a new mission. The Party continually promises not to meddle in SOE affairs, but it just can't help itself. Recently it proclaimed that "Strengthening and improving the party leadership is the fundamental guarantee for speeding up the reform and development of SOEs." How can the self-assigned vanguard of society not become involved in perhaps the most important problem China faces?

We know that the Party will not retreat. "In the long practice of building up state-owned enterprises, we have gained rather effective management experience, which should not be discarded," says President Jiang. Maybe so, but the Party does not have much experience in restraining itself and releasing the energy and initiative of its professional managers. This is one area where practice does not make perfect; the Party is still getting it wrong. That's a shame because the ongoing conflict within SOEs between the Party and professional management retards change. Many managers know what to do and have the resources to do it. They cannot move, however, because the Party apparatus inside their enterprise blocks change. The obvious solution is to eliminate Party cells within state-owned enterprises. That, however, is not possible in China, at least at this time. It is now clear that Jiang Zemin is resisting any reform that will undercut Party authority. Because most change must, there is little that can be done.

These two goals, separating the Party from SOE management and unburdening SOEs of their social welfare obligations, are structural in nature and deserve a more flattering label than "tinkering." But it is giving the Party too much credit to say that it is trying to accomplish them. The reality is that these goals have fallen into the "too difficult" box and illustrate a recent tendency of the Party's announcing, but not implementing, broad reforms. The general policy initiatives being discussed now (better management, incentives for employees, and the like) have been discussed and tried in the past. The issue is whether this time China can implement these general prescriptions better than before.

While the Party figures out what to do next, cadres do anything to avoid the need for fundamental reform. When all else fails, Marxists fall back on science. Therefore, Beijing can get excited about the hope offered by high technology and demand that SOEs become technological. "The core of international economic competition today is knowledge and technological renovation and the industrialization of high technology," says Jiang Zemin. Technology has always had a special appeal to China's leaders, who as Marxists claim a "scientific" basis for their socialist ideology.

Technology does offer hope because, if properly utilized, it will permit SOEs to leapfrog their global competitors and help put China firmly in the twenty-first century. Especially since the end of the last decade, China's leaders have refocused their efforts to develop homegrown high technology and encourage Internet usage. As a general proposition, their strategy makes sense.

There is a limit, however, to what science can do for SOEs. China's leaders talk about the application of technology to business as a mechanical process, almost as if there were some objective formula that could be applied. That concept naturally follows from their general belief that there is a "correct" way of doing things. Here, as in other areas, ideology centered on the objective nature of the universe can get in the way.

The Chinese government, once having identified the initial steps to a larger goal, is second to none in achieving those first steps. China can, and will, develop high technology. It is only a matter of time now that Beijing has put its full weight behind this effort. It remains to be seen, however, whether China, after achieving interim steps, can develop a modern industry based on that technology. Early indications are that its industrial policy needs to be "rectified," to borrow a phrase in vogue in Communist Party circles. In most people's minds the image of the ailing

SOE is of some gargantuan enterprise making commodity products based on 1950s technology with hundreds of thousands of ill-trained laborers. Some SOEs fit this description, of course, plenty of them, in fact. Nonetheless, some failing SOEs are modern high-tech companies that, for one reason or another, are just as uneconomic as the mastodons of China's rust belt. A good example is China Hualu Electronics, which was launched in 1993 with plenty of funds and the latest technology from Matsushita. With little market in China for its high-end products, however, Hualu produced mainly bad debts, which were subsequently canceled.

As the Hualu example indicates, high technology does not a modern corporation make. Technical superiority, like any other element of a modern business, cannot by itself ensure success. In the two decades of reform, Chinese enterprises imported some of the world's finest technology and most modern equipment. Some of the enterprises that did so are benefiting today. Others, however, are in ruins. All the programs to upgrade SOE technology are just new versions of China's failed industrial policy.

This is not to say that Beijing's emphasis on technology is wrong. Plainly, it is not. Why should China confine itself to the basement just because it is blessed with low-cost labor? Party leaders should remember, however, that in the world they wish to join, businesses are judged by the profits they generate and the shareholder value they create and that technology is but one ingredient in the stew. Jiang Zemin is failing in his struggle to make the lumbering SOEs viable in an Internet world because his industrial policy has been efficient in destroying that value.

SOEs are especially experienced in destroying value when given the slightest opportunity to spend central government money. And the guardians of China's sunset industries have just sensed a new way to get it. Beijing's recent emphasis on high technology as an answer to SOE problems is being learned too well. Angang, the steelmaker, is trying to diversify into computers and semiconductors, and of course it is asking for central government help. Is it realistic to think that this rust belt relic can make a smooth transition from steel to silicon?

The Party exhorts SOEs to strengthen their "scientific management." Who can argue with that? But business is an art as much as a science. Success these days is as much about strategy, marketing, and organization as about technology. Jiang Zemin warns enterprises to "avert risks." Business is about taking them. Now you know why there is a problem.

Modernization, socialist style, can succeed; it is not impossible. Small steps are sometimes rewarded. More than seventy thousand cadres and bureaucrats visited the facilities of Handan Iron & Steel Group, or Hangang, in Hebei Province in 1998 to learn how to transform minimal profits into gigantic ones without laying off a single worker. The secret? Hangang imposes cost controls and sets financial, as opposed to output, incentives. Hangang proves that tinkering can result in increased efficiency. Nonetheless, Hangang would be even more of an economic success if it would reduce its workforce.

Today tinkering is the order of the day as Chinese leaders "cross the river by feeling the stones." There are, of course, a few success stories as they move forward cautiously. Beijing touts Hangang as a model, but for every Hangang there are a thousand Angangs. One will not be enough: China will need hundreds, if not thousands, of Hangangs to modernize its industrial sector. In the absence of real reform, the odds of that happening in the future are not good.

Yet even if the country can beat those odds, the price may be too high. In its drive to modernize its economy of the past, China steals from its future. Privately owned enterprises, for example, need funds for expansion, but the state diverts capital to SOEs instead. The establishment of a "second-board" stock exchange, designed to permit smaller and privately owned businesses to raise money, has been repeatedly delayed on account of fears that the newer bourse will attract funds that would otherwise go to the main boards, where large SOEs list their shares. The new exchange should have been in operation long ago but now has been delayed to the indefinite future. Yes, China's economy could have a bright future, but the state sector will have to get out of the way first.

THE FUTURE

You can see the future if you look hard enough today. It's there at Shanghai's airport of the past, Hongqiao International. If you want to see what happens when things go wrong at state-owned enterprises, try to take a taxi from there.

As boom turned to bust in the late 1990s, the number of cabs in Shanghai mushroomed. About forty thousand taxis now roam the streets of that metropolis, many more than are necessary. Shanghai must be the only major city in the world where you can find a cab in the rain at rush hour. Many drivers know little of the city's roads and, worse, cannot find the important landmarks of which the municipal government is so proud. They look as if they would be more comfortable pouring molten steel than trying to find their way around the narrow roads or even the main highways. That's because many were doing just that before they found their new profession on the streets of Shanghai. The city channeled its newly unemployed into cab driving, and they received little training.

In a perfect world, these drivers would not be forced onto innocent, and unsuspecting, visitors. In our world, however, the solution was as good as any that could be devised. If you had arrived at Shanghai's aging Hongqiao airport in October 1999 with luggage, you would have fought your way through the crowds, and eventually you would have found the front of the taxi line. You would have been directed to a cab, if you were lucky, by a surly female traffic monitor who was responsible for matching bewildered folk like you with annoying drivers. The driver would have argued with you because in addition to the problems that he, or she, had had with the spouse that morning, you simply had too much luggage to fit comfortably into the cab. The monitor, however, after three minutes of conversation punctuated by threatening arm and leg gestures, would have prevailed, and you and your luggage would have traveled together.

Arrive one month later, however, and you would have thought you had entered a parallel universe. There are now more armband wearers, many more than needed. You are guided to the same taxi line, and the same driver, who is not getting on any better with his or her spouse, tries to fit you, and all of your luggage, into the vehicle. You are bewildered. An armband wearer, in a firm tone, commands that you hire another cab for your luggage, and it is now the driver arguing that he or she can take everything. Out of the hearing of airport officials you will be told by your driver that, almost as a matter of official policy, the municipality is trying to increase cab usage at the expense of passengers. Visitors are no longer allowed to travel with their luggage or even their loved ones. Drivers hate the new practice because ultimately they suffer. Visitors grumble, but there is nothing they can do except skimp on tips.

Unemployment has become a serious problem in China. You learn that when you have to relieve yourself. There are, in addition to more cab drivers and airport monitors, more toilet attendants. Restaurants in Shanghai revived the practice of the bathroom attendant as state-owned enterprises searched for ways to create employment for excess workers. Unnecessary congestion in Chinese toilets will not, on its own, bring down the system, but Chinese business cannot afford, at least over the long run, to tolerate overstaffing. In the absence of a comprehensive nationwide system for the unemployed, Shanghai has created meaningless jobs as a stopgap. And you can tell how fast city leaders will push the reform of municipal enterprises by observing the taxi lines. If cabs are scarce, it means that the municipality can issue more taxi licenses. In this case, the city can sponsor more reform, which will inevitably lead to more unemployment. That unemployment will be relieved as more workers drive cabs. It is fear of the jobless that determines the pace of change in China.

Hu Angang, the noted Chinese economist, says that unemployment is China's most important issue. But unemployment is only the symptom—it is SOEs, the creators of unemployment, that are the number one problem. Reform, then, should be considered the most urgent task. That is not the case, however. The possibility of disorder haunts the regime, so for the most part officials put change on hold and just wait for the next disturbance.

Senior leaders used to rule, but now they merely react. That's because the Party, in the area of SOE reform, is in long-term retreat. First, it permitted small township and village collectives, many of which were really privately owned enterprises, to engage in productive businesses. Then, in the early 1980s, foreigners were allowed to joint-venture with SOEs, effectively beginning the sell-off of state assets that continues to this day. In the 1990s, the Party experimented with the sale of minority stakes in the bigger enterprises and then endorsed the outright sale of small and medium-sized businesses. The Party may hail a change as "a new conceptual breakthrough," but the conceptual breakthrough, if any, is the ability to call a retreat and declare victory at the same time. Today the Party has failed with SOEs as a group and is now trying to work with a smaller number of them, as if a lack of concentration of its effort had been the problem. So cadres cling to a precious few of the bigger SOEs, hoping to accomplish with them what they so far have failed to do. That, we know, is not realistic.

At each retreat the Party has been adept at molding its ideology to fit practical reality. Yet the continual stream of tortuous explanations of what socialism means only serves to highlight that ideology's terminal condition. Chinese leaders have not been able to recognize what the rest of the world already knows: socialism, with or without "Chinese characteristics," does not work.

But there is no consensus to make an admission of that sort. On the contrary, the Party at the turn of the century talks about SOE reform as if it will increase the role of the state sector in ten years. The current mood of orthodoxy has led to the replacement of Deng Xiaoping pragmatism with Marxist-Leninist faith. And that is why, at this time, further change of any consequence is so hard to implement. The comrades at the upper reaches of the Party, an extraordinarily brittle lot, are no longer seeking truth from facts. They are merely saying to themselves that they cannot retreat from Maoist ideals much more. The leaders therefore will not part with either management or control of their state-owned enterprises. And so, as the reforms fail, they part with time.

But time is even more important as China enters the World Trade Organization. China's leaders talk about the benefits of WTO membership but are not taking sufficient steps to prepare SOEs for the drastic changes that accession will bring. Perhaps they believe their own reports of glowing success in transforming state enterprises or do not realize the magnitude of the changes that WTO membership will bring.

And so the Party, afflicted by wishful thinking, keeps hoping that something will actually work if it continues tinkering. The risk is that the Party, stuck somewhere between the old and the new, will talk about further change but instead opt for the status quo. A period of consolidation is turning into one of stagnation as the pain of an incomplete transition prevents further progress. What cadres know, but cannot say in public, is that few in China care to keep the Stalinist system of industrial development and even fewer worry about theoretical correctness. Party leaders simply do not want, and are afraid, to make that-admission. And in the current climate, they cannot. Jiang Zemin's increasing reliance on obedience and ideological orthodoxy not only makes reform more difficult to achieve but also restrains debate. He asks the Party to "talk politics," but discussion about economics, not politics, is what will help SOEs.

Today Party cadres think they can afford their ongoing spasms of orthodoxy. In the future, faced with the stark choice between ideology and power, the Party may become pragmatic. By that time, however, pragmatism may not be enough. While Beijing dithers, China's financial condition continues to erode as SOEs by the tens of thousands continue to call on the central treasury in one way or another. It may not be evident in the official statistics on enterprise profitability, but it is clear from information about the nonperforming loans of the state banks. The grim news is that most of these loans are of 1990s vintage, created in the reform era as a result of gradualist SOE policies. Through delay, Beijing is simply making a bad situation worse.

SOE reform is not merely a question of fixing particular factories. If that was all there was to it, the job would have been finished long ago. Consider the challenges. First, Beijing has to junk the utopian model of self-sufficient communes and restructure SOEs so that China can reap the benefits of efficiencies of scale. At the same time it must make redundant millions of workers (and bureaucrats as well) and find the money to upgrade industrial facilities. Local governments will have to absorb the social welfare obligations now borne by the SOEs. Then someone has to figure out how to get the Party out of business and stop the meddling of local officials—all this in a system that discourages meaningful change and while cadres cling to an ideology that everyone else recognizes is exhausted. Although the leadership talks about reform in the run-up to WTO accession, China must translate intention to action where it counts—on the factory floor and in local Party halls.

Bai Dehua was blunt. Commenting on Zhu Rongji's promise to return SOEs to profitability within three years, Golden Summit's chairman at the time said, "I feel that no one has yet found an effective way to turn around state-owned enterprises. If they have, I haven't seen it." Dong Tao, a Hong Kong–based economist, is optimistic: "Once China has tackled the SOE and banking sector successfully, its pace of development will surprise the world." That prediction is spot on, but when that happens, the Party will no longer rule. None of its answers is anywhere close to the answer. History tells us that: the Party has debated state enterprise reform since 1975, when the Four Modernizations were first discussed. There has never been a shortage of ideas or even of money, but the system that reigns today cannot permit the change that must occur.

Where will the rest of the world be when China finally jettisons Mao's legacy? While China now struggles with theoretical orthodoxy and practical fears of worker unrest, the pace of SOE reform is beginning to resemble continental drift. Conforming an outdated ideology to reality takes time. The rest of the world, which does not have to learn how to adapt Marxism to the twenty-first century, powers ahead, while China falls further behind. There are many who will say that China is making progress, and that is true. Yet it is also true that much of the world is progressing faster than China. The issue is relative speed, and these days China is losing out.

The sparrows have won a reprieve and are now safe. SOEs, on the other hand, still face extinction as modern China, even on the eve of accession to the WTO, has not been able to come up with the right formula to save them. Worse, the Party has not even been able to articulate to others why they should be rescued in the first place.

4

future@china.communism

Is the Communist Party Ready for the Internet?

> The Internet breaks a 500-year Latin American pattern of monopoly, monopoly of information, economics, social, religious power. It fundamentally gives power to the individual, which is a new development in Latin America.
>
> —FERNANDO ESPUELAS

MARRY THE EUPHORIA of the Internet to the lure of China's markets, and you have the hype of the century. Add China's accession to the World Trade Organization, and the excitement really gets out of hand. China, built on the foundation of steel and coal and heavy industry, has entered the Internet age and is seeking its place at the top of the class. Nothing is too modern for a country that claims to have the world's oldest culture. And foreign business is buying the story.

Shenzhen, in rich and strong Guangdong Province, is at the center of China's tomorrow. It is there that China's high-tech and Internet future will shine—or be extinguished. Hong Kong sits next door, separated from it by a zone ringed with steel and barbed wire, the type that once divided Europe into two. Impassive Chinese soldiers with machine guns still patrol this boundary, although these days the guards are a bit of an anachronism. Once, thousands swam the Shenzhen River, really just a large creek, to freedom on the other side. Hong Kong soldiers, the famous Gurkhas, walked the British bank of the stream, waiting to intercept the poor "IIs," illegal immigrants, as they risked all for a better way of life. Now few on the Chinese side want to leave because it is Shen-zhen, not Hong Kong, that has hope.

Shenzhen is where China's future is happening, but on Saturday, No-vember 13, 1999, the country's tomorrow, for the moment at least, was being determined elsewhere. In Beijing, U.S. Trade Representative Charlene Barshefsky met with Chinese Premier Zhu Rongji as both tried to reach an agreement to permit China to enter the WTO. And on that day Guangdong's high-tech world was not in Shenzhen; it was an hour's train ride to the northwest. The capital of Guangdong is Guangzhou, better known in some circles by its former name, Canton, which evokes memories of nineteenth-century opium trading and vice peddling. The Communists rid the city of those evils, at least temporarily, and even re-named the metropolis. The provincial capital is more modern in appear-ance now and few of the landmarks remain, but the freewheeling spirit of old Canton survives.

That pleasant November morning in Guangzhou was a busy one at the aging White Swan. Once the toast of the town, the hotel has stood still in a frontier city pushing China headlong into a new age. Looking at the decoration in the lobby, you can pretty well guess the year it opened (1983) and figure out that it was one of the first foreign-funded hotels in New China, as the People's Republic sometimes calls itself. The White Swan, dominating a small island of prerevolutionary buildings, sits at the intersection of two branches of the big and muddy Pearl River, the artery that connects and enriches Guangzhou, Hong Kong, and Macau.

At this aging hotel Governor Lu Ruihua was hosting the Inter-national Consultative Conference on the Future Economic Development of Guangdong Province, a powwow of chief executives of American and European multinationals, many in the high-tech area. It is fitting, in a his-torical sense, that Lu, chief of Guangdong, China's "information prov-ince," had chosen Guangzhou for this honor. That city was one of the handful of trading outposts, at the margins of Chinese territory, to which Manchu emperors of the Qing Dynasty restricted foreign traders. China, being the center of civilization in its own estimation, once allowed for-eigners only to the edges of its domain. In 1999, the foreigners, no longer repelled by the Chinese, were invited in as honored guests.

To many, the conference at the White Swan was a pale imitation of the Fortune Global Forum, held the previous September in Shanghai on the eve of the fiftieth anniversary of the People's Republic. The Guang-zhou conference was not nearly as grand or flashy as the Shanghai gath-ering, attended by China's president, Jiang Zemin. But like all things Shanghainese, the Global Forum was too much of everything, show-casing all, and then some, of what China had to offer. The Guangzhou conference, on the other hand, focused on Guangdong's high-tech fu-ture, out of sight of international television. While noisy Shanghai bragged about itself in a brand-new convention center, practical Guang-dong got down to business at the dingy White Swan.

The Guangzhou conference might have had its eye on the future, but it had all the hallmarks of old China, where *guanxi,* a network of rela-tionships, is the medium of exchange. After the opening-morning ses-sion, businessmen were herded together for the mandatory group photograph with Communist Party cadres, a practice that China bor-rowed, and ritualized, from the West. "You can use the photograph to gain access to departments of government to help you with your busi-ness," said provincial Party Secretary Li Changchun. Li, definitely a politician from the old school, has close ties with President Jiang Zemin—so close that some say that he could be China's next premier, al-though there are about five others determined to prevent that from hap-pening. A picture with Li could be worth a thousand words. This is how China has worked since time began.

At the White Swan that evening, twenty-first-century China is at work at A Taste of China, the grand-class restaurant upstairs. There, at a table in the unadorned corner next to the kitchen, two of China's promising netpreneurs and their accountant are about to get a taste of publicly raised money. Zhang Jingjun is the boss of an Internet company, Guangzhou Feihua Telecoms Engineering, best known as the operator of China's fourth most popular Web site, 163.net. That name has a power-ful appeal in China: 163.net was the first free e-mail service in China and is the largest. Ms. Zhang is there with the permission of her only child, a boy of nine. Zhang's husband is supportive of her career; her child, Lu Xiao, is not. He, like all of China's "Little Emperors," products of China's "one child" policy, demands, and usually receives, the full atten-tion of his parents. But there's something afoot tonight, so she is not at home.

If 163.net were in any other business, the boss would be Lu Xiao's father, not his mother, and he would be a lot older than thirty-six, Ms. Zhang's age. But this is no typical business, and there are no rules in a start-up operation in a start-up industry. In that industry thirty-six is somewhat old for someone in her position, but even though she may not fit the usual profile, Zhang runs the show at 163.net. She has drive, foresight, and a dominating personality, and she has Guangzhou municipal support. She plays in the hottest industry in China and is one of its stars. We call all of that fame, and this evening it attracts the boys—the boys with the money, of course.

Typical of business dealings around the world, the last to arrive are the moneymen, an investment banker from Hong Kong, Sing Wang, and another, the representative of a fund manager from the New York area. The fund manager, who represents the real financial muscle, is more than an hour late, but he doesn't care—the party cannot start without him no matter how famous Ms. Zhang is.

There is almost no small talk, and what there is centers on the emerging telecommunications industry, a far cry from the usual dinner conversation in chatty, gossipy China. Soon Ms. Zhang and her colleagues are intently listening to Wang as he explains how the purchase of 163.net will have to be structured so that they can eventually float the company's shares in an initial public offering. Then Wang, whose day job is at investment banking giant Goldman Sachs, mentions that he needs an "exit strategy," a means of turning his investment in 163.net into cash if, for any reason, an initial public offering becomes impossible.

Zhang's dark eyes are now motionless, her stare uncomfortably intense. For someone who is about to become wealthy in a nation of peasants, Zhang shows no trace of joy. This business is her passion, more than just a vehicle of short-term enrichment. Clearly, she is not from Hong Kong. Scratch any person in the former British colony, and you will see the blood of a day trader. Li Ka-shing, for instance, the most prominent businessman in a city where business is the only thing that truly matters, thinks long-term only about the future of his sons. What he owns he has no attachment to. He makes deals. He makes money. He doesn't make investments. And he may not even believe in his native Hong Kong—it is, after all, just a place to be used to accumulate wealth. Zhang, however, cares. She cares for those with whom she works and cares for the business she conceived and built. She is a true believer.

A true believer who is attracting the attentions of the best of Hong Kong's investment banking community. Two prominent groups are courting her with the currency of their realm: money. One is Merrill Lynch; the other is Wang's newly formed consortium. Wang's group has the edge and are the ones at dinner tonight. Only Zhang can really say why, but in all probability it is because she is devoted to her work and Merrill, for all its strengths, failed to see that. Wang, with less money at his back, looked for other ways to snare a star, and he is evidently succeeding.

Ms. Zhang and Henry Ford shared something, and Sing Wang could see that. Once when Henry and his son Edsel were discussing the sale of all of Ford Motor Company, the father said, "Supposing we do sell. Supposing we do get these millions. What will we have? We wouldn't have a job!" The Fords never sold all of Ford, and Zhang wants to make sure that she will keep control of her company—or as much of it as she can under the circumstances.

The discussions are involved. Sing Wang is concerned that in the future Ms. Zhang may not want to sell at any price, thereby making it difficult for him to dispose of his investment. He tries to persuade her that, even if she is forced to sell, she can always "retire to Bermuda." She finds that idea completely unappealing. Ms. Zhang wants to work because that is her life. Wang says she needn't retire for life, she can always go back to work after a noncompetition clause expires in three to five years. Zhang retorts, "In the Internet business, three to five years *is* a lifetime!"

Will she and her colleagues sell? In true Chinese fashion, the conversation continues over food; sometimes there is no other way to communicate in China. The parties meet the next morning over brunch in the enormous White Swan coffee shop, which has the best indoor view in Guangzhou of the ugly Pearl River. That eatery is famous, for it is here you can find all the Western couples with their newly adopted Chinese newborns. New parents must wait in China until they get approval to go home, and the White Swan is where local adoption officials say they must stay if they want Guangzhou babies. Devoted mother Zhang Jingjun does not notice the infants as they crawl around her feet, for this is the most difficult part of the negotiations. She, Wang, and the New York fund manager talk about the terms of employment for her and her senior managers. She fights over compensation, and the moneymen fight back.

They argue that the payoff is not now and not in the form of salary; it will come when her company is floated on the public markets. Zhang does not buy the argument.

Unlike most southern Chinese, Zhang is tall and strongly built. Her hair is cut short, and now her demeanor is adversarial. When animated, as she is this November Sunday, she is formidable. She speaks with conviction. She is persuasive.

And she appears to have persuaded Sing Wang. That evening Wang is upstairs in his smallish room at the White Swan huddled with his lawyers and the fund manager. It's fortunate that there is not much conversation about whether to give in to Wonder Woman—it's standing room only for the participants of this meeting, and everyone is tired. Wang decides to relent, and he decides to tell Ms. Zhang the following day. Earlier in the afternoon, at the coffee shop, she had made a case that salaries in high-tech China are higher than Wang had realized. But it is neither persuasion nor her dominating presence that wins this battle. She prevails this particular day, as she will prevail throughout the negotiations, because the moneymen want in and she already has a piece of the industry.

And what an industry it is! The statistics don't do it justice. Materials that Zhang has prepared for investors say that to reach 50 million users, it took almost a hundred years for telephones, thirty years for television, but only five years for the Internet. As 2000 became 2001, there were about 22.5 million Internet users in China, more than double that of the year before. In a land of exaggerated hopes and promises, the statistics may actually understate the penetration of the Net. Multiple users per Internet account mean that many are uncounted. At current growth rates, it is estimated that the number of netizens in China will surpass that in the United States sometime around 2005 (although some say earlier). By that year one of China's portals estimates that there will be 500 million users. That sounds a little far-fetched, but still, it will be only a matter of a few years before that prediction becomes fact. Sometime early in the new century, perhaps around 2015, Chinese will be the most commonly used language on the Net. The oft-quoted Edward Zeng of Sparkice, a high-profile Chinese Internet company, says that will happen *by 2004, if not earlier.*

On its face, that seems impossible. Today Internet usage in China is hobbled by the prohibitive cost of PCs. The average comrade in a city has to work for almost two years before he can afford to buy a Chinese-made PC—if he doesn't purchase anything else, such as food. His country cousin needs more than four. Due to a combination of factors, phone and Internet access charges are high.

And then there are stiff government regulation and strict censorship. In the White Swan Hotel five members of the Gong An, the police, march almost in unison into A Taste of China and sit themselves at the table next to Ms. Zhang's. The coercive power of the state has arrived, although this evening it doesn't look so fearsome as the boys are obviously looking for a good time in their smart green uniforms. Old and new China coexist, each unaware of the other that Saturday in November. On the Net, they do not live together so easily.

Mao sought absolute control over the Chinese population; his successors, living in a different age, are less ambitious and more realistic. Jiang Zemin knows that he cannot stop the Net and still have economic progress; he will have to try to harness it and make foreign technology serve China. The backbone of the country's economy, the state-owned enterprises, is dying, uncompetitive even in China's highly protected economy. Beijing is pinning its hopes on high technology and the Net as a means of catapulting China into the future. China, after all, gave the world paper, gunpowder, and, most important, spaghetti. While it slept for hundreds of years, the West took over the mantle of innovation. Now it is China's turn to relearn invention.

High technology and the Internet, however, have a dark side, as far as China's leaders are concerned. They now know that the Falun Gong adherents who surrounded Zhongnanhai, the Party's leadership compound in Beijing, had organized themselves over the Internet. And through the Internet that group, now branded "an evil cult" and outlawed, has continued its protests. Observers wonder why China's state apparatus is bedeviled by a group armed only with spiritualism and one another's e-mail addresses.

As a result, the central government in Beijing faces an unresolvable dilemma, a "contradiction," to use the correct Maoist lingo. Will it be growth and the Internet or political control? Or can it be both? The Internet is based on availability and diversity. The notions that underpin China, however, are monopoly—the Party's monopoly—and isolation, upon which the Party's power is founded. Mao built his China upon the concept of self-sufficiency, which ultimately implies isolation. The countryside commune was transplanted to the city, where it was reborn in the form of SOEs, little communities that manufactured many, if not most, of the things their workers needed for daily living. By edict, Mao banished the concept of comparative advantage.

Rutger Palmstierna, at the time a Swedish diplomat in China, relates the dynamics of typical communes in the 1970s based upon his observations in the countryside and his own study. He noted that everything either coming into or going out of communes was carried on the backs of commune members. Party secretaries organized commune labor and thus controlled all access to the outside world. Consequently, they reigned supreme in the communes, unchallenged by anyone. Things changed once the communes began to enjoy success, however. They then bought tractors, which were used for transport as well as farming. As the tractors' mechanics became responsible for transport to the outside world, their technical expertise gave them power to challenge Party officials. What started in a small way with tractors is continuing on a larger scale with newspapers, satellite television, and the Internet.

The control over information was once easy for the Party, even in the electronic age. The first modern office structure in Shanghai was the Union Building, close to the historic Bund, the strip of grand old buildings fronting the Huangpu River. On the roof there are dozens of antennas because that was where all the phone lines of foreigners in the city once converged. And on the top floor, unconnected by elevators to the rest of the building, all of their phone conversations were monitored. Now not every conversation is overheard. In the world's most populous country there are simply not enough government monitors for all the foreigners and phone lines.

Say that you are a foreigner living in the most populous city in the most populous country in the world, Shanghai. You get your official *China Daily* in the morning, unadorned by packaging. Subscribe to a foreign publication, however, and it will come in the afternoon in brown wrapping paper, stapled or sewn shut after censors have removed any offending pages. CNN will, from time to time, go off the air, the official reason being satellite malfunction. And every once in a while the state enforces its ban on satellite dishes. Increasingly difficult though it may be, the central government is still attempting to manage information.

And Beijing is trying to control the Internet. Maybe China doesn't listen to every phone call today because it has diverted its resources to patrolling something even more sensitive: the growing number of domestic chat rooms. It's easy for censors to delete comments deemed offensive, but it's increasingly difficult for Beijing to control every Web site. That was also Poland's problem a decade earlier. Says Lech Wałęsa, "The truth is, communism exhausted its possibilities. It was based on censorship, but at that time satellite television was introduced, the Internet, cell phones, and they would have to multiply their political police force by at least five. They had no money to do it."

China may block sites on the Net, but, as Wałęsa notes, no government, no matter how diligent, can keep up with the task. One Citibank officer in Shanghai, looking for model airplanes for his son in 1999, typed "model" into his search engine. China, which blocks pornographic sites, apparently missed one of the most flagrant. And that is how Li Hongzhi can run the Falun Gong, an organization of millions in China, from as far away as New York, where he lives in exile. China blocks his known sites, but the Falun Gong can always stay one step ahead. Li, who claims to be the incarnation of the supreme divinity, undoubtedly uses his supernatural powers to keep the faithful together, but when he wants to speak to them he uses the power of the Net.

Can the Party both promote the Net and maintain political control? So far no Communist state has tried as hard as China. The Party, which has no blueprint, employs various approaches to achieve what appears to be the impossible dream. In addition to patrolling the Internet itself, it is also falling back on smothering regulation, a time-honored tactic in the People's Republic. In January 2000, the Party's Bureau for the Protection of State Secrets issued comprehensive Internet regulations that, among other things, require prior government approval before the disclosure of "information" and prevent the release of "state secrets." The rules are breathtaking in their breadth and, if enforced, would essentially shut down the Internet: no unofficial news could be disseminated, except after weeks of delay, and few would dare e-mail anything controversial or important because a secret is anything the state says it is. Of course, Beijing neglects to enforce the rules, but they still bewilder the online and business communities and stunt the growth of the Net.

Just as bad, within a week of the issuance of these rules, China's encryption registration requirements went into effect. These are so strict that, on their face, they require any foreigner in China, other than diplomatic personnel, to register their cell phones and laptop computers with the State Encryption Management Commission and obtain approval for their use. Again, these requirements are simply impossible to enforce, so they are not.

The state secret and information rules and the encryption requirements create uncertainty, and as long as that sort of atmosphere exists, China cannot fulfill its potential. Such restrictions show the limits of Party policy and make one question how much progress China is really making. "Fifty years after China went through a Communist revolution, it's going through a different sort of revolution, a technological and telecommunications one," proclaims Riz Khan of CNN. Yes, there are more phone lines and Internet subscribers now, but these vague and sweeping rules lie in wait for unsuspecting victims in the future, demonstrating that China is still not really ready for the Internet world. "In order to inspect the Internet, we must control it," says China's Public Security Bureau. Has China undergone a "revolution"? Perhaps not.

Nonetheless, Beijing knows that if it only tries to censor and regulate, it must ultimately lose. Therefore, it is also taking another approach. It's better to win the hearts and minds of the people, the reasoning in Beijing goes. Showing its flexibility and a bit of realism, the Party has ditched Mao, Marx, and Lenin (at least for this purpose). An organization that prides itself on the scientific basis of its beliefs and its unyielding modernism is now reaching back to someone who lived before the birth of Christ, Confucius. That most famous of Chinese sages, whose thoughts were banned in earlier days of the People's Republic, taught many things, but the most important in the eyes of the Party are his beliefs on the importance of obedience. As China confronts a new age, it is looking back to an old one to find comfort. Call this desperation or call it genius—it's actually a bit of both.

But whatever the source of the inspiration, it's a dangerous game for the Party. Deng Xiaoping was good at quoting Mao to tear down Maoist institutions. Similarly, Confucius can be used by the regime's friends and foes alike. If your politics puts you at the unorthodox end of the spectrum, you can remind the Party that Confucius also talked about the Mandate of Heaven, the concept that the people could overthrow unjust rulers. The sage also left little time bombs for the Party. Consider this small gem from *Analects of Confucius,* suitable for creating an unfavorable comparison with the current crop of rulers in Beijing: "If I were given the opportunity, it would only take me a single year to administer a country well, and remarkable achievements could be made in three years." The Party, in contrast, has had more than fifty.

We now know that the Party realizes that it has run out of ideas. The devotion that sustained all of Mao's campaigns has been exhausted. Today that spirit has been, in a sense, rekindled as millions follow the teachings of a former clerk now banished to New York. It's Li Hongzhi's Web sermons versus Confucius's thousand sayings. Both preachers are good at sound bites, and this contest is far from over.

Let's say, purely for the sake of argument, that the sage of all ages helps the Party control the Net because the Chinese no longer entertain dangerous thoughts. Is China then ensured of a high-tech future? After the Party gets through with Confucius, he will sound like a stern father, to be sure. Will obedient netizens be able to think and imagine their way to innovation in such a system, all for the future development of the Motherland? Consider these words from Lech Wałęsa:

> In the past, you could stand with a gun behind a man who had a pick and a spade and tell him to dig a hole two hundred meters long. But you can't put a man behind someone working creatively, behind a computer, and tell him, "Please devise something original." There is no way to do it, and I took advantage of that.

Jiang Zemin certainly hopes that there is no Wałęsa among his flock and that innovation and socialism are compatible. The Chinese president is currently using the awesome powers of the state to start a Silicon Valley in Zhongguancun, near Beijing's great universities. And China is pushing its best minds into technology. Such as Zhang Jingjun, for instance. She went to college at the early age of fifteen. Upon graduation, she was directed to work in Guangzhou's telecom bureau because that was where Guangdong wanted its best minds to go. She didn't complain.

It is perhaps no coincidence that Silicon Valley, the original, is located in mostly freethinking, uninhibited California. That does not sound like the China that we have come to know. As a theoretical matter, there does not have to be a linkage between political freedom and innovation. Nonetheless, in the last two centuries there has been a strong relationship between the two. Of course, the Party is not without its resources and political will, and it is definitely no coincidence that the years of the greatest growth of the Internet in China have also been a time of political suppression and censorship.

Yet for all its strengths, no authoritarian system of beliefs, even those of a wise man, can survive an interactive future in the long run. Teaching will be different in the wired classrooms of the twenty-first century with the young exposed to so many competing sources of information. Will Confucius, or anyone else for that matter, be able to tell them what to think?

In any event, the Party's top leadership, to its credit, has decided to support Internet usage by the entire population. In a country where political stagnation has meant the deferral of most difficult questions, that is no mean accomplishment. More surprisingly, China arrived at a reasonable solution, a rarity in these days of ideological rigidity. There was, of course, a reason why China did so. The same Internet that permits the Falun Gong to organize silently is also permitting China to change its industrial model from state-owned brontosaurus to high-tech start-up. Promote the Net, the reasoning goes in higher Party circles, and China will once again grab the lead in the race for technology. Then the Chinese will lead the world in both steel and silicon.

It is now Tuesday, November 16, one day after the single most important event in the twentieth century, at least according to some. U.S. Trade Representative Charlene Barshefsky and her Chinese counterpart, Foreign Trade Minister Shi Guangsheng, have trouble maintaining eye contact at the ceremony, but no one cares now. China and the United States have signed their agreement paving the way for China's accession to the WTO. Every Internet entrepreneur in China is now potentially worth millions of dollars more.

Our Ms. Zhang included. She even looks wealthier than she did three days ago at the White Swan, where she sported a snazzy African thatched print jacket over a cool black T-shirt. Today she is decked out in a power suit of southern China in tones of white on black, the better to reflect her enhanced power. She is at another restaurant, this time on the other side of Guangzhou. The Lee Gardens, which shares the name but not the parentage of a once famous hotel in Hong Kong, is a maze of private rooms wrapped around main dining areas. She is in, of course, a private room, one befitting the major occasion that it is.

Zhang has just signed an agreement of her own today with Sing Wang. Twenty months to the day that 163.net officially started, she has sold most of the business at an unrealistically inflated price, millions and millions of dollars more than it can possibly be worth. And Ms. Zhang is celebrating the only way the Chinese know how, with a traditional banquet of an uncountable number of courses. Waitresses in their twenties serve each dish, but only after they show the delicacy to the guests by a twirl around the lazy Susan in the center of the table, as ritual and restaurant policy dictate.

A few of the participants—perhaps all of them—think of this as an event to be endured. The irony is that if culture did not demand this ceremonial function, all would scatter and be much relieved. The New York fund manager, for example, would undoubtedly find the comfort of nonspousal companionship, as he did a few nights ago, when he could not be reached (guilt was pronounced when, the next morning, he was painfully defensive as his alibi folded under light questioning). In any event, he is wearing thin on his compatriots' nerves, starting with being hours late for the White Swan dinner. Of all the people from around the world who are eager to invest in China's Internet sector, why does it have to be him? After all, there are thousands who would take his place to back Ms. Zhang.

At least the fund manager is paying for dinner. For all the significance of the event, there is surprisingly little joy this evening. South China's new etiquette requires karaoke, but this particular gathering watches the news on CCTV, state television. The talk around the table is equally serious, focusing mostly on the WTO agreement signed the day before. There are few people in China who will benefit more from that agreement than Ms. Zhang. Money will pour into China's Web, making her remaining stake in 163.net worth more than what she had before the sale.

At the table that night are more lawyers than clients, surprising given the conventional wisdom that law is not important in Chinese society. Unfortunately, they are needed to structure the extraordinarily complex arrangement by which 163.net is being sold. One of those advisers, not being particularly tactful, mentions that farmers and workers at SOEs will be hurt by the agreement. What he did not say, but did not have to, was that the social stability of China, Zhang's China, was at stake. The lawyer, if he had thought about what he said, would not have cared; he represents the fund manager, not Ms. Zhang.

Zhang's transaction will proceed with or without China's accession to the WTO and with or without a legal basis for the complicated structure the lawyers helped devise because "dot coms" are hotter than the sun. Her industry is regulated by the Ministry of Information Industry, and MII, as it is called, is headed by ultranationalist Wu Jichuan. Minister Wu, a 1950s thinker in charge of a twenty-first-century industry, is the single biggest roadblock to China's development in this area.

Wu's passion is control, and the object of his affections is the Directorate-General of Telecommunications, a state-owned enterprise providing services under the China Telecom name. Until 1994, China Telecom enjoyed a complete monopoly over China's then-archaic telecommunications industry. In that year China United Telecommunications Corp., better known as "Unicom," began operations, but government regulation deliberately starved the upstart competitor. As a consequence, Unicom turned to dozens of eager foreign companies that had been seeking entry into China.

As they do now, Chinese regulations prevented foreigners from directly owning, operating, or managing telecom networks. In response, Unicom cleverly skirted the rules by establishing so-called China-China-Foreign joint ventures (CCFs). Although these arrangements took various forms, CCFs were usually made up of joint ventures layered one on top of the other and involved the payment of fees to foreign parties. The fee structures permitted the foreigners to receive payments without acquiring actual ownership, which would have violated Wu's regulations. Under CCF schemes, Unicom, with Wu's knowledge, raised about US$1.4 billion (70 percent of its total funding) from the world's largest telecom operators. This allowed it to somewhat loosen China Telecom's stranglehold. More important, Unicom got foreign technology. And there was one other thing: foreign investors perfected the art of using fees to avoid Chinese ownership restrictions, an art that would be used in ducking similar restrictions in the closely related Internet sector.

Once telecom technology was safely in the door, Wu declared CCFs "irregular" and ordered them disbanded. It took more than two years after Wu's declaration for foreign investors to reach a resolution with Unicom over how much they should be paid. Some of the CCF partners call it expropriation in light of the valuable rights they were forced to surrender. However you look at it, this is a disgraceful chapter in China's relationship with foreign investors.

Wu's success with Unicom naturally encouraged him to take on the Internet operators that were buying ownership stakes in China's fledgling industry. Everyone was at this party, including the giants such as America Online. Even ordinary folk got to drink from the punch bowl: the stock of China.com Corporation, listed on Nasdaq in July 1999, more than tripled in value on the first day of trading. The intersection of technology and China is called hysteria, and in those days the stock price of Chinese dot coms traveled in only one direction.

Foreigners, however, were having too much fun at this gathering, at least according to Wu. In September 1999, he announced that all such investments were illegal, single-handedly igniting a fire in the ballroom as he had done earlier with Unicom's CCFs. There were consternation, rage, and disbelief as foreign Internet investors wailed upon hearing Wu's pronouncement. The conflagration ultimately had to be doused by President Jiang Zemin himself as he sealed November's WTO agreement with the United States. Foreign companies will be able to own up to 49 percent of Chinese Internet companies one year after accession (and 50 percent after two years). Yet the agreement also means, as a practical matter, that existing investments, as illegal as they may be, will not be disturbed.

The convoluted structure that Sing Wang and the lawyers created may no longer be necessary. But business, especially when it's tech-related and has something to do with China, has a momentum and logic of its own. Seven out of ten deals will crash and burn, Wang says as he sits at the White Swan Hotel. The remaining three will make you rich. Zhang's deal will go forward with its ungainly structure. "Close fast" is the mantra, and close it does—so fast, in fact, that Wang does not even have time to visit Zhang's premises before he commits millions of dollars with his signature. It's as if he were buying this Internet company over the Internet. Investors, says one Hong Kong lawyer, "aren't even waiting for the details, as soon as they hear it is an Internet company they ask where they can wire the money."

If anyone needs proof that China has been isolated for most of its history, it is on the table at the Lee Gardens. Dessert is a collection of fried brown balls filled with gooey sesame paste, each ball presented on its own sheet of cheap pleated paper, the type that surrounds cupcakes. After five thousand years of "uninterrupted civilization," is this the best China can do? Even many Chinese won't touch them short of famine or hallucination. Surely any society that was allowed to trade and interact with foreigners would have done anything to import desserts in these desperate circumstances.

Long before the advent of the Internet, China shut itself off from the rest of the world. Commentators like to pinpoint moments in history when perceptions change. With China, Admiral Zheng He's voyages in the mid–fifteenth century were the high-water mark of China's outreach to the world. After that, his fleet, the mightiest in the world, was disbanded and China retreated into itself. Contentment and an antimercantilist outlook ensured centuries of isolation, and that eventually led to decline. China completed a wall to repel foreigners, and Mao, as noted, built the Party upon the bedrock of isolation. For the last five hundred years, the Chinese have been nothing if not consistent.

By isolating its citizens from one another, the Party has been able to ensure that they hear its version of history first. "The only thing I can remember about June 4 is watching television and hearing that riot police had died," said Lu Jing, referring to the Tiananmen Square massacre of 1989. "I don't believe any students died," she volunteered. "China in this respect is democratic as China wouldn't hurt its own people." The Internet will cure the ignorant like Lu, a sixteen-year-old. When it does, what will she think of the regime?

The one thing the Net will not do is change ingrained attitudes—at least not overnight and maybe not even in decades. Many of today's youths are nationalistic to an extreme, even fanatical. Expose them to information from abroad, and it is not necessarily true that they will believe what they read. They are, after all, a product of the same society that gave us Wu Jichuan. He has had plenty of contact with the West, and he is still unrepentant.

Not everyone who logs on will become an instant dissident. "My choice cannot be independent from the patriotic colours in my blood," proclaims Juliet Wu, China's most famous netizen (she left her position as Microsoft's general manager in China for a post at a state-owned company). Ms. Wu may be a little more jingoistic than your typical "Net bug," as they are known in China, but she shows that Chinese can be resistant to foreign influences even though they live online. China is, for the most part, centered on itself (and worse, on its past). The Net will not change that, at least in the short term.

"What do you want the Internet to be?" asks Nortel Networks. If you're Carlos Santana, the answer is "[a] road to a world with no borders, no boundaries, no flags, no countries. Where the heart is the only passport you carry." If you're Jiang Zemin, you want a means to rejuvenate industry and a way to ensure the dominance of the Communist Party. Juliet Wu and Wu Jichuan convince him that he can have both. Over the long term, however, that is not possible. A system based on isolation cannot live in an open architecture. The Party smothered the media with its incomplete view of the Taiwan election in March 2000, but when Chen Shui-bian triumphed, many of the inhabitants of China's Internet world got their uncensored news on the night of the vote, news that did not exactly correspond with the Party's. And there's another reason why the Party cannot prevail in an open age. As Mao taught us, you don't need a majority to sit on the throne in Beijing; a small group will do. To bring the Party down, only one determined person online needs to find out the truth—a person like Mao Zedong, for instance.

So which will it be? For all its commitment to modernization and progress, there is one thing more important to political leaders in Beijing. The Party's decision to crush the demonstrations in Tiananmen Square in June 1989 was not an aberration or a mistake. The Party, if it is anything, is determined to survive. If Jiang Zemin and his successors must make a choice—and they will have to—they will choose retaining power over keeping the Internet. When you believe that you are the only path to progress, the choice is easy to make. And when they make that choice, their consciences will be clear, but China will fall even further behind.

The choice is also easy for Zhang Jingjun and her colleagues. Chat rooms may be full of nationalist ranting against foreign domination of China's Internet industry, but she is happy to bring outsiders into her company and even give them the control they seek. Even after WTO accession, China will not permit foreign investors to own more than 50 percent of an Internet business, yet in the Internet world actual stock ownership is not necessary. The industry has ingeniously developed means of allowing foreign parties to obtain what they want within the confines of China's regulations, which have yet to catch up with the clever mechanisms of foreign investment banking talent. Wu may prohibit, but foreigners can innovate. Both are relentless, but only the latter have history on their side. In a world that is increasingly open and interconnected, Wu will eventually be doomed.

And so will those who do not move fast enough. Events move quickly in Internetland, and although she has just closed the sale, Zhang Jingjun must now plan the next stage of financing for 163.net. If she does not do this well, the company will need an obituary. Her son does not like it when she travels, but Zhang needs money. That means she must go to the Hong Kong Special Administrative Region, as that city is now officially called by China.

Hong Kong has a high-tech future, but one that is different from the Mainland's. The city remembers the flood of Chinese immigrants streaming south in the 1950s and still views itself as superior to Shenzhen, the city just north of its border, and the rest of China. Those on the Hong Kong side of the steel boundary are the same as their Guangdong cousins. They speak the same language, share the same superstitions, and observe the same rituals. Fifty years of Communist rule have had little lasting effect.

Now, as one century blends into another, in southern China it is Shenzhen that has grasped the vision of the new millennium. Hong Kong talks about the Internet but sounds unconvincing. It should be the high-technology center of Asia, but it has failed to distinguish its future from its past. With regard to the development of technology, Hong Kong is merely copying what it has done before: serving as China's intermediary with the outside world. The only significant piece of high-tech business that Hong Kong will get is financing China's winners.

Financing China's winners is exactly what Hong Kong is doing on November 27. Ms. Zhang and her accountant take the train to Hong Kong that morning to meet in the tasteful offices of Sullivan & Cromwell, a New York law firm that represents the fund manager. That same firm was retained by Unicom to argue that foreign investment in CCFs is illegal under Chinese law, but today it is on the other side, helping a whole new group of foreigners throw cash at a Chinese dot com. High above Queen's Road Central, one of Hong Kong's main arteries, representatives from the various groups gather. For purposes of closing the earlier transactions, Ms. Zhang and her colleagues hired a well-known London firm. Today they will meet their foreign lawyers for the first time—after, not before, her agreement to sell is signed. In Zhang's Internet world, face-to-face contact is avoided if it costs more. That's what the Net is all about.

This time it is Zhang who is late, by almost an hour. She enters the conference room, smiles at everyone, and, without an invitation, sits at the head of the table. There is no ritualistic chitchat; she is all business. Even though the purchase was consummated less than two weeks ago, there is so much future to think about. Hours of planning take place over muffins and tea. With China's WTO accession expected within months, Zhang must raise money to compete with the impending challenge of dozens of foreign companies coming to invade her home turf. In a year's time Wu Jichuan may not be able to protect her. She will need every last dollar the public markets will provide.

In spite of the strategic importance of the matters under discussion, Zhang leaves this meeting in the early afternoon to go back home so that she will be on time to have dinner with her son, as he has commanded. Whatever is left unfinished can be handled by her lawyers. She is doing business Western style now.

Even clichés are sometimes true, and Zhang and her new foreign friends are proving one of them. People who work with one another over time develop understanding, and understanding will result, at least ultimately, in a China integrated into the world. When Zhang goes abroad to list shares of 163.net on a public stock market, she will expose her employees to the benefits of belonging to a community larger than any they have seen. Her initial public offering, perhaps in Hong Kong and maybe even on Nasdaq, the stock exchange of choice for China's Internet industry, will create one more contact for her and her young employees.

What will prevail over the long term is the Chinese eagerness to learn and the openness that implies. The Gong An's green uniforms bore POLICE in English when they marched so ceremoniously into A Taste of China on November 13. Even more remarkable, a few years ago Shanghai introduced new winter uniforms. Their brown leather jackets, modeled on Chicago's, say POLICE on the back, in English only. For a society that divides itself from the rest of the world, it still has the capacity to surprise. Open China just a little, and great changes can occur. Who knows where the people will be able to take their country?

The Great Divide in the world is not East versus West, as we often assume, but something else, maybe young versus old. All the culture of the young, which is so easy to label "Western," is in reality not. Modern popular culture first developed in the West and Elvis sang in English, but that was merely an accident of history. It developed there first because societies in North America and Europe were freer than in Asia. It could have started anywhere, and if by accident of history it had first developed in, say, China, only the language of the music would have been different. The young around the world are basically the same, and their culture reflects that essential fact. Let the young be young, and they become almost indistinguishable. Beijing does not yet appear to grasp this point. The Internet will drive it home for the cadres working there.

At the height of 1999's version of the Taiwan crisis, when President Jiang Zemin had just given the "shoot first" order to frontline fighters patrolling the Taiwan Strait, what was the biggest attraction in Beijing? The People's Liberation Army Marching Band? No. Taiwanese pop star Zhang "Ah Mei" Huimei. Forty-five thousand fans jammed the Workers' Stadium to see her, the hottest ticket in town. It was the end of the first week of August, and a government, one that was trying to convince the world that it was about to launch a war against Ah Mei's homeland, looked a little bit silly.

The Internet is merely the medium. Today the West is exporting "its" culture to China. Tomorrow the West will be on the receiving end from a China then an inseparable part of the world. Yes, the Net poses a danger to the government in Beijing, and so do its online young.

So now the race is on. Can the Party get from the Net what it wants before the Net does it in? Perhaps the answer is in Shenzhen. Deng Xiaoping picked that city to be one of China's first Special Economic Zones in 1979. SEZs, which pioneered China's development, are on their last legs these days, but Shenzhen is breathing new life into this aging concept by adding a high-tech element. The presence of central government leaders at the first China Hi-Tech Fair, held in October 1999 in Shenzhen, confirmed that city's favored position. "If other cities can catch up with

Shenzhen, then China's Gross National Product can surpass that of the United States and Japan," said China's premier, Zhu Rongji. With China's outsized ambitions, it is not clear whether he was referring to each country alone or both collectively. In any event, it seems that every hamlet in China is now high tech, or at least announcing that it is, and holding a fair of its own.

Beijing and Shanghai are playing catch-up. They are reduced to sponsoring beauty pageants. They held the Miss Internet contest in conjunction with the selection of Miss Internet Knowledge, Miss Enterprise Information, and, best of all, Miss Home Online Shopping.

The real Miss Internet, our Ms. Zhang, leaves Hong Kong with all her papers from the meeting and a few more besides. She is now on a great adventure, one that could take her anywhere. "Where do you want to go today?" asks Microsoft. "The future" would be her reply.

"Are you ready?" asks another Zhang, Zhang "Ah Mei," as she warms up the crowd in Beijing. She is. So is Zhang Jingjun. The Party thinks it is, but, no, that organization built on isolation and now floundering in the Internet age, is really not.

Sing Wang knows he's ready—ready to sell 163, even though he purchased it just two weeks before. A dot com, flush with cash, has just offered to buy the free e-mail service provider and provide a handsome profit to Wang and his group. Before he completes his sale of 163, however, Wang is off to Shenzhen on still another Internet deal, and Ms. Zhang is continuing to do what she loves. These are good times, very good.

They are good not only for Zhang Jingjun and Sing Wang, but for all Chinese as well. The Internet is the force that will bring about change in the world's most populous nation, for it is where all that is positive in China converges. The regime may patrol cyberspace, but it cannot help but be changed in the process. The Net is not only enriching investors, it is energizing one of the world's oldest civilizations as well. As the chief executive of one of the leading dot coms in Asia recently said, "China needs the Internet more than any other developing country."

Maybe so, but China apparently doesn't think it needs the many talents of Zhang Jingjun. It is January 2000, and now the Guangdong provincial government has stepped in to stop the sale of 163 to Sing Wang. Zhang and her colleagues are now under investigation.

Guangdong Province alleges that the sale to Wang was not properly authorized and that the purchase price was too low, thereby resulting in a loss of state assets. The key to both issues is who owns Guangzhou Feihua Telecoms Engineering, the seller of 163.net. Guangzhou Feihua is a collective, and it is owned both by the state and on behalf of Guangzhou's telecoms employees. Ownership isn't exactly clear, and that's the problem with many other start-ups in China, such as those in Zhongguancun.

The fact is that 163.net was losing money and needed help fast. Advertising revenue, essentially its only source of income, was stagnating. If it had not gotten funding quickly, competitors would have savaged its free e-mail service and then there would have been little or nothing left. Yes, it was valuable, but it was like a rose in full bloom without water. In an immature, volatile market where there are no fixed notions of value, who can say whether the sale price was fair? Yet one thing is clear: the sale was at the top of the curve for dot coms. A few months later the worldwide sell-off in Internet stocks would reduce the values of nonlisted companies such as 163.net. Zhang's sale of 163 resulted in the best price that Guangzhou Feihua would ever get.

The state, however, does not really care about such things. The price wasn't the real problem, it was just an excuse. The sale of 163.net is thought to be the first of an e-mail service provider in China. The investigation is the result of the notion that valuable assets should not be in private hands at all. The state just cannot let go. In the case of most state assets, it isn't clear what rules apply, so it's not known who can authorize a sale. When no one is sure who owns what, few transactions involving state assets are ever really final.

There is one aspect to this matter that is final, however. Guangzhou Feihua dismissed Ms. Zhang on February 1, 2000, and her colleagues left soon thereafter. The hardest part of this ordeal for her is not losing her livelihood; it's explaining the circumstances to her nine-year-old, Lu Xiao. He asked his mother whether she had been fired because she had done something wrong, and she did not know what to say.

To everyone else Ms. Zhang says that the business could not have grown unless there had been a sale because the strictures of the state prevented 163.net from realizing its potential. Zhang is fond of using the term "framework" when she mentions the restrictions of China's system. "The framework does not allow any further development, whether it's for the individual or for 163," she says. Referring to all the Party cadres and bureaucrats who resist change, Ms. Zhang notes that "there will be people who are upset" by any sale. So the state always fights reform.

And it never relents. Beijing opted to connect to the Internet in the early 1990s but retained so much control that some argue that China still does not have a true Internet. Some higher-ups, however, are having second thoughts about having opened the country even this far, and Jiang Mianheng, son of President Jiang Zemin, has sounded the alarm. "China must build a national network that is independent of the Internet," he said. The Chinese Net, says the American-educated engineer with the famous dad, will be in the Chinese language and run on locally developed chips and protocols. And it will have local content supporting the Party's message. There you will not be able to find any "electronic heroin," as it is sometimes called. Jiang Jr. was not merely engaging in idle chatter. In January 2001, Beijing announced the formation of the China C-Net Strategic Alliance, which will develop an Internet-like network just for the world's most populous country. C-Net, when it is formed, will be in line with Jiang Sr.'s campaign against the dangers of globalization and China's preoccupation with its sovereignty.

Our Ms. Zhang is not impressed. The process of development of the information industry is "a historic trend," she says. "It cannot be stopped." These days, she should recognize that it can. Her predicament is proof of the continuing power of the state to resist change. Today Zhang appears weary, as if she has lost something—which she has.

And so has her country. The hope she embodied for the renewal of the Chinese state is gone. Because she's had to leave 163, she's no longer pioneering the country's Internet industry and serving as a model for the nation's young. And her situation is all so unnecessary, she thinks. "If the 163 transaction had any problems, including legal problems, including the so-called state asset problem, et cetera, any problems, this transaction would have been reversed a long time ago," she says in June 2000. "There are no secrets in the 163 transaction, no secrets at all," Zhang notes. "So that should be the end of it."

It's not, unfortunately. There has been no conclusion to the investigation into the sale of 163.net, Wang's subsequent sale of 163 to the cash-rich dot com has not gone forward, the Internet boom in Asia has burst, and 163 has lost much of its value. So China continues to hobble privately owned Internet businesses, but in the process it injures its own future. And with C-Net, Beijing will once again try to cut China off from the rest of the world.

Ready for the Internet? No, the Communist Party is not.

5

Life Everlasting

Industrial Policy Grants Perpetual Existence to the Inept

Crime wouldn't pay if the government ran it.
—UNKNOWN

THE CATEGORY IS "Communist Organizations." The question is "How many of them exist in the world today?" If you're former tennis great John McEnroe, the answer is two. He could name only North Korea and the ATP, the Association of Tennis Professionals. Others go even further. Jonathan Alter, writing in *Newsweek,* declared that communism is "gone."

McEnroe and Alter can be forgiven for forgetting China. After all, even most Chinese don't believe in communism, and each year change takes the country further from its socialist roots. The central government seems to announce a major reform every third day, and some of them it actually implements.

Now that we have been told that communism has disappeared from China, should we suggest to Communist Party General Secretary Jiang Zemin that he apply for a post at the ATP? Well, communism may be having a few bad decades in China, but don't worry, Comrade Zemin, you still have a job in Beijing, and the Party still maintains a system that it rigidly controls. Today cadres struggle to rejuvenate ailing state-owned enterprises, direct the process of reform, and develop new enterprises and technologies for tomorrow. They are doing everything but letting go. They perpetuate a system that needs them.

The people, however, don't need them. They can, if the truth be told, get along without the meddling of their leaders. When residents of Kunming in southwestern Yunnan Province heard that Deng Xiaoping was talking economic reform during his Southern Tour of early 1992, the effect was immediate. Like a "swarm of bees" the people took matters into their own hands. Overnight, private vendors put up strings of white lights along roadsides and began selling trinkets from card tables during the evening. The populace then realized that there was no turning back from *gaige kaifang,* the policy of "reform and opening to the outside world." Before the tour, no one had been quite sure, and everyone was waiting for a sign. In symbolism-rich China, Deng's trip could mean only one thing. And the people didn't need to be told twice.

And that's where the case for optimism about the People's Republic starts. Many see all the signs of modernization visible today and say that eventually the country will grow into a modern market economy. China has "the most promising market in the world," says Phil Murtaugh of Shanghai General Motors, the biggest Sino-U.S. joint venture. "It has by far the highest growth potential anywhere in the world, and that's why we're here and why everybody else wants to be here." Extrapolation, especially in the hands of the optimistic, can lead one astray, however. Most of the change occurred during Deng's years. His successor, the orthodox Jiang Zemin, has been responsible for far fewer advances. He is continuing along the path that Deng charted, making adjustments here and there. Yet he has just about reached the limits of reform that he will tolerate.

For all the change that Deng and Jiang have wrought since the end of 1978, they have done surprisingly little to modify the underlying assumptions about the role of the Party and the central government in leading development in China. Beijing still retains the massive planning apparatus that Mao developed from the Soviet model. Now, as China progresses from its Ninth to its Tenth Five-Year Plan, it is evident that the nation cannot progress much further within the Party's conceptual framework. The world is racing at Internet speed; China moves forward in carefully orchestrated five-year blocks of time. The concept of a multiyear fixed schedule is outmoded when things change by the day, but Beijing soldiers on in its pursuit of orderliness toward the goal of development. In the Chinese capital there is an apparent confidence, lacking most everywhere else, that it is possible to know—and control—the future. As planners go about directing the workings of an entire economy with little sense of urgency, China is falling behind, misreading the ever-changing environment. And while that happens both old and young enterprises suffer.

THE ANGEL OF NANCHANG

In the dark Chris Tibbs cannot tell just how old the Ferris wheel is, but in the glow of the decorative lights the rust is visible, and he can hear the scraping of tired steel as another turn is made. At the top of the arc his gondola rocks in the breeze, and he doubts the wisdom of entrusting his life to this ancient piece of machinery. Yet there is nothing Tibbs can do at the moment, so he looks out over drab Nanchang, the capital of poor, inland Jiangxi Province in the southern part of the country. This is heroic China. Not far from Tibbs is a revolutionary monument in the middle of a large square, for it is near here that the legendary Long March began.

Tibbs is no tourist; he is in Nanchang on a mission of mercy. If it were daytime, the American from Citibank might just be able to see the sprawling plant of Jiangling Motors from his swaying perch. When compared to other enterprises in its home province of Jiangxi, Jiangling is powerful, a colossus even. The light truck company has the latest technology and modern facilities, and it makes money. There's a fatal problem, however. When compared to other vehicle manufacturers in China, Jiangling is small.

Sun Min, Jiangling's chairman, knows that Beijing wants to consolidate China's highly fragmented vehicle-manufacturing industry. The country's economic planners look at the United States and see three car companies. In a much smaller market at home they have, in the middle of the 1990s, more than 120 enterprises assembling cars and trucks. In a decade, fifteen years at most, there should be only four or five. The technocrats in the Ministry of Machine-Building Industry will, by fiat, make sure that happens, and, as a consequence, Jiangling will not survive as an independent enterprise. It may not even survive in any form. Chairman Sun, as powerful as he is, realizes that. Bureaucrats in the capital of China spend their busy days willing enterprises into existence and decreeing them closed. Unless something is done quickly, Nanchang, and Sun, will lose Jiangling.

That's why Sun had Tibbs called to Nanchang. Sitting at the top of the Ferris wheel, the American thinks he has the right answer. The issues are economic, but the solution in China, he knows, is political. Tibbs has a simple plan, and Sun likes the idea. Over the course of half a year, both of them will convince longtime Citibank customer Ford Motor Company to buy a large slice of stock in Jiangling and, at the same time, to begin manufacturing its Transit line of vans and light trucks in Nanchang. It's a match made in Heaven. Ford needs a foothold. Alex Trotman, its leader from 1993 through 1998, once said, "I can't go down in history as the Ford chairman who missed China." Sun is gambling that his new relationship with Ford, one of the strongest vehicle manufacturers in the world, will prevent Beijing's technocrats from closing, merging, or otherwise interfering with the pride of Nanchang. And he turns out to be right. Since 1995, when the first transaction with Ford was completed, Jiangling has led a charmed life as far as Beijing is concerned, just as the angel from Citibank contemplated. Today it doesn't matter that Jiangling loses money; it is safe from the intervention of the central government.

Luoyang Mining Machinery Group, another Old Economy business, is safe too. "They are," says one retired worker referring to this enterprise's managers, "treating a heart-attack patient for ingrown toe-nails." It's an apt description, and, as a result of giving everlasting life to the ailing industrial concern, the state is destroying a business, an economy, and a society. Luoyang Mining, based in Luoyang in Henan Province, was one of 156 "key enterprises" formed pursuant to the First Five-Year Plan of 1953–57, and it built itself into China's largest mining equipment manufacturer. An ill-conceived, poorly executed diversification in the early 1990s left the company limping. In a market economy the solution would have been simple: fire bad management, sell extraneous assets, and spend money to upgrade the core business. If that strategy didn't fix the problems, then through bankruptcy or other means there would be a rebirth. The business might not survive, but the assets would end up being productive one way or another.

In China's "the state knows best" system, the state had another plan, which in broad outline looked like Tibbs's tactic: find a politically powerful shareholder. China International Trust and Investment Corporation, better known as "Citic," took over Luoyang Mining in 1994. Luoyang got a new name, Citic Heavy Machinery Corporation, but little else. For Citic, the investment arm of China's State Council or cabinet, the acquisition was painless: it paid little or nothing and assumed no financial responsibility. The rebranded Citic Heavy remained an independent legal entity so that Citic itself would be shielded from its new subsidiary's debts.

The Ministry of Machine-Building Industry, Luoyang Mining's department-in-charge, exited the picture after losing control of the enterprise and no longer steered orders its way. Unfortunately, the new owner, Citic, with no financial exposure, didn't pay attention to its new acquisition. Citic was supposed to help out by expanding overseas markets, but the foreign mining equipment orders that it generated were at prices that could only lead to losses. Citic Heavy could legally have refused to fill them, but, as a practical matter, it could not defy a powerful central government shareholder in a system where politics almost always trumps economics. Jiangling Motors, on the other hand, is struggling today, but at least it has a chance to succeed as Ford introduces technology and management know-how. Yet Jiangling had to go to extraordinary lengths, bringing in a multinational bank as a consultant and then one of the world's most capable manufacturers, to give it a chance to survive.

Citic Heavy, by contrast, is sinking further because government officials offer political answers. Yet in China that may actually be enough, given the way the state bails out failing enterprises with handouts from the state treasury and loans from the state banks. Why should Citic Heavy change? Especially for this particular enterprise, there are no sanctions for failure. Bankruptcy is the obvious next step. The creditors, however, cannot opt for that remedy. Under Chinese law, creditors cannot put a SOE into bankruptcy without the consent of its government department-in-charge. Moreover, bankruptcy is not generally available when an enterprise is "public" or when it has "an important bearing on the national economy and the people's livelihood." The law also institutionalizes delay. The bankrupt enterprise's department-in-charge can take up to two years to fashion a "reorganization," but in any case the law's technical provisions are not enforced by the People's Courts. The end result is that state enterprises are effectively beyond the reach of creditors. Worse, creditors' rights are often subject to outright government interference. Consider the case of Zhengzhou Baiwen Group, the first publicly listed company to face insolvency. In a landmark event, a bankruptcy petition was filed against this department store chain in March 2000, but the proceedings were superseded by an arrangement forced on all parties by the Zhengzhou and central governments a few months later. Creditors waived most of their debts as part of the plan.

That is not to say that enterprises do not exit from the economy. When they do, it is usually the result of the central government's industrial policy, not the workings of the market as enforced by the bankruptcy laws. Beijing is fond of closing the small to protect the large regardless of economic viability. Low-end refineries, for example, have been shuttered to enforce a duopoly in the oil industry. The state thereby increases its involvement in the economy and takes the nation in the wrong direction. As the large take over the small according to administrative decision, they often choke on the acquired enterprises, and China's politicized economy slows as indigestion occurs. Should anyone be surprised?

The concept of bankruptcy does not sit right with the Party's brand of socialism, which holds that its own cadres, and not the forces of the market or judges sitting in bankruptcy courts, should determine the fate of state enterprises. The aversion to bankruptcy is also cultural. One trait found among Mainlanders, and even among Chinese generally, is an unwillingness to admit a mistake. Call it "face" or something worse, but it shapes policy in the People's Republic. Combine that with communism's glorious visions of the future and the Party's attempt to project an aura of invincibility, and you have a good part of the answer why bankruptcy is not a favored option. Cadres refuse to admit defeat in all but the most hopeless cases. In 2000, there were only 7,528 bankruptcy filings in all of China—this in a nation where few state-owned enterprises can pay their debts and a year of deteriorating economic conditions. This is not a system that confronts its problems.

What the system needs is a "Neutron Jack" Welch of General Electric. The American is accomplishing with GE what Mao Zedong sought to do with China: create a continuous revolution. Welch never stops examining the company he leads so that he can remake it over and over again. He harnesses the destructive energy he unleashes and uses it to build value for shareholders and even society. Welch constantly confronts problems; China has not yet learned to do so.

As a result, dozens of ways are employed to avoid admitting failure. The nation's securities regulators often require a company to absorb a failing enterprise before obtaining permission to list stock on a public exchange. Municipalities, provinces, and sometimes the central government lean on the banks to continue lending money to businesses that have been dead for years. Sometimes failing enterprises are even strung together, as if cripples who are bound to one another will then be able to walk.

This process of avoiding bankruptcy, says Cao Siyuan, who is considered China's foremost expert on this subject, only slows the inevitable. He likens it to laying straw and flowers over a minefield: everything looks better—at first. Despite whatever appearances are created, China cannot expect investors, whether domestic or foreign, to acquire idle assets until they are confident that the laws, and especially the bankruptcy laws, will protect their legitimate interests. Until these assets change hands, recovery will be postponed. The ongoing saga of Citic Heavy teaches us that sometimes there must be death before there can be life.

This also holds true for China's newborn. High tech and the Internet are China's hope, but for there to be success entrepreneurs will have to take risks. When they fail, they will need to be able to pick themselves up off the ground and start over again. Good bankruptcy laws permit that. Today that sort of rejuvenation cannot occur in China. Spring does follow winter, but not there. When officials seek to avoid the inevitable, they make success impossible.

When bankruptcy comes in China, it is often the result of political disfavor, not economic failure. Our Angel of Nanchang, Chris Tibbs, was assigned by Citibank in 1999 to look at the books of Guangdong International Trust and Investment Corporation, one of China's ten original "window" companies granted easier access to foreign debt markets. Gitic, as it is known, borrowed and built and borrowed some more as it helped Guangdong Province pioneer China's headlong dash out of the past. Foreign banks and others fell over themselves to lend to the investment arm of mighty Guangdong Province. Yet out-of-control provincial officials directed the investment of borrowed funds, and eventually Gitic was hard pressed to repay. It eventually choked on its debt because the investments it made did not produce enough income to repay its many creditors.

The People's Bank of China, the central bank, administratively closed Gitic in October 1998 and in January of the following year put it into bankruptcy. Gitic's end was truly historic. With the equivalent of about US$4.7 billion in debt, this bankruptcy was by far the largest in the history of the People's Republic, a record that stands to this day. It was also the first bankruptcy of a financial institution in the history of New China, and, to top it all off, Gitic had the honor of being considered the first borrower in that country's history to default on an international bond.

Even after Gitic was declared bankrupt, Western bankers thought that a rescue was possible. So Tibbs from Citibank and his counterparts at Hongkong and Shanghai Bank, another creditor, regularly traveled to Gitic's headquarters, a skyscraper dominating its surroundings in bustling Guangzhou, to see if they could fashion a restructuring with the help of the remaining staff. Yet even Tibbs's impressive skill as a banker proved inadequate. As he and everyone else knew, there was plenty of money to pay back Gitic's creditors: rich Guangdong Province was ready to step in and put things right with its own funds. Premier Zhu Rongji, however, would have none of it. The story goes that Deng Xiaoping, to consolidate his position, had made a deal with Guangdong Province's leaders two decades earlier. Since that time the province had run itself with minimal interference from Beijing. Zhu was angry with the mess that Gitic had made in the intervening years, and nothing this side of Heaven could save it. Beijing blocked all efforts by creditors to attempt a reorganization, a process that is authorized by the bankruptcy law. Like many others in China, Tibbs was defeated by politics. The central government wanted to rein in free-spending, high-flying, and all-too-independent Guangdong. There were good policy reasons for doing so, as China's provinces needed financial discipline. Nonetheless, the point remains that even today, life or death in the marketplace is mostly determined by politics in Beijing, not economic forces.

And that's especially true as China prepares its industries of the past for the future. But you wouldn't know that by reading *The Economist,* which tells us that "Socialist China has the world's brashest capitalist economy." It's true that central planners, despite their bias for central planning, saw that China had no great interest in who in the country made washing machines or microwaves. As a result, in the 1990s the Party let certain segments of the economy slip beyond the bounds of socialist orthodoxy. But sectors considered strategic are still under firm management by the state. Government-sponsored monopolies survive to this day, especially in sensitive sectors such as armaments. It is remarkable that the failure of central planning in China appears to have gone unnoticed in Beijing. In those areas deemed to be the most important, the central government is still seeking to apply concepts that have, over a long period, obviously failed.

Even in those parts of the economy where free-market philosophy is supposed to rule, government bureaucracies seek to restrain competition by one means or another. Sectors once abandoned by Beijing to the forces of the market have been taken back; they are now regulated by legislation regulating the prices of commodities and manufactured goods. In other sectors, government intervention is more direct. Take civil aviation, for instance. At one time the country had only one airline, which went by the awkward name of Civil Aviation Administration of China. That, not coincidentally, was also the name of the government agency responsible for nonmilitary air transportation.

The second airline of the People's Republic was established in 1984, but the division of the industry did not begin in earnest until 1988, when Air China, the flag carrier, was carved out of CAAC. The process eventually resulted in thirty-four airlines as provinces and even municipalities got into the act. A period of overexpansion, characterized by excessive purchases of aircraft, produced losses in 1998. CAAC, acting in its regulatory role, responded by stepping between the combatants to halt most forms of competition. Beginning in early 1999, CAAC used its administrative authority to restore profitability to the industry. It restricted fare reductions, banned hidden discounts, and required reductions in the number of domestic flights.

It took only a few months for the airlines to begin flouting the rules. In response, CAAC dished out punishments, even suspending some carriers from flying their routes. Widespread noncompliance did not prevent CAAC from trying to hold the line on fares. It decided to take the Party at its word and institute communism in China on the first day of April 2000. Its policy required 80 percent of revenues from each of 108 important domestic routes to be divided among the carriers on that route based on the number of flights operated and seats available. "Our purpose is to prevent the airlines from offering discounts and to reduce competition among Chinese carriers," says one blunt CAAC official. CAAC is doing its best to eliminate discounts, but the new formula, with its mechanism to punish that practice financially, is a tacit admission that discounting will continue. "From each according to his ability, to each according to his needs," said a man named Marx, who would undoubtedly approve of the shared-revenue scheme. Evidently the revenue-sharing policy was also meant to stabilize earnings as a way of facilitating mergers. CAAC now wants to take the industry almost full circle, if not to duopoly, then at least to oligopoly. The agency wants the industry to consolidate into just three domestic carriers. That's the wrong approach, but CAAC regulators look like trustbusters compared to their colleagues overseeing the alumina industry. In February 2001, Beijing consolidated all of its alumina enterprises into one giant, the Aluminum Corporation of China. China has just created the third largest alumina producer in the world—and a monopoly in its home market. Technocrats evidently believe that to build competitive enterprises they must first eliminate competition.

Beijing is like a nervous referee in a boxing match, rushing in to stop enterprises from competing at the first signs of nosebleed. Accordingly, CAAC is not only unwilling to let major airlines go bankrupt, it is even unwilling to let them suffer the mildest effects of competition. The experience so far indicates that although government officials are willing to experiment with competition, they have never lost their suspicion of the market. In short, the central government views itself, not competition, as the regulator of industry.

In the domestic oil business, Beijing's aim is to eliminate competition, not merely restrain it. Monopoly is the road to prosperity here. Up until the middle of 1998, China Petrochemical Corporation, better known as Sinopec, was China's monopolistic oil refiner. China National Petroleum Corporation, which goes by its initials, had the monopoly on onshore oil exploration and production. In a giant swap of assets in July of that year, the two became vertically integrated with "upstream" and "downstream" operations. Bureaucrats in Beijing divided the country along provincial lines, with Sinopec in the eastern and southern parts of China and CNPC in the northern and western regions. The ultimate goal is to create two giant companies that will, sometime in the far future, compete with the best the world has to offer. In the meantime, however, competition is not part of the plan. Both companies are essentially monopolies in their respective territories.

The ink on the swap was barely dry before central planners quickly learned that even government-controlled entities will, if left to their own devices, engage in cutthroat competition. Beijing ruled, at the time of the swap, that CNPC could sell surplus oil in the south, but only through Sinopec. CNPC, however, sensed a business opportunity. Only one month after the swap was announced, CNPC began to offer lower gasoline prices at the pump in Sinopec's territory in Jiangsu Province and Shanghai. Sinopec retaliated by dropping its own prices and selling gasoline in CNPC's territory in northeast China.

The central government's plan had been ruined by what it termed "ruinous competition," and it ordered CNPC and Sinopec to stop competing with each other. In Beijing's view, these two enterprises could expand by putting small operators out of business, but they could not attack each other. As soon as they were pulled apart, however, CNPC began rebuilding its retail operations in Sinopec's territory, especially in Guangdong Province. Beijing's edicts were no match for the competitive instincts of state-owned enterprises. Finally, in March 1999, Beijing arranged an agreement between Sinopec and CNPC to settle the price war. "We can sit down and talk about our next price move in a very cooperative manner," a senior CNPC marketing manager remarked. The agreement, of course, did not halt the competition between the two giants, and they continue to struggle with each other. Now technocrats should realize what the rest of us know: ambition and self-interest almost always overpower carefully formulated government plans.

Like officials in the oil sector, telecommunications regulators favor monopoly. Once there was just one provider of telecom services. China Telecom enjoyed a monopoly in the strictest sense of the term. Citizens complained about high charges and lousy service, but Beijing took notice only when it realized that China was falling behind the rest of the world in telecoms infrastructure. At least as a technical matter, Unicom ended the monopoly when it was formed pursuant to a 1993 State Council decree. Unicom was supposed to provide competition, but it was not able to do so. Regulators protected China Telecom by deliberately starving the upstart.

So the State Council moved toward further reform by decreeing in February 1999 that China Telecom be dismantled. Many hailed its breakup as the end of monopoly in China's telecommunications industry. It would be more precise to say, however, that the division of China Telecom, as contemplated by the State Council plan, would result not in the destruction of a monopoly, but only in the creation of smaller ones. As originally envisioned, China Telecom would be split into four firms that would each have a near monopoly, or dominant market share, in a particular field (fixed lines, satellite communications, wireless paging, and mobile communications). There would be no competition among them, according to the plan, as each of the four firms would be restricted to its own area.

Rapid developments, technological and otherwise, ruined Beijing's careful policy of managed competition. Officials now realize that the plan to create four monopolistic firms is nonsense in today's world and tomorrow's telecom sector will look nothing like the plan contemplated by the State Council in early 1999. There will be more participants, competition, and openness. Regulators, relenting to the inevitable, have subsequently granted more licenses, but they're now using their powers to enhance the market position of dominant China Telecom. Beijing, even at this late stage, is still trying to stand in the way of change.

That's because central government technocrats have a hard time letting go. They correctly see that the world's economy is dominated by multinationals and that Chinese companies must also be big to compete. Consequently, they seek to build, by administrative fiat, large domestic enterprises. Beijing's policies assume, or hope, that size will ultimately breed success and that both can best be attained without domestic competition. Central planners, however, have stood reality on its head: the truth is that size is the result of, not the cause of, success and that both are the children of competition. Size, Beijing should know by now, is the prize for winning. Experience in all sectors of the Chinese economy also shows that bulk without strength is ultimately unsustainable. Beijing may talk of an Internet future, but the Silicon Valley model of development, continual division and growth, is alien to China's economic planners. Beijing is comfortable only with gargantuan enterprises that operate in its carefully controlled environment.

China peers outside its borders and sees a world of hostile competitors for its homegrown enterprises. The instinct of the central government is to protect its young from a harsh world, and it thereby finds itself managing, but mostly restraining, competition in its domestic economy. The Long March veterans in government have retired, but they have left behind younger cadres trained in Soviet-era economics. Those who have studied in Moscow are no friends of competition. What Beijing largely fails to comprehend is that China's enterprises need to sharpen their skills in the marketplace and do it now. "There will be progress only if there is competition," says Zhang Jingjun, the former boss of 163.net. China's technocrats can ignore her views, but the nation's enterprises face an overriding reality: at some point they will have to stand, and compete, on their own.

If only Beijing's bureaucrats had studied Chinese philosophy. Before *laissez-faire* there was *wu wei*. "Practise not doing and everything will fall into place," says the *Tao Te Ching,* Taoism's primer. The Chinese today could use a bigger dose of their own medicine, ancient medicine at that. The country that invented the right way to manage (or more precisely, not manage) must relearn its own wisdom.

If the central planners won't listen to their own ancient sages, perhaps they will accept the advice of the Angel of Nanchang. Chris Tibbs and countless other foreigners are full of ideas to help develop a modern economy for China. Tibbs's efforts in Nanchang and Guangzhou may be just the beginning. The creative banker knows what is needed to put things right. But China is not going to have the benefit of his expertise. His boss moved him to Seoul in July 2000 so that his talents could be put to better use. Tibbs thought that Shanghai would be his last posting in Citibank as there was so much to do in a developing China, but the bureaucrats in Beijing resisted change and the prospects for the foreign banks dimmed. So after more than half a decade in Shanghai, Tibbs is now changing banking somewhere else. That's the tragedy of China. The country will progress, but in its own way and in its own time.

MR. ACCELERATOR

Beijing's industrial policy not only keeps old enterprises alive, it chokes young start-ups. If Xing Fei thought about it, she would agree because she is unaccompanied tonight in New York's Tribeca district at the opening of a gallery devoted to contemporary artists from China. America is probably not ready for the work of nihilistic Chinese who use human corpses in their sculptures or spear dozens of live reptiles at a time and dangle them from wires in the name of performance art, so that type of stuff is not on display this evening in June 2000. Also not in Tribeca is her husband, Dinyar Lalkaka. He's left his artist wife and their one-year-old child and is off on one of his many trips to Shanghai, where he is struggling to accelerate the opening of his Internet "accelerator" or "cyber-incubator," as he calls it. At the gallery Xing Fei asks visitors from Shanghai how her husband is. It seems that the couple knows more about him these days than she does.

The sins of fathers may be visited on their sons, but so are their passions. And Dinyar has inherited those of his father—the passions, that is. The father, Rustam Lalkaka, worked for the United Nations Development Program and was the first person to introduce to China the concept of "incubators," which help start-ups get going by providing seed capital, know-how, management, and the dozen other things that new businesses need. He brought the idea to Beijing in 1987, and now there are some 120 government-sponsored incubators in China. Only the United States and Germany have more incubators. Rustam Lalkaka also introduced the concept to his native India, where it did not take root. Especially when there's a large role for government officials, China will try anything modern these days.

Now Rustam's son, Dinyar, wants to introduce his dad's concept to China, but this time adding a private-sector element. So the son travels to Shanghai regularly to see if he can establish the first privately funded incubator in the country for high-tech and Internet start-ups. There he hooks up with Professor Qian Zhenying from prestigious Jiao Tong University, Jiang Zemin's alma mater. Qian is perhaps the busiest man in the busiest city in China. He runs an entity called Shanghai Withub Hi-tech Business Incubator, which is the university's foray into the sea of entrepreneurship, as well as the Withub Technology Park. "Withub" is the combination of "wit" and "hub," and that is actually a fractured English translation of "Intelligence Valley," the name in Chinese. Qian's intelligence tells him to usefully employ the talents of the Lalkaka clan in the service of the Motherland, or at least the part of it that he runs. Qian's Shanghai wants to support incubation in universities, and the Lalkakas, father and son, present a perfect opportunity to ride the newest wave in innovation-crazy China.

Although approaching retirement age, the good professor's hair is pitch black except for a few millimeters of gray at the roots. So Qian shares one trait that is common among the rich and famous males of the Communist Party: any cadre important enough to have his picture taken has picture-perfect black hair, regardless of age, so a wonderful mane must be the dominant trait in the Communist gene pool. Dinyar Lalkaka, on the other hand, is younger than Qian by more than a decade, but the refugee from New York is gray reincarnated except for his thick black-rimmed glasses. Dinyar obviously would look younger had he been born a Communist.

The younger Lalkaka, however, is a capitalist. Along with his father he established Business & Technology Development Strategies, based in Manhattan. The father and son call themselves "international consultants," and the business has a staff of two (themselves), but, as the son notes, "we have a brand name." And Qian likes the brand. So Withub and the Lalkakas decided in early 2000 to create China's first private cyberincubator, an incubator for Internet companies (although they will "incubate" high-tech companies as well). They have a snazzy name for the historic business: Dakang, the Sinofied version of "dot com."

In a country where technology is white hot, the press goes wild. *China Daily*'s headline tells the whole story: ON-LINE INCUBATOR IMPLEMENTED. That paper tells us that China's first cyberincubator was formed with the help of "a global pioneer in the field of small business support and entrepreneurship development": the Lalkakas' Business & Technology Development Strategies. What a great development for China! And so it does appear. Withub has arranged the purchase of an old shoe factory and its conversion for Dakang's purposes. Dakang will get what is surely the most favorable lease ever offered to a foreign party, and it will run for fifteen years, an eternity in ever-changing Shanghai. Even more important, Jiao Da, as Jiao Tong is known, is one of the preeminent technological and engineering institutions in China, and it can channel its students and faculty to Dakang. They are the inventory of any incubator. So Dakang has just about everything it needs to capture the world.

And the news travels fast. Everyone, it appears, wants a piece of Dakang. You can almost see the dollar signs in Professor Qian's eyes as he listens in September 2000 to an eager American, Larry Rinaldi, describe how much money he and his allies can shovel into the hands of Dakang's current owners. The smooth talker intersperses his message with phrases such as "commingling of interests," but Qian is quick to discard the chaff and grasp the essence of the pitch he is hearing: his Withub will have even more funds for its important high-tech and Net initiatives. "China is huge market," Qian tells Rinaldi. "So attack China." The American smiles. So does Qian.

There's a problem, however, if Rinaldi and his friends want to buy in: Dakang does not exist. The Lalkakas want to include the phrase "Business Accelerator" in the name of their new venture. The Shanghai municipal authorities, however, won't permit them to register it. His choice of name, Dinyar Lalkaka explains, is considered by government officials to be "too innovative." Today the name is still unapproved.

This problem is just a detail, however. "I don't care what the government does," the younger Lalkaka says. "This," referring to private incubators, "will happen one way or another" because the trend is "inevitable." It's good he feels that way because another problem has cropped up, and this one is a bit more serious: his incubator would be illegal, Lalkaka is told by Professor Qian. The Lalkakas have already invested some funds to get Dakang going, and they have employed a team of seven. What will happen to the employees when the authorities close the Lalkaka operation down?

That doesn't seem to bother Qian. He's fifty-seven, and retirement age is sixty. Qian explains to Dinyar Lalkaka that if he takes a risk to get Dakang going, he won't be rewarded under the system that the Chinese state maintains. If, however, Dakang fails, he could easily be punished. But the ever-resourceful Professor Qian has come up with a plan that involves no risk to his retirement pay. He knows what to do in a state-managed economy: bring in the forces of the state. There is no reason why a privately owned incubator in China cannot be owned by the government, he reasons. Qian wants the central government, through its various ministries, to take a large stake in Dakang. Along with the ownership of Jiao Da, the state will have an overwhelming majority interest if the good professor gets his way because Jiao Da is itself state-owned. The Lalkakas, who were going to own half of the incubator according to their original arrangement with Qian, will end up with less than a quarter. "Jiao Da is begging them to interfere," Dinyar Lalkaka says, referring to the Shanghai Science & Technology Commission, which Beijing is using to channel money to Dakang. "Tell us how we can help," the overeager Ding Xue Xiang of the commission urges the younger Lalkaka.

The Lalkakas' plight was virtually inevitable in an authoritarian state that still wants to own everything. Dakang's competition has figured this out from the beginning. The Boston Consulting Group teamed up with Shanghai New Margin Venture Capital to launch what they also call China's "first" incubator, a claim Dinyar disputes. New Margin is controlled by Jiang Mianheng, son of Jiang Zemin. In the society where politics is still in command, it is best to retain the offspring of the political commanders. The Lalkakas will soon learn that China has not changed as much as it appears. China and India can lead the Internet world, says Dinyar Lalkaka. Yes, China can do anything it wants, anything at all as long as the state is in control. To this day Dakang is still a dream despite all the headlines, which were premature. It has yet to be formed. In today's China, good news is announced days, or years, before facts have a chance to catch up.

The Lalkakas now know the meaning of "inevitability." With all the rules in China against private ownership, they know that Dakang will be formed only if they accede to Qian's suggestion to bring in the state. What started out as a private incubator will inevitably turn out to be a state-owned business. Because Dakang will, according to its business plan, take an ownership interest in the Internet and high-tech companies it incubates, the state will take an indirect interest in them as well. In short, these "New Economy" companies will become partially state-owned and maybe state-controlled as well. But that's just par for the course in a country where the state supplies 80 percent of the venture capital.

It seems that the march of technology is unstoppable in China. The Chinese see that a high-tech future will permit their country to leapfrog over other nations. Mix high technology with cheap labor, and you produce an intoxicating cocktail. Here is real hope for an ancient civilization that is seeking to regain its glory.

As technology marches on, so does the state. China's brand of socialism, premised on the notion that the few can control the economic actions of the many for the benefit of all, is the ultimate expression of human optimism. Whenever an economic goal is set, Beijing believes it can be achieved. It is the power of positive thinking at its most powerful. Central government planners can do what they set out to accomplish. They can pour concrete, string wires, even grow grass. If you can draw it on a blueprint, they can make it happen. Not only can they build it, but they, the rulers of an authoritarian state, can also make you go there.

And they are building it. You can find it in the northwest corner of Beijing. Jiang Zemin himself is personally attending to the details. It has to be a success—it is a major part of his legacy to China. No doubt it will be written up that way. Not far from the Summer Palace of the Qing Dynasty emperors is China's first state-level high-tech development zone. Like the Dalai Lama, China's Silicon Valley, as it calls itself, is a reincarnation. In 1988, the State Council, taking its first stab at industrializing the products of its universities' research, set up a development zone in Zhongguancun in northwest Beijing. Soon there were similar zones across China, but wide replication did not lead to success. Zhongguancun mushroomed into a center for stores offering pirated software and "screwdriver shops" where no-brand PC clones were assembled. The technology was about 99 percent foreign. The story was, and still is, generally worse in the other high-tech zones. Some of them are essentially real estate developments with futuristic names. And in China, most anything these days is considered advanced technology, including, or maybe especially, herbal breast enlargement.

Beijing is trying again. The old zone was replaced by a new and much bigger one, but like much in China, the materials in the foundation are of dubious origin. In this case, the new zone was built on China's "biggest securities fraud." Hainan Minyuan, a diversified property company listed on the Shenzhen stock exchange, frittered away most of its assets and then fabricated about 95 percent of its reported earnings for 1996 to support its stock price. In the following year the central government decided that its controlling shareholder, the science and technology commission of the Beijing municipal government, should be held responsible (just why was a science commission in northern China investing in a property concern in the south?). The commission was forced to rescue Hainan Minyuan, even though that course of action had little economic justification. The company should have ended up in bankruptcy, but that didn't happen—officials were concerned that 108,000 angry shareholders might take to the streets if their stock in the company became worthless. And there was a complication: the scandal touched two of the members of the family of Deng Xiaoping.

The only party interested in a rescue was state-owned property developer Zhu Zong. To make a deal possible, the commission promised to designate Zhongguancun "a model science and technology park" and to appoint Zhu Zong as the lead developer. The 108,000 shareholders got stock in a company developing Zhongguancun. So China got a high-tech zone and part of a national economic strategy in an effort to save embarrassment to one municipal commission and two important relatives.

Now that those objectives have been accomplished, what about the future? This time the hype is reaching Wagnerian proportions. Any Beijing official connected with the zone will tell you that the "21st century belongs to Zhongguancun." And as an adviser to Jiang Zemin says, "Zhongguancun can become a hi-tech city that is as big as Hong Kong." China expects its zone to grow quickly, perhaps more quickly than any other country has ever managed. "We're trying to build Zhongguancun into one of the world's leading science parks, a hot cake for both capital and human talents in 10 years," said Ren Ranqi, an administrator of the zone, in 1999.

So far the result looks pretty good. This time around, the buildings in Zhongguancun are shinier, of course, and there are more of them. There are also many more companies, 8,224 in early 2001, almost double the number at the end of 1999. Output at Zhongguancun was up 27 percent in 1999 and almost 47 percent in 2000. Some companies in Zhongguancun have done well, such as Legend, the computer maker that has taken Asia by storm. Officials, of course, are pleased; they say that Zhongguancun is as inspired as the nearby Summer Palace and the other wonders built by China's emperors.

But do those facts tell the real story? Communist cadres can make anything look good for a while. After all, even state-owned enterprises appeared successful at first. Is it any wonder that Zhongguancun, the new version, is off to such a fast start? The real test for the zones will not be their initial results; it will be performance over the long term for the country as a whole. An increase in the production in the high-tech zones will not help China if they merely rob progress from other areas.

For Zhongguancun and the other zones to own any decade, much less the entire twenty-first century, they must employ two critical ingredients to bake their "cakes": people and money. "Forget oil, gold, land, the ocean floor or the reaches of outer space," says American futurist George Gilder. "The single greatest untapped resource in the world economy is the Chinese people." The country is awash in talent, and much of it is near Zhongguancun. There are more than 100,000 scientists nearby in 68 universities (including China's two most prestigious, Qinghua, the nation's MIT, and Beijing) and 213 scientific research institutes. Utilization of these talented people, however, remains a big problem. "When I meet the heads of Peking and Qinghua universities, they talk about using science to build the nation. But which one—China or a foreign nation?" asks Duan Yongji, another official in the zone. "In Qinghua, 82 per cent of graduates of some science faculties leave for developed countries and in Peking University it is 76 per cent." According to official sources, only about a third of them return to China. The country is not an especially attractive place for anyone, scientist or street sweeper. Beijing announces, with distressing regularity, preferential programs to entice those overseas to return to the Motherland, but it won't really succeed until it creates a society where people want to live.

China has lots of money, too. The problem is accessing it. Most of the country's capital is tied up in small bank deposits. Banks have traditionally ignored private enterprises and only now are beginning to lend to them (with government prodding, of course). The state banks, in a reckless move reminiscent of their efforts to rescue SOEs, have committed themselves to supporting Zhongguancun, exhorted by no less than the head of China's central bank to heed the Party's and State Council's call to help the zone. The concept is that banks will make loans to the zone itself and the zone will then pass along the money to qualified start-ups. Fundamentally flawed, this plan has the makings of still another loan crisis. Government administrators are not especially good at picking tomorrow's success stories. And are risky ventures the appropriate place for the already insolvent banks to entrust the life savings of small depositors to? The answer, apparently, is "yes." It is no surprise that thousands of the nation's failing state-owned enterprises see an important opportunity: they merely call themselves high tech so that they can borrow again.

China will need more than bank loans to nourish the thousands of start-ups in Zhongguancun and the fifty-two other state-sponsored zones. It will also have to attract foreign capital. There are, however, complications. "It is more important to create an ideal structure than to simply allow capital inflows," said Deng Xiaoping's daughter, Deng Nan, speaking about venture capital. While China creates that ideal structure, the hope of a nation languishes. Her father, looking at the world as it actually was, knew that nothing was ideal and that it was better to just get on with things. His daughter, however, can be forgiven. She lives in the orthodox and rigid China of Jiang Zemin, and she must reflect the mood of her times in word and deed.

There are now about ten venture capital funds in Zhongguancun, but they are small and mostly government-sponsored. China will need the resources of hundreds of foreign venture capitalists. They have capital, experience, know-how, and judgment. They are the straw that will stir the drink. The country will also have to permit its high-tech companies to access foreign equity markets in order to sustain their initial growth. The high-tech community can look at its Internet cousins and see that the prognosis is not good. Internet firms are having an extraordinarily difficult time listing their shares outside China due to bureaucratic infighting and fears of foreign domination of that new industry. Controversies delayed planned stock offerings of Chinese portals so that their Nasdaq debuts occurred only after the Internet boom. That meant they raised a lot less money than they could have. If high-tech companies face the same problems, Zhongguancun will wither. Beijing is looking at the issues, but progress in these matters, so crucial to the high-tech zones, is little short of appalling. The Party exhorts but does not provide.

There is a complication that must be solved before foreign investors will throw much money at high-tech China. About half of the enterprises in Zhongguancun suffer from "ownership rights syndrome"—what happens when hazy legal rules meet a cultural instinct to avoid clarification. Privately held enterprises inhabiting the zone need capital, and that will be hard to attract until entrepreneurs can prove that they can pass title to investors. Legend, Founder, and Stone, the domestic high-tech companies that are the bedrock of Zhongguancun, all started out with state ownership and had to suffer delays as the state reduced its holdings in them in preparation for foreign fund-raisings. Unfortunately, in a country that is still hostile to private capital, even of the domestic variety, that process often takes a long time. Officials at some of the government-sponsored incubators have tried to privatize their operations by announcing that they are now for profit, but that's just untrue, Dinyar Lalkaka says.

Suppose that Zhongguancun can marshal talent and money. And suppose that China can stop the piracy of intellectual property and develop a good framework of investor protection laws. There is one more matter to consider: Can there be innovation in an authoritarian society? The Soviets, and the Chinese themselves, proved that under some circumstances there can. After all, they developed weapons of mass destruction. The fate of Zhongguancun, however, will be decided in a freer world than the one in which those advances took place. Theoretically, the Party can permit the openness necessary for scientific innovation and still operate a closed political system. It is unlikely, however, that the scientific and financial elites needed will accept this deal. People want to breathe free air all the time and, if they have any choice, won't live where they can't. Jiang Zemin, however, thinks that socialist China will have no problem becoming a technological leader. In June 2000, in a speech urging even more development of science and its industrialization, he noted that Marxism is a scientific body of thought and therefore enhances discovery.

Of course, it would be unfair to compare Beijing's zone with California's high-tech areas, even though the official media invite precisely that by using the "China's Silicon Valley" label in connection with Zhongguancun. Yet Zhongguancun pales when measured against India's Bangalore, where government-sponsored development efforts started at about the same time. Today Bangalore produces original product, which domestic companies in Zhongguancun have not yet mastered, and Zhongguancun's output badly trails Bangalore's. That's just a reflection of something fundamental: "modern" China cannot keep up with "backward" India when it comes to information technology.

Today you can still buy fake identification and pirated software in Zhongguancun, and Chinese homegrown technology is a rarity. The zone still has its shabby backstreets, and the place is a slum in more ways than one. Incredibly, Zhongguancun is becoming a sleazy haven, hawking its special tax status to companies that are not even located in the zone. Now it becomes obvious what was, and still is, wrong with China's industrial policy. In many ways, little of substance has changed. Of course, anything can happen by 2010, when the ambitious schedule says that Zhongguancun will be leading the world. By then, if the past is any guide, Beijing will be thinking about how it can bail out China's high-tech industry and its development zones. Because of government intervention, most of the high-tech enterprises that are being created today will become tomorrow's mistakes. Beijing, wedded to outdated notions from the Stalin era, is using the same tools to develop technology that it employed five decades ago to build heavy industry.

There is nothing intrinsically wrong with government incentives, which, in one form or another, exist everywhere. Silicon Valley, not the Chinese one, grew on federal government grants, for instance, but those were only seed money. Eventually, the businesses there became self-sustaining, as did the entire area and industry. On the other hand, the Shenzhen Special Economic Zone, the first zone to be created in the Deng era, still exists after more than two decades and is now making plans for the next three. Long ago it accomplished its purpose of triggering the development of Guangdong Province, but special privileges remain in place many years after they are no longer needed. Today China has a quilt of about twelve thousand such zones, so many that the central government in Beijing has lost track of them all. The zones have become institutionalized, and a political party that needs to control is loath to take the steps necessary to create a freer, and better, system. Why can't all of China be one big zone?

Because China is not, the current high-technology initiatives will probably fail. The truth is that central planners have run out of fresh ideas when it comes to the conceptual theory of economic development. The high-tech zones look uncomfortably like Mao's agricultural communes and state-owned enterprises: they are set apart from the rest of society and expected to develop with strong state support. It's easy to see why technocrats like to wall off a patch of real estate and call it a development zone when they want to accomplish something. China's economic system, with all of its prohibitions and restrictions, is hostile to growth and development. It is much easier to grant concessions to a limited area than to do what is really needed, which is to change the basic structure of the entire economy. A zone allows planners to experiment on a small scale, and that appeals to the instincts of a cautious system. There is, however, another reason why planners encourage economic development by granting exceptions: they can maintain control by determining who benefits.

So Zhongguancun is merely an echo of the past masquerading as China's future. Therefore, it is natural for Beijing to develop its high-tech start-ups in a compound separated from the rest of society—and with direct aid in many forms. Accession to the World Trade Organization should kill all the zones because of the trading group's rules prohibiting discriminatory treatment, but Beijing is nonetheless planning to enhance Zhongguancun and other zones in the future. The state, after all these years, is still guilty of subsidy abuse and can't kick the habit.

Now the question is whether China's high-tech technocrats can break the patterns of the past. The three most important inventions in the history of the world, at least according to Francis Bacon at the beginning of the seventeenth century, were gunpowder, the magnetic compass, and printing. All were invented by the Chinese, but their country, for various reasons, did not take advantage of them. The Middle Kingdom stopped inventing, and it even stopped learning as it shut itself off from a world that was too foreign for the Ming and Qing emperors. It had all the elements needed for an industrial revolution centuries before it would occur in Europe. Yet, for one reason or another, China stumbled. Why did the world's dominant civilization falter on the verge of an even more glorious future? It is one of the greatest mysteries of history, and scholars will ponder the question for years to come. Jiang Zemin is no scholar, but he is wasting no time making sure that his country will succeed this time. Perhaps China did not try hard enough a millennium ago.

Rustam Lalkaka can see that China won't make the same mistake this time. The Chinese incubators he visits in October 2000 have plenty of support. That much is evident. The funds the state provides are often free, so the incubators, like state-owned enterprises before them, have no sense of the cost of capital. Therefore, the incubators have all the best

in marble decoration and their use of space is "extravagant." Their premises look like the offices of Fortune 500 companies, they are that lavish.
"There is no attempt to make them self-sustaining," the elder Lalkaka
says. In fact, one of the government-sponsored incubators Rustam visits,
run by Shanghai Internet Incubation Investment Co., Ltd., spent so much
money that it needed a government bailout soon after it was formed. To
jump-start the Internet industry in Shanghai, the municipality created
the Zhangjiang High-Tech Park in a lonely part of the Pudong district to
spur development there, but the location is so remote that this incubator
and other zone inhabitants are struggling. China is trying too hard and
trying to accomplish too many objectives all at once, and as a result the
country will fail again.

Today New China has wholeheartedly embraced the development
and commercialization of high technology. Thus Zhongguancun will become "one of the world's most advanced science parks by 2010." How
will it get there? "We're persuading the government to give us more
privileges such as those for Shenzhen and Shanghai," said Ren Ranqi, a
zone administrator. Jiang Zemin's slogan tells us that science and technology are "the first productive force," but those in charge of science and
technology seem to think that government intervention is the key to
progress. Jiang may not let China repeat the mistakes of the Ming and
Qing emperors, but he is following the path of a more recent ruler, Mao
Zedong. And like his illustrious predecessor, Jiang gets high marks for effort but low ones for results: high-tech businesses account for less than
2 percent of China's economy today.

"Today no one wants to work for the state when they graduate," says
Dinyar Lalkaka's dinner guest. "Perhaps that's what Marx meant when he
said that the state would wither away," replies the host, who is in Shanghai in April 2000. Lalkaka the younger has flown to China from New
York to announce the formation of his incubator, which can give hope to
New China. He has yet to hear Professor Qian tell him that the state
should own almost all of Dakang. Today the state should wither, but, of
course, it won't.

HOPE OF A NATION

"If I compare China today with the China I saw in the last days of the Mao era in 1976–79, it's so vastly different it's unimaginable," says Lee Kuan Yew, Singapore's senior minister. It is a clear night, and the grand old man is sitting on the east bank of the Huangpu River. Behind him are the night lights of Shanghai, brash and bright and magical. When we are dazzled by the lights, we assume that China will continue to progress and that success is ensured. We, like Lee Kuan Yew, remember what China once was, so we assume that the trend must continue.

And when the night lights sparkle it is easy for us to believe Jiang Zemin, who can sound so enlightened these days. The official media assure us that he is working constantly to make 1.25 billion people prosper. That is the question that China should think about every day, he says. Yet we know that he, in fact, does not. If the people's prosperity were his real goal, he would immediately free the economy so that millions of Chinese could go about improving their own lives. Yet we know he will not do that. "The Communist Party has stayed in power since 1949 through stages of revolution, construction and reform because it is a 'vanguard production force,' " he also tells us. The truth is that the Chinese people themselves are leading their nation into the future. The Communist Party has stayed in power not because it is a vanguard of any sort but because it restrains them with all the powers of a police state— or sometimes pushes them too far.

Seeing Communist cousins fall in Europe as events passed beyond their control, Jiang is doing everything he can to prevent another revolution in China. When forces move just a bit too fast, he knows, the game is over. Jiang has already taken the biggest risk in his tenure in Beijing, for the cause of building his legacy, and supported accession to the WTO. He cannot afford to endorse any other bold economic measures, so there will be none. Central government domination of the economy, although a concept grown tired, will remain. He adheres to the past as if that were enough to preserve the current system. Strengthening the Party is his solution to all issues, economic and otherwise.

The solutions we hear are almost all from a bygone age because Jiang sees the political shades. Beijing closely manages the economy because this, like almost everything else in China, can be framed as a matter of survival for the Party. Any solution in the economic sphere must there-fore pass through the filter of ideological correctness. The Party has told the Chinese people that it, and it alone, correctly understands the forces of history and can make China economically strong. How can the Party let it appear that market forces, the sum of millions of acts by ordinary individuals, can do the same thing? Market competition, by its very na-ture, is chaotic. Jiang, however, demands order, especially in these days of turbulence. His planners, not competition, will decide which enter-prises are created and which destroyed.

So politics remains in command of economics as China embarks on its ongoing adventure in socialist planning: remaking state enterprises. At least Jiang can claim some credit for one of his campaigns. There are smiles at planning ministries in Beijing as SOEs report profits for 1999. Start spreading the news about the success of low-tech textiles! Six years of losses were ended in 1999, one year earlier than planned. If the state can make its policies succeed here, it can make them succeed anywhere. The first month of 2000 was not over, however, before textile industry officials were calling for even more help from Beijing. "If the central gov-ernment halts policy support for industry reform, all previous efforts will be wasted and the textile industry will return to poverty and trou-ble," local officials say. In fact, there has been no turnaround. The indus-try is, as ever, completely dependent on government support. In a China unhurried by the constraint of time, enterprises, large and small, feed from government treasuries and weaken the state day by day. The nation is seeking to free itself from the burdens of the industrial SOEs, but at the same time it is adding new offspring such as zones and their high-tech companies to its load.

And there are others that will one day need central government aid. State media and government regulators are now trying to cash in on the Internet by establishing their own Web sites. Will they survive? "Entre-preneurs work twenty hours a day and have invested their own money," says one who runs a privately owned Web site for Chinese surfers. "The public sector will never be able to compete with that." But it will try. "This is another example of the government pushing its way into an in-dustry that it should just leave alone," says a reporter of a newspaper in-volved in such a site. "With the level of regulation they want to impose, the site is virtually doomed to fail." Worse, there is some possibility that the government sites will band together and refuse to provide content to privately owned ones in order to gain a competitive advantage. That would choke off the development of the vibrant private side of the Web. Moreover, rules issued by Beijing in January and September 2000 were designed to force private portals to close or be acquired by official sites. So the cycle is starting again. First it was heavy industry, now it's the Internet. When will the state learn?

So, Comrade Jiang, you still have a job after all. John McEnroe was mistaken, and communism still prevails in China. There is one problem, however: the category is "Communist Organizations," but there are no right answers.

6

The Banks That Sank

Chinese Banks Will Fail

> The Chinese government is not stupid enough to allow the state-owned banking system to collapse.
>
> —LAURENCE J. BRAHM

THEY ARE A SYMBOL of the failure of Maoist planning and the most vulnerable link in China's economy today. If Yao Caifu had been in charge of China's struggling state banks, however, the situation would have been different.

According to the official Xinhua News Agency, Yao, a banker from Longyan in coastal Fujian Province, approved more than three thousand loans totaling ¥220 million (about US$26.6 million) in his remarkable eighteen-year career. During that time, there has not been one single default and, even more impressive, not a single late payment.

Yes, if Yao had been running things then, China's banks would not be hopelessly insolvent and the central government would not have to confront a financial system in disarray. It is here, in the banking system, that the end of the modern Chinese state might well begin.

In the meantime, the banking system begins where the sand dunes end. A banner, painted in red characters on a white background, looks like those of an earlier and unhappy era, but the message is more friendly and the people now listen. "Welcome You to Participate in Your Rural

Credit Cooperative," it says. The single-story mud-brick building, what passes for a financial institution in Dunhuang in western Gansu Province, appears frail against the encroaching desert. The huge sand dunes across the narrow road could bury the shack any day, but the people still come to place their money there. They always have.

They also come to the Bank of China's headquarters in the heart of Beijing. American architect I. M. Pei designed this monument to China's modern banking industry. His father founded the bank's Hong Kong branch in 1918, and in the 1980s the son designed a building for the bank in Hong Kong, too. The bold structure in Hong Kong, not far from where Pei was born in southern Guangdong Province, is even more impressive than the one in Beijing. The Hong Kong tower starts at the ground as stone blocks arranged like a medieval fort. From this foundation emerge metal and glass, arranged in triangle patterns that Pei would later use for the headquarters in Beijing. The Hong Kong structure, incorporating an innovative design admired by architects worldwide, has been hailed as an architectural triumph. It was the fourth tallest building in the world when it opened and is the seventh now.

From the grand Bank of China to the humble cooperative in Dunhuang, China's banking system is swollen with deposits. This is where hundreds of millions of individuals have entrusted their life savings, the wealth of a great nation. China has one of the highest savings rates in the world, averaging, year after year, about 40 percent. In contrast, Americans put away next to nothing. At the end of 1999, the amount of household deposits in all of China's institutions was equivalent to approximately US$720.9 billion.

The deities gave China's banks a nation of world-class savers with few alternatives. If they had stopped there, Chinese bankers would have been treated as royalty, the envy of their colleagues around the world. Unfortunately, the gods set bankers on a barren throne. All dressed up with few places to go, China's financial barons had no place to lend their money other than state-owned enterprises and other parties favored by the central government. So the banking system is both the beneficiary and the victim of a closed system.

It's their "assets" that are the banks' greatest liabilities. The loans made by the banks, "assets" in bankers' terms, are mostly "nonperforming," a polite term used by the financial community to describe loans in default. State-owned enterprises cannot, or will not, pay back the banks, so today there is a silent crisis. What is the extent of the damage that China has inflicted on its banking system?

Don't ask the People's Bank of China, the central bank, if you really want to know. The technocrats at the PBOC, as that institution is known, have been possessive of information, even to the point of hiding the truth from themselves. At the end of 1999, they said that 25 percent of the loans held by the state commercial banks were nonperforming, but no one took that figure seriously. A year later the PBOC told the world that these banks had unloaded ¥1.3 trillion (US$157.0 billion) of nonperforming loans in 2000 pursuant to a government recapitalization plan. Yet even after the state commercial banks did so, Beijing's central bankers stated that overdue loans still comprised 25 percent of their portfolios. In other words, the biggest bank recapitalization in China's history had no apparent effect on the health of its banks.

So what is the real condition of the state commercial banks? Foreign estimates of nonperforming loans at the end of 1999 topped out at 70 percent, a figure mentioned by Standard & Poor's as the upper limit. The consensus of estimates actually hovered around 40 percent, but that was certainly too low. Deutsche Bank, the German financial services giant, concluded in a recent analysis that 50 percent of China's loans were nonperforming, and Standard & Poor's believed that the 50 percent figure was at the low end of the range. "The more I knew, the more pessimistic I became," says Johannes Schoeter, head of Deutsche's China operations at the time of the study. Today we don't know much about the true condition of the state commercial banks. The best that can be said is that the US$157.0 billion recapitalization must have reduced the percentage of nonperforming loans from, say, the 50 percent level to about 30 percent during 2000. In contrast, the overall percentage of nonperforming loans at American banks these days, if loose Chinese standards were applied, would be negligible, perhaps even as low as 1 percent.

And how much can Beijing recover from these soured loans? Beijing's technocrats estimate at least 30 percent and maybe 40 percent, but that's delusional. When it comes to banking statistics, China has simply lost its credibility. Recent foreign estimates put the recovery figure at 10 percent, a figure more consistent with experience in bankruptcies in China. Assume that 20 percent is the correct percentage and the amount of unrecoverable debt in the entire banking system is somewhere in the vicinity of US$490 billion. That's a huge number, but the most frightening aspect of the problem is that no one really knows the true state of China's fragile banking system. "There is no simple answer to finding the level of nonperforming loans among state-owned banks," admits a high-ranking official at one of the largest of them. How can China's economic planners plan when even they are in the dark?

Beijing's senior cadres do not seem to be worrying too much about the situation, though. Premier Zhu Rongji says that the financial institutions are generally in good shape, and Deputy Auditor General Liu Jiayi of the National Audit Office agrees. "According to our audits, China's banking sector is operating soundly," he assured China in early 2000.

China, says Dai Genyou of the PBOC, is solving its banking problems by "seeking truth from facts." The facts, as the PBOC sees them, are so much better than they appear to the rest of the world. It's a problem of definition. A country that considers itself "democratic" also considers that the loans held by its banks are good. China's loan classification system gives new meaning to the term "optimism": loans that have been in default for years are still classified as performing, as are loans to bankrupt institutions. To its credit, China is improving the loan classification system, but that may not matter much. The really bad loans are merely rolled over every year so that they look fresh on the banks' books.

Those who are serious about knowing the truth view the situation with more gravity. "For many observers, the Chinese banking problem is one of the most serious in the world and perhaps *the* most serious," write Rudi Dornbusch of MIT and Francesco Giavazzi of Bocconi University. Only *perhaps* the most serious? In any free economy, the banks would have failed long ago. In China's abnormal financial system, Beijing postpones systemic failure by maintaining strong walls around itself and limiting real alternatives to the banks. As the central bankers defer solutions, the problems fester and get even worse. The Industrial and Commercial Bank of China, China's largest, has started offering financial planning services to its customers. Shouldn't it be telling them to take their money out of China's banks altogether?

Perhaps not, because the banks, ill as they are, look like the picture of health in the family portrait. Unfortunately, there are other sick children in this house. The 42,000 rural credit cooperatives, the backbone of

China's financial system in the countryside, are dying. Some say that their percentage of bad loans is about twice that of the commercial banks. That does not seem possible, but the entire rural financial sector is in a shambles, to be sure, and definitely insolvent, as even central bank statistics admit. The PBOC is formally in charge of the cooperatives, but it does not exercise control as a practical matter and seems to pay little attention unless hysterical peasants start a run against one of these deposit takers.

Nor does the central bank seem to be doing much about the family's unmentionables, illegal deposit-taking companies. In the semi–police state that Beijing operates these days, it is inconceivable that anyone can, without a required license, start a little company and then openly compete with established banks for deposits. Yet it's done all over the country, even by local units of the Communist Party. Central government bureaucrats are obviously losing their grip on society. The central bank sets the rate of interest that deposits may pay, and now the rates are low to stimulate a sluggish economy. The deposits at the illegal companies pay interest well in excess of the PBOC maximums. That's why the companies are so popular. The western city of Chongqing, for instance, has seen more than 160 illegal deposit takers established since 1993—and more than its share of unrest.

Almost every week brings a story of the failure of one of these companies. Poorly managed and undercapitalized, the illegal deposit takers are unstable. When they fail, depositors take to the streets. And the state buys time by paying off the mob. When the PBOC closed Guangdong International Trust and Investment Corporation, the notorious Gitic, foreign creditors were stiffed. Yet Guangdong Province did honor one class of Gitic's debt—that owed to local depositors—even though the deposits themselves were illegal. Beijing just hates to see unauthorized expressions of its citizens' anger, and nothing brings them onto the streets faster than a failure of a deposit taker. Now we know why Beijing is beginning to execute those who offer high rates of interest. It would, however, be preferable to relax commercially unreasonable restrictions and let the market set deposit rates. The PBOC can dictate, but the market will, one way or another, prevail. Call them illegal, and the central bank does, but interest rates in excess of its low limits are inevitable.

The PBOC took a stab at shuttering illegal deposit takers when it closed Gitic. Since then the central bank has shut down a few other "itics," international trust and investment corporations, and merged still others, but there has been scant progress in helping this troubled sector. Comprehensive reform remains far off as China's bureaucrats prefer to defer. "Isn't slower better?" asks Dai Genyou. Slower is better, but only if you wish to see the People's Republic fall.

TIGER IN A CAGE

In the beginning in Maoist China, there was one bank. In a republic belonging to the Chinese people, there could be only one name for their bank: the People's Bank of China. It was both the central bank and the sole commercial banking institution. To round out the picture, there were also the rural credit cooperatives (which did not lend very much), the Bank of China (which was, in reality, part of the PBOC), and the China Construction Bank (which, despite its name, was not a bank but a disbursing agency for the Ministry of Finance). The history of banking in the People's Republic has generally been the story of the creation of diversity.

But not too much diversity. Today, instead of one giant there are four. The PBOC is no longer a commercial bank and the rural credit cooperatives still exist, but four commercial banks, entirely state-owned, dominate the landscape. At the end of 2000, the Big Four together held about 68.4 percent of the deposits and made some 71.0 percent of the loans in the banking system. Among them, they have a staggering 150,000 branches.

So are the Big Four insolvent? Definitely. Are they dead? No. Not only are they alive, they are actually thriving. Their story shows that when a country designs a system free from economic constraints, almost any situation, even one completely divorced from reality, can exist.

The problem with the banking system is not, for the most part, a problem with the banks. They are still backward by world standards, but they are modernizing. In the middle of the 1990s, they were uncompetitive even on their own protected turf. Today they at least look up to date with their ATMs, cobranding deals, online services, and other badges of modernism. An American banker in Shanghai tells how his American bank gave a copy of its internal credit manual to the PBOC and within nine months each of the Big Four had issued its own (for the first time). Not long afterward, Big Four bankers to foreign-invested enterprises were applying rigorous credit analysis and asking pointed questions of these customers, things that had not occurred in the past. The ongoing transformation of the four largest banks shows how much can be accomplished, even within a moribund system.

The real problem is the state-owned enterprises, the pride of Chinese socialism. As mentioned, Beijing forced the Big Four to "lend" to the SOEs, thereby replacing direct government subsidies with loans. Banks, therefore, became the conduit by which Beijing propped up enterprises with essentially free money, keeping China's industry on life support. Some call this gradualism, but in reality it was postponement of the solution to a critical problem.

Many people focus on the fear of unemployment as a reason for this postponement of reform. But there was something more fundamental at work: a failure to confront and admit the faults of socialism as practiced in China. The banks offered a convenient way to avoid, at least temporarily, uncomfortable matters, and the "policy loans" were like morphine for the mortally wounded. The worsening plight of the banks is, therefore, a symptom of the weaknesses of the system itself and the Party's approach to problem solving.

The SOEs were uneconomic during the era of government subsidies, and they are uneconomic now during the era of loans. The only difference is that the problem has been, by government decision, transferred to the banks. The SOEs are still sick. The only difference is that now the banks are as well. It was a financially transmitted disease.

To Beijing, it was a matter of indifference who suffered. Loans from the central government's banks replaced direct subsidies from the central government's treasury. It's just a matter of accounting if you sit high atop the apparatus in the Chinese capital. In another sense, however, transferring the problem to the banks makes all the difference in the world. Most of China's individual depositors have money in the Big Four, and that gives them a special interest in the banks that they do not have in the central treasury.

From an objective viewpoint, there should be no possibility of a bank run in the People's Republic, especially not against any of the Big Four. Douglas Red, then head of ING Bank in Shanghai, said it all: "The bad news is that the Big Four are insolvent; the good news is that they're sovereign." Technically, no state-owned commercial bank in China enjoys sovereign backing. In practice, however, the Big Four, as weak as they are, are as solid as China itself. As long as the government stands, so will those banks, because Beijing knows that it cannot withstand the collapse of any of them. Would the People's Liberation Army shoot ordinary citizens whose only crime is demanding the return of their life savings? No one knows for sure, and Beijing does not want to find out. As Doug Red says, the Big Four are as good as China itself.

Yet for all the sense that it does not make, depositors in China have, from time to time, lost confidence in the banks. Bank runs, essentially stampedes with passbooks, don't happen often, and at least up to now they have been easily contained, but they do occasionally occur as a reminder of how things can go wrong, even in an environment as tightly controlled as China's. It was April 1999, and rumors, once whispered person to person in a village, were now zipping across China at Internet speed. There was a run in Zhengzhou in inland Henan Province at the state-owned Bank of Communications, one of China's strongest commercial banks and a pioneer in banking reform. The excitement was over in a day as the bank pumped cash into its seventy subbranches, which stayed open throughout the night to permit withdrawals. By the time it was over, however, China's fifth largest bank had lost the equivalent of US$108 million in deposits. The run had been sparked by rumors of official fraud posted on the Net. The state countered by putting the bank's managers on television to issue denials. The Internet won. Of the amount withdrawn, "only a portion" was returned when the hysteria had run its course.

Anger and resentment over corruption, whether real or imagined, is explosive these days, but the troubling aspect of this affair is that rumors could have rocked one of the best of China's state banks, even if only temporarily. Suppose it had been one of the Big Four and someone had told the truth on the Net by saying "insolvent" instead of "fraud"? Something close to that happened in June 2000 just outside Beijing, when officials of Luan County withdrew government funds from China Construction Bank, one of the Big Four. The run lasted four days at six of

Construction Bank's seven branches as individuals panicked when news of the county's withdrawal spread. There is no deposit insurance system in China, and the authorities are in no hurry to put one into place. No insurance means that the Chinese have only one option to protect their savings in times of uncertainty, and that is to stampede. No wonder observers, worried about "a disaster of epic proportions," have called deposits the "tiger in a cage."

It's one thing for the banks to be insolvent. In China's *Alice in Wonderland* banking system, that does not mean much, perhaps only an accounting entry. It's another thing, however, to be illiquid. A substantial portion of the "assets" in the banking system, and especially in the Big Four, are loans to the SOEs. They're long term as a practical matter: whatever the maturities, they must be rolled over to avoid precipitating a crisis. Most of the banks' liabilities (essentially deposits), however, are short term, and it is the new deposits that are funding withdrawals. That's the classic formula for collapse. Today, Chinese banks must limit withdrawals from time to time, and when the banks' condition becomes a common subject of dinner conversation in China, the situation will become precarious. At that point, a message on the Net could turn into a run, but one that is nationwide and that history books will record.

Then Beijing will have only two choices: to maintain public order by the gun or print money fast. Either choice will spell the end of the Communist regime, if not immediately then over a relatively short period. A Tiananmen Square solution just will not work these days. Although most Chinese might have a hard time identifying with the democracy activists of 1989, there will be no lack of sympathy for other ordinary citizens. Force, as a practical matter, is no solution in such circumstances. The central government is simply no match for all its citizens. Severe inflation, the result of printing money to save the banking system from collapse, is not an appealing alternative either. Any dislocation of that sort would severely test a government whose legitimacy rests on its continuing ability to provide for people's material well-being. So saving the state banks is a critical item on the to-do list for the Party and its government.

Call it coincidence, and maybe it was. Just a month after the April 1999 run on the Bank of Communications, the PBOC quietly began to prepare to use its local currency reserves in "emergency situations where more than one bank is having a problem." It also began to implement an early-warning system intended to give regulators information on assets and deposits over a real-time network. All this sounds as if someone in Beijing, despite all the brave talk, is getting worried.

And there is plenty of brave talk in turn-of-the-century China. When Dai Genyou of the PBOC is at home and quarreling with his wife, he probably says, "Honey, you just don't understand me." In the office, when he must speak the language of central bankers, the same thought comes out like this: "But classic economic precepts can not be applied in analysing many of China's problems because the origins of the problems are quite unique." Resorting to the last refuge of a Chinese bureaucrat, Dai is trying to explain to the West why China's financial system is not headed into a crisis. The pessimism expressed by foreign analysts, Dai says, can be attributed to their lack of comprehension of China's economy.

According to Dai, the liabilities of state-owned firms are not the result of poor management; they exist because of the transformation of the economic system. The debtors are not in danger, Dai assures us. Can the man be right? When the central treasury keeps all vessels afloat, the state banks and the state's commercial enterprises are as seaworthy as the state itself. Dai correctly reminds us, although this was not his intention, that China's whole system is unusual.

But even in an abnormal system nothing insolvent lasts forever. Obviously the banks needed to be recapitalized, and in 1998 the central government took one small step in that direction when the Ministry of Finance injected a sum equal to US$32.5 billion into them. Without providing details, the PBOC said the recapitalization had lifted their capital adequacy ratios to 8 percent, the international standard. It was a fib, but at least China was trying.

The following year the central government announced what was supposed to be the real deal. Beginning in April 1999, the Ministry of Finance formed one asset management company, or AMC, for each of the Big Four. The AMCs then bought from the banks debt that met certain standards. The debt could be repackaged into securities and sold or converted into equity of the borrowers, mostly state-owned enterprises. If debt was converted to equity, the AMCs would become owners of these enterprises and could then use their new shareholder powers to force improvements in their operations and management. In theory, these enterprises would become princes again after existing in froglike form for decades.

The AMC plan has all the outward appearances of reform. It even acknowledges paternity for the mess by returning fiscal responsibility to where it belongs, the central treasury. In a country where the government rarely admits mistakes, it's hard to overemphasize the significance of the AMC plan. Moreover, the plan even has the best bloodlines. The AMCs were modeled on the successful Resolution Trust Corporation of the United States. In the early part of the 1990s, the RTC acquired assets from failed savings and loans and sold them at discounted prices to private parties, contributing to a speedy recovery.

The plan worked well in America. It is failing in China. When it comes to restructuring banks, one lesson has been learned time and time again around the world: only decisive action works. Do it quickly, do it big, and do it just once. It's even better not to restructure at all than to do it in stages. Dentists don't fill cavities until they remove all the decay, and partial recapitalizations don't change bad lending practices. In fact, they are thought to encourage reckless lending because bankers know that there will be further bailouts. The RTC worked because it was a very American solution: recognize a problem, take losses quickly, and move on. But in the People's Republic all the instincts are to proceed cautiously. Beijing's solution is to implement slowly and in many small steps, and as a result its program to save the banks itself needs rescue. The aftershocks of a banking crisis are felt for years even if a government moves fast. When it does not, the crisis never ends. That's China. The AMCs are a study in slow motion, when the critical element is speed. Recovery of the banks, critical to China's future, has been postponed yet again.

So even when Beijing strikes out and adopts bold ideas, it more often just strikes out. The AMCs are proof of that. First, the program is not nearly big enough. "I consider the establishment of the asset management companies as the last dinner for the state-owned commercial banks," said Dai Xianglong, head of the central bank. "I know some people are expecting midnight snacks or breakfast the next morning, but I don't think this will be possible." Here's news for you, Governor Dai. They will be back, and you, or your successor, will feed them. The central government originally said that the program would be limited to ¥400 billion

(US\$48.4 billion). That was not nearly enough to clean up the balance sheets of the banks, and, as it turned out, there was an additional meal after all. The AMCs eventually acquired about ¥1.3 trillion (US\$157.0 billion) in nonperforming debt from the Big Four. Even that increased figure was woefully insufficient, however; the nonperforming debt held by the Big Four was more than twice that amount. If Governor Dai is as good as his word, the Big Four must someday fail. If he's not, there could be no end to the cycle of bank bailouts.

Second, the AMCs don't have a chance in China's politicized economy. Local government officials, patrons of state-owned enterprises, are fighting to keep control over their debt-ridden business empires. Localities have been able to protect their enterprises from the reach of the asset management companies, even preventing them from talking to SOE managers. Because the home teams have the upper hand, SOEs don't take the threat of restructuring by the AMCs seriously. To them, the AMC program merely looks like another preferential policy, so they have rushed to unload their debt. Hundreds of SOEs sent delegations to Beijing to be included in the plan. Enterprises have even defaulted on their obligations in order to obtain debt relief, and the announcement of the formation of the first AMC was preceded by a big increase in the number of late payments. This isn't merely a "free lunch," as it's often called; it's a refund for a decade's worth of meals. And a coupon for another decade's worth: those who have swapped debt for equity are first in line for new bank loans.

Third, AMCs have forgotten their larger purpose. They should be trying to acquire and dispose of debt as quickly as possible to speed up rejuvenation. As profit-making enterprises themselves, however, AMCs have given first priority to strengthening their own financial condition. For example, they're concerned that when they swap debt of SOEs for equity in those enterprises, they will lose out. So they're arguing with the SOEs over the number of shares they are to receive upon conversion of the debt they hold. As a consequence, the AMCs are seeking, from the SOEs and local governments, guarantees protecting them against anticipated losses. In addition, AMCs have been asking for preferential treatment from concerned localities eager to prevent layoffs at hometown SOEs. Some complain that in their eagerness to protect themselves against loss, the AMCs have been "blackmailing" local governments. On another front, the AMCs are quarreling with the banks. The AMCs want to buy the better doubtful loans from the banks, but the banks are trying to sell them the lowest-quality ones. The result is that the AMCs, putting themselves first, have become mired in disputes and are not getting on with the cleanup job they were set up to do.

Fourth, the program, designed to do too much, is unrealistic. It was announced as a plan to help the banks, but in reality it is structured to aid state enterprises as well. The State Development Planning Commission, a central government body, established rules for the type of debt the AMCs can acquire. The debt, among other requirements, had to be is-sued before 1995 by one of the country's key state-owned enterprises whose products were marketable. The losses of the enterprise had to be largely caused by high interest payments. If Beijing's plan was meant to aid just the banks, the AMCs would simply have been charged to buy the worst loans held by them in order to provide a fresh start.

"As a shareholder of the indebted firm, Cinda can exert pressure on management to produce a better financial return," says Fang Xinghai, who heads a committee coordinating matters between China Cinda Asset Management Corp., the first AMC, and China Construction Bank. "Cinda's main mission is to help enterprises restructure, because an out-right liquidation will bring losses to creditors and hardship to the work-ers." Fang ignores the reality that losses have already occurred and that the remedies he suggests have been tried before without success. How can he think that the newly created AMCs, as minority shareholders, can bring about meaningful change when the central government, as a sole or majority shareholder, was not able to reform the SOEs much over two decades? Moreover, Fang thinks the AMCs should help *SOEs*. He forgets that they are supposed to rescue the *banks*. China already has investment bankers for ailing enterprises. Now it needs debt collectors for the Big Four. Common sense persuades us, but not Mr. Fang, that the central government will recover less the longer it postpones its collection ef-forts. The AMCs should take nonperforming debt, and *all* of it, off the books of the banks now. It's time to forget the guidelines and dispose of the trash. If that helps the SOEs as a by-product, that's fine, but curing the SOEs and saving the banks are two entirely different matters.

That, however, is not how the central government sees it, and the first AMC deal highlights much of what is wrong with its plan to help the banks. In September 1999, Cinda agreed to take equity in Beijing Cement Plant, and China's controlled press hailed the accord as a sign of accelerating SOE reform. Cinda exchanged debt of the plant (originally acquired from Construction Bank) for shares in a newly constituted cement enterprise. The concept is that the new enterprise will eventually buy back those shares from Cinda, thereby effectively repaying the original debt. The intriguing aspect of this transaction is that at the same time, Construction Bank agreed to extend financing to another new entity, China United Cement Co., which was established in Beijing to hold cement plants. The bank granted a two-year interest-free period in addition to other financial concessions to China United.

This solution bore the hallmark of Chinese gradualism: postponement to the indefinite future. Cinda agreed to wait years as Beijing's overgrown cement industry wanders to economic rationality. Worse, Cinda's deal involved Construction Bank increasing its exposure to a business that had caused it problems in the first place. The related Beijing Cement and China United deals may further the restructuring of the sick cement industry in the Chinese capital, but they do not do much for Construction Bank. They will even make matters worse for that financial institution if the new debt, like the old, goes bad.

Months later it turned out that the deal between Cinda and Beijing Cement was not yet agreed upon. In fact, many "agreements" between AMCs and SOEs, announced so proudly in the controlled press, have been little more than statements of intent. The accord between Cinda and Beijing Cement was not finalized until late June 2000. When it was announced, it was revealed that Cinda would own 71 percent of Beijing Cement but have no management role. How can AMCs do anything when they're not even allowed in the front door? Implementation, if it ever occurs, could take years as local power struggles involving the AMCs rage.

But don't tell that to the central bank in Beijing. "We hope that in a matter of two years, the non-performing loans of our state banks will fall to international average levels," Dai Xianglong said in late 1998. Two years have come and gone, and China is even further behind. The AMCs, according to Dai's own timetable, are not working. Their creation is evidence of a long-overdue admission, but let's not mistake them for a solution.

Even if they were the solution, the AMCs cannot solve the crisis if the government forces the banks to churn out new bad loans. Restraint is the hardest virtue for the Communist Party of China to practice. Since 1949, the cadres have been issuing orders; they're not about to stop. They don't even rest on weekends. And they'll go just about anywhere, even to the Sanjiang Dong Autonomous Prefecture of the Guangxi Zhuang Autonomous Region in western China. Here, what passes for a financial institution doesn't look like a bank. It's even more humble than the mud-brick credit cooperative in Dunhuang: only a table with a sign saying COUNTER FOR SMALL LOANS. The women of the Dong ethnic minority, dressed in their dark jackets and simple white headdress, are going to do something really special this Saturday night. The Agricultural Bank of China, generally thought to be the weakest of the Big Four, is handing out loans, and the women are going to join China's modern economy as the bank participates in the region's antipoverty efforts.

They should be called "policy loans." They aren't as big as the ones that shore up steelmakers Angang and Hangang, but the concept is the same: government policies determine who receives credit. Beijing calls the tune and the banks follow, whether the goal is to alleviate poverty in the barren hills of the interior of China or to save an aging steel mill on the Chinese coast. Even if the AMC plan works as advertised, the plan will still be inadequate. AMCs are not supposed to acquire bad loans made after 1994. Presumably that's because China's Commercial Banking Law, adopted in the following year, made the banks responsible for their own operations and freed them from outside interference. "No government agencies or individuals should be allowed to interfere with banks' business," said Wang Xuebing when he was head of the Bank of China.

That sounds good in theory. In practice, however, the PBOC and other government departments still meddle. In June 1998, for example, the PBOC generally ordered commercial banks to support SOEs that made marketable products. In January 2000 the State Council ordered them to stop lending to certain enterprises manufacturing polyester. These instances are exceptional only because the instructions were put into writing; most of the time government or Party commands are informal—and, of course, contrary to the Commercial Banking Law.

The central government treats the banks as a "secondary budget," a convenient place to find funds with which to paper over problems of the past. Fixing sick state-owned enterprises is only the starting point. There are, in addition, high-tech zones to build, rivers to dam, and anything in China's western region to be developed. State leaders expect the state banks to do their part. If they were really serious about reform, as they say they are, they would stop telling the banks what to do.

The leaders of modern China won't restrain themselves, so we can forget all the optimistic statements from central bankers about how the AMCs will work. Hope, by itself, won't help the banks. Let's bring on Yao Caifu, our model banker from Fujian Province. Not content with his own spotless loan record, he is reported to have collected ¥1.29 million (about US$155,800) in bad debts left by his predecessors. Yes, Yao Caifu knows what to do. He is, we have been told by official media, perfect in every respect.

But wait: Even if Yao was in charge of China's reform efforts, would everything be okay? After all, it's not the people who are at fault for China's banking mess; it's the system. So even a perfect banker like Yao Caifu cannot save China's banks. Is there anyone else?

BIG FACE AWAITS

How about another banker, Christopher Tibbs, our Angel of Nanchang? This former U.S. Marine Corps major is hard at work behind his desk in June 2000. He's alone with his small corporate finance team in the Union Building, the first modern office high-rise in Shanghai. In the 1980s, most foreign businesses in China's largest city had their offices in this tall brown structure. This is where you would have found Citibank, Bank of America, and a dozen other financial institutions, along with scores of multinationals, which were customers of all these banks.

Until the mid-1990s, all the banks had their operations in Puxi, Shanghai west of the Huangpu River, in the Union Building or close by. Now the banks are in Pudong, on the east side of the river. They moved over, almost all at the same time in 1996 and 1997, because the central government wanted to make that part of the city China's financial capital, the "dragon's head" as it is called. So Citibank and its main competitors moved from the run-down Union Building to Pudong's brand-new Marine Tower, right across the street from the also new Shanghai PBOC headquarters, a powerful stone-clad building designed to look like a chair—a throne, actually.

The foreign banks are determined to change China's banking system, and you know that because, in June 2000, you couldn't find the marine in Marine Tower. Tibbs was left behind by his buddies. He and his team are the only Citibankers not to make the move across the river, and they inhabit a tiny corner of the aging Union Building. There are no other offices on the otherwise deserted fifth floor. What has this man, perhaps the most knowledgeable banker in Shanghai, done wrong?

Nothing. Tibbs is merely holding down what may eventually prove to be the most important position in Citibank in China. He's warming a spot until the revolution begins. He even knows precisely when it will happen. In fact, the date is contained in an agreement signed before the cameras of the world. Five years after China's accession to the World Trade Organization, foreign banks will be able to take deposits from local Chinese. Tibbs is sitting behind his desk at the Union Building because Citibank wants a retail branch in Puxi, and his boss at the time, John Beeman, figured that keeping someone in place on that side of the river would make the licensing process easier. So Tibbs must cross the Huangpu to Pudong whenever he wants to see his colleagues, and the world's greatest retail bank lies in wait.

That's when the revolution will begin. Will China's banks be ready? Today the Big Four depend on fresh deposits for liquidity. Some portion of that flow will find its way to the foreign banks, and if you listen to local bankers, that portion will be large. Chinese banks, says a Mainland banker, "don't have much retail banking experience as we mainly serve as cashiers taking money from depositors and putting the money where the Government has directed."

Let's say you're Chinese and live in China. You have most of your life savings in your bank account. There's a whisper on the Net that the Industrial and Commercial Bank of China is gagging. You keep your money in one of the other of the Big Four, but you know they're all the same. There's a branch of Citibank in town. Now that you have a choice, what will you do? Keep your money with an insolvent institution or one that can pay you back? Will you take the risk that you will not be able to send your son to school? You know that Citibank has a more capable ATM, but you don't really care about that. What's important is that it's run by people who actually worry about paying you back. It's time to stand in line with the millions of others at the withdrawal counter of your domestic bank, and that's exactly what you will do.

No liquidity, and the system will collapse. This is the first lesson in Banking 101. So you would think the PBOC would be doing all it could to prod the local banks to revitalize themselves. But it's not, even though by now it's clear: competition in the home market is the only way the state banks can bring themselves into the twenty-first century. The PBOC, however, is mostly taking the opposite tack. China talks the talk about competition in the banking sector, but it's not walking the walk. In 2000, the central bank began to further restrict the ability of the foreign banks to compete by trying to impose all sorts of additional annoying prohibitions. That can be only a short-term strategy—and a gravely mistaken one. PBOC regulators can protect state banks for only so long because the clock is ticking. Foreign banks will be able to conduct business in local currency with domestic enterprises two years after WTO accession and with domestic individuals after five. Geographical limitations on where foreign banks may establish branches will be scrapped within five years. The country's top think tank, the Chinese Academy of Social Sciences, warns that accession could result in state banks' losing their best customers to their foreign competitors as well as substantial numbers of employees.

Although Beijing could prevent the impending cataclysm, there's nothing that Big Face can do. Therefore, he's spending his time planning a gala. Jean-Pierre Raynaud is a big man whose jowly cheeks are covered by a full salt-and-pepper beard and mustache. He doesn't understand Chinese, and that's just as well because his staff has given this jolly man the rather uncomplimentary nickname of "Big Face." He heads the commercial banking operations in China of French bank Crédit Agricole Indosuez, and by November 1998, he's been planning a celebration for almost a year.

This is Raynaud's night. Shanghai's Garden Hotel is managed by the Japanese, but it's the center of that city's vibrant French community. That's because part of the hotel, the elegant part, was once the French Club. And that's where Indosuez is celebrating its one hundredth anniversary in China. The night glitters that November as France's elite in China gathers in what was once the city's French Concession. Raynaud has even gotten the French ambassador to fly down from Beijing.

The ambassador, Pierre Morel, is everywhere, or so it seems. His face appears on the wall at the most famous Chinese restaurant in town, but tonight he is live at the Indosuez gathering. The tall, handsome diplomat is addressing the crowd in his native French. He is urbane and witty and clearly enjoying the spotlight, but he is going on much too long. People want to sample the delicacies or talk to their friends. Raynaud and his staff, however, have other thoughts on their mind. They are eager to work the large crowd that they have assembled in this ornate setting. But they can't make a move while Morel continues with his erudite, and long-winded, chatter. Even the amiable Wong Yu-May, the Cantonese manager of Indosuez's branch in Guangzhou, is getting a little anxious. His father, grandfather, and great-grandfather have all worked for this bank, and he sometimes moves a little slowly, secure in his sinecure. He usually has time to socialize, but on this gala evening he fidgets while he waits to get on with the business at hand.

Like most foreign banks in China, Indosuez can do little at this time, even though it has one of the precious licenses to transact business in the coin of the realm, the renminbi. Those licenses, though prestigious, confer little economic benefit because the PBOC prevents the licensed banks from accumulating the local currency needed for lending and absolutely prohibits them from dealing with most potential customers. Raynaud, whose office is also in Marine Tower, would not have far to go if he wanted to protest to the reserved, soft-spoken Hong Pei Li, his designated contact at the PBOC. She is, after all, just across the street. She might as well be in Pakistan, however; the PBOC is that intransigent.

Raynaud won't complain to the officials across the street. He prefers to entertain. This sly fox—his last name is almost the French word for that predator (renard)—knows that harsh words won't move the emotionless bureaucrats at the People's Bank, so he goes about building up his customer relationships with fine food and drink. And he plans for the time when WTO rules will come into force so that he can begin to compete in earnest. He knows that time is his friend. Therefore, Raynaud, like a fox, patiently awaits his turn. In the meantime, however, he will have to wait for Morel to wind up his turn at the microphone.

Finally the distinguished ambassador finishes, and Raynaud returns to work before the applause fades. Indosuez is a big-game hunter, going after corporate business only, and Raynaud saves the best customer for last as he zeros in on the tall, aristocratic head of the Shanghai operations of Alcatel, the French telecommunications company. Chinese banks don't have much time left before Big Face, and even Wong Yu-May, will be able to go on the attack—and before the retail army of Citibank relieves the corporate finance team waiting in Union Building for the revolution to begin.

If China's domestic banks have a future, Cinda and the three other AMCs not only must succeed, they must succeed now. If they don't, China will end up with a reformed financial system. But it won't be run by the People's Bank. Big Face and all his colleagues at the foreign banks will be in charge.

NO CULTURE

China claims a civilization that is five thousand years old, but today it has no culture—credit culture, that is. There is nothing in their past that makes the Chinese a race of welchers, but over five decades the People's Republic has made them so. Few in the state sector want to, or feel they should, pay back their loans. One customer of the Agricultural Bank of China claims that he is the only borrower at his branch still paying interest. Only two years after the PBOC directed the banks to make consumer mortgage loans in Shanghai, about one third of the homeowners were already in default. Among borrowers there is a philosophy that "it's better to repay late than repay early, and it's better not to repay than to repay late." China, in short, is in the process of creating a society "based on the repudiation of debt," warns a prominent Beijing scholar.

And why should anyone repay? Courts generally won't decide against a state enterprise, and even if they do, court orders routinely go unenforced. Bankruptcy rules are meant to protect debtors owned by the state. SOE managers know the benefits of an economic system in which political influence is the main currency: they do not have to pay back the banks, even when they have the money. So many of them in fact do not.

"Banks can show torture instruments, and the blood would come out," says Johannes Schoeter, the former Deutsche Bank manager. "In China, there are hardly any torture instruments for bankers." The situation has gotten so bad that repaying a loan would put a borrower at a competitive disadvantage with all those who do not pay. This we know: banks cannot continue to lend without the prospect of being paid back. It does not work elsewhere, and it won't work in China.

Children learn from their parents, and in China everyone takes his cue from the state. And the state is not paying back either. There are many reasons for the historic failure of Gitic, but the one that stands out, especially in the minds of creditors, is that Beijing forced that institution to repudiate its debts when it could have paid with the help of its parent, Guangdong Province. Foreign creditors, such as Chris Tibbs and his colleagues, were especially unhappy, but the central government decided that the province would not be permitted to honor Gitic's obligations.

The way the PBOC closed Gitic reinforced the notion that debt repudiation is acceptable in the People's Republic. So we shouldn't be surprised that China's banking system has, in the words of Nicholas Lardy of the Brookings Institution, "deteriorated dramatically in recent years." That's only one of the reasons why the most interviewed American in Beijing, except perhaps for the ambassador, is not very convincing. Laurence Brahm, celebrity consultant, writes books with titles such as *China as No. 1: The New Superpower Takes Centre Stage,* which gives you some indication where he thinks the People's Republic is headed. Banking crisis? It doesn't seem to bother him. "The Chinese government is not stupid enough to allow the state-owned banking system to collapse," he assures us. But it is not stupidity that will cause the end of China's banks. Central bank officials, like their colleagues all across Beijing, are intelligent, perceptive, and knowledgeable. They know what should be done. They have attended all the right international conferences. The world's leading multilateral organizations volunteer advice to them.

Yet little is done. Beijing's officials can't stop meddling with state bank lending decisions; they can't even publicly admit the full dimension of the problem. By adopting partial solutions, they are making matters worse. They can spend public funds, but they will not solve the problems of the banks. They don't have enough money, and now, with WTO accession, they don't have enough time. They have the right to ignore valuable lessons and common sense, but then they must face the consequences. That means they will fail. China's banks are doomed.

What is the Communist Party's response to all this? To ensure greater control, it has inserted even more of its cells—formal groups of members dedicated to ensuring adherence to Party policies—into financial institutions, including the only privately owned national bank in China, Minsheng. Cancer spreads. The Party, of course, continues to intervene in internal bank matters whenever it pleases. "You must put politics in command," said Mao, and his successors have. Maybe that is what Liu Mingkang, then a PBOC official, was referring to when he said that "there is no perfect recipe for strengthening the banking system of a country like China." For a country like China, there may be no recipe at all.

When China's banks fall, there will be no excuse. The pattern is visible for all to see. China's first banks were established by private businessmen in Pingyao, in inland Shanxi Province, which became home to four hundred of them by the middle of the nineteenth century. Pingyao's bankers, who boasted of their close ties to Qing officials, lent substantial sums to the rotting dynasty, which it could not repay. The banks failed. Today, just a century later, the same process is at work.

It is true, as author Laurence Brahm suggests, that Beijing will do everything in its power to keep the state banks alive. That, however, does not mean that they are assured of survival. It just means that of all segments of the economy, banking will be the last to fall.

7

Biting the Snakes
The State Attacks the Private Sector

One winter's day, a farmhand found a snake frozen by the cold. Moved by compassion, he picked it up and put it in his bosom. The snake was revived by the warmth, its natural instincts returned, and it gave its benefactor a fatal bite. The dying farmhand said, "I've got what I deserve for taking pity on an evil creature."

—MAO ZEDONG

FROM THE TOP of his bowling pin Chen Rong can see the world. It has to be one of the tallest sculptures anywhere, and it is visible for miles, at least on clear days. The pin is, of course, standing next to a rather large bowling ball, and both dwarf Chen, though not his sense of pride in his new bowling center.

The orange ball and the red-and-white pin are attached to each other and form the front entrance to Chen's new facility, which holds a record of sorts. Chen claims that his bowling center, in the Huamu district of Shanghai, is the biggest single-floor alley in the world. Under the roof are 108 lanes. To put that into perspective, that is two more than can be found in the largest bowling alley in the United States—located in Las Vegas, of course—and just thirty-three behind the world record holder, a center on five floors of a building in Japan. Chen's center is tremendous but is obscured from the road by two large grubby buildings. He opened the center so quickly that he didn't have time to tear down those two eyesores, but he will do so soon.

The road from Nanhui, where he grew up, to Huamu is but a few miles, but it has taken many years for farm boy Chen to make the journey. Unlike many who call themselves Shanghainese, Chen really is. The true Shanghainese are found in the farming areas surrounding the city center. The urban dwellers, for the most part, are originally from somewhere else. Nanhui is within the jurisdiction of the sprawling Shanghai municipality, but it is, for all intents and purposes, another world. It is about as far east as you can go, sitting at the edge of the East China Sea, and if there is not much traffic, it is an hour away from Puxi, the center of the brash, money-grubbing, sophisticated, and naughty Shanghai. If the roads are crowded, the trip will seem to take the better part of a day—or perhaps a lifetime.

For Chen, it took only a few decades to make the journey to the bright side of Shanghai. Things did not start well for him, though. He was an unpromising child in a large family, and when he was six his parents sent him away to be raised by an uncle. He's possibly the richest person in Shanghai today because he was utterly incompetent as a boy. He tried to commit suicide at nine by electrocuting himself but failed. "My life seemed like an endless nightmare," he said. He was even rejected by the People's Liberation Army because his poor parents were considered counterrevolutionaries.

It took Chen ten years to save ¥2,000 (then about US$625) from his farm and jobs at a glove factory and a municipal bureau. In 1984, he used that sum to start a small garment business, which he illegally operated as a "collective" instead of as a private business to avoid punitive rules. He sold in 1989 in the aftermath of the Tiananmen Square massacre, worried by the government's crackdown on entrepreneurs. He took his sales proceeds, a hundred times what he had put into the business just five years earlier, and invested half of them in Shanghai's and Shenzhen's newly opened stock markets. He multiplied his stake hundreds of times by what the Chinese call "stir-frying"—speculating. If to get rich is glorious, as Deng Xiaoping told the Chinese people, then Chen Rong is Shanghai's candidate for Mr. Glory.

Chen Rong got out of the market at more or less the right time. In 1994, he wanted to get back into business. By then, people had enough money for entertainment, and bowling, an Egyptian game that goes back before the beginning of China's recorded history, was the newest sports craze in the People's Republic. In Shanghai in those days, Chen recalls, locals were not welcome in five-star hotels. But he'd been able to try the sport at a hotel in Guangzhou, and when he returned to Shanghai he learned that he could use the bowling lanes at the Equatorial Hotel, which was close to his office. Chen would usually treat his guests to bowling after a good meal. Karaoke, China's favorite form of legal post-dinner entertainment, was not an option. "I can't dance or sing," he explained. "Each time I entertained, I spent a couple thousand on food and only two hundred on bowling," Chen noted. "But then they would forget everything, they only remember the fun of bowling, that Shanghai had bowling."

That left "a deep impression" on Chen. So in April 1995 he went into the manufacture of pinspotters, the large gadgets that pick up pins from the end of lanes and reset them in the familiar pattern, and other bowling equipment. And as a means of promoting his business, he started his own bowling centers. In the mid-1990s, foreign companies, such as industry leaders AMF and Brunswick, looked as if they would capture China's market for bowling equipment. That is not what happened, however. Chen's timing was perfect—his Zhonglu Industrial targeted the fastest-growing segment of the market, grabbing about a 75 percent share of the sales of low-end lanes. AMF and Brunswick, on the other hand, found themselves competing to sell higher-quality machines to fewer and fewer potential customers. Not only did success bring more wealth to Chen, who's now listed by *Forbes* as one of the fifty richest entrepreneurs in China, but he also became famous for his ability to succeed against world-class foreign competition.

RONG AND RANDY

Mao Zedong succeeded on the battlefield with his brilliant military strategy, but he captured the imagination of the Chinese with his vivid written imagery. As 1948 turned into 1949, he borrowed an Aesop fable and recalled the snake that bit and killed the farmhand who had saved him from the freezing cold. At the time, Mao was referring to domestic and foreign enemies of his proletarian army. He soon triumphed over all of them, of course. Yet today Mao would feel the need to repeat the fable of the snake, for new foes are threatening his republic. This time they are private entrepreneurs, who are poised to change the structure of the Chinese economy.

Mao eventually eliminated private enterprise in New China. In 1978, when Deng Xiaoping wrested control from Hua Guofeng, virtually all industrial assets were in public hands. That began to change. Today, after two decades of dazzling transformation, the private sector has grown to such an extent that even the Communist Party has had to come to terms with its importance to the Chinese economy.

State-owned enterprises, old, inefficient, and obsolete, are dying. They don't really matter anymore, many foreign observers believe. Privately owned businesses, such as Chen Rong's Zhonglu Industrial, will surely take their place. It's just a matter of time, the reasoning goes. Now, bitten by the snake, China's socialist system is wounded—many say mortally.

The statistics support that story. The numbers are not precise because China is still a hostile environment for statisticians, but best estimates show that private enterprise accounts for about 45 percent of China's nonagricultural gross domestic product. Experts argue over the precise figure and the range of disagreement is huge (from 25 to 75 percent), but the point remains that private enterprises have become a significant, and steadily growing, factor in China's economic rejuvenation.

New investment by private domestic entrepreneurs should be where China becomes "rich and strong" again. This is the path the Chinese should take to their future. Yet we have not heard the last word from a state that is determined to protect its own struggling industrial enterprises. China talks capitalism but breathes socialism. The new entrepreneurs such as Chen Rong will help China develop, but sometimes the state bites the snakes.

For protection against the state, private entrepreneurs tie up with foreigners. Chen Rong's latest chapter begins with one of them, Randy Daniel, a sandy-haired Virginian whose full name ends in "IV." His patrician background is rather different from Chen's, but they get along. Neither understands the other's language, but both sense that the other can be trusted to be fair.

Daniel's passion is golf, but his business is bowling. If it was up to this rangy son of Richmond, AMF, the American bowling company, would have moved its manufacturing to China long ago. Management in Virginia had other priorities then, however, and it is Chen Rong who now owns the largest bowling equipment manufacturer in the People's Republic (and claims to be the third largest in the world). "If you want to be the world leader in your industry, you must be the leader in China," says Jack Welch, the legendary head of General Electric. Randy Daniel agrees. "With a population of 1.3 billion people, it holds the largest potential for bowling in the world," he says. Now it is up to Daniel, president of the manufacturing operations, to see if he can put AMF back on the map in China.

And that is an urgent task. Goldman Sachs, the Wall Street investment firm, bought control of AMF in 1996 in a leveraged buyout and then took the company public, selling shares on the New York Stock Exchange the following year. These sophisticated financial moves were premised in part on continued strong Asian profits, but those disappeared in 1998 as the Asian financial crisis shook AMF and sales to China, already hurt by increased tariffs, continued to plummet. That's why Daniel has been talking to Chen Rong about linking their companies together in some way.

Like Chen, Randy Daniel is both tough and sincere. The two trust each other, but the interests of Zhonglu Industrial and AMF are, for the time being, diametrically opposed. In June 1999, the two of them are sitting in Mechanicsville, the site of Civil War battles on a ridge outside the old Confederate capital of Richmond, on opposite sides of a long table in a colorless conference room. Chen Rong and his colleague Jin Wei Dong are enduring a week of long meetings and do not quite know what to make of the American way of negotiating. That's why they've asked a friend, Steve Lo from Dallas, to help them through the process. They share no meals with Daniel and his supporting cast except for sandwiches at lunch. If this was China, there wouldn't be just shared meals, there would be banquets and toasts and ceremonies. Chen Rong is not in China now, and he doesn't even bother to eat the Americanized "Chinese" food that Richmond offers. He's partial to Virginia's big steaks.

They have a deadline because Randy Daniel must go to Bowl Expo 99 in Orlando and has to leave early in the morning on the thirteenth, just five days from the time they start. Contract provisions are discussed in detail one by one, and at times it looks as if they will need weeks longer to finalize the documents. "AMF Always Means Fun" is the corporate slogan. No one thinks so at this particular time.

As the thirteenth draws near, however, the pace picks up and agreement, even on difficult points, becomes easy. Negotiations take place during the day, and documents are produced overnight by AMF's team of lawyers in Hong Kong, where it is daytime, while Mechanicsville sleeps. It is eleven at night on Saturday, the twelfth, in Virginia when Chen and Daniel finally agree on the last word of the last clause of the last sentence. Zhonglu becomes AMF's exclusive distributor in Mainland China, and AMF becomes the exclusive distributor for Zhonglu everywhere else.

Chen and Daniel meet at 6:30 A.M. on the thirteenth at the Jefferson, a magnificent hotel in downtown Richmond. Amid ornate but tasteful Victorian splendor, they begin to initial hundreds of pages of contracts. Hotel guests stare as a flock of people huddle over two figures surrounded by piles of paper neatly laid in stacks in the main lobby. In two hours the contracts are fully signed and the two briefly shake hands. It's a historic occasion for both companies, but the parties don't stand on ceremony. Randy Daniel almost runs out the front door as he heads for the airport. Chen Rong looks at the massive marble columns and thinks about having some made for his new home in Shanghai.

He can buy the whole hotel if he wants, columns and all. Chen Rong, after all, is a Shanghai success story, and he has just vaulted even higher in the Chinese corporate hall of fame. Chinese enterprises have come a long way in the world and, like Zhonglu, are challenging their foreign competitors. The central government measures success by how many of its enterprises are included in the Fortune Global 500, a list of the largest companies in the world. Zhonglu is not among the nine Mainland Chinese firms that are on the list, but that could be just a matter of time.

AMF is not on that list either, but Roland Smith, its determined chief executive, is definitely doing all he can to be included. On April 6, 2000, the AMF van is on the way to Zhonglu's manufacturing facility in Nanhui. On board is Smith, who wants to see Zhonglu's site for himself. He is bringing along Randy Daniel and Wen Kang, his China manager. When he first arrived from Arby's to take control of struggling AMF, Smith

vowed to learn how the business worked. "I'm going to go put on a bowling shirt and spend some time working in a bowling center," Smith said at
the time. He's not wearing his bowling gear now, but, just shy of com-
pleting a year at AMF, the new chief is out in the field and learning about
business in China from the ground up as he goes to visit his Chinese business partner, Chen Rong.

Wen Kang, to pass the time on the long ride to the plant, begins to
explain the symbolism in Zhonglu's logo. He's learned the story from
Chen Rong's boastful employees in idle conversation, and it's time to
pass the information up the corporate chain. The logo has three roads
pointing to the sky at a slight slant to the right. The two on the outside
are blue and represent AMF and Brunswick, the world's two largest
manufacturers, Kang explains. The one in the middle is green, and that's
Zhonglu, which means "Middle Road." There's a Chinese saying that
roughly translates as "Green comes from blue but is better" (meaning
that the student is better than the master). It's no surprise that Chen
Rong did not explain the symbolism to AMF before the signing in Richmond.

Today Zhonglu is the student, and it is learning quickly. A decade
ago, no Chinese company was competitive outside China except at the
lowest ends of markets. The story is different now as the Chinese rapidly
acquire foreign technology and learn foreign management techniques.
Even in relatively unprotected segments of the Chinese economy, some
local companies have managed to shine.

Such as Zhonglu, for instance. In a few short months in 1995, Chen
Rong studied the technology of both Brunswick and AMF and chose the
latter because it was more advanced. In a couple of years he had mastered pinspotters and lanes and the hundreds of other things that go into
bowling. He was so good at adapting AMF products that AMF sought him
out to discuss a possible partnership. Brunswick, which sold more lane
packages in China than AMF, also wanted to do a deal with Chen, but
Zhonglu's boss pursued the discussions with Randy Daniel. These days,
the Chinese want the best technology, and that was AMF's.

"JOHN" AND JERRY

"Let the past serve the present, let foreign things serve China," said that famous servant of the people Mao Zedong. Mao did not let foreigners serve China, apart from the Soviets, and he even got tired of them, pushing his troublesome northern neighbor to the point where it recalled its advisers in 1960. It was Deng Xiaoping and Jiang Zemin who first redefined and then perfected the art of receiving tribute from those beyond China's borders. The foreigners now serve the cause of China's economic rejuvenation. AMF, for instance. A history of cooperation starting on June 13, 1999, will inevitably help Zhonglu become a stronger competitor in world markets.

It often seems as if foreign companies can't get enough of China. The number of potential consumers mesmerizes; it always has. Even though China's markets may not be as big as they sometimes appear, they are nonetheless essential to multinationals, which need to constantly grow their sales beyond their saturated home markets. China will be one of the biggest growth areas for AMF in the coming decade, which is why Roland Smith is going to Nanhui. Bowling is declining in popularity in America and suffering most everywhere else. It is the Chinas of the world that will keep Smith's five hundred workers in Mechanicsville busy. The company celebrated its centenary the month before Smith's visit, and if it wants another hundred years, it will have to do well in foreign markets such as China.

Foreign investment is important for China as well, of course. It brings money, technology, know-how, and improved management techniques. For all its advantages, however, foreign investment has been controversial in the People's Republic. Its government, for one thing, was founded upon Mao's ideal of self-sufficiency and socialist notions of public ownership. And there are other reasons.

The Chinese people have always hobbled foreigners in their midst. There is an aspect of economic self-interest and suspicion in this, but that exists around the world. In today's China, however, the resentment of outsiders is unusually strong. The issue is not whether the country's attitude is understandable—it is in light of the history of foreign invasion and domination—but whether its outlook will prevent it from progressing as fast as it needs to.

Up until now, there has been no hard deadline for progress. With WTO accession, there is. In the past, foreign businessmen moaned about the hundreds of restrictions that kept them weak. Today they chortle as they see that Chinese enterprises are unprepared for real competition as a result of the country's closed system. In the end, the restrictions on foreign business hurt Chinese companies more.

The need for reform has never been more immediate, but the response from the central government has been slow. Although the people's collective memory of unhappy contact with foreigners retards reform, the Party has added its own impediments to needed change. Senior cadres fear the "long nose," the outsider, and nowhere is the apprehension more evident than in the Fortune Global Forum, held in Shanghai, in 1999. Time Warner, the parent of *Fortune* and *Time,* is hosting this event, and its entire board of directors has flown in for the occasion. The hype, which serves the interests of both that company and China, is getting way out of hand. For China, this is an opportunity to showcase itself at an important juncture: while the event was being planned it became clear that foreign investment would fall dramatically in 1999. Jiang Zemin himself flies to Shanghai to give the keynote address.

The forum is being held in the last days of September, which means on the eve of the fiftieth anniversary of the founding of the People's Republic. Various news organizations roll out issues commemorating the event, as do *Time* and its sister publication, *Asiaweek.*

We may one day know why China was offended by *Time*'s commemoration of the People's Republic, but now we can only speculate. A short essay authored by the Dalai Lama appears in those pages, as does one by Wei Jingsheng, who some consider to be the father of the dissident movement in China. In December 1978, the same month Deng Xiaoping pushed aside Hua Guofeng, Wei coined the term "Fifth Modernization" to refer to democracy, a delicate subject in the China of both then and today. Wei wrote in *Time:* "No weapon can wipe out the truth." That's true, but the state can suppress its dissemination. During the forum, China bans the sale of *Time*'s issue. And *Asiaweek*'s for good measure.

This was too much for some to bear. Time Warner had already been criticized for keeping political issues off the agenda of the forum, and that controversy dominates media coverage as reporters find little of interest during its bland sessions. CNN, another Time Warner unit, talks to one of the victims. "I'm disappointed not for *Time* but for China," says *Time Asia* Editor Don Morrison, interviewed against the backdrop of Shanghai's Huangpu River and the Puxi skyline. "I hope someday that China is going to feel comfortable doing for information what it's now doing for the rest of its economy."

CNN does not stop there, but this time the result does not appear rehearsed as this is live broadcast journalism. Riz Khan, CNN's veteran journalist and host of *Q&A*, has invited Lee Kuan Yew onto his show. Lee is blunt, especially for a high government official and especially for one in Asia. The father of modern Singapore and now its senior minister, Lee does not mince words. Elder statesmen can afford to voice their thoughts. Khan, referring to China's ban on *Time* and *Asiaweek*, says to Lee, "Although the parent company Time Warner hosting the forum as well is trying to, I guess, encourage the business community, it's kind of ironic, isn't it?" "It's ironic that Time Warner has not pulled out," Lee retorts.

And it is sad. In one quick reply Singapore's Lee illustrates why bullies can roam schoolyards with impunity. Although Time Warner publicly displays weakness in the face of tyranny, it has also demonstrated to the tyrant, once again, that foreign business is responsible for transmitting ideas subversive to the state.

Not all foreigners are so easily cowed. Call him "John," though that is not his real name. This American working for a multinational in China is not diplomatic; "forthright" is a better term, "pugnacious" an even better one. He will not dilute his feelings. One of John's Chinese coworkers has launched into a tirade against the United States for the May 1999 bombing of the Chinese Embassy in Belgrade, and the American has no time for it. They are on a business trip at a hotel in Kunming in southwestern China. "You go to your room and watch CNN," John says. "Come back tomorrow, and we'll discuss it." The next morning his colleague, who "spent eight hours" watching coverage of the campaign in Yugoslavia, apologized to John. He told the American that he had not heard any of the background from the state media.

In one brief conversation, John has justified the central government's fears about the presence of foreigners: they spread their ideas and undermine the message of the state media. In public they may kowtow like

Time Warner, but in private some, such as John, show no respect for the modern Chinese state. And the state, of course, figured that out a long time ago.

China's current leaders know that they cannot remake China's economy on their own, as much as some would like to try. They are also correct in thinking that they need to go beyond what they have already done in opening up their country if they are to maintain any momentum. That, however, is where their realism ends. Senior Party leaders still harbor the notion that they can maintain strict control over society while they go about modernizing the People's Republic. Every day they calculate how much economic development they can afford and still keep themselves in Beijing.

Despite all their careful plans, they cannot succeed, for it must be one or the other: economic progress or Communist Party control. Wei Jingsheng stated in 1978 that without the Fifth Modernization, democracy, the other four would be merely promises. So far it would appear as if he were wrong because the Party has been able to modernize the economy without ceding political power. Nonetheless, in a few years the exiled Wei will look prophetic because Beijing's leaders cannot allow much more economic development and still retain control—their system is just about at its limits for change. From Mao to Jiang, China's Communist leaders have known the dangers of incremental reform, and they are on their guard. "The Western countries are staging a third world war without gunsmoke," said Deng Xiaoping. "By that I mean they want to bring about the peaceful evolution of socialist countries towards capitalism." He assured us that socialism remained the goal, something that Jiang is fond of reminding us.

So Beijing's leaders are always on guard against the erosion of their power and their ideology. And they know that foreigners are the agents of change. When they want to open up the economy a little more, they see New York lawyer Jerry Cohen everywhere they look. He's hard to miss, always appearing when the agenda says "China." He visited the People's Republic even before Mao passed from the scene, and ever since then he has been outspoken in the defense of the rights of humans in the country that has the most of them. Cohen's partners are fond of saying, even though they may not be fond of him, that the Ministry of Justice would have approved the establishment of their Beijing office years earlier had it not been for his activism. Cohen says that foreign business often goes to bat for human rights in China, and maybe that is true. It matters little, however. What does count is that Beijing's leaders see Cohen wherever they look and wonder how to preserve their monopoly on power with so many foreigners underfoot. Beijing wants the money and technology that foreign business leaders provide but not their politics and ideals. It must have all or nothing, and eventually it will choose the latter because its own survival is what is really important.

CHEN RONG COUNTRY

Everyone, it seems, has had his picture taken with Chen Rong. There's Xu Kuangdi, the ebullient mayor of Shanghai. Even higher still in the political pecking order is Huang Ju, Shanghai's faceless Party boss. And isn't that fellow over there Bill Clinton? In a country whose economy is run by politics and whose politics are governed by connections, it is photographs that count. That's why you can find them blown up almost as large as life in the Zhonglu administration building in Nanhui.

Chen Rong built his business mostly by himself, but now that he's done so he needs the Party and the support of those in the photographs. As important as he is, he's not about to cross them. The real currency of the People's Republic is not the renminbi; it is political patronage, which can give you all that money can buy and a few things in addition. "You have no idea how tiring it is to sit at banquet after banquet wining and dining these cadres, feeding them shark's fin soup, goose liver, and all the most expensive dishes money can buy," says one owner of a factory in Henan Province. Yes, it is, but he nonetheless eats and eats to burnish his *guanxi* with local officials. Chen Rong has great *guanxi,* but that is not helping him this evening as he stands by himself at the fringes of the crowd on the great lawn of the Taiyuan Villa in Shanghai. James Harding, the Shanghai correspondent for the *Financial Times,* is returning to London. Harding is the first foreign correspondent who interviewed him, so Chen Rong attends this farewell reception held in September 1999. Chen really did not have to show up; after all, he has been interviewed by journalism's elite around the world.

China works hard to craft the image that the world sees, and it is the Party that has thrust Chen Rong into the spotlight. The readers of the *FT* now know what New China can accomplish. Chen serves as proof of the correctness of its policies.

Zhonglu's boss does not know many at this reception, just Harding and a few others, so he mostly stands alone. In a group dominated by mangy foreign journalists, that's a safe place for him to be because the topic dominating the conversation this evening, apart from Harding's imminent departure, is the disappointment over the results of the Fourth Plenum, a meeting of the Party's leaders in Beijing. The hope had been that the leadership would move beyond its stylized phrases and address economic issues of substance, but that has not happened. Even Chen Rong thinks that more could have been done, and he says so at the reception. Otherwise observant journalists, engrossed by one another's cleverness, pay no attention to Chen and miss his forthright comments, which would have made good copy.

Optimists say that private entrepreneurs such as Chen will become a force for change in China, but that hope is, at least for the next few years, unrealistic. These businesspeople have become beholden to the Party in one way or another and depend on its system for their continued success. Most of them support the state fully for the same reason that foreign business does: they just want to make money. Chen, in a very important sense, is different. He is one of the few successful entrepreneurs in China who is willing to speak his mind.

Jim Rohwer, Asia editor for *Fortune,* is at Harding's gathering at the Taiyuan, and he is talking about the upcoming Fortune Global Forum. China works hard to craft the image the world sees, and it has demanded the right to choose the local participants. *Fortune,* contrary to its usual practice, caved in. Therefore, Chen Rong will be there, and he will, of course, be interviewed by CNN. Somehow China always manages to get its success stories into evidence in the court of world public opinion.

Chen will be on display at the forum and, in the future, at a dozen other forums and on a dozen more magazine covers. Now, however, he is playing the host, and the guest of honor *du jour* is Roland Smith, AMF's chief executive, on his first visit to Shanghai in April 2000. Chen is holding court at what some people consider to be the best Shanghainese restaurant in Shanghai, Xiaonanguo, whose literal name is "Small South

Country." Smith is there to talk bowling; Chen prefers to discuss film. The most prominent entrepreneur in the small country that is Shanghai reveals to a surprised Roland Smith that he also owns a movie company. Chen's latest production is a story of a con man who steals from the rich to give to the poor. Chen is rich, very rich, but when it comes to getting richer still he does not mind making films that cut against his class interest, proving once again that Lenin was right when he said that capitalists would sell the rope that is used to hang them.

Chen Rong's film company is Shanghai Xie Jin Zhonglu Film & TV Co., Ltd. The "Xie Jin" in the name is that of the director of *The Opium War,* one of the most successful local films in the history of the People's Republic. Xie made that epic in time to coincide with the handover of Hong Kong in 1997, before he joined Chen. *The Opium War* is not propaganda, Xie maintains, but it served an interest deemed important by Beijing: denigration of the British and, by implication, their accomplishments in the colony. Since then, Xie's patron, the cash-strapped Hengtong Group, has not been financially able to support his filmmaking activities. So it appears that the state has found another way for Chen Rong to serve it. He won't say why he took on Xie Jin, but the state always takes care of its own.

And Chen is finding ways to take care of himself. Now that he has a film company, Chen is making the best of it. His hands flail, his voice quickens, his eyes widen; Chen is now talking about his next vision. The Zhonglu boss hopes to bring the Hollywood way to Shanghai. "My childhood can be made into a movie," he says, referring to the hard times he went through. You can see that he's going to turn that period of adversity in his life into an opportunity. Soon the world, not just Shanghai, will know what he endured. In the process, he will do for Chinese filmmaking what he has done for Chinese bowling.

Yet for him to do so, he must enter a business that the Party deems sensitive, breaking one of the self-imposed rules that made him wealthy. He will have to use all his political skill if he is to succeed this time. As is his custom, Chen Rong looks for safe areas. In the spring of 2000, he tries to take advantage of his country's most important obsession. The topic is still nationalism, but instead of the British, the enemies are Chinese this time, splittists in Beijing's jargon. Come March and April of that year, Chinese propaganda lashes Taiwan almost daily and Chen Rong looks for scripts featuring the island "province." Unfortunately, Beijing seems to be getting nowhere with its unrelenting denunciations and Chen cannot find any films he wants to bankroll.

Chen's search for scripts on Taiwan goes beyond his pursuit of the almighty renminbi, however. He's a believer, like many Chinese raised on Mainland news. April 2000 finds the entrepreneur telling his guests from AMF, Randy Daniel and Wen Kang, his version of Chinese history regarding the island. The Manchus who conquered China and established the Qing Dynasty did not control Taiwan at the outset, Chen Rong points out. According to him, they waited thirty years and then took over the island by military force. Wen Kang, who is Taiwanese, turns to Daniel and says in English, just loud enough so that Chen can hear him, "That's not true." Fortunately, Chen Rong cannot understand English. This is an important business meeting, and AMF would like to keep the tone civil.

Chen Rong may be independently wealthy, but he is not independent. And he knows the secret of making money in China's supposedly new economy. Chen Rong observed that the government favored bowling because it was viewed as a healthy sport. Other businessmen know the name of the game too: doing what the government wants and accepting its largesse. "I just want to make money by taking advantage of government policies that are favorable to businessmen," says Qi Bing, who set up a chain of clothing stores in Beijing. "Making money, that's my goal." That is also Chen Rong's. That's why he's looking for safe scripts.

Like other Chinese entrepreneurs, Chen Rong has diversified in his quest to make more money. He knows the second secret for China's emerging new class: keeping out of the way of government enterprises. All of his lines of business are in areas in which state enterprises are not involved. Yes, there is a fast-growing private sector in China, but it is fragile. It has been allowed to prosper where the state has little or no economic interest of its own.

Keeping out of the way of the government means, among other things, respecting the state's population policy by having only one child. It's not illegal to have two or more, it's just that doing so is officially frowned upon in "one child" China. The newly rich can easily afford to have a second and bear the financial penalties imposed by the state, but this is not a question of money. One wealthy Chinese entrepreneur, a man whose name and face are familiar to the Chinese people, has two children but admits to only one for fear of offending the Party.

Chen Rong's son is at dinner with Roland Smith. Chen Jr. bears more than just a little resemblance to his father—it's almost as if he had been cloned. Chen has a company that does that to sheep. Zhonglu Bioengineering also claims to have transplanted human genes into that barnyard animal. Yet when it came to his own offspring, Chen presumably stuck to more traditional methods. For that particular task he employed his wife, a pleasant-looking but plain woman. She and the Chen Rong clone are at dinner with Roland Smith in Shanghai. She doesn't pay much attention to the American chief executive; she has her hands full with the fidgeting child. The boy absorbs the attention of everyone at dinner, as always happens in a country culturally preoccupied by its young, and soon the conversation around the table turns to children in general.

Little Chen stands to become one of the richest people in China if he can outlast his parents—and depending upon what the state does regarding inheritance. When everyone was "poor and blank," there was no point in taxing inheritances. Today the story is different. "Some people in rural areas and cities should be allowed to get rich before others" is a famous Dengism. Chen Rong and others have taken advantage of Deng Xiaoping's leniency, and now there are disparities in wealth that were unimaginable just a decade ago.

So the Party of Jiang Zemin has decided to level society. The first attack against little Chen began when the "real name" rules went into effect at banks on April 1, 2000. Up until then, China's savers could open an account in any name they chose. There was no requirement to produce identification on establishing an account, an anomaly for an otherwise strictly controlled society. The real-name rules pave the way for the establishment of an inheritance tax. There can be no such tax if the state cannot locate assets.

But a tax is more than meets the eye because, in the words of jurist John Marshall of the U.S. Supreme Court, "the power to tax involves the power to destroy." The state does not intend to destroy the newly emerging class of private wealth in China, but this tax is not just a revenue measure. Entrepreneurs will find themselves with a new heir, the state, and the state will find a new tool of control. Highly selective enforcement, already a feature plaguing China, will be just another means of reining in the rising entrepreneurial class. Chen Jr. need not worry about his next meal when his parents finally depart this world, yet he will undoubtedly have to surrender a sizable portion of his birthright, perhaps as much as half.

But what's going to happen to Zhonglu when the state seeks to collect its new tax? With much of Chen's wealth tied up in his principal enterprise, his heirs may have to liquidate the business to pay off the inheritance tax. It's way too early in China's development process to tax the engines of rejuvenation. As jurist Marshall also noted, "the power to destroy may defeat and render useless the power to create."

That is, however, only a future worry. In the present Chen Rong is enjoying himself. His visitors from AMF are having a good time, too. He is showing off, something he does not do often. He bought a floor for the corporate headquarters of Zhonglu, and it is located, of course, in the new building housing the Shanghai Stock Exchange in Pudong. This is one of the things that James Harding of the *Financial Times* interviewed him about: Zhonglu is, according to Harding, the first privately owned business to move into this building, the center of Shanghai's new financial center. For Chen, working in this building is like living in his hobby, which is what stock trading is for him these days. If you want to see Chen Rong, you have to make an appointment *after* three in the afternoon, when the stock market closes.

Everything is modern here, including the walls of his corner office. They are opaque now, but in a moment the greenish walls become transparent. Another second, and they are opaque again. All it takes is a click of a button on the remote control that Chen Rong is holding in his hand. The technology, he explains to his visitors, is American. Randy Daniel thinks it must have something to do with the polarization of light. The Virginian is impressed, but it doesn't appear that he wants to replace the solid walls of his office in Mechanicsville with those employing some scientific secret.

Unfortunately, the rest of Chen Rong's operations are not as high tech. On his April trip Roland Smith finds that out as he takes a tour of Zhonglu's facility at Nanhui. In one of the larger buildings he can see rows of metal lathes that are not computer-controlled. So Chen's parts are not as precise as they could be. In practical terms, the imprecision means that Zhonglu's pinspotters are not yet of the same standard as AMF's. Smith can see all that. But in this particular building there is something he does not notice. He cannot read Chinese, so he walks right by the Party's messages carefully chalked onto boards at the entrance. As a general matter, the Party would like Zhonglu's quality to be the best in the world, but it is more important to the cadres that workers see the Party's messages all day long. That's essential. Zhonglu is a private business, but the Party is never far away.

Chen Rong's tour seems to take forever because his manufacturing and assembly operations are housed in building after building in a campus setting with a Great Wall motif. Along the route Chen does not point out the metal-cutting machine. It looks lonely in the dim light. In a large one-story building with a high ceiling, it is the only object inside. Smith does not say whether he noticed the solitary metal cutter, but he quickly gets a sense of the overall picture. "Nowhere else in the world do we have the luxury of so much space," he observes. Chen does not tell his guest the reason for this unusual layout: he wants to take maximum advantage of what few government incentives exist for his low-tech industry. The more buildings Zhonglu uses, the more taxes Chen saves.

And the more it is apparent that Zhonglu is not doing as well as it once did. There's not much activity during his tour because it is late in the afternoon and the workers have already left, but Smith, who knows more about marketing than manufacturing, can sense that even at peak hours, the facility is not that busy. If it were, machines would fill all the buildings and there would be more partially completed pinspotters and other bowling equipment in the workshops.

After the Nanhui plant tour is over, Chen Rong takes Roland Smith and the rest of the AMF team to Huamu to visit his newly opened bowling center. The policeman standing in the middle of the busy intersection loses his concentration. He watches Chen Rong's black Rolls-Royce purr past him as it heads east, forgetting the traffic whizzing by inches from his feet. Chen and his guests arrive at the center with the gigantic bowling pin at the entrance. Zhonglu's boss is obviously proud of what he has built.

From the outside, Chen's business looks healthy, but all we see is a facade. Inside, Smith gets a look at the true state of Chen Rong's, and China's, affairs. That country has made great progress in building its industry in the past two decades, but now there is too much of most things, including bowling lanes, because foreign and domestic investors and central government technocrats have gotten carried away in their investment decisions. Inside, Chen's center is dreary. It's much too dark, and it lacks a feeling of excitement because it's so empty. There are no more than a dozen bowlers when Smith and the others visit, and 108 lanes look, well, deserted in the cavern that Chen has constructed. The place is bleeding cash for sure, and Chen Rong cannot be happy about that. He built the world's biggest single-floor alley, it appears, so that his manufacturing operations would have something to manufacture. His factory at Nanhui didn't look busy because his product is not selling well either in China or on the international markets. World demand for new bowling equipment is just not good in 2000. Not good for Brunswick, not good for AMF, not good for Zhonglu. Brunswick is dropping its prices, and Zhonglu will have to as well because these two companies compete at the lower end of the market.

But there is more to Zhonglu's problems than the world's poor appetite for bowling. Chen's company could sell more lanes in China, but all sorts of government rules keep the price of bowling equipment, and most everything else, relatively high. The consequence of that, of course, is that the Chinese do not have the money to bowl as much as they would like. That depresses the demand for new lanes that Chen's workers could produce. Until the Party understands this elemental point, Chen will have to figure out what to do to keep his employees gainfully occupied in Nanhui. Chen can, after all, build only so many bowling centers to take up the slack.

When they have walked outside Chen's bowling center in Huamu, Roland Smith looks skyward toward the top of Chen's monumental bowling pin. He wants to know just how high that sculpture is, and he figures out how to do it. He stands right against the building and determines that he is about as tall as a pane of glass. Randy Daniel counts the number of panes to the roof and then estimates how many more there would be to the top of the pin. The consensus is that the oversized pin is eighty feet tall. Smith tells Chen that it just might be "the tallest in the world." Chen breaks out into his boyish grin. Smith works for AMF, but he could have been a diplomat. Chen is Chinese, and, like all the rest of his countrymen, he enjoys praise from foreigners. The two men are made for each other.

From the top of Chen Rong's bowling pin we can see a long way, even into the parallel universe where Party policies are more important than the laws of economics. And where farmhands bite snakes. In June 1998, Cheng Wen, at an auction, bought Shenyang Micro-electronics, a plant located in the capital of industrial Liaoning Province, after having turned the operation around when he served as a manager there. The sale, supported by current workers, was bitterly opposed by those who had been laid off before Cheng's arrival. Claiming that their interests had not been protected in the auction, they staged continuous protests. On one occasion they blocked Shenyang's main roads for about six hours. About three months after the auction, local government authorities unilaterally annulled the sale and reclaimed the plant for the people. Disputes after the unilateral confiscation led to the halting of the plant's operations. There are five thousand similar disputes in Liaoning Province alone. "A state firm is always a state firm," says Fang Xuanbing, who had to abandon his investment in Anyang Lude Pharmaceutical Factory in December 1999 after being roughed up in his office by rampaging proletarians who opposed plans to restructure the business. "Whatever I do will be ineffective; I will always be a stepmother," he noted. "Once it has money, the firm will find a real mother." Fang reminds us that no private entrepreneur in the People's Republic is really secure.

"When people ask me whether I'm positive or negative about China, I ask 'Which China?' " says Jack Perkowski, one of the country's most prominent foreign investors. "What I am positive about is what the new breed of China can accomplish." The modern, dynamic China we see, Chen Rong's China, is the one we want to perceive. It gives us hope. But it's not the only China that exists today. For all the progress in the last quarter century, socialism still prevails in higher government and Party circles—and in the Shenyangs and Anyangs in the provinces. We hear Beijing's leaders talk about socialism and dismiss their words as so much verbiage. Words, however, are important to a political organization based on ideology. And that ideology, ingrained by decades of Maoist campaigns, strikes a responsive chord in many, even today.

Today China constrains the private sector as if it were an orphan. It rations capital, denies legal protection, and bars access to business opportunities. "The 21st century world belongs to the non-state sector—at least in places where the emperor doesn't show his face very often," says a Guangdong Province cadre. Where the emperor, or Party secretary, visits frequently, the world belongs to the politically favored, the state sector.

Beijing's leaders use a dash of free-market thinking to help them build socialism, not capitalism. Mao permitted private ownership for a while. His successors are doing the same. In their minds, private-sector reform is only a temporary tactic. "It can be said that Jiang Zemin, Zhu Rongji, they are not standing by the side of private enterprise," Chen Rong says. He knows that companies such as his are tolerated by the regime for as long as they are useful. "They do not really believe," he says.

Chen Rong doesn't have President Jiang Zemin's photograph in his collection, and he knows he never will. Jiang simply doesn't visit real private businesses, he notes. And Chen's picture with Huang Ju, Shanghai's influential Party boss? He came only after a "debate," Chen explains. "Because I have made a contribution to Shanghai, especially my conversation with Clinton was very good, so they know me, so he came," Chen notes. "He is a Party secretary, so he does not easily come to a private enterprise." As a result of the Party's ambivalence, China's private enterprise will develop slowly, much more slowly, than it should. As will China itself.

From the top of his bowling pin Chen Rong can see the future, and it's not clear that he likes the view. As Roland Smith departs China in April 2000, the Party begins to wind down its latest campaign against those seeking faster reform. At first it appears that Chen and the thousands of other Chens across China should be happy. Jiang Zemin is ending the campaign, however, because die-hard Maoists are taking advantage of the situation to renew calls for "a new class struggle." Deng Liqun, the outspoken leader of the leftist faction of the Party, believes that private and foreign owners are exploiting their workers. Chen Rong's employees seem to be happy, but the old guard happens to be right. Working conditions are harsh in many of China's factories, and the state's labor rules are rarely enforced in the private sector. Conditions approximating slavery, where people are imprisoned and forced to labor without pay, have even reappeared in the country's privately owned factories. You won't hear much about this in the official media: Jiang, adopting his best Maoist style of governance, has ordered the media not to publicize Maoist views on the exploitation of workers.

Chen Rong, like tens of millions, suffered during the Cultural Revolution and knows that despite appearances, the important things have not changed. He can see the Party's persecution of entrepreneurs when they lose favor, even today. And he knows how China works. Chen says that China used to have a "red economy." The West's economy is "white": transparent and fair. Today China's economy is "gray." There are laws, Chen says as he begins to explain his choice of colors: "In different situations, at different times, to different people, the laws can change."

And he can see that the Party wants to further infiltrate private businesses. Zhonglu is big enough that it already has a Party cell established inside, and Chen has to pay the salary of the cadre who runs it. It's now May 2000, and other entrepreneurs are about to share in this fate. Jiang Zemin called for cells to be formed in private businesses "to guarantee the healthy development of the [private] sector." These cells "should work hard to unite and educate entrepreneurs to advocate various policies of the Party, run the businesses according to law, and protect the employees' interests." It's as if Jiang thinks that the snake and the farmer should share the same bed.

Chen is powerful now, but perhaps that is only temporary. He knows that because he has already seen what can happen in China. "The Party can do what it will, both for good and bad," he says. Even today, after nearly a quarter century of reform, the story remains the same. The Party giveth and the Party taketh away, but it is always the Party that decides.

8

Highway Girls

China's Economy Stagnates

> Until the tide goes out you don't know who's swimming
> naked.
>
> —WARREN BUFFETT

Prostitutes no longer stand in the middle of China's main roads. Their absence is a general sign of progress, of course, but it also reveals why the country faces economic troubles. The girls won't be missed, at least by most of us, yet China's technocrats probably long for the days when the prostitutes were blocking traffic. Life was easier for Beijing's planners in the days when females ruled the roads.

It is late 1995, and the setting is the main road leading east out of Hangzhou, the capital of prosperous Zhejiang Province on China's eastern coast. This city has been the capital of China from time to time, and in the 1100s it was the most populous urban center in the world. Marco Polo described the city as the most graceful anywhere, but by 1995 it is just another large Chinese metropolis, a bit grimy and shabby like all the rest. Hangzhou, however, has a tourist industry because it sits on the shores of West Lake. The lake is picturesque, but the city has encroached on its banks with high-rise hotels, and the area has lost much of its natural charm. Chinese, however, still visit West Lake, and many come by the roads.

The main road east of the city is two lanes wide and not divided. A few miles out of town on its south side are small restaurants of white tile and concrete, set back on a gentle slope. They are run-down, like most of the rest of this area. In the middle of the eastbound lane are two girls in their late teens, perhaps early twenties, with the pure white skin favored by local truck drivers. Their lips are bright red, of course, and they are not particularly attractive, just good enough for this type of work. Gorgeous or not, they have courage. As they face the oncoming traffic, they smile as if this game were fun. If they are successful, they take you back to one of those white tile buildings for quick servicing. Vehicles that don't stop have to swerve, as the girls never entirely surrender their patch of one of China's main arteries.

Today the main artery connecting Hangzhou with the east looks like an interstate, a road as modern as can be found anywhere. The ninety-mile trip between Hangzhou and Shanghai, once seven hours, is now less than two. There are no stoplights, no right-angle turns, and no girls standing in the road. Asphalt and cement in seemingly endless strings are beginning to bind China together. And for the first time in Chinese history, it is possible to think about the nationwide distribution of products.

China is creating a national economy, and the result is a massive—and painful—restructuring of industry and society. The strong drive out the weak, and efficient producers are continually able to lower their prices to consumers. Competition across provincial boundaries is becoming a reality. As a result, the country is experiencing deflation, a continual decline in prices.

As prices fall, the economy stagnates. The rosy statistics from China's capital mask fundamental problems. Beijing's feeble programs have not done much to restart the economy or ease deflation because technocrats choose the wrong solutions as they misperceive the problems. China needs healthy growth to absorb the unemployed and underemployed and give jobs to those entering the workforce. If the People's Republic does not do these things, it risks economic failure.

RABBITS ON THE ROAD

We think of China as "the world's biggest market," but in reality it has been many small ones. In the past, each Chinese city was largely self-sufficient, with one car manufacturer, one steelmaker, one of everything. Each city's requirements were relatively small, so efficiencies of scale were sacrificed to the god of self-sufficiency. Mao had one model of development, the commune. He transplanted that model to urban areas and created state-owned enterprises. Cities, in the Maoist state, were collections of industrial communes.

Because transportation of goods over long distances was not feasible, a steelmaker in Liaoning Province in the northeast could not compete with one in, say, Sichuan, in the southwest. So every city resembled a minicountry as far as economic production was concerned. By one means or another each locality protected its own industry and was largely economically isolated. That's how, for instance, China ended up with about 8,000 of the world's 9,500 cement producers.

Now China has good roads and railways and airports, so there is, for the first time, substantial intercity and interprovincial commerce, even for food and other perishables. Efficient producers in one city can compete against backward manufacturers in another. Consequently, we have recently witnessed the rise of national domestic brands. Guangdong Kelon sells its domestic appliances far from its southern base, and you can find televisions made by Sichuan Changhong across the length and breadth of the country. These forces affect the foreign investor, too. The brave, the first of them, built small-scale operations because of the difficulty of selling products far from the point of manufacture. Tomorrow's foreigners will build big to dominate the emerging national market. The early foreign investors may therefore end up being too small to survive in China's changing marketplace. So much for "first-mover advantage."

Efficient producers are able to lower prices to consumers. China is moving forward as it restructures. Its industry is becoming more competitive and the nation more modern. Good transportation makes that possible. As highways grow from two lanes to four and then to eight, the prostitutes are consigned to the back roads. No matter how attractive, they can no longer block the nation's vital traffic on the main arteries. The only ones who can do that today are rabbits. It is the Year of the Rabbit, and a horde of cute white bunnies is certainly taking advantage of its prominent position on the Chinese calendar. The bunnies have just escaped from a big tour bus, and the fugitives are now blocking the Suzhou-bound traffic on the Huning Expressway. Their bus is astride two, perhaps three, lanes that should be open to traffic but unfortunately are not. As the rabbits scamper around the pavement, the driver and onlookers from the toll plaza try to figure out how to put them back into their cages. China looks more modern these days, but those who make decisions are stuck in the old times. Like those who decided to allow the critters onto the bus in the first place—and those who let them out.

The rabbits, however energetic, can stand in the way of the nation's progress for only so long. In China, the only creatures that can really block forward momentum are the leaders of the Communist Party. Zhu Rongji made his career by taming inflation, which reached an annual rate of 21.7 percent in 1994. In a China where everything is political, inflation took on dark overtones, so in the eyes of many senior cadres Zhu is credited with saving the Party. In 1994, inflation was higher than even in the pre–Tiananmen Square period, when eroding incomes added to the general discontent of the time. Zhu solved the inflation problem and, as a reward, became premier soon afterward.

Yes, he solved the inflation problem; however, he did it too well. Deflation occurred on his watch and is now *his* problem—and he is panicking. Consumer prices began their downward trend in October 1997, the first time that had happened in China in twenty-five years (when measured on a year-on-year basis). In 1998, consumer prices fell by 0.8 percent, and in the following year the decline was 1.4 percent. He has also presided over declining growth: 1999 marked the seventh consecutive year in which the growth rate fell. China's economy grew by 7.1 percent that year; that was half of 1992's rate of 14.2 percent. These alarming trends explain the lengths that Zhu will go to these days to reinflate the economy.

China is suffering deflation as cadres scurry to correct the Party's past mistakes. For one thing, the process of restructuring is itself deflationary. Mao's system of communization of the cities was in large part responsible for the gross inefficiencies that kept consumer prices high. Remedying this structural flaw through nationwide competition has naturally resulted in lower prices. Curing the banks, made sick by the attempt to salvage state-owned enterprises, means restricting their lending, and that's deflationary too, especially when it takes place in times of decelerating growth.

And there has been another problem. In the Deng Xiaoping era China had the highest growth rates in the world, but it now appears that much of the investment in the last quarter century was economically useless. The result of that era of exuberance is too much of everything today. "War is hell," said General William Tecumseh Sherman of American Civil War fame, but it's nothing like competition in the beer industry in China. It is a Tuesday night in a cold January in another tourist destination in the eastern part of the country. "In Heaven there is Paradise," the Chinese say; "down on Earth there are Suzhou and Hangzhou." Hangzhou we've just heard about, and in Suzhou there are charming gardens and picturesque canals. But also in Suzhou there is Phoenix Street, which is bustling as people jump out of the way of motor scooters traveling at high speed—on the sidewalk. The street is no better: it is terror for pedestrians and drivers alike. China is getting ready for the Year of the Rabbit to give way to that special time in the Chinese calendar, the auspicious Year of the Dragon.

On Phoenix Street in the busy Wanjiadenghuo Restaurant an enormous tortoise, almost three feet long, is not stirring as he hugs a portion of the ground floor near the entrance, but everything else is in overdrive, especially the girls selling foreign beer. There is Miss Steinlager, a small, thin lass wearing a velour pants suit in that beer's official color, dark green. She is running between the various floors of the restaurant, pushing New Zealand's most famous beer in China, but she has to work hard because there are two sturdy-looking young women hawking Asahi, the Japanese brew, in red dresses and short white jackets.

And who will sell more beer tonight? It depends on the night, because, as Miss Steinlager says, "People have a brand loyalty for beer." If her patrons come, she will be run off her feet. If they don't, Asahi will sell more. She doesn't have time to explain; she's off to the next table and the one after that.

It is clear that the foreign brands have found their way to Phoenix Street. There are about fifty of these brews sold in China, and it seems that most of them have found the Wanjiadenghuo. The restaurant boasts a refrigerated display case from Steinlager—and one from Asahi as well.

The green menu cover is imprinted with the logos in gold of both Beck's and Guinness, and the inside cover has a full-page advertisement for Beck's (with a space-age theme, bottled beer in orbit). Surprisingly, none of these brews is actually listed on the menu. That honor is reserved for Sapporo, Heineken, and Budweiser. The ashtrays are from Budweiser, the glasses from Asahi, and Asahi pennants decorate the spiral stairway to the second floor. Either the decorator chose a beer motif, or this is ground zero of one of the fiercest commercial battles on earth.

Already there have been casualties, and soon there will be more. Britain's Bass exited the China market in 2000. Guinness is withdrawing from its licensing arrangement, and Australia's Fosters has shuttered two of its three breweries in China. Others have scaled back operations. Only one or two foreign brands make money. Foreign beer makers in China now have only one choice: to get bigger and go national or close. Market leader Tsingtao, a domestic brand, is less optimistic of their chances. Says Peng Zuoyi, Tsingtao vice chairman, "We can say with certainty that the retreat of the foreign beer makers from China is irreversible."

That's too bad for the foreigners, because it will not be long before the Chinese brew more beer than anyone else. China's just a shade behind the United States, and its output has been growing a staggering 25 percent a year for the last decade, the fastest in the world. Profits in the industry, however, have been elusive, and not just for the foreigners. Price competition has wrecked the margins of the almost 550 remaining local brewers. Beer, of course, is just one of the many industries in which supply exceeds demand.

Those who drink too much at the Wanjiadenghuo might seek the refuge of a nearby hotel. Suzhou is said to be home to the country's prettiest girls, with the statuesque figures and white skin so favored by most Chinese men. Two of these stunning examples of female pulchritude are standing behind the reception counter of the Cao Qiao Hotel, tucked into a back road a block from chaotic Phoenix Street.

Opened in 1997, the hotel occupies a five-story building. On the outside, the structure is undistinguished, impossible to differentiate from tens of thousands of other white tile boxes that mar China. The inside, however, is a different story. Somebody obviously went to great expense to decorate this three-star establishment. Its reception area is enormous, dominated by an atrium that ends in a massive skylight. The marble floor contains an intricate, visually exciting compass design. The wood and stone surfaces were designed and crafted with taste and care. The Cao Qiao has all the standard amenities and facilities. The place has everything—everything, that is, except guests.

The hotel's 102 rooms are almost all empty. One of the guest floors has been closed, and the others are deserted. The bathroom taps obviously have not been used in ages—the water runs a rusty orange. The gift shop is enormous, but the only person there is an extremely bored girl behind the counter. She can probably remember every person who wanders into her domain, they are that few. If you want to spend a night in Suzhou, the "Venice of the East," and have forgotten to make hotel reservations, try the Cao Qiao. The whole hotel will be at your disposal.

And if the Cao Qiao does not please you, there are tens of thousands of empty hotel rooms across Suzhou and the rest of China's eastern coast. Take your pick. You are the principal beneficiary of one of the twentieth century's most irrational building campaigns. Start from Suzhou and continue down the road past the rabbits that escaped from their bus, and you will find in China's greatest city all that is hollow in China's greatest economic boom.

Twice as populous as New York and at times twice as fast, Shanghai is "a city of superlatives." As anyone who lives there will tell you, Shanghai, the "Paris of the East," is China's premier city. Other Chinese will disagree, but Shanghai is, in fact, the most populous city in the world's most populous country. "Nothing more intensely living can be imagined," Aldous Huxley said of the city.

Shanghai has intensely overextended itself in its own inimitable style, building the equivalent of all of Hong Kong's office space within eight years during the 1990s. Folly, maybe, but one must admire the city's ambition. It already has the world's third tallest building and third tallest structure, but this is no third-class city. Predictably, Shanghai is about to construct the tallest building in the world. A few years ago Shanghainese loved to boast that 20 percent, some even said 80 percent, of the world's construction cranes were at work in their city. They now brag that they have more skyscrapers than New York, a dubious claim. But true or not, it says a lot about their vision for the future.

"The culture is tomorrow," says one foreign businessman, referring to Shanghai. The Shanghainese certainly built as if there were no tomorrow. "We Shanghainese are shrewd and smart," says Ruan Yanhua, a Shanghai municipal official. Well, maybe not, because the boom ended in vacancy rates approaching 70 percent in some parts of the city, such as Pudong's Lujiazui district, the "Manhattan of the East." The exuberant mayor, Xu Kuangdi, justifies his prolonging the building boom this way: "You make them a little too long and maybe next year the clothes will fit."

As bad as the situation is in Shanghai, it is much worse in other parts of China. In general, the Party followed Nike's famous slogan. The cadres not only just did it, they overdid it. Time will remedy the results of the Party's unrestrained enthusiasm as eventually China will grow into its new premises. The inevitable consequence of the gross overinvestment of the past will be that growth rates in the future will decline as China makes the adjustment. China lurches from scarcity to excess and now to economic failure. That's the result of development by mass campaign.

It will be harder for the cadres to remedy another cause of deflation, one that cannot be solved by mass action directed from Beijing. Simply put, the people of China look around them and feel insecure. They can see what is happening. Their country is undergoing wrenching transformations from a Maoist economy to a semimarket one and from an agrarian society to a string of urban centers. And the old "iron rice bowl" system is breaking down. Once the state provided workers with most essentials for life. If you needed a bar of soap or a towel, for instance, your employer would provide that in addition to housing, schooling, health care, and a hundred other essentials. Maoism might have smothered the Chinese people, but they did feel secure in its embrace.

That's a lot less true these days as the Party stumbles toward a freer economic system. Hardship, the consequence of change, has convinced millions that they must provide for themselves. Today they save and save and save some more. Americans are allergic to putting money away for the future; the Chinese, on the other hand, are collectively among the world's greatest savers, stuffing away some 40 percent of gross domestic product year after year. That, if anything, is a big vote of no confidence in the state's ability to provide.

Beijing's technocrats should be praised for trying to remake China's economic system, but they could, and should, have put a safety net for workers into place beforehand. That, of course, would have avoided much of the human pain of restructuring. Moreover, the central government should be pushing through with reforms at something faster than molasses speed. As it is, Beijing, by dithering, is prolonging the agony. If there was a safety net of some sort, progress could be faster because worker unrest is a major factor slowing necessary changes. With a net of some sort, workers' spending would be higher and deflation less of an issue. Zhu Rongji wants the nation's social welfare system to be "perfect," and maybe that's why it's taking such a long time to put one into place. The point remains, however, that this groundwork should have been accomplished long ago by a government established for the proletariat.

So the proletarians must fend for themselves. And they are thinking on their own, too. China's populace has concluded, correctly, that the vicious price wars will continue. Entry into the World Trade Organization only reinforces the "things will be cheaper tomorrow" mentality. The state-owned media try to give the impression that accession will not result in price declines, but that is counterintuitive in light of the scheduled tariff reductions on imports and the hundred other reasons why enhanced trade in accordance with WTO rules will lower prices.

Perhaps that's why manufacturers have to resort to tricks to get people to buy their products. Take Tianjin Automotive, the maker of a small car rather appropriately called the Charade. That manufacturer announced in January 2000 that it would reduce prices for members of certain professions. The reduction was not, the company insisted, a price cut, but a "reward" for past support. But people soon discovered that in fact they didn't have to be policemen, journalists, soldiers, doctors, or teachers to buy Charades at the lower prices—the discounts were available to everyone.

Not even discounts work these days, as the problems in the economy are deep-seated. Because deflation is the result of faulty economic policies, it should come as no surprise that the official media label this phenomenon "inevitable," as if the Party had been a bystander all these years, and call for even more government control of the economy to solve the situation. That approach, however, has not been working. Central government technocrats, led by Premier Zhu Rongji, have tried virtually everything to little avail. Their monetary policy has been a flop: seven successive reductions of interest rates, a big decrease in bank reserve requirements, and other maneuvers have had little effect.

Then there is fiscal stimulus. The Chinese have always been preoccupied with taming their great rivers, which both enrich and ravage them. In this respect, the leaders of the People's Republic resemble those who preceded them. Yet if you go to Fulong Temple in Dujiangyan, a city just northwest of the Sichuan capital of Chengdu, you will see how the People's Republic differs from its predecessors. It is at the site of this temple that Li Bing, a master of hydrologic engineering, subdued an evil dragon. At least that is what legend says. Here by this impressive structure Li also subdued the mighty Min River in the third century B.C. In Dujiangyan they brag about Li's ingenious use of topography and water patterns to control flooding. They boast that it is the only water conservancy project in the world that does not use a dam. Chen Zonglin, a *xiagang* worker, now gives unofficial tours of the wonders of Li Bing's project. What really excites him is not the scope of the undertaking but how the ancient engineer set the stones in a channel that to this day still carries away the silt. "The way the stones are laid, no need for concrete," the middle-aged man says proudly.

Today, another famous water engineer named Li, Communist Party stalwart Li Peng, also brags, but now the boast is about the gargantuan scope of the Three Gorges Dam, which will tame the Yangtze River. China's media recite statistics on the amount of concrete to be poured, the volume of water that will fill in behind the dam, the number of people to be resettled, the area of land to be submerged. And especially the cost. It is the biggest ongoing civil engineering project in the world today. China is building big in the first decade of the new millennium, and it is proud of its dams. The economical methods of Li Bing's project in Dujiangyan aren't of interest. What is important is statistics, not efficiency. The leaders in Beijing need projects, and they like them big.

The bigger the projects, the better, because they can then spend lots of money. A program of massive fiscal stimulus has been Beijing's primary hope of ending deflation. Central government planners are doing what decades of training have taught them to do: plan the economy centrally by shoveling money into the public sector. Technocrats build roads, increase the salaries of civil servants, rearm the armed forces. They sprinkle funds onto thousands of other projects across the nation and channel money into state-owned enterprises, thereby increasing the size of the public sector. They are accomplishing all they set out to do: China, predictably, has more highways now, more weapons, and richer civil servants. Their spending is accomplishing a lot, but it is not ending deflation. In that task they are failing. Fiscal stimulus is not working.

Spending money is not doing the job, so they're employing additional tactics. Because supply has outstripped demand, the central government is simultaneously constricting supply and increasing demand. Experts say that China no longer has a command economy, but the technocrats are commanding what they can. To reduce supply, Beijing is closing productive operations around the country by administrative fiat. More than 30,000 coal mines and 5,600 oil refineries have already been shuttered, says the official *China Daily,* with even more headed for the same fate. Many other industries are targeted, such as cement, glass, sugar, and saccharine. But central government technocrats shouldn't celebrate just quite yet. Closings work better on paper than in real life. Local officials seem to be able to protect their enterprises from a central government that often cannot enforce its will outside the Beijing municipal borders. It's rather a paradoxical position for a Communist state to have arrived at.

And Beijing has devised a dozen other means to prevent the market from determining prices. The plants that aren't being closed are being restricted by other administrative measures such as output ceilings, and imports are subject to curbs and outright bans. New investment in certain areas is prohibited. And the technocrats have simply declared deflation to be illegal. They are using their new authority under the Price Law to fix prices. Moreover, they are allowing producers to do the same. After a secretive meeting in Beijing in March 2000, for example, nine of China's largest steel producers announced a coordinated price increase of about 5 percent. The cartel agreement, arranged by the Ministry of Metallurgical Industry, was patterned after a similar agreement in the summer of 1999 among all eight of China's producers of television tubes. Then the Ministry of Information Industry jumped on the bandwagon and announced in 2001 that it would decree cuts in the production of televisions, thereby resurrecting a private cartel agreement that had failed in the previous year. Who says Communist leaders cannot learn from the private sector? Today there is ambivalence in Beijing about the advisability of permitting private cartels, but the fact that there is even debate shows how far the Communist Party has fallen.

The technocrats are leaving no stone unturned, or power unused, in their fight against the demon deflation. In addition to everything else, they are also busy increasing demand—or at least trying to. That will be difficult, however, because about 900 million people live in the country-side, where more than half the peasants survive on about US$0.73 per day. Incomes there have been declining since 1997, and the end of this trend is nowhere in sight. That means peasants and rural workers, who comprise most of the people in China, don't have extra cash to spend. Although many city dwellers do, Beijing's political commanders, even in an authoritarian society, cannot command consumers to consume. As a consequence, central government planners are reversing decades of planning that thwarted spending. And they have had to resort to novel tactics in places far from Beijing.

Not long ago you needed a map, and perhaps a guide, to find the Shanghai Stock Exchange. Down the famous strip of buildings that form the Bund and past the historic Peace Hotel you would cross the old steel-truss Waibaidu Bridge over the foul Suzhou Creek and then make a sharp right turn onto narrow, winding Huangpu Road. Just before a bend in the street, on the left-hand side, stood a prerevolutionary building of weathered grayish stone. Inside, the lobby was dark and cold, with wooden benches along the dingy walls. But hidden away in a maze of rooms were well-lit rows of terminals and wall-mounted display screens—all connected by the most modern trading system in the world at the time. In the mid-1990s, stock exchange officials would regale you with stories, entirely true, about how their electronic matching system was days faster than the archaic procedures of the New York Stock Exchange.

Now that old building is home to a hostel, and the exchange, as part of the central government's master plan, is at the crossroads of Pudong in another grayish building, this one modern with a big hole through the middle. Inside, replacing the rabbit warren on Huangpu Road, is the world's largest trading floor. It is here, and on the floor of Shenzhen's stock exchange, that Premier Zhu Rongji planned in early 1999 to make his last stand in the fight against deflation—a fitting venue, considering that Pudong suffered some of the highest vacancy rates in the world and thus contributed to China's deflationary environment.

In the late 1990s, the premier could see that Americans, buoyed by their unrealized stock gains, were spending their country to continued economic success. Zhu thought that what Americans could do, Chinese could too. In early 1999, he decided to inflate the equity markets and thereby make domestic investors feel rich. This "wealth effect," he reasoned, would make them want to spend again. Faced with the failure of his other remedies, the premier embraced the notion that stock exchanges could be an integral part of China's "socialist market" system.

Through old-fashioned exhortation and some tinkering with rules, Zhu Rongji engineered an impressive stock market rise that began during the middle of May 1999. And the upswing in the markets succeeded in capturing the attention of the people. Zhou Xiaoyi is sitting in a kitchen on a low stool. She is at work as an *ayi*, a housekeeper, in the home of foreigners in Shanghai and has finished most of her chores for the day, just waiting for the laundry's dry cycle to end. Zhou is listening to the day's stock quotes over a transistor radio through earphones so she won't bother her employers. She is doing exactly what the leaders of her great nation want her to do, speculating some of her money in stocks. Zhou was one of the lucky ones: she made about ¥2,000 (about US$240) in 1999. Only a third of Chinese investors ended up ahead that year, even though it was the Year of the Bull on the two Mainland exchanges. Zhou, however, did not consume more with her winnings: she left them in the market, where she lost her profits (and much more) in the following year after the artificial run-up in share prices came to an end. On a larger scale, consumption was largely unaffected by the temporary stock gains, and retail prices continued their downward trend.

Central planners will do just about anything to manipulate stock prices, even backtrack on reform. In July 1999, for instance, the China Securities Regulatory Commission, the country's stock watchdog, announced that state-owned enterprises would be allowed to acquire stock in initial public offerings. A few months later, in September, the CSRC announced that it would permit SOEs to trade shares in the secondary market—a reversal of the May 1997 policy banning them from speculating in stocks. China's planners had spent a long time getting the SOEs out of the market. It was a sign of desperation that Beijing was allowing them back in. The banking system was also called upon to do its part in keeping the equity markets high. In 1999, securities houses were allowed to access the interbank market (thereby permitting them to borrow from the banks). This was good for the markets but not so hot for the banks, which were pressured by the government to enter a risky line of business after having been forced out of it just two years before.

Since 1999, regulatory improvements have been announced weekly as China's technocrats seek to make the markets work better—and boost share prices. After all the rule making and cheerleading, however, China has little to show for its efforts. The markets established a pattern of soaring on the news of regulatory changes and then falling back soon afterward. Investors know that the stock exchanges are wacky, and, as a consequence, they have made big money and lost it too. The one thing that they have not done, however, is spend their profits, the purpose behind the government's campaign.

FROM THE ULTIMATE HEIGHT

Through 1999, the central government's economic policies didn't work, and the slide was beginning to look dangerous. But as dawn broke on the millennial year of 2000, something wonderful happened in China: the economy roared back to life. Growth picked up, and deflation eased. "China's stars have never seemed in better alignment," said one foreign economist in the middle of 2000. "China's time is now."

What on earth could have caused the upturn? Maybe it didn't occur on this planet; perhaps it was the supreme being himself, the Falun Gong's Li Hongzhi, who engineered the miracle. "My *qigong* level reaches the ultimate height; and I understand the truth of the universe, see through human life, and can tell and predict the past and future of humankind," he boasts. Yes, that must be the explanation: the heavens were involved.

Or maybe the technocrats were lying. "The figures are so good, I just cannot believe them," says a Chinese economist working for one of the state banks. "How can things turn around so quickly?" Even Master Li, with all his divine powers, could not have pulled off all these macroeconomic feats by himself. He would have to have had help from China's statisticians, who, like all the other officials in China, say whatever is demanded from above.

Official statistics may tell us that retail deflation bottomed out in early 2000, but some analysts disagree, and few really think that prices in China were on the rise. "What's going up?" asked Shanghai resident Matt Miller in September 2000. In China's largest city, one of the most prosperous in this country, the prices of everything were headed downward, the veteran newspaper reporter knew. The truth is that none of the strategies of the central government has had a lasting effect on deflation because in China today there is too much of almost everything that is for sale; the country's economic miracle was not as miraculous as it looked.

Central planners are doing dozens of things wrong, but the worst is their deficit spending, which is draining the nation's resources. Fiscal stimulus does not work, because bureaucrats can spend but they cannot spend efficiently. Beijing has always wasted money; that's an old story. Now, however, there is a new dimension to the problem: the economy is hooked on government spending, and China cannot continue the current pace of expenditure for much longer. At first glance, the situation looks manageable. Official figures show that the central government's 2000 budget deficit of US$31.4 billion was 2.9 percent of announced gross domestic product for that year (US$1.1 trillion). The total public debt of US$246.6 billion was 22.9 percent of 2000 GDP. Both percentages are within internationally recognized safety limits (3 percent for annual deficits and 60 percent for total debt), but the statistics severely understate the severity of the situation.

China's total indebtedness would be substantially larger than the official numbers indicate if the central government's hidden obligations were added to the books. Take indirect loans to the state, for example. Beijing has essentially borrowed from the nation's depositors by forcing its banks to make loans to state-owned enterprises and other entities controlled by the state. The central government will have to continue to accept responsibility for this indebtedness unless it is prepared to see its banks collapse, which is simply not an option. These indirect loans amounted to about US$860.8 billion in 2000, which by itself was 79.7 percent of GDP for that year. Also excluded from the official statistics is a portion of the rapidly growing expenditures on the military, a closely guarded secret. Some think that about two thirds of the budget for the People's Liberation Army is not revealed; others say that 90 percent is hidden from view. Then there are unfunded pension obligations (which, by themselves, are about US$850 billion or 79.4 percent of current GDP) and the losses of state-owned enterprises, both of which should be included in the budget if we want a realistic assessment of China's financial picture.

Moreover, China's output statistics are not reliable. The 1999 gross domestic product numbers were issued before the end of that year, an impressive feat in any country, especially one as far-flung as China. China's statisticians were much more respectful of appearances in announcing GDP for 2000: they waited until January 1, 2001. For many reasons the numbers overstate GDP as they always do. Outright fabrication remains a serious problem: GDP growth may only be a quarter of what official statistics claim. Lying, however, is not the primary cause of distortion. China's GDP statistics lose their meaning because some substantial portion of real growth is economically useless and shouldn't be included in GDP if we are trying to use this measure to gauge the nation's ability to continue its deficit spending. There are empty buildings in Shanghai, the wasteful Three Gorges Dam, and all the unwanted goods that now sit in warehouses. All of these increase GDP, but they are, for the most part, economically useless. As a result, the traditionally used ratios of deficit to GDP and total debt to GDP, as computed using the official numbers, grossly overstate how much more debt China can incur to jump-start its economy. How can Beijing's technocrats know what they're doing when their statistics hide the truth?

So no one knows just how much more debt the central government can take on because no one's working from the facts. But let's make a few adjustments to official numbers to get a better idea of China's true financial condition. First, we need to include, as a direct government obligation, the unrecoverable loans in China's banking system (about US$490 billion) and the unfunded pension obligations mentioned above. When we do that, China's total accumulated debt of US$1.6 trillion is 146.7 percent of GDP, a figure that exceeds the internationally recognized safety mark by more than two times. By making only these adjustments, we are still understating the problem, but at least we can begin to see the dimensions of the situation. If all the other necessary adjustments are made, China's financial state looks precarious, perhaps critical. We won't know the nation's true condition until Beijing produces reliable GDP statistics and reveals the true size of all the expenditures and other obligations that should be included as part of the central government's budget. Even if the optimistic official statistics were correct—and they're not—observers say that China's spending spree must end soon, something even bureaucrats implicitly acknowledge. They must know there's a problem in Beijing, because servicing the debt requires more and more of the central government's revenue, a situation *The Economist* calls "scary." And so is the increase in China's sovereign public debt, which zoomed up by 25.7 percent in 1999 and 16.2 percent in 2000. Even though central government officials know that they can't splurge forever, they also can't stop: the budget deficit for 2001 will top 2000's record shortfall. Finance Minister Xiang Huaicheng says that the economy will move "into a virtuous cycle in 2001," but if that were the case he wouldn't need to take China deeper into the red. He knows that he must spend all he can so that his economy won't grind to a halt.

China's fiscal situation is shaky for another reason: the central government garners less revenue than it should. Although tax collections jumped by 13.4 percent in 1999 and 22.8 percent in 2000, China is still behind almost every other nation in its ability to collect revenue. Moreover, the good news is somewhat unreal: deceptive practices, such as collecting future taxes in advance, have inflated the recent statistics. Whatever improvement there has been, the recent uptick in tax collection will be short-lived, as central government officials admit. Much of the increase was the result of a onetime gain in customs duties resulting from the recent crackdown on smuggling. More important, admission to the World Trade Organization will reduce customs duties, at least at first. In addition, the stepped-up drive for revenue is choking the recovery of the nation's enterprises, especially its insolvent banks and also triggering widespread peasant unrest in the countryside. Jiang Zemin himself unintentionally tells us how precarious China's finances are these days when he notes that profits and tax revenues from state-owned enterprises account for 50 percent of the country's fiscal income. But the SOEs' profits are illusory once state subsidies are subtracted.

Let's pretend for a moment that we believe all those wonderful things Beijing's technocrats say about their economy. We can nonetheless see that growth in China is not good enough. Premier Zhu Rongji set his GDP annual growth target for the 2001–05 period at around 7.0 percent, a full percentage point below 2000's 8.0 percent. China needs

GDP growth to increase, not decrease. It's too bad for the swelling ranks of the unemployed. China needs robust growth to absorb the millions who are being thrown onto the streets, but the statistics paint a picture of a listless economy. Then there are the tens of millions of underemployed and those entering the workforce for the first time. Job creation is, in short, Job One for the cadres.

That makes restarting the economy an urgent task. As the ill-conceived stock market manipulation program failed, Beijing officials tried simpler tactics, employing both the carrot and the stick. First they taxed people's savings by imposing a 20 percent levy on interest as of November 1, 1999. At the same time, they gave people more time off from work. It's called "holiday economics," and among all the desperate tactics employed by the central government, it is the one that has probably had the most visible effect. Beijing rearranged the calendar to create weeklong holidays beginning National Day in October 1999. People traveled, and spent, in record numbers, and Beijing's central planners celebrated. The concept is that the people can consume China out of its economic doldrums. That's an extremely tall order for China's world-champion savers, however.

"The holiday season boom will not be a persistent phenomenon," said a Chinese professor quoted in the official media in May 2000. And he was right: consumer spending during the next weeklong holiday, which occurred in October of that year, was disappointing, and even the official media suggest that the central government doctored the results to hide the decline. And the tactic looks as if it's going to lose even more altitude; today the Chinese are significantly increasing their level of saving. A Western diplomat called holiday spending an "economic sugar-high" because the effects wear off quickly. Very quickly, in fact. "Does the big-vacation policy help consumption?" asks a professor at a think tank at Beijing University. "The answer is no."

The other quick fix is export growth, which Beijing heavily subsidizes with a raft of rebates and subsidies. Today China depends almost entirely on exports to lift its GDP, but the trend is not sustainable. All the government incentives are expensive for the country, and WTO accession will end some of the discriminatory export practices. Moreover, an expected slowdown in China's foreign markets will inevitably reduce the demand for Chinese goods. The export drive, like all of the other temporary tactics, will soon run out of steam. That's already happening: China's trade surplus declined in both 1999 and 2000. The trend has become so apparent that even central government officials realize that there is a problem, and WTO membership could ultimately result in deficits as Beijing loses the ability to closely manage trade flows.

Getting the economy moving again will be hard; there are so many other factors working against the technocrats. The Chinese, for example, have little confidence in their government to get the job done. State-owned enterprises and the wealthy smuggle money offshore at every opportunity they get. And the people themselves are leaving. Many depart legally, others not. In June 2000, fifty-eight Chinese were found dead in the back of a truck in Dover, England, after fleeing the People's Republic. Human smuggling from China "has no parallel in any other country."

And why should the people have any confidence that the future will be any better? China must continue restructuring if it is to have a tomorrow, but the central government is not doing much to address the fundamental problems that afflict the economy today. All the easy reforms have been implemented, and now Beijing is at a loss as to what to do next. State-owned enterprises are ugly: they are slow, inefficient, and unreformable in the present political system. They devour enormous resources and are now threatening the banks, which, as we have seen, are insolvent and survive only because the government dares not let them fall. Central planners, in their effort to save the current system, are stifling efficient private entrepreneurs and foreign investors by diverting even more resources to the public sector and employing a hundred other tactics. China needs more competition and openness, but Beijing is restraining those forces for change as well.

In addition to the structural problems that remain from yesterday, there are other barriers to tomorrow's growth. China's impressive economic development, for instance, has been purchased at the cost of severe environmental degradation. China boasts, if that is the right word for it, nine of the world's ten most polluted cities, including the one that may just be the worst, Lanzhou, the capital of central Gansu Province. The nation's good earth cannot stand much more; recent flooding, droughts, and deforestation are proof of that. Somewhere between 4 to 8 percent of GDP is lost through destruction of the environment. About 350 million of China's citizens, more than a quarter of the total, remain desperately poor with little relief in sight. It will be difficult for the nation to progress economically without alleviating their poverty. The state does not provide education or health care for hundreds of millions in rural and urban areas. China is proud that it can send doctors to Guinea, but it desperately needs them in the southern Guangxi Autonomous Region, where health care is "worse than in Africa." At some point, Beijing will have to find the funds for all these social services, especially because the state-owned enterprises are trying to shed these burdens. In a rapidly aging China, it will be expensive, but no country can progress for long without providing essential services to its people. And then there is worsening corruption, which is inevitably slowing growth as the undeserving prosper and competitors are turned away from the market. Hu Angang, the prominent Beijing economist, says that corruption cost China about US$150 billion over the past decade.

In a time when fundamental problems confront the People's Republic, there is little realism in Beijing. The central government is spending the resources of a nation on building monuments to itself. The National Theater in the center of the Chinese capital, to name just one of them, will cost the country nearly US$430 million. That's just a drop in the bucket compared to the billions of dollars that China has already expended on its bid to host the 2008 Olympics (and the more than US$20 billion that the country has pledged for facilities should it be awarded the games). Beijing spent around US$4 billion on its preparations for the National Day celebrations in 1999 marking the fiftieth anniversary of the founding of the People's Republic. And the Chinese program to send a man to the moon requires untold sums. These extravagant expenditures are of questionable value to the economy, but then again, the government of Jiang Zemin has always been out of touch. And we see that all the time, even in the fight against deflation. In August 1999, Beijing's technocrats unveiled their ultimate weapon to keep prices high: regulations that put teeth into the comprehensive Price Law. The new rules authorize consumers to file complaints against those who sell at prices that are too *low*. No wonder Communist Party functionaries are having such a hard time solving China's economic problems.

In view of all these trends, growth in the future will slow, consumer prices will decline, exports will stagnate, foreign investment will fall further, and the economy will stagger. Beijing can, by decree, postpone the onset of the symptoms, but eventually the laws of economics will apply: at some point the central government will simply run out of money. When that happens, China will have the same half-reformed economy and will have to tackle substantially the same problems it faces now. The only difference is that its financial condition then will be ominous. We are but a few years, perhaps five, from that time.

While foreign experts tell us that everything's just fine in China, the Mainland's own analysts are becoming worried. The economy could collapse, warns Lin Yifu of the China Economic Research Centre of Beijing University, the nation's most prestigious institution of higher learning. He sees all the trends close up and, despite the pressure to make rosy pronouncements, tells us that deep-seated problems could cause the central government's economic policies to fail. Recent growth won't mask China's structural defects, Lin argues. The time for Beijing's leaders to worry is now, argues Yang Fan of the elite Chinese Academy of Social Sciences. "We already face major crises of income disparity, corruption and flight of capital, thanks to the government policies of the past ten years," he says. If the central government doesn't act, Yang predicts these problems "will explode within five years and could bring everything down."

In the meantime, at least China's emperors have new swim trunks. "Until the tide goes out you don't know who's swimming naked," says Warren Buffett, the American investor. The tide is going out, and soon we shall see who's been in the water without his gear. But of course we already know.

9

Trade Charade

WTO Accession Will Trigger Collapse

History is a nightmare from which I am trying to awake.
—JAMES JOYCE

HIS JOB IS to tell the truth to the world, but now he's going to lie. In a moment of inspiration, he thinks of the perfect answer. "I'm Swiss," he says. The lanky American is safe, but only for the moment.

Peter Wonacott, China bureau chief for Dow Jones Newswires, has already been punched by an angry protester once this evening. His moment of inspiration saves him from another assault at the hands of an enraged youth who demanded to know his nationality. Wonacott finds himself, however, between a line of grim-faced policemen, arms linked to channel the protesters away from the grounds of the compound, and rioters, surging back and forth to an angry rhythm. The mob is packed so tightly that it is hard for him to move. Escape for the reporter flying Swiss colors is not possible.

Wonacott is at the north end of Beijing's famous Silk Alley on Sunday, May 9, 1999. Most days, shoppers from all over the world congregate around hundreds of merchants operating from corrugated metal stalls. Street vendors openly sell pirated compact discs and software by the fence guarding the American consular buildings, just down the street from the embassy itself. That Sunday, however, the merchants and ven-dors are gone and the crowd is on the verge of violence. American war-planes have just bombed their embassy in Belgrade, and students and workers are venting their anger at the scattered American diplomatic compounds in the Chinese capital of Beijing.

Protesters are standing on the roofs of the stalls, stomping their feet in encouragement to those trying to ignite an American flag by throwing flaming bicycle tires over the consulate's fence. They miss, and all they can do is set a nearby tree on fire. The rickety stalls threaten to collapse onto the crowd below. Demonstrators form a continuous wall stretching for blocks around the American diplomatic compounds. The group at the Silk Alley end of the block would have been even larger if not for the fact that some are throwing stones at the Irish Embassy, mistaking it for the back of the American one. In front of the main gate of the intended target dozens of youths try to scale the fence, but Chinese policemen pull them back down. The police don't catch all of them, however. A protester who made it onto the lawn of the American Embassy is pinned to the ground by a marine, just a boy himself.

Wonacott, still trapped, sees that a group of protesters is marching out in a line, and the crowd, still packed tightly, makes way for them. He falls in behind them and slips through to safety. As soon as he is clear of the crowd he hears a familiar voice—familiar to him and millions of oth-ers. "What's it like in there?" asks Rebecca MacKinnon, CNN's tall, sturdy Beijing bureau chief as she dials her cell phone. "I wouldn't go in there," Wonacott advises. MacKinnon wades into the crowd nonetheless; she is about to go on the air and needs some background atmosphere. She finds it—or it finds her. Moments later a protester, shouting obscenities, slaps her on the side of the head while she is broadcasting live from her phone. Her glasses fall to the ground. Marina Kolbe, at CNN Center in Atlanta, tells MacKinnon, while the world listens in, to find her way to safety.

Beijing is aflame with passion, and Wonacott and MacKinnon are not the only victims. China's most important annual gathering of investment managers is in a shambles. It is the morning of May 12, and foreign speakers have canceled, afraid to travel to the Chinese capital for the Credit Lyonnais Securities Asia China Forum 1999. No one quite knows if the officials from the central government will show up either. The crowd waiting in the auditorium of the China World Hotel numbers just over a hundred, far short of a normal turnout. The China Forum, Jing Ulrich's premier event, is in jeopardy. She doesn't have time for pleasantries now; it's almost a crisis. The tall Mainland-born woman is moving at Olympic speed, and her long black hair is flying in the wind behind her as she moves from phone to phone. She knows what's at stake: she is voted the best China analyst every year in part because she attracts the cream of the Mainland business community and top government officials to her conferences, where they mingle with the many customers of her investment advice. But now the big names look as if they will skip her show, and her customers from around the globe will surely be disappointed.

Oh, thank goodness! Ulrich finally hears that the central government officials will arrive, but they will all be late—they have to attend some emergency meeting. Now she must completely rearrange the schedule. The unflappable Chris Murck, a managing director of Chase Manhattan Bank, will have to begin his presentation earlier in the day to accommodate the officials who have been given his afternoon slot. And he will have to do it without one of his panelists, a rather timid fellow from the Bank for International Settlements. He was supposed to fly in from Hong Kong but now has given a rather lame excuse for not attending.

The audience at the China World is expecting to hear about assessing financial risk in China, but first they'll hear a well-rehearsed personal message that Murck wants to deliver. "As an American citizen, I can only repeat to my Chinese friends the apology and expressions of regret and condolences made by President Clinton and other NATO leaders to the government and people of China," Murck says. "The anger and distress of the Chinese people are entirely understandable." His apology inadvertently tells us that the real risk in China is not financial but political.

The risk is political because China's recent relationship with foreigners has not been easy. The humiliations of the nineteenth and early twentieth centuries, when foreign powers bullied China, still rankle the people and their government and distort their perceptions of the twenty-first. China, preoccupied by its past, is failing to adapt quickly enough to the present. By joining the World Trade Organization, China is at long last entering the global trading community, taking a momentous step that will change this ancient land for generations to come. Yet the Chinese, imprisoned by their anger and distress, are unprepared for the challenges ahead, challenges that will shake the government to its foundations.

Mao Zedong built his party on the bedrock of isolation, and there it could have lived indefinitely. As the Party takes China out into the world, however, it does so at its peril. "No nation was ever ruined by trade," wrote Benjamin Franklin, and that is true. Yet the wise American never said anything about trade's effect on a political party. Trade will not ruin China, but what will it do to the seemingly invincible Communist Party?

REMEMBER THE SUMMER PALACE!

Foreigners ransacked her country and subjugated her ancestors. Chen Yan has not forgotten that. Nicholas Howson, a securities lawyer, is proudly telling his Chinese visitor, a potential client, about his family's long history in China, starting with his grandfather. Chen, the head of a New York–based finance subsidiary of a state-owned trading company, smiles and politely acknowledges the comments. After Howson leaves the conference room overlooking Radio City Music Hall, Chen turns to her colleague and says, "His grandfather must be one of those people who burned our Summer Palace." In fact, Howson's grandfather was a flying instructor and carried no lit torches in China, at least none in anger. The conversation in New York, in late 1996, took place 136 years to the month after marauding foreign armies attacked and burned that famous landmark in Beijing.

Two centuries of contact with foreigners have left the Chinese, to use one of their favorite words, humiliated, and events long past have been etched into their consciousness with acid. History is never far away. Any issue in China is ripe for historical introspection of the worst sort. Defective Toshiba laptops? "The Chinese people fought for eight years against the Japanese to counter unfair treatment," shouted one e-commerce firm as it announced that it would no longer sell that company's products. "This is no longer a simple commercial dispute. It bears directly on the honour of the Chinese people!" Any matter can become emotional in China once it has been linked with the devil of history.

History haunts this great people, and history has not been kind. *Time* labeled China the "Worst Victim of Globalization" because Britain forcibly opened the Middle Kingdom's markets with opium trading in the 1840s. But that is not the point. Yes, the British burned the Summer Palace and the Chinese have a right to be angry. Yet the British also burned the American capital, but when was the last time you heard anyone complain about the War of 1812? The Chinese talk about events in the distant past as if they had taken place yesterday and focus on their suffering, but they are being left behind by the rest of the world, which is largely unburdened by historical concerns. Mao Zedong liked his people "poor and blank." Perhaps he had a point.

Say what you will about the Cultural Revolution, it is not a time to be defended, but one should, in fairness, mention this: if the Red Guards had succeeded in eliminating all of China's historical memory, New China could have flourished. Unfortunately, their goal of erasing the past completely was not possible, and the zealous youth of 1960s China only added to history's toll on the present.

"We remain a new nation," said American President Bill Clinton in his 2000 State of the Union address. "And as long as our dreams outweigh our memories, America will be forever young." The Chinese also dream of the future, so they can no longer afford to be old. Their civilization spans millennia and they cannot change the past, but they should retain only the best of their long inheritance if they want to be great again. "Happy the people whose annals are blank in history-books," wrote Thomas Carlyle, expressing the same thoughts as James Joyce, who likened history to a nightmare. "History repeats itself" in countries around the world. In China, it not only recurs, it kills the future.

Peter Wonacott is safe now. In a small local restaurant near the embattled embassy, the journalist who temporarily assumed Swiss nationality waits for his colleague, Karby Leggett. It is the following Tuesday, May 11, and the protests have, for the moment, died down. But Leggett is nowhere to be seen. That's because he is in a hotel elevator trapped by a snarling Chinese youth, who has just asked him if he is an American. Leggett, over six feet tall and well built, does not need a moment of inspiration. He answers yes and then hears the same anger that assaulted Rebecca MacKinnon and others. Wonacott and Leggett fear that the following hours could be worse—the remains of the three journalists killed in the Yugoslav capital by the NATO bombing are to arrive at the airport in Beijing on the following day. There could be more emotion in the hours ahead, and they will have to go back to work soon.

"Are you American?" At a different time, that would be a friendly question, but in those days of May it was the prelude to the expression of an ugly sort of nationalism that has festered for centuries. Americans are proud of their heritage and what their country stands for. The Chinese, who have much more history to boast about, seldom are. The sons and daughters of the Middle Kingdom express nationalism in terms of the humiliation of two hundred years of colonial encroachment, not the great accomplishments of five thousand. They speak eloquently of their violation by invading foreign armies but mention little else. Did history for this country really begin only two centuries ago?

As Chris Murck tells us, Chinese anger is "understandable." Yet those who look at China in a broader perspective know that the sharp emotions witnessed by Wonacott and MacKinnon are hindering this ancient nation. In the short term, the protests following the Belgrade bombing slowed China's admission to the World Trade Organization. In the long term, nationalist attitudes close minds and retard the progress that openness and receptivity bring.

China now talks about the future as if it will attain greatness once again. Yet that appears to be just an illusion for a people burdened by their history. "We can advance to the future only through looking at the past clearly," says Jiang Zemin. Actually, the best way to advance toward the future is to look toward the future. For China, yesterday poisons today and robs tomorrow. Great nations, if old, are inspired by their history. China, however, is haunted.

And it is not just humiliation that haunts the Chinese. They are persecuted by their greatness too. "No culture can live if it attempts to be exclusive," said Mahatma Gandhi. That, in fact, is precisely what China tried to do. In the mid–fifteenth century, the Middle Kingdom stood as a colossus astride the world, generally acknowledged as superior to every other civilization of that era. It was a time when China looked beyond its borders, as all great powers do. Admiral Zheng He commanded a fleet of more than three hundred vessels, some of them the largest the world had known up to that time. For three decades, from 1405 to 1433, he explored in the name of the Ming Dynasty, reaching as far west as the port of Aden on the Arabian peninsula. Zheng settled local wars, surveyed surrounding lands, tamed pirates, and subjugated nations along his sea routes. Tribute flowed to the Ming courts from lesser states. But suddenly China had seen all that it cared to. In the 1440s, a Ming emperor, listening to his Confucian advisers, ended sea contacts with the inferior outside by imperial fiat. The "treasure fleet" was dismantled, the records of the seven voyages were destroyed, as were the designs for the vessels, and the shipyards were converted so that China could no longer build those magnificent ships.

Some speculate that the fleet and the voyages were a financial burden on imperial treasuries. That is possible because trade, the one thing that could have supported the expensive ventures, was largely forbidden by the Ming. The most interaction the Chinese would allow with the outside was receipt of tribute and the giving of gifts in return. Tributary trade could not sustain a great navy, however. And a country that forbade private trading, and thus exposure to new things and ideas, could no longer progress or innovate.

Historians debate why the Ming turned inward, but one thing is clear: China's decision to scrap the fleet began centuries of decline. "Cultures can't remain static," says Buzz Aldrin, the second man to step onto the moon. "They evolve or expire, explore or decline." And decline China did. It was not apparent at first, but its inward-looking society stagnated, and soon China was unable to defend itself against invaders, who were made of sterner stuff than the complacent Ming rulers. The Manchus from the northeast breached the Great Wall, but soon they themselves became Chinese, establishing the Qing Dynasty in 1644 after displacing the Ming. Yet some foreigners refused to be assimilated. Adventurous Europeans reached China by sea, and this country without a great navy found itself defenseless. The invaders looted the Summer Palace and a thousand other sites and marched over the country almost at will. The Europeans marveled at China's ancient culture, but they refused to kneel to the emperor, and they had no intention of becoming Chinese.

Like Chen Yan, the Chinese to this day remember the shame of national weakness. Yes, China was violated in the past and the conduct of the foreign powers was inexcusable. But is China the worst victim of globalization, as *Time*—and China itself—would have us believe? No, it is not. In the long run, the opening of the Middle Kingdom was both inevitable for the country and beneficial for the Chinese people, however painful it might have been. Ironically, the Chinese themselves proclaim that this is true. After all, they genuinely think that they are doing the Tibetans a favor by bringing this backward people into the modern age. If they're right, the invading foreign powers must have done them a favor, too.

The Chinese don't quite see it that way. Yet they should peer across the East China Sea at their island neighbors. Whatever the Japanese thought of Commodore Matthew Perry, they embraced modernization and in short order created a strong nation. The Japanese defeated China in 1895, just about four decades after Perry sailed into Tokyo Bay in 1853 and forced their country open. Perry's incursion, the Chinese should note, was well after the time when the West first encroached on China. Many of us look at the great advances in the People's Republic since 1978 and feel confident about China in this new century. We forget that the Chinese have been modernizing for about 150 years and have not yet succeeded. And that is unfortunate for them because now, in the first decade of the third millennium, the Chinese stand at a critical point in their history. Ready or not, membership in the World Trade Organization is upon them.

SLOW ROAD TO THE WTO

Mao Zedong, as powerful as any Ming emperor, ended most trade with foreigners. The "Bamboo Curtain" he put into place isolated China for decades. His successors, first Deng Xiaoping and then Jiang Zemin, took a different tack and let foreigners serve China. And serve the foreigners did. But investment from abroad was tightly controlled, and, as a consequence, foreigners posed a competitive threat only in limited sectors.

It took a decade after Mao's death for Beijing to reapply for membership in the General Agreement on Tariffs and Trade, from which China had withdrawn in 1950. For the Chinese, readmission would be unattainable in the Deng Xiaoping era. A China driven by his pragmatism, however, would liberalize on its own. *Gaige kaifang,* the policy of "reform and opening to the outside world," eroded the Bamboo Curtain.

Now membership in the WTO, GATT's successor, means that Mao's drapery, which outlasted its iron cousin in Europe, will cast a much-diminished shadow. China's border is still made of rules and controls that restrict the flow of commerce and people, but the trend is clear: the People's Republic, for the first time in its history, is opening itself to the world in accordance with the foreigners' rules.

China's economic miracle has been built largely on one-way trade with the world. Deng Xiaoping wanted to make China "rich and strong," and that desire translated into ever-increasing trade surpluses. Selfish trade contributed to staggering foreign exchange reserves of US$165.6 billion at the end of 2000, the second highest in the world behind mighty Japan. That's impressive by any standard, and so is China's trade surplus with the United States—no other country, not even Japan, had a more favorable balance with America in 2000. Yet the days of unequal trading will end, and China will need its hoard of foreign currency for the trade deficits that will occur. That's precisely why so many countries around the world have been pushing for China's admission to the WTO.

And the world's excitement is turning to euphoria. Short of taking nonprescription pharmaceuticals, talking about China's entry into the World Trade Organization is the easiest road to ecstasy. More than twelve hundred attendees gathered in Shanghai in May 2000 to hear Chinese Premier Zhu Rongji give his views on the WTO in a speech delivered in conjunction with Jing Ulrich's China Forum 2000. There would even have been more people in the audience, but Chinese Communist protocol demanded that this crowd be smaller than the one President Jiang Zemin had addressed at the Fortune Global Forum in this same room a little over seven months before. When it was all over, it was Gary Coull's turn to deliver the closing remarks, but no one was listening anymore. They should have been. Coull, Ulrich's boss, gave his assessment in a monotone that could barely be heard over the growing chatter of the restless crowd: ". . . and we believe over the next four or five years the shape of the economy and the capital markets will change as much as in the last two decades."

That assessment is simply astounding. How could there possibly be that much change in such a short period of time? There are two reasons. First, accession will bring about a fundamental liberalization of trade rules. China will either slash or eliminate tariffs across the spectrum of industrial and agricultural products. That, however, is not the big news. The most sweeping changes will liberalize existing rules affecting trade and investment. Most quotas and other nontariff barriers will be eliminated within five years of accession, and many will be phased out within two to three years. Foreign firms, for example, will be permitted to import and export most products themselves, no longer required to go through a state-owned intermediary. And foreigners will be able to engage in wholesale and retail activities by themselves. Ownership restrictions will be relaxed in a broad range of sectors, such as securities and telecommunications. Many export subsidies, such as for agricultural products, will be eliminated. Moreover, local barriers to trade as well as national ones will fall as each province and city will have to dismantle the trade walls it has erected against its domestic neighbors. Any of these changes would be important in and of itself; together they are, well, revolutionary. It is difficult to overestimate the effect they will have on China's economy.

For the second reason why change will be dramatic, ask Robert Kapp of the U.S.-China Business Council. His words may not be elegant, but he explains why Gary Coull just may be right: "The point about WTO is that it puts China fully on a track of commitment to international standards and universally agreed-to standards of trade and economic behavior and to the reconstruction of the way its own state deals with its own economy." In other words, China is giving up control. Beijing is making specific commitments that are enforceable by an international organization based outside its borders.

China produced its economic miracle by a deft handling of private entrepreneurs and foreigners. In this task, Beijing was accountable to no one. It set the rules and refereed the game. Thus it obtained more or less the desired results. Those days, however, are over. Love means never having to say you're sorry, and WTO means never having to listen to the Beijing bureaucrats anymore. Rules-based trade and investment, novel concepts for the Chinese, herald a new age for the People's Republic.

And China looks prepared for the dawning of the Age of Aquarius. "I went to a bookshop on Chang An Avenue to buy a volume of Mao's collected works—and they didn't have one—but there were about seventy books on WTO," said one shopper in Beijing recently. Academicians are writing on the subject. Consumers are eagerly awaiting the lower prices that competition and open access will bring. Jiang Zemin is waiting to hear the applause of history for his decision to back accession. And Zhu Rongji looks prepared, too. He has been reforming the laggard state-owned enterprises ever since he became premier in 1998, working hard to make them ready for the impending battle. "All these measures will help most of the large and medium-sized loss-making SOEs out of their predicament this year," says Premier Zhu in his speech at China Forum 2000, summing up all that he has done.

Afterward, Karen Elliot House of Dow Jones begins, in a crisp voice, the postspeech formalities by thanking the premier "for his outstanding remarks" and "the trademark candor of his comments tonight." At first glance, it appears that the only outstanding aspect of the premier's candor this evening is its absence. Everyone knows that the state enterprises are still sick. Yet Ms. House was right because the premier was perfectly sincere in his assessment of the SOEs. That he could be both candid and so far off the mark shows the slippage between perception and reality in the abnormal system that China's leaders have created. As Zhu said, most of the larger state enterprises reported profits. But those were profits generated by fabrication and measured by the lax standards of Chinese accounting, which ignore government subsidies and a hundred other things. Now, as his three-year deadline for finishing SOE restructuring has come and gone, Premier Zhu has made the numbers look better. The enterprises are all dressed up, but he has not fundamentally improved them. Most state enterprises are in no position to compete in the difficult years ahead.

During Mao Zedong's Great Leap Forward, senior cadres in Beijing demanded good news, so that is what they received. Millions of people, tens of millions actually, starved and died as a consequence. Today, four decades later, China's senior cadres believe that China is ready for accession. "China is fully capable of participating in global competition," says Jiang Zemin. That is the Party's party line. So it is no surprise that Zhu Rongji says that the state-owned enterprises can withstand the foreign challenge after accession. Based on this perception, the People's Republic is willingly entering a world trading order that is unforgiving and is joining the world on the world's terms. If the People's Republic cannot succeed, it would not be the first time the Chinese leadership has been trapped by idealized notions of its own accomplishments.

There is another problem, too. "Solid and down-to-earth preparatory work is scarce," says Lu Zhiqiang of the State Council's Development Research Centre. Despite the senior leaders' optimism, lower-level technocrats in Beijing are unhappy with the WTO preparations of state enterprises and government ministries. And they should be. The top leadership, badly divided on accession in the first place, has yet to reach a consensus on a strategy for implementation. That means the technocrats can't do much now. As a consequence, preparations have been agonizingly slow where it counts, in government ministries and state enterprises. This is where the WTO battle will ultimately be won or lost for the Chinese state. And this is where there has been the most resistance to membership in the first place. It has been reported, for example, that about half of the SOEs have no WTO plans whatsoever and merely assume that, whatever occurs, the government will protect them. One large fund manager in Hong Kong predicts that only a few of the thousand or so publicly listed firms will survive accession. Even domestic enterprises that are market leaders could crumble under the pressure.

There is more than just a little irony here. If anyone in China has had the clearest crystal ball about what WTO membership ultimately means, it has been those in the ministries and the SOEs. They have been saying all along that accession would allow foreigners to dominate important segments of the economy. Yet now that accession is upon them, they are the ones least prepared for all that they have foretold.

It takes time for perceptions to change, and that is especially true in the ministries that are part of Mao's legacy. Yet it is not only the old bureaucracies that suffer from arteriosclerosis; the new ones do as well. Look at the China Insurance Regulatory Commission, for example. It was created in 1998 to assume the oversight functions once performed by the People's Bank of China. The PBOC contributed some forward-looking individuals to the CIRC to help it regulate an industry still dominated by the People's Insurance Company of China, the old monopoly. Inside the CIRC, PICC loyalists, who have no desire to open up the industry, have been disposing of their liberal colleagues who originally came from the PBOC. The process started first in Beijing, then spread to Shanghai. The purge means that when foreign companies are unleashed by the WTO, China's domestic insurance companies will still be uncompetitive.

Yet sometimes it is better that the bureaucrats not make preparations, for they often make a bad situation worse. The People's Bank of China, for instance, is trying to turn back the clock by further restricting foreign banks, thereby making those banks even less competitive. But that is the shortest of short-term solutions. Some of the restrictions may survive WTO's phased-in rules and others may not, but one thing is certain: the domestic banks will not be prepared because the PBOC is reducing the incentive for local institutions to reform themselves. Accession will be shock therapy for them, and the PBOC is turning up the voltage. "I doubt the time-frame is long enough to turn its banking system fully around," says a foreign banker, referring to the period before China opens the banking sector under its WTO agreements.

Ministry after ministry is mimicking the central bank. Even on the eve of accession, senior cadres think that it is premature to permit competition as a means of preparing domestic industry for the inevitable foreign onslaught. And bureaucrats flout the spirit of free trade while they still can. Foreign makers of sealants, for example, must now sell to a newly formed government company, China Yuanwang Corporation, which imposes fees that look like a 100 percent tariff and make it economically impossible for foreigners to sell in China. Sales to China for one foreign sealant company "dropped to zero" after the new restrictions were implemented in late 1999.

As they get ready for tomorrow's WTO world, Party cadres won't abandon their five-year plans and precepts from the Mao era. They apparently cannot see their own failures over the past five decades, so they insist on commanding as if they still had a command economy. In steel, mobile phones, and a hundred other industries domestic players are receiving subsidies or special favors, even though these solutions landed China in this mess in the first place. China's other grand industrial strategy is to make the big still bigger by forcing even more consolidation in the Chinese economy. In its pursuit to build world-class competitors, however, China has stifled competition, the inevitable result of bureaucrat-led mergers. By delaying the establishment of freer markets, Beijing is postponing the strengthening of domestic enterprises and making them less ready to take on foreign businesses. Yes, as a general matter Chinese companies should be larger, but making them bigger artificially often makes them less competitive by, for example, increasing the burdens on already overtaxed management and diverting financial resources to uneconomic activities.

Jiang Zemin has commanded the cadres "to fully understand what it means for China to gain WTO entry." If he really wants them to know, he should have them talk to foreign journalists, who can't stop asking about unemployment. Experts go quiet when they are questioned, and sometimes the evasion is obvious. Other times it is the hesitation that gives the true answer away. Yet one need not have to interpret the expressions of experts to find the anxiety: Jiang should also instruct the cadres to talk to the workers themselves. Accession means one thing, says a member of China's struggling proletariat: "More unemployment." About a third of China's state-sector workforce is not productively employed now and will undoubtedly face redundancy as enterprises close down in the wake of entry to the WTO.

Yet as bad as conditions are in the cities, they are far worse in the countryside. The sector that will be hardest hit by WTO, everyone agrees, is agriculture. As much as 18 percent of China's land under cultivation will be taken out of production after entry into the world trade body. Accession will devastate rural China because Beijing's agricultural policies have utterly failed. The official media recognize that the nation's system is "irrational" when, even in good harvests, the peasants cannot benefit. In recent years rural incomes have slumped, with some peasants earning only half of what they did just three years ago.

It's not that there are too few crops—today there are simply too many. But what the peasants grow, often as dictated by the Party, is unprofitable. The source of the problem is that central planners don't care about efficiency; they just want to stockpile huge quantities. As a result, China is storing mountains of agricultural products, many of them unmarketable as the nation's tastes and needs change and as supply swamps demand. For example, some analysts estimate that the state and peasants are holding 500 million tons of low-grade grain, much of it unsalable. Others say that the correct figure is 1.3 billion tons. In any event, the government's system of price supports cannot be sustained after WTO accession. Beijing, seeking to achieve the Maoist goal of self-sufficiency, has made its agriculture uncompetitive. Analysts now say, for instance, that Chinese rice will not be able to compete with that grown in Australia— even in China's domestic markets. So no one thinks that primitive Chinese agriculture, as badly mismanaged by Beijing, has a chance.

Especially the peasants themselves, which is why they're leaving the countryside already. Today, the number of surplus rural workers is somewhere between 150 to 200 million. Beijing estimates that 9.7 million more farmers will be forced to leave the land after accession, but others think that the real number will be four times that. In Huangqiao, a town in Jianli County of central Hubei Province, about 90 percent of the peasants have abandoned their homes and fields. Some have even abandoned their lives; suicides are on the rise, and a whole family drowned themselves in despair.

"I have met old people who held my hands and told me tearfully that they preferred to die early," wrote a township Party secretary, Li Changping, "and I have seen the sad sight of children kneeling before me saying they want to attend school." In Li's Qipan, also in Jianli County, society is failing because of the decline of agriculture. Li wrote a direct plea to Zhu Rongji about conditions in his area. That was futile because the well-intentioned Zhu has little power in Qipan and most other places in the countryside. The premier can bark out orders, as he likes to do, but local officials can ignore him because he does not control their funds. Today Zhu more or less understands what to do to fix the immense problems of Chinese agriculture, but he doesn't have the power to implement his solutions. And even if he did, imminent accession to the WTO means that there's no time left for his plans to take effect. That's too bad because those with the real power, the local cadres, won't help the peasants.

Only those who offer jobs can do that. The service sector will create employment, so there will be some gains to offset the losses after entry into the WTO. Marketing and distribution personnel, for example, will be in demand as multinationals seek to sell throughout China. Job creation will be primarily in white-collar positions, however. There won't be enough of such workers, and there will be too many blue-collar and unskilled ones as well as countless migrants from rural areas. The transformation of employment in China will be wrenching, even more than it has been up to now. "You cannot just put a farmer in a factory and ask him to assemble computers," said Shawn Xu, a research chief at an investment bank in China.

The biggest domestic winner from WTO will be textiles, says the consensus. Yet surging exports from this sector will not generate as much employment as first appears. In today's closed shop, textile companies buy their raw materials from domestic producers. In a WTO world, however, they will source from cheaper foreign suppliers, as China's largest producer, the Zongheng Group, plans to do. So in the years after accession, workers producing synthetic fibers in South Korea, Taiwan, and Japan stand to gain at the expense of the Chinese proletariat even as the Chinese textile industry makes the nation proud.

WTO accession will bring one other change that will remake the face of China's industry. Economist Andy Xie of Morgan Stanley Dean Witter notes that Beijing is only beginning to understand that by the middle of this decade foreign enterprises may largely own China's economy. In the closed system of the People's Republic, Beijing could make and enforce the rules that would hinder strong foreign competitors. In a post-accession world, that prerogative will be restricted, in some cases severely. China has thousands of laws, rules, and regulations that must be eliminated or liberalized so that its control mechanisms, built up over five decades, will meet WTO norms. And many ownership restrictions will be phased out under the terms of entry.

Increased unemployment, as serious as it may become, and foreign domination of domestic industry, no matter how widespread, are not the real risks for the regime. It is xenophobia, the ugly side of nationalism, that the regime has to fear. China will gain little present economic advantage from WTO accession. Prestige and a place in the sun go with WTO membership, but not much that is tangible. It is foreigners who will reap virtually all the gains at first. So who will defend the Party when workers lose their jobs in the WTO economy? Will some economist from Beijing University explain trade deficits and the concept of comparative advantage to an angry mob as it marches on the Communist leadership compound of Zhongnanhai?

The angry nationalist tide that caught Wonacott and MacKinnon in its path may also sweep others aside. The Chinese have disposed of governments that have not defended the Motherland. The Qing, violated by foreign armies, fell to Sun Yat-sen's Revolutionary Alliance. The Kuomintang, the successor to the Alliance, in turn fell to the Communists for being soft on the Japanese, who were also allowed to have the run of China. The Communists, who are letting foreigners in and permitting them to march across their land in a different way, will be at risk, too. Senior cadres will be trapped in their own country, cornered by the nationalism that they themselves have encouraged and exploited in the past.

Unless, that is, they can keep their economy going. About the only realistic way they can do that postaccession is to increase foreign domination. Many predict a boom in foreign investment once ownership restrictions are relaxed. Goldman Sachs economist Fred Hu sees annual foreign investment more than doubling in about a five-year time frame. Increased investment from abroad, so the theory goes, will employ those who will be victimized by foreign competitors. It is the same process that is occurring now; the prediction is that the phenomenon will accelerate in the future as ownership and other restrictions are relaxed.

Even more foreigners? Dinyar Lalkaka, who is seeking to establish a privately owned incubator, and hundreds more like him will find their way to the Shanghais and Shenzhens of China to invest in the Internet and high-tech sectors. Some multinationals will build bigger manufacturing capability to take advantage of the emerging national marketplace. These solutions, however, will be exceptions. The argument that there will be a flood of new investment ignores the realities of China—and the world—today. First, China has too much of almost everything already. Who will want to invest in a country already plagued by industrial overcapacity? Second, the world at large is also suffering from excess production. As Chinese trade barriers fall, the compelling solution will be to use existing foreign plants and sell into China. Referring to all the changes to be brought about by accession, President Clinton noted, "As a result, we will be able to export to China from home, rather than seeing companies forced to set up factories in China in order to sell products there." That's what General Motors plans to do, even though it already has manufacturing capacity in China.

Accession also means Chinese will buy what foreign factories make. Imports through Shanghai surged by almost 150 percent when China decreased tariffs on cars in January 2001 by a small margin. The increase in imports on accession will be even more dramatic. "Once we get into

WTO, I will be able to get rid of this bad Santana car and buy a Japanese one, preferably a Honda," says a taxi driver in Shaoxing in coastal Zhejiang Province. That's bad news for Volkswagen's Shanghai joint venture, which sold the junky Santana. The German carmaker expects to incur substantial losses in China after accession, as its manufacturing costs are about 30 percent higher there than elsewhere in the world. Therefore, China's tariff reductions mean that Volkswagen won't be able to match the prices of imported vehicles. The world's most efficient plants, in Japan, are just two days away by ship.

That's why Volkswagen will do almost anything these days to sell cars made in China. The two German women are obviously enjoying each other's company. The one with short black hair has her hand on the blonde's stomach, and their legs are intertwined. The blonde is touching her breast with one hand and fingering her scarf with the other. Her eyes are closed and her mouth open, and you can tell what's on her mind. Maybe the two will get it on, but not now and not here. This is Auto China 2000, a trade show in Beijing, and both young models are in front of a new Audi sedan, also made by Volkswagen. Hearts pound and pulses race, and no one's paying attention to the car. Although the models may be stimulated, auto sales are not. No matter what manufacturers do these days, it's not enough. People are waiting for accession, when prices will surely fall—an inevitable consequence of tariffs' dropping from the current 80 to 100 percent to 25 percent.

Patrician Randy Daniel won't hire a lesbian sex act, but he is just as eager as Audi to sell in China. The president of the manufacturing operations of AMF, the American bowling company, is Chen Rong's guest for dinner, and Chen, the head of Zhonglu Industrial, always gets the best, a corner room. One can look out of the big windows of Room V7 of the Lulu Restaurant in the Pudong district of Shanghai and see two of the world's tallest structures, but Randy Daniel is not into the view this evening in December 1999. AMF missed its moment to manufacture bowling lanes and equipment in China, so Daniel is thinking about tariffs and the WTO a lot. AMF saw its exports to China drop sharply when China raised its tariffs in 1997. When tariffs fall upon accession, Daniel sees a "long-term bonanza" for AMF. In the city that never stops building, he can't stop thinking about the future. So at dinner he asks Chen about the effect that WTO will have on the Chinese economy.

AMF may never know what Chen Rong thinks about WTO membership. His answer meanders, and when he is finished no one in the room quite knows what to say because it's not quite clear what Chen has just told them. If Chen had been forthcoming, however, Daniel would have heard about competitive pricing in a hostile environment. Brunswick, AMF's main competitor, has been dropping its prices around the world, thereby narrowing the cost differential between its own products and Chen's. Add to that a big decrease in Chinese tariffs on bowling products (they will be cut by more than half) and the elimination of the expensive middlemen that AMF and Brunswick now need to use in China, and you have the potential for a vicious price war for Chen. Yet Chen once captured the bowling market from these two multinationals, and he and other private entrepreneurs can give the foreigners a good run for their money even after accession. They are not about to let up just because WTO accession will change the rules against them. The Chens all over China, after all, are nimble.

The managers of state-owned enterprises, on the other hand, are not. Saddled by Party instructions and bureaucratic rules, they cannot make the quick decisions necessary for survival in an ultracompetitive climate. Officials in the provinces want autonomy to deal with the changes that accession will bring, but central Party leaders insist on more control from Beijing as they continue their efforts to recentralize the economy. They underestimate the pain that accession will bring and are not willing to loosen the reins on the state sector. The shock therapy of accession can work only if managers of state enterprises are free to act in an economically rational manner. Beijing's political commanders don't seem to appreciate that a free-trade environment is unforgiving. Rejuvenation can result, but there can be spring only if the Party lets the seasons change.

So the cure will be especially excruciating if the cadres in Beijing do not come to terms with the probable effects of accession. Mainland sources, extolling the WTO, say that accession will boost China's growth. Not everyone agrees, especially with regard to the next few years. Daryl Ho, a prominent economist in Hong Kong, estimates that China's economic output could be reduced by 0.8 percent per year over the near term as foreign companies increase their exports to China after accession. That probably understates the effect of accession, but whatever the real figure is, Ho is certainly right when he makes one judgment: "The next few years would be a rough period." The rosy Mainland vision of the future is, on its face, more propaganda than prediction. After all, how can anyone expect that curing half a century of gross economic mismanagement will be painless?

All the pain can be avoided if China just cheats and dishonors its WTO commitments. Yet senior cadres don't plan to do that. An endless parade of them assures us that China will honor all its WTO obligations. The Chinese leaders may be shortsighted, intransigent, and unlikable, but they are proud as well. They will do as they say. Nonetheless, there will be problems of enforcement. "Let a hundred flowers bloom," said Mao, borrowing an ancient exhortation; "let a hundred schools of thought contend." And that's exactly what will happen as thousands of officials come up with their own interpretations of what WTO rules mean. Let a dozen ministries write new regulations, and we will have a hundred new ways to defeat the foreigner. And a thousand new disputes tomorrow. Chinese officials have a special genius for honoring obligations, but only as they interpret them. Each ministry in Beijing, each province and town, will act beyond the effective supervision of Beijing's senior leaders. It is happening today, and it will happen tomorrow. Trade promises mean nothing to local cadres seeking to protect the homeboys. One agreement to join the WTO is not going to change a history and culture that date back thousands of years.

Does that mean that the implementation of free trade will be just a charade? No, it does not. This time the foreigners will strike the empire back. They're sick and tired, and they won't take it anymore. Multinationals, which campaigned so hard for WTO around the world, will not be denied. Now, armed with enforceable rights, they will litigate if need be. Of course, central government bureaucrats and provincial officials can delay and argue and fight—and they will—but the foreigners will ultimately prevail because senior Chinese leaders know that countries successful in WTO disputes can retaliate unilaterally against states that don't comply with their trade obligations.

Today WTO members Japan and Korea maintain partially closed economies and thereby demonstrate that accession does not necessarily open markets. The Japanese and Korean approach is no solution for China, however. Opening only halfway after accession will deny China the benefits its leadership is seeking. More to the point, it will prolong the agony the Chinese currently endure. The leadership in Beijing is using WTO to force changes in the SOEs, which employ about 41 percent of the urban workforce. One reason to opt for accession now is that today the Party can still control the inevitable consequences of ever-increasing unemployment. A few more years down the road, and it may not be able to maintain social order as tens of millions are thrown out of work. There is, in short, a limited window of opportunity to counteract the pain that WTO membership will bring. "It's in China's own interest to comply," says the European Commission's ambassador to Beijing, Endymion Wilkinson, at Jing Ulrich's China Forum. Because the tall diplomat is being more than just diplomatic, fair trade will eventually come to China.

And China will be the better for it. A year has elapsed since Peter Wonacott was trapped behind enemy lines, and it is May 2000. Patriotic Chinese always remember anniversaries, and students in Beijing are set to take to the streets to remind the Americans that they have not forgotten the deaths of the three journalists in Belgrade. This time, however, the glorious Communist Party of China reins them in. The power of trade as a force for peace is already working: the inhabitants of Zhongnanhai don't want youthful zeal to jeopardize the upcoming vote in the American Congress over permanent normal trade relations with China. Party leaders tell the students to study, build a strong nation, and leave the patriotic posturing to them.

The Party's stance, though unpopular, is effective, and the students do not march. A year before, in 1999, Americans were angered by the image of their ambassador looking out from the window of their scarred embassy in Beijing. Now James Sasser is gone, replaced by Joseph Prueher, the admiral who sent American carriers into the waters near Taiwan in March 1996 to tell Beijing to back off. On the first anniversary of the Belgrade bombing, Prueher and his wife pointedly walked the three blocks from their residence to the embassy alone, except for the reporters and photographers who also remember anniversaries. Yet the Party's suppression of first anniversary demonstrations is only temporarily successful; Beijing University students burn in silence and then march over something else just a few days later.

Peter Wonacott has been promoted and transferred to Hong Kong, so he doesn't report on the new ambassador's pleasant stroll to work or the student protests. The ace reporter is out of harm's way, but the Party is not. It could soon become encircled by the patriotic fires it once stoked and now tries to contain. "Some 150 years ago, a weaker China was forced at gunpoint to open to the West," says a *China Daily* commentary. "It is under the leadership of the Communist Party that China finds its own feet and gains world respect." That's how the official media want the people to see accession. But will they? It took courage, or perhaps recklessness, for Jiang and Zhu to support WTO membership, and it will take skill, and definitely luck, to keep their country together in the years ahead. Those who say that accession will result in the loss of sovereignty will blame the Party when hardship occurs. "If the government's domestic policies hurt the interests of our people, people are more likely to endure it," says a university undergraduate who protested at the U.S. Embassy in May 1999. "But if the government betrays us to an outside country, conducts evil business with a foreign government, we cannot stand this."

So WTO had better work. If it doesn't, Gary Coull will be right and change in the next few years will be unimaginable, with the consequences for the Party unthinkable. The problem for the cadres is that admission to the WTO "will take the command and control out of communism." Today the Party is surviving by deferring economic problems in a thousand ways and in any manner it chooses, such as providing generous subsidies for both production and export. After accession its freedom to act will be severely restricted by general WTO rules and the specific promises it made to gain admission. For the first time in the history of the People's Republic, leaders will no longer be able to indefinitely defer the problems inherent in their own brand of socialism.

"No communist nation has successfully managed an economic transformation of the magnitude China is now attempting without triggering massive political upheaval," says a *Business Week* editorial. "Not one of 134 member countries saw its economy collapse because of entry into the WTO," notes *Beijing Youth Daily,* ignoring China's unique and severe economic and political problems. Maybe the influential paper believes it is correct because the state is arming itself even further. Each province and large city in China is boosting its policing capabilities in the run-up to accession. In any event, we'll soon find out if Chinese socialism will survive and if Gary Coull is prophetic.

In the meantime, Coull's employees are no longer in a tizzy. Now, one year after the bombing of the Chinese Embassy, Jing Ulrich even looks at ease. She is in her element now. Her China Forum 2000 is in Shanghai, the city with buzz. It's all about networking, and this year there are so many more people to network, more than twice as many as showed up the previous year, when the protests in Beijing forced cancellations and chaos in her speaking schedule. The forum is held in the world's third tallest building this time, a futuristic tower capped by Art Deco spikes. The Jin Mao Building stands at the main entrance to Pudong, where it shines as a beacon of modernism in a city striving to be up to date.

"Optimism" does not even begin to describe the mood at Ulrich's gathering. Euphoria is in the air. "We are the electricity that drives the economy," boasts one young man, whose company has nothing to do with the power industry. It seems each person at the microphone must utter an even more outlandish claim than the one made before. But it is not until the evening of the first day that the distortion—or self-delusion—reaches truly historic proportions. That's when Zhu Rongji, the world's favorite Communist Party leader, gives his speech praising his own success in reforming SOEs.

Yet there are moments, just a few, when sober reflection takes over. The subject turns to WTO membership, as it has so many times during the day, and the mood shifts. Jing Ulrich, now on stage, pauses for a moment. "The SOE reform process is going to be a long one," she says.

SECRET JOURNEY

It was a secret journey to Beijing by a man who hates to travel. But when his Chinese backers demanded that he receive his instructions in person, he had to come. So in May 2000, North Korean leader Kim Jong-il made his first trip outside his country in seventeen years. And like a vassal he went to the capital of the Middle Kingdom.

China's leaders do not want a unified Korea, one that would be controlled by the rich and prosperous South. They need a dependent state on their border, a country to serve as a buffer between them and a hostile world. Yet today's isolated North Korea, that buffer, cannot survive on its own. Beijing's rulers demand that North Korea trade so that it will become stable, but it must not trade so much that it becomes allied with foreign powers. So the reclusive Kim Jong-il traveled to Beijing to receive the advice of his only meaningful ally before the upcoming summit between the two Koreas.

How much contact should North Korea have? It is a dilemma for Beijing's leaders, just like the dilemma they face at home. They understand that China must trade if it wishes to progress, but they know that there is a point beyond which they can no longer remain in control. "Just how much trade can *we* have?" Jiang Zemin must ask himself almost daily. How can he advise his Korean ally when he does not know himself? Because Chinese leaders do not know where the line is, they are making special preparations for accession: government departments responsible for ideology, culture, and the media have been developing plans to counter the "Western influence" that WTO membership will bring and progressive scholars are being purged or disciplined as a precaution. For every step forward in the economic arena, there must be one back in the political.

Mao wanted his people to be poor and blank; he also wanted them isolated. When the people were cut off from the outside world, senior cadres could maintain their hold on political power indefinitely. Yet in an increasingly interdependent, globalized, and trade-dominated world, they cannot. As China's economy becomes more integrated with those of its trading partners, its abnormal system will increasingly clash with "global norms," argues The Economist. This will create "unprecedented pressures" on the political system. "The reform of the government system must be speeded up with the advent of WTO accession," liberal economists, still afraid to use the term "political reform," were quoted as saying in June 2000 by a semiofficial news agency. But that view, also shared by realistic cadres, does not reflect the opinions of senior leaders in Beijing. They move backward, as if that were an option in today's world.

China's current crop of leaders, not seeing the obvious, remain adamant about their right to rule. And that means, in the face of the forces of change, suppressing virtually all dissent. Klaus Schwab, the founder of the World Economic Forum, asks, "How do you make sure that human rights are observed, and that violations of those values are penalized, wherever they take place?" The Party, either because it's Chinese or because it's Communist, has scant capacity to absorb advice about how to run its country. Schwab can advise, but Jiang Zemin will bristle.

The Republican congressman from southern California understands this essential point. "We do not make a liberal by hugging a Nazi," says the outspoken Dana Rohrabacher, referring to the Chinese leaders. Yes, Congressman Rohrabacher, you are right. All the engagement in the world will not make Jiang Zemin a democrat. It will make him proud, it may even make him arrogant, but it will not make him open-minded. Nonetheless, you miss the point. Engagement makes the Chinese want to live like your prosperous constituents in Orange County. That's why Americans engage others in the world with trade. Jiang may suppress, but consumers will prevail.

And that's why Klaus Schwab is wrong when he says that in an interdependent world, "Everyone must be a winner." You don't have to go to Beijing to know that the Party leaders cannot win forever. Not even all the power at their disposal can protect them for long. "As China's people become more mobile, prosperous, and aware of alternative ways of life, they will seek greater say in the decisions that affect their lives," wrote President Bill Clinton. When the people all want more freedom, how will the Party maintain itself in power? Sorry, Klaus, there will be some losers.

Richard Nixon knew something about losing. He also knew that in the modern world there is no such thing as just a little freedom. Today there can be no economic freedom without political freedom. "Freedom is indivisible," he once explained. And there is no such thing as just a little integration with the outside. When Nixon left China in 1972, the White House did not take back the communication and satellite systems it had installed for his historic visit. "You know, that was like leaving a Trojan horse behind, because the result of that China saw the world, the Chinese people, and the world saw the Chinese people," he later noted. "Tiananmen Square, for example, was on living color in television. If it hadn't been on living color, there wouldn't have been the reaction against it."

And because there was Tiananmen, there was Deng Xiaoping's decision to open to the world even faster. Deng's successor is continuing that policy and, with WTO accession, is accelerating the process. Yet Jiang, unlike Deng, is no realist. Today's leader will fight political change as hard as he can. He told Kim Jong-il during the North Korean's visit to Beijing, "Snuff out all challenges when they are still at the embryonic stage." Adlai Stevenson is no friend of despots, but he could agree with Jiang Zemin on this point. "The time to stop a revolution is at the beginning, not the end," said the famous American politician. The People's Republic, however, is no longer at the beginning. Its leaders will cross that line by joining the WTO, and the matter will soon be out of their hands.

10

Sentences Without Verbs

Ideology and Politics Restrain Progress

Ev'rythin's up to date in Kansas City
They've gone about as fur as they c'n go!
—OSCAR HAMMERSTEIN II

"MAOISM, EMBODYING ITSELF within the peoples of the world, is marching unstoppably to command the new great wave of the world proletarian revolution." These words came from Maoists, but they are not Chinese. Abimael Guzman Reynoso, better known to his fellow Peruvians as Chairman Gonzalo, uttered that sentence as a rallying cry. Even though his guerrilla movement known as the Shining Path has been subdued, its scattered remnants still have more ideological vitality than Maoists in Mao's home country.

Communists in China don't speak like Gonzalo anymore; their sentences have lost their flash. We no longer hear that "Maoism marches" or that anything "commands great waves." Today the verbs no longer inspire. The Communist Party whispers when it talks about ideas, and then it speaks mostly to itself. When it must address the Chinese masses, it sloganizes in the hope that the people won't notice. The Party knows that its ideology is out of gas, so it is left with "We can work it out." That is not exactly exhilarating, especially for an organization that professes to be revolutionary. The Party's exhausted political philosophy is supposed to cover everything from democracy to privatization, but it provides no answers for the cadres in the present world.

Mao Zedong set the pattern. His successors can modify what they inherited, but they cannot change the framework. With no ideas of their own, senior cadres can only repeat what they've heard before. That's ideology in China these days, the past's claim on the future. And that's why the leadership grasps onto anything that might save the ruling theology. Today it's one slogan; tomorrow it's another. Senior leaders will not, however, confront the truth: the Party has nothing new to say.

Visitors to China marvel at what has happened in the last decade, and so they should. The Party—Deng Xiaoping, actually—realized what had to be done to stay in power after the slaughter in Tiananmen Square in 1989. Extraordinary change was the result of extraordinary times. In return for political obedience, Deng promised, and delivered, economic prosperity. He did that by ignoring much of Mao's ideological legacy. His colorful phrases contained vibrant thoughts that energized the Chinese.

Today, Jiang Zemin is administering Deng's compact with the people. The emergency has passed, and Jiang, the cautious Party politician, is adhering to the old ideas. He tells us that, like Deng, he has taken socialist thought to a new level, but his words are nothing new. Jiang certainly won't jettison the Party's ideology, even though that is obviously the right thing to do during this time of constant change as China embraces the rest of the world. We will need to see a bolder leader before China abandons the outmoded concepts it has inherited from an earlier, isolated age.

DESTINY

Can the Party, despite all of its ideological history, see its way through to democracy? Deng Xiaoping, in the most revolutionary words he ever uttered, said that there would be national elections in China in fifty years. That was in 1987. Will China get there by 2037?

Some days one might think so. The Party now talks about "various forms of democracy," and that's okay—democracy is not a "one size fits all" concept. Moreover, senior cadres are learning to listen to the proletariat. Premier Zhu Rongji says that President Jiang often reads letters sent to the Bureau of Handling Letters and Visits. That's an important part of "Chinese-style democracy," Zhu tells us. The Party even goes so far as to employ high technology to solicit opinions, using state Web sites to poll residents about policy issues. There's also something called "inner-Party democracy," a series of little reforms relating to the selection of Party officials. And far more important, there is "grassroots" democracy. That refers to village elections in which peasants get to choose representatives. Such elections are even starting to spread to the towns and cities.

Once the door is open, all sorts of reforms can be tried. Why can't the Party let two or more of its members compete for the same post in open elections? Someday, the Party might split into factions that vie for power, much like the Liberal Democratic Party in Japan. And then may come an even bolder reform. Technically, China is not a one-party state. Apart from the ruling Communists, there are eight "democratic parties." Today, they are sponsored and controlled by the Communist Party and participate in China's political system through the Chinese People's Political Consultative Conference, an essentially meaningless body maintained to show broad-based support for the regime. Tomorrow, if allowed, they could become real forces for change.

Another force for change in China is performing in the Special Administrative Region of Hong Kong. With slightly less than five hours to go before the year 2000 arrives, three girls are singing "It's a Small World" on a large stage set up in the middle of Chater Road in Central, the business center of that still-vibrant city. Like the song, the teenagers are cute, but this evening they seem to be testing the limits of official tolerance.

The girls are wearing matching black sweatshirts with white lettering. The two words displayed across their chests are assertive; the imagery used is crudely sexual, even pornographic by the standards of that community. The words emblazoned behind the trio are more than just assertive for ideologically rigid China. They are even defiant: DEMOCRACY AND RIGHTS 2000. Later that evening, Hong Kong's brightest democracy stars take the stage, and taped messages from the world's leading dissidents are played.

The trio and their song went largely unheard in the last hours of

1999, however, and later that evening activists could field a crowd of only three hundred. In nearby Lan Kwai Fong, just a few blocks to the south, eighty thousand revelers greeted the new millennium in perhaps the most raucous celebration in Asia, but that gathering had nothing to do with politics—other than sexual politics, of course.

That's not to say that Hong Kong's people don't want democracy. Once a sixth of the entire population, about a million, marched for democracy in a line that snaked across Hong Kong Island. Those times, the Tiananmen days, are gone, however. Today Hong Kong people are just pragmatic. China has gently deadened political debate in the former British colony; it's now clear that only the pro-Beijing parties have a voice. And as Beijing's strength in Hong Kong grows, it becomes more brazen. Beginning in 1999, Mainland leaders publicly issued instructions to Hong Kong people, restricting their exercise of freedom of speech as well as freedom of association. There were attacks on freedom of the press as well. Since then, the central government has missed few opportunities to interfere.

It was inevitable that Hong Kong's fragile notions of self-rule would suffer after integration with the Mainland. China does not want a functioning democracy on its doorstep; the contrast would be too much. So Hong Kong's government is, at Beijing's behest, stifling efforts to introduce greater popular participation in the political process, as contemplated by the Basic Law, Hong Kong's "mini-constitution." The trio's members can sing, but they'd better do it while they can. And they shouldn't take their act north of the border with Shenzhen, because there the coercive power of the state, rather than subtlety, shapes the political equation.

In Mainland China, just a few miles away from Chater Road, where the trio sang, there have been emperors, warlords, and general secretaries, but over the centuries the model has remained the same. Political authority is supposed to have resided in one individual. True, there have been transitional intervals during which power has been shared among caretakers, and some leaders have been weak, but society has always looked to one man. Sometimes he was supposed to be divine; other times he has been recognized as mortal. But there has always been one. And in this regard today's China, even though power has become a bit diffuse, is a direct continuation of the past.

The Communist Party has not done much to change China's traditional notions of governance, and the result has been more sorrow for the Chinese people. Tiananmen was neither the last nor the most tragic result of dictatorial rule during the Communist era. It's been more than a decade since the momentous days of the Beijing Spring of 1989, but the Party remains unrepentant.

Being in power in Beijing means never having to say you're sorry. Deng Xiaoping, who ordered the assault on Tiananmen Square, was not going to express any regret, of course. But the world expected more from Jiang Zemin. Here was the first leader who was not from the Long March generation, and he had had no involvement in the 1989 slaughter. Unburdened by the past, he was free to reverse the Tiananmen judgment and modernize China's political system. It has not worked out that way, however. Time has passed since those tumultuous days, but China's political development has remained essentially frozen.

One has to wonder why. Maybe because it is weaker and more insecure than it has ever been since 1949 and thus cannot afford to stain the memory of Deng. Moreover, because the Party retains power due to the compact Deng reached with the people, it can do little to atone for his sins of those dark days. As a practical matter, democracy cannot progress until the Party comes to terms with June 4, 1989. Because it either won't or can't, China today is no closer to 2037 than it was in 1987. The Party's intransigence may not matter, however. "History alone will make a judgment," says Cao Siyuan, a leading advocate of political reform and the nation's most famous gadfly. Cao, who obviously does not want to spend any more time in a Chinese jail, is too polite. What he'd probably like to say is that the Chinese people will render their verdict.

At first glance, the people's verdict is that the 1989 massacre should be forgotten. "Look, Tiananmen is behind us," says one who suffered. The mood in the country is different now. Attaining some measure of economic well-being is the first and foremost priority for most Chinese today. In the large coastal cities, the parts of China that are the most influential, there is little pressure for political reform. The illegal China Democracy Party, small and ineffective, has not struck a chord. So do the Chinese really want a freer political system?

Despite appearances, they do. "Silence," Che Guevara told us, "is argument carried on by other means." The Communist Party is deeply unpopular. "I don't know anyone who believes in the Party anymore," says one whose job it is to keep tabs on such things. Worse, many, if not most, consider the organization irrelevant. It is telling that cadres will not put matters to a vote or even "let a hundred flowers bloom" and ask the people what they think. Any opposition, organized or not, is quashed. If the China Democracy Party hasn't gotten off the ground, it is only because it has, for most of its short life, been hounded by security forces dedicated to its elimination. Outside the big cities of the coastal east there is simmering discontent. "Sometimes I come across an account of a county in Sichuan in which over a period of five years fifteen different political parties have been established and broken up, one county," says American businessman turned activist John Kamm. These days, there are constant disturbances across China, and because its policies are the policies of the government, those protests are tantamount to challenges to the Party itself.

It is inevitable that the Chinese will reverse the Party's verdict on Tiananmen Square; the only issue is when they will do so. Although most people may not think about this tragedy in their daily lives, there are some who will not relent. If the people won't relent, will the Party? "I am the state," said Louis XIV of France. Once you start from this point, it is hard to allow for democracy. Louis XIV was not Chinese and no one in the Chinese Communist Party is known to have said those words, but the arrogance of that utterance is typical of what comes from China's leading political organization. There are five stars on the flag of the People's Republic. The big one, the one larger than the other four, stands for the Party.

The Party—and this should come as no surprise—has its own version of " L'état c'est moi." It is its historical mission and destiny as it sees it. "The force at the core leading our cause forward is the Chinese Communist Party," begins the first quotation in the publication popularly known as *The Little Red Book*. Without the Party, Mao argues, there can be no socialism. Because there must be socialism, the people must permit the Party to discharge its historic role to lead China. It is really that simple. If you have a role, you must fulfill it, as inconvenient as that may be for the governed. China's Constitution speaks of "the people's democratic dictatorship led by the working class" and "the principle of democratic centralism," but the drafter could simply have used the word "destiny." That would have been clearer. How many people does the Communist Party think it takes to change a lightbulb in China? About 63.5 million, the number of its members.

When Mao spoke, the Chinese people listened. They responded to his commands with their hearts. The Great Leap Forward and the Cultural Revolution are proof of that. Few mortals, maybe none, have ever held such sway over a nation's soul. Jiang Zemin, a less charismatic man who will not be buried in Tiananmen Square, has less hold over the populace because the Party's ideas no longer inflame or excite.

In the Party's weakened condition, will the People's Republic evolve into a democratic state? That is, after all, what many, both inside and outside China, expect. And so their assessments are getting a little extreme, their judgments too simplistic. "The Internet tolls the eventual death knell of one-party rule as it is now practiced in China," says one unnamed Party official. Thus the current thinking is that today's embrace of modernity in China, from stock markets to the Internet, must change Chinese communism over time.

The predictions are that the Party will evolve, but that won't happen. For there to be evolution, the Party must give up what it holds most dear, the tenets that gave Mao's peasant army the strength to defeat a vastly superior enemy. Senior cadres remember the power of the Party's ideology, and they will not abandon it now. In their eyes it is the basis of their own legitimacy and therefore the last thing they will, or can, surrender. The Party can, as a tactical matter, allow a temporary retreat, such as village elections, but it cannot give up its leading role in society. That's its destiny.

And that destiny is why the Mainland cannot follow Taiwan's example. In Taiwan it took someone of vision, and more than just a little power, to begin the reform of the repressive regime the Kuomintang had created. Chiang Ching-kuo, the generalissimo's son, did so after he took over from his father. Unfortunately, Jiang Zemin, the self-described "core" of the Chinese leadership, is too weak and too orthodox to try anything like that. Even if he was stronger and more innovative, the Party's theory of destiny would get in the way. When one has a historical mission to lead society, one must fulfill it. Destiny can be as inflexible as the immutable laws of history that Marx was able to discern. The Kuo-mintang did not have a destiny, so it could evolve. The Communist Party, burdened by its role assigned by history, simply cannot.

Those who buy the theory of evolution point to the village elections. Those elections, however, are more apparent than real. They're often rigged, and elected representatives clash with Party officials, who, de-spite the trappings of democratic safeguards, retain real power. And then there's another roadblock on the road to reform. "They said they are only here to talk, but they have a very bad attitude," said Wang Lingyun, mother of Tiananmen dissident Wang Dan. Policemen arrested her hours before the expected announcement of the 1999 Nobel Peace Prize merely because her son was in the running for it and they wanted to pre-vent her from speaking to the press. As Wang's comment shows, China's police state misses no opportunity to be vigilant. Jiang's tenure has seen the bureaucracy of repression grow rather than diminish. So much for any moves toward democracy under his leadership. Finally, there is the Kuomintang factor. After that party's loss in the March 2000 presidential elections in Taiwan, the Chinese Communist Party, having learned all the wrong lessons, decided that reform would be the path to ruin. Since then, it has stiffened its position against changing China's political sys-tem.

So the Party brooks no opposition, and, left unchecked, it has become what you'd expect: arrogant, corrupt, hated. Go to the small villages and towns of China, and you will find thousands of local officials who act as if they were the embodiment of absolute power, levying their own taxes, dispensing justice as they see fit, and, as unbelievable as it may seem, issuing their own currency. Go to Beijing, and you will see all of this, only on a grander scale. The Party is, at all levels, an organization out of control.

It's really not too hard to understand how the People's Republic got into such a mess so quickly. Mao and Deng had too much power, as Jiang does now. Party leaders at the center talk about self-discipline and vigilance as a means to reform, but they have already tried those and they have failed. There is a much better medicine: the competition of democracy—democracy, that is, not in the Chinese or North Korean sense, but as the rest of the world has come to understand the word. We all know what absolute power leads to.

The cure is as simple as the diagnosis. The patient, however, will have none of it, acting as if ideology were all it needs. "I do not see a clear linkage between corruption and one-party rule in China," said Zhu Rongji in March 2000. If he cannot, he should speak to a taxi driver in his own capital city of Beijing, who notes, "We live in a dictatorship where there is no control over the party. The higher officials are, the more corrupt they are." What matters is not whether the premier is sincere or not. The point is that the leadership cannot come to terms with the root cause of pervasive corruption. The Party can be self-righteous, intransigent, and arrogant; it cannot, in the final analysis, be self-aware.

Thus corruption flourishes in the People's Republic of China, as it has from the beginning. The first movement against this ill, the Three Antis campaign, was launched in 1951. The late Party statesman Chen Yun once remarked, "Not fighting corruption would destroy the country; fighting it would destroy the Party." Deng Xiaoping, making a bargain with the Devil, permitted corruption in southern Guangdong in return for its provincial leaders' political support for his reforms. It's pointless to argue whether, in the context of history, he did the right thing. Now the issue is what the Party will do to reduce the rising tide of corruption that is threatening the regime more than ever. As Jiang Zemin has noted in connection with the Kuomintang's recent fall, a corrupt party will soon lose its power.

So the Communist Party, in the midst of one of its periodic campaigns, strikes hard against venal cadres. Officials are jailed or executed daily. Yet little has changed. The nature of prosecution today remains political because China remains politicized. In 1998, Jiang Zemin had Chen Xitong, the party secretary of Beijing and Politburo member, jailed for corruption, and he deserved incarceration, to be sure. Yet Chen was prosecuted because he dared to oppose Jiang politically. That was, in reality, his crime. Two years later Beijing Party boss Jia Qinglin, a Jiang ally, escaped any form of punishment for the Xiamen smuggling affair, even though he, and especially his wife, were both implicated in what is called "China's biggest corruption scandal." The leadership is seeking to reform the Party through sloganizing and exhortation, but cadres know the reality of the political system that operates today. It is, in essence, the same that has been in existence since 1949. So it comes as no surprise that Jiang Zemin said recently, "It is imperative that we combat corruption; yet it is equally important to maintain stability." What he's really saying is that senior Party loyalists are beyond prosecution.

China will make real progress in the fight against corruption only when prosecution and conviction are separated from politics. That means when the Party truly embraces the rule of law. There was much ado in the world's press about the incorporation of the rule of law into the Chinese Constitution in March 1999. Many hailed the amendment as historic, but the change was vague and of little significance. In reality, the rule of law was already enshrined in the Constitution in specific and clear language before the amendment. In any event, the Party, despite its high-minded rhetoric, still views its will as law as if nothing had ever changed. Li Peng, the infamous "Butcher of Beijing" for his role in the Tiananmen Square massacre and now China's top legislator, equated the Party's word with the country's law at the 2000 session of the National People's Congress, thereby negating the national constitution and two decades of efforts to institutionalize the rule of law. Others in the leadership may not repeat Li's words, but they too believe that the Party stands supreme. The truth is that there is no law binding the Party; there are no constraints of any kind. Jiang Zemin, backing away from the rule of law, now talks about the virtues of "the rule of virtue," and Party theorists, taking their cue from Jiang, promote collectivism over individualism. In this climate, how can there be democracy by 2037—or, for that matter, by any date?

History has called Deng Xiaoping bold, but his changes, however dramatic, were in the context of the system that Mao devised. His reforms were essentially tinkering. It is said that the Holy Roman Empire was not holy, Roman, or an empire. The People's Republic of China is certainly Chinese, but is it a republic belonging to the people? Without democracy, it cannot be.

THE PRIMARY STAGE OF SOCIALISM

Mao's state-owned enterprises are struggling. A conceptually simple solution, privatization, could fix them. That remedy, however, is ideologically faulty: a fundamental tenet of the Party is state ownership of the means of production. What happens to the "Party of Public Assets," better known as the "Chinese Communist Party," when all public assets are in private hands? No wonder privatization is termed, by official media, "suicidal."

So Party leaders remain dead set against this obvious solution. "The rights of an overwhelming majority of people would be guaranteed if state-owned enterprises were in the hands of Marxists and Leninists," wrote China's most prominent Marxist-Leninist, Deng Liqun. Deng, once propaganda chief, does not hold the reins of power, but those who do listen to this influential elder of the Party. Such as Comrade Jiang Zemin. "We must actively open up new opportunities, have the courage to keep forging ahead, but never engage in privatization," said China's current leader in 1999. That inspiring statement, so clear in its meaning, appears to be the final word on this subject. And it comes from an authoritative source. China, it seems, will not privatize its state-owned enterprises.

If that's the case, someone should tell the Party. Cadres in Beijing and in the provinces are, in fact, selling off Chinese industry in initial public offerings in domestic and global financial markets and by private sale. In other parts of the world, this is called "privatization." In China, at least in the realm of higher Party officials, it is not.

Why must adults play word games? As cadres dispose of the pride of China's Stalinist past, they encounter the "contradictions" of a China struggling to harmonize the economic realities of today's world with their ideology. One political faction in the Party's leadership, then another, seeks to establish the "correct" socialist position. Debate, medieval in its theological ferocity, continues while the economy trends downward. The earth revolves around the sun, except, of course, in Beijing, where many live in a theoretically constructed universe with its own unique set of rules.

Foreign commentators often say that China, despite its socialist foundations, has embraced capitalism, and they usually do this in the context of phrases such as "There's no turning back the clock." Like doctrinaire Marxists, they speak of "inevitability." If the Politburo was to take a long vacation, China would surely privatize all of its enterprises. It is the obvious solution. The Party, however, cannot adopt that answer, no matter how much sense it makes. Although the state religion preaches that objective economic laws govern the universe, economic considerations must take a backseat in the China of today.

If Jiang Zemin is the leader of the Party of Public Assets, why is he permitting the sale of stock at all? The offering of stakes in large enterprises, those that are "public assets," if any can be said to fit that description, is an extraordinary move given the ideology of the Party. How could that happen in an institution with such strong roots in Marxism? The answer is truly clever: as Jiang notes, China is still "at the primary stage of socialism."

By referencing the first stage of socialism, Jiang was saying that, in this early period, the Party should emphasize economic development, even if that means tolerating private ownership. In March 1999, the Party, working through the National People's Congress, boosted the private sector by amending the country's Constitution. Prior to that constitutional amendment, the private sector had been considered a "complement" to the socialist public economy. Postamendment, it took its place as an "important component." Nonetheless, the Constitution enshrines socialism, not capitalism. Although it seems inconceivable to many in the West that China would ever revert to true socialism, that is not out of the question for the Party's leadership. Apparently Jiang views the existence of the private sector as transitory.

Karl Marx believed that socialism presupposed capitalism; in other words, that society has to undergo capitalist transformation before the correct conditions for socialism can exist. That was not a message that Mao and other revolutionaries in underdeveloped societies wished to hear. After all, they wanted to avoid, to the extent possible, the worst aspects of brutal capitalism. Mao was also impatient, willing to wait only four years before trying something really ambitious: the overnight transformation of a feudal agrarian society into a socialist industrial state.

Mix a dose of an outdated nineteenth-century philosophy with a dash of Chinese genius, and you have an explanation of how, in a society where socialism has triumphed, capitalism is on the rise. One explanation, true to Marx's own beliefs, is that China's jump to socialism in the 1950s was premature. Marxists, the Chinese variety, now believe that Mao tried to short-circuit the objective laws of history and was therefore doomed. "In China the state took control of too much so the current task is to reduce its role," notes Li Junru of the Central Committee's Research Centre on Party History in Beijing. Hence, even committed Communists can support privatization, in substance if not in name. In this context, today's privatization is merely just a step backward to capitalism so that China can eventually attain communism along a more conventional Marxist pattern. An economy containing privately owned businesses is just one of those things, like adolescence, that one has to go through.

How long will this capitalist phase last? Deng Xiaoping said that socialism "will require persistent struggle by many generations, a dozen or even several dozens." Jiang Zemin, believing in a more ambitious timetable, estimates that "hard and enterprising work of 100 years" will "by and large bring about socialist modernization" although he has also been quoted as saying that "tens of generations" might be needed. "In the future, the state's control of the economy will be like the head of the dragon which will move the whole body," says Dr. Fang Zhulan of People's University. If that's the case, the capitalist phase, however long, will be temporary if China's Marxists have correctly interpreted the history of class struggle.

True pragmatists dismiss all this as ideological window dressing, as do Marxists outside China. Li Junru notes that European Marxists "can't grasp why we still claim to be a socialist country." Many would agree with Lee Kuan Yew, Singapore's outspoken senior minister, when he says, "If you are going to have socialism, then as a matter of principle, you can't have a free market."

Undeterred by the past, China's Marxists still believe they should control tomorrow. In Party schools across the country where cadres are indoctrinated, the faithful are still taught that the ultimate goal is communism. Foreigners may think that no one in China is really that idealistic, but there is no support among senior Party leaders, or at least any that is visible, for taking the next step and overthrowing the ideological baggage that Mao (and even Deng) dumped on China. If that happened, thousands of Marxist scholars such as Li Junru and Fang Zhulan could begin to do something productive with their lives. There are more people studying Marxism in China (an estimated 240,000 in addition to schoolchildren) than in any other country in the world. Although China is short of the people it really needs—scientists, economists, doctors, teachers, practically everybody, in fact, except Indian chiefs—it employs its best and brightest in thinking how to update its theology. A mind, as the saying goes, is a terrible thing to waste.

So thousands spend their time conforming Marxism to the realities of present-day China. Ideology may not be important to most Chinese, but it is to the leaders in Beijing. It's bad enough when a country's universities engage in endless theoretical debate. It's worse when a country's leadership participates as well. China faces serious problems from every side, and even in an ideal world, finding solutions that work and implementing them in time would be difficult. The process is made virtually impossible by forcing everything to pass the narrow test of ideology (or, as is often the case today, molding ideology to fit the solution). China, acting as if the world will wait for it, obviously believes it has the time to afford doctrinal purity in all matters of state. Time waits for no country these days, however, not even one as important, or unimportant, as China. Nero fiddled, Jiang theorizes.

Whatever words or concepts are in vogue in Beijing these days, the central government is, in fact, finding a way to privatize the larger SOEs. The ideological explanation for this most un-Marxist of developments is that stock ownership is merely another form of "public" ownership. As Jiang Zemin said as early as 1996, production can be public if it is run for the benefit of many people. One has to admire the mental agility of Communist Party cadres as they struggle to privatize without admitting to such antisocialist behavior. Take former Shenyang Mayor Mu Suixin, who claimed that his city's massive transfer of enterprises to the private sector was not "privatization" because the enterprises were being sold to corporations and not individuals. By this definition, that bulwark of free enterprise, the United States, with its Microsofts and General Electrics, has adopted, perhaps even perfected, socialism. Not surprisingly, there are a few who do not accept this rather innovative breakthrough in socialist conceptual thinking.

The notion of "socialized public ownership" sounds like a rationalization at best. Government ownership is public ownership; ownership by individuals is not. As a theoretical matter, that should be the end of the story. But in China, all things, including theory, serve the Party and its views of the moment, no matter how far-fetched they may be. If the broad masses owned the means of production through public markets, there might be a practical justification for socialized public ownership.

Unfortunately, the facts do not seem to bear this out. There are approximately 55 million domestic shareholders in China's stock markets, about 4.2 percent of the population, but the number of active shareholders may be under 5 million. Shareholders are, for the most part, rich by Chinese standards, and they are decidedly unproletarian in outlook. Some workers have taken shares in their employers, but not many. Only when pension funds control China's markets, as could happen one day, will the notion of socialized public ownership have a factual basis. In the meantime, it is obvious that the keepers of socialist orthodoxy are in denial.

Jiang Zemin says that "only socialism can save China." Singapore's Lee Kuan Yew confides, "Between you and me, I find that a little off-key." Jiang's proposition sounds so ludicrous after two decades of economic reform that many assume he is being insincere. Only Jiang knows what he is really thinking. Fortunately, we don't have to. It's not whether he's trying to fool us that counts—it's what's actually happening that matters.

All this talk of socialism, whether genuine or not, is slowing down the process of rejuvenation of China's industry. That is critical. China does not have the time to waste. Hu Yaobang, a general secretary of the Party under Deng Xiaoping, remarked, "People don't care if this is a socialist or a capitalist country. They don't even want to debate it." The Chinese people don't, so why should the Party? Jiang and his colleagues have moved back into Mao's world of theoretical constructs while change elsewhere in the world accelerates.

Instead of debating theory, cadres should focus on making privatization, or whatever they're calling it, work. If they completely sell off the smaller state-owned enterprises, good things can happen. If they insist on retaining control, privatization, Chinese style, falls flat. The Party cannot bring itself to part with the larger enterprises, so all it does is sell minority stakes in them. The result of this sort of partial privatization is predictable: it ends up having little effect on modernizing the underlying business operations. At the Party's Fourth Plenum in 1999, Deng Liqun's conservative faction argued, with statistics, that SOEs' efficiency does not necessarily improve after privatization. The conservatives may be exaggerating to prove a point, but the gist of Deng's message is sound. Timid privatization, the type being practiced in China, is not especially effective.

The arrival of private investors should, in theory, have some reformist effect on the SOEs, but except for the rare offerings involving strategic investors who take management positions, this has not been the case. Passive portfolio investors have relatively little day-to-day interest in the companies whose stock they buy. Moreover, the Party, consistent with ideology, makes sure that SOEs are run for the benefit of the state and workers, not minority shareholders, and in accordance with its own doctrine. All that happens in most partial privatizations is that SOEs upgrade their facilities by using the cash that public markets bring to the table. Modern equipment, however, does not make modern enterprises. SOEs need, first and foremost, modern management. Without it, fresh funds from private investors end up as unproductive investments made by SOEs or in the Swiss bank accounts of corrupt officials.

Moreover, China's crippled courts won't enforce what few rights minority shareholders have. Consider the recent fate of China's first shareholder suit based on fraud. In late 1998, a domestic investor filed a lawsuit against Chengdu Hongguang Industrial Company for making allegedly false statements in its offering prospectus. Hongguang, a telephone component maker, claimed net profits of ¥54 million (about US$6.5 million) for 1996. In fact, the China Securities Regulatory Commission determined that Hongguang had had an actual loss of ¥103 million (about US$12.4 million) for that year. Nonetheless, in May 1999, a court in Shanghai denied the investor's claim for stock trading losses of ¥3,136 (less than US$400). The decision claims that there was no connection between the reportedly false statements and the losses (even though the stock price clearly tanked after Hongguang's claims of profits were revealed to be false). More important, the court ruled that false claims were the business of the CSRC (in other words, the central government) and not the courts. Since the Shanghai case, other Hongguang shareholders have been denied compensation for their losses.

The case illustrates the predicament of minority shareholders, who are often left without redress for egregious, even criminal, behavior on the part of SOE managers. It will take years for China to develop laws protecting shareholders. China's new Securities Law, intended to modernize creaking legal rules, is a disappointment in this regard. It implies the existence of, but does not clearly set forth, important shareholder rights. It is unlikely, especially in the near future, that courts will respond to the implicit invitation in that law and create those rights. The courts won't help because the Party will not cede them enough power. Jiang Zemin is resisting reforms that would weaken Party authority over state enterprises. Is he really going to empower private investors, whether domestic or foreign?

Not all is bleak, as the China Securities Regulatory Commission has stepped in where the courts cannot tread. In a series of enforcement actions the CSRC has been punishing bad management, such as that of Chengdu Hongguang Industrial. The CSRC, in the first known instance of government sanctions relating to a public stock offer, fined that enterprise, confiscated assets, and punished individuals. Real hope, however, is misplaced. There are now about 1,100 companies listed on China's exchanges. The CSRC has only about twenty investigators. But even if it had twenty thousand of them, the CSRC would still be shorthanded. Because the Party won't let private shareholders help enforce the laws by permitting them to sue bad management, the only solution to the ills of partial privatization is complete privatization. Cao Siyuan, the reformer, applies the analogy of the leaky faucet to state ownership: "What do you do? Fix it quickly, to prevent too much water from being wasted? Or fix it slowly?"

This is one area where we should take our cues from the Party. "One thing is clear, people expecting overall privatization in China will continue to be disappointed," say the official media. "The dominating status of the publicly owned economy is protected by the national constitution." Ideological statements such as this can be dismissed, but it's undeniable that those who have predicted a fast pace of privatization have been wrong. Some of their forecasts were simply preposterous, others merely intriguing. Pessimists, however, have always been closer to the mark.

It's not all that hard to figure out what's going on. So far, Beijing has been living in what Deutsche Bank, in a recent advertising campaign, called "the Age of All." Investors have bought SOE equity and have not challenged state managers. From Beijing's perspective selling equity has not hurt because it has not had to surrender control of what it considers important. "The idea is that this is money for nothing," says Duncan Clark, a partner of an advisory firm in Beijing.

One does not need to be Nostradamus to see what's going to happen. The pace of stock offerings will continue to be leisurely. There will be some progress in reducing state ownership—the Party will continue privatization by reducing the number of industries considered strategic and by limiting the number of SOEs within such strategic industries that will remain state-owned. And something else is predictable: ideology will continue to pollute China's modernization efforts. Jiang Zemin will preside over a debate that will result in postponement of any new initiatives as he seeks to avoid controversy. Cadres will defer the day of reckoning, making the situation even worse. With the slow pace of sales, it will be decades before China gets to the point where it has to think of surrendering control. What Beijing fails to realize, however, is that it will also be decades before it begins the rejuvenation of larger state-owned enterprises in earnest. The best prescription is to take the medicine now: SOEs need the discipline of supervision by shareholders.

"And it can all be yours," say Deutsche Bank's advertisements. That may be true for Deutsche's customers, but certainly not for the Communist Party. For the Party, the Age of All is all but over. China can have an ideology or a future, but not both. Which will it be, Comrade Zemin?

China has been modernizing at its own pace for around 150 years. The Qing Dynasty, failing to realize the urgency of the problems it faced, collapsed before it could catch up to the Western colonial powers and Japan. The Communist Party, a century later, finds itself in essentially the same situation. Now it believes that China can reform gradually, as if the rest of the world were standing still or just didn't count. In the meantime, the cadres worry about appearances. By the Party's own reckoning, if it cedes control of the SOEs it will be a public admission that its ideology has no practical application to the twenty-first century. The cadres do not have the luxury to worry about appearances at this stage. They should simply do the right thing and let the Chinese people be the judge of their stewardship. Otherwise, they will go the way of the Qings.

AS FAR AS THEY CAN GO

The middle-aged man didn't have much choice. The square itself, where so much Chinese history has been made, was off limits, surrounded by a seven-foot fence of corrugated metal. Everywhere members of the state's security forces were standing a few yards apart from one another. If he was to be successful, he would have to be clever—and quick.

So he walked across the ancient stone bridge, the one under Mao's portrait, toward Tiananmen Square. Then he unfurled his umbrella. It was white, the Chinese color of mourning. The symbolism was evidently lost on the ranks of grim men guarding the state. The words on the umbrella, however, were unmistakable: RETURN STATE PROPERTY TO THE COMMON PEOPLE and REMEMBER THE 10TH ANNIVERSARY OF THE STUDENT MOVEMENT.

It took about a minute for police to realize what was happening, but then the People's Republic was safe again. A uniformed officer put his arm around the waist of the protester and, with his plainclothes colleague, led him firmly to a car kept waiting for an incident such as this. In a moment on that day, June 4, 1999, it was over.

On the day to commemorate democracy and freedom in China, the message on the umbrella seemed odd at first glance; in 1989, the students and workers wanted many things, but privatization of state assets was not their concern. For many in the Party, however, the issues of democracy and privatization are almost the same. Privatize everything, and the Party loses its grip over the people, the reasoning goes. The end result is freedom, and true democracy cannot be far behind. Therefore, the leaky tap described by Cao Siyuan is being fixed slowly.

At a time when China needs practical solutions to immediate problems, the answers from its leaders are ideological and reminiscent of an earlier age. Politics, after all, gave birth to the People's Republic. Turn the clock back several decades, and Communist guerrillas have just bungled a raid on a rail line as they fight the Japanese. Michael Lindsay, a British academic fighting alongside Mao's troops, observes to a general that his soldiers need more military training. "You don't understand our movement at all," the general replies. "The first job is political organization." Mao had a point when war was being waged over a terrain filled with civilians. Today the struggle in China is different.

But Jiang Zemin remembers Mao. "Talk politics," today's leader says, evoking memories of the first days of the People's Republic. During the summer of 1999, Jiang essentially shut down the central government so that Party members could participate in his Three Stresses (sometimes translated as "Three Emphases") campaign, which focused on studying

Marxism, promoting righteousness, and being politically correct. There were extensive study sessions and group and individual self-criticisms, and important government tasks were accomplished, if at all, only on weekends, at lunchtime, or during the evening. The president of the Bank of Communications, the bank that had suffered the disastrous run in Henan Province, spent his summer participating in 118 meetings as part of that Maoist-style campaign. Provinces had their own Three Stresses campaigns, as did factories and colleges. Said one retired man who noticed that the beaches near the capital were empty in 1999, "The adults are all in 'three stresses' meetings, and the children are all rehearsing for the National Day parade."

The Three Stresses campaign had not run its course when Jiang began another. The Three Representatives campaign, launched in May 2000, instructed the Party that it must always be representative of the foremost productive forces in society, of the most advanced culture, and of the fundamental interests of the people. Again, all Party and government units were instructed to hold study sessions.

And so Jiang Zemin is returning China to earlier times. Jiang, living in a more modern age, is more modern, yet he imitates the style, and sometimes the substance, of the founder of the People's Republic. And that imitation subtracts from his commitment to the future. His answer to China's problems is to strengthen the Party. That is the "top priority." "Adherence to the party's leadership is a basic political principle and a fundamental political guarantee for our success in all undertakings," he says repeatedly and with conviction. "The more complicated the international situation is, the more weighty and arduous the task of reform and development, the more necessary it is to strengthen the party's leadership." This is not mere talk: the Party is currently spreading its cells to all but the smallest organizations in China. This is, in sum, an echo of the past.

There is a difference between the Party's old campaigns and the new ones. Then, Mao Zedong's stirred a people. Today, Jiang Zemin's are mocked. "Who do these guys think they are?" asks one government official who resents all of Jiang's campaigns. When Jiang says, "Talk politics," he is addressing the men and women of the Party, and his message is one demanding obedience. The last thing senior cadres want in these days of alienation and unrest is for anyone, least of all ordinary citizens, to think more about politics.

Foreigners who care to notice all this often dismiss China's retreat to the past as rhetoric or, at most, just a phase. They are missing the point. The fact that there is so much rhetoric highlights the inherent ideological and political nature of the Party's rule. But ideology today just won't work, especially now that China is on the eve of joining the World Trade Organization. Accession will mean accelerated reform, which will erode the Party's power. So these days are characterized by repression. Beijing blacklists academicians, restricts the press, steps up indoctrination in the schools. It closes, censors, and tightens regulation of Web sites. And it continues to imprison.

The people are unimpressed. "We swallow our consciences and excrete ideology," sings rock musician He Yong. "Talk politics," replies Jiang Zemin, reminding his audiences of Mao's infamous instruction to "put politics in command." He Yong and Jiang Zemin are both from the same country, but one of these men is out of touch.

Today's Party, however out of touch, remains focused on theory. It's as if the cadres have been reading the works of another great thinker. "Don't part with your illusions," said Mark Twain. "When they are gone you may still exist but you have ceased to live." There are, however, limits to the power of illusion: "ideology cannot supply rice," said Deng Xiaoping during 1992's famous Southern Tour, which fueled China's explosive growth during the early part of the last decade. Now that the Party has produced rice, it needs an ideology to survive, and unfortunately, rice cannot supply ideology. Simply put, supplying rice is not an ideology, as much as Party ideologues have tried to make it one. Until it has the courage to make a fresh start, the Party will cling to the old ideas, however out of step they may be with today's world. Ideology, by itself, is holding back China in all aspects of modernization, both political and economic. Cadres no longer use Mao's words, so why must they keep his ideas?

And his system? Rae Yang is now a professor at Dickinson College, but once she was a Red Guard. "I believe a lot of people in my generation became completely disillusioned of the Cultural Revolution, and we started to think like who was responsible for this great disaster for our country." It's *what's* responsible, not *who,* Professor Yang, and that is un-doubtedly the reason why you are teaching in Carlisle, Pennsylvania, today. The people responsible for that most absurd of upheavals are gone, but you did not return to China when it was over. If it was just a person at fault, you would have gone back to your homeland years ago. Of course Mao was abnormal, but why was he allowed to start the Cul-tural Revolution in the first place? And why today, when China is so "re-formed," did the Chinese state imprison your colleague Song Yongyi for merely trying to study that turbulent period?

Yes, in Kansas City they've "gone about as fur as they c'n go." That's also true in turn-of-the-century China. And that is the critical problem the Party faces. Mao's army captured a semifeudal, fragmented society and shook it to its roots, but they had to use ideology and force to keep it together. Of course today's cadres can modernize a Leninist state, but they can take this model of society only so far. Today the Party has re-formed the system about as much as it can. Go much further, and the Party will have to disavow its ideas. Don't do enough, and the system will collapse. One way or another the People's Republic will not survive. The only question is how it will die.

"Of course our party is committed to economic construction and re-form," Jiang Zemin's heir apparent, Hu Jintao, said. But then he added, "However, economic development must not be achieved at the expense of ideology." When the Party's very ideology stands in the way of rejuve-nation, Hu's statement can mean only one thing: the People's Republic will one day run out of time.

I I

Emerging in the East

Can the Chinese State Evolve?

The laws of history tell us that only when the old is gone can the new take its place.

—WEI JINGSHENG

A MINIBUS APPROACHES the inspection station at the border of coastal Jiangsu Province. An officer, in the drab green uniform denoting the authority of the state, motions it to a special lane by pointing to the ground with his left hand, and the bus stops where directed. It's not hard to understand why this vehicle, among the thousands that are traveling that day, is being pulled over: it's dangerously overloaded. The young conductor in the front has a sharp smile with no warmth, and the effect is enhanced by his narrow eyes. Those eyes are always looking for more fares, and sometimes his head, and even his body, is extended far outside an open window on the right side of the bus while it is on the move. "Quickly!" he shouts to the poor folk who want to go to points northwest in Jiangsu—and who are willing to pay his price. They run to catch up and jump onto the moving vehicle, only to be directed to where the aisle once was. There ought to be a law, and in fact there is. So the driver is fined at the inspection station. Yet after crossing into Jiangsu the minibus picks up still others. The conductor gives up his seat in the front to a new passenger and then sits on a stool blocking the door. Soon he has to give up his stool to still another passenger, so he now stands as the bus works its way into the farmlands of Jiangsu. China's new economy is at work.

And so the country grows and moves to a faster rhythm. There are many Chinas, living side by side. One is run according to five-year plans and ideological campaigns; the others are powered by entrepreneurial drive and a defiance of the first. Every day we see them all and marvel that they coexist in the same land. The Chinese are moving in so many different directions all at once; it's exhilarating just to watch. Who can tell where they will eventually end up?

It's no wonder that many argue that China will peacefully evolve to a better society. The case for that proposition starts with the energy of its people. They are charting new courses and their government must follow, we are told. This is already occurring today as the nation moves forward. After all, as Singapore's senior minister, Lee Kuan Yew, tells us, "this is a better China than ever has been for a very long time." And as Robert Kapp, president of the U.S.-China Business Council, reminds us, we shouldn't be so "mesmerized" by the tragedies of the country's recent history that we can't acknowledge how far the Chinese have come. Kapp is also right, of course.

Many try to predict the future by looking at the recent past and extrapolating. When one does that, one can even imagine China regaining its position astride the globe, a colossus of a country. As respected authors Nicholas D. Kristof and Sheryl WuDunn write, some observers need to be tied down "so that they don't float away with their own enthusiasm." Even the sober-minded, however, believe that there will be a good outcome for the one-party state. "The most likely scenario for China's future, and the fondest hope of many Chinese, is continued evolution along the path that China is already taking, rather like the trajectory of other quasi-fascist countries—South Korea, Taiwan, Chile, and Spain," write Kristof and WuDunn. The Chinese government can almost agree with that assessment. "A powerful, democratic and civilized socialist China will emerge in the east," Beijing assures the world. So is all the turmoil finally behind this great country? And will change, for once, be positive and peaceful?

The Chinese people are the greatest cause for optimism, but they're also the strongest argument for even more tragedy. It is precisely because the people have been so successful that the authoritarian state cannot evolve much further. In the future forces will collide, the Chinese and their government. A democracy would bend, but a half-reformed dictatorship will resist. "The laws of history tell us that only when the old is gone can the new take its place," wrote Wei Jingsheng in "The Fifth Modernization." China's most important dissident is really saying that before the new can claim its place, it will have to *shove* aside the old. Change, in other words, will not be evolutionary.

The progress we have seen since 1978, or most of it, is the people's, not their government's. It is true that the state had the foresight to embark upon a phased retreat of its management of society, but that retreat was intended to prevent the people from demanding an even greater one. And it was the people who took advantage of the withdrawal. They showed true genius by exploiting the situation and forcing additional change. As a result, the country's economic growth was explosive. The Chinese ignored constraints and surged through society. And now they don't want to stop.

"When we look into the history of a billion people's lives in China, we cannot help asking ourselves 'Why?' " says Yang Lan, one of China's richest women. "But when we look into their future, we want to say to the world 'Why not!' " As Yang tells us, her people have great aspirations for tomorrow. Yet she should know why the Chinese will not be able to achieve them under the current system of governance. "The potential is there for everybody to see," says Lee Kuan Yew about China, "but the potential has not been realized to the maximum because of so many obstacles." As the founder of modern Singapore, he knows something about the development of nations and has just told us the essential truth about China.

The "great, glorious, and correct Communist Party of China" understands so little of what it has wrought, and for all the change in China itself, the Party has changed so little. We can see that when the cadres celebrate. They marked the fiftieth anniversary of the founding of the People's Republic in 1999, and nothing was going to get in the way. They unilaterally abrogated advertising contracts and then tore down all the signs along the parade route. Party officials stopped nearby industry for two weeks to clean the air and cut off all cell phones and pagers on the day of the event. They censored news coverage. They closed the heart of Beijing many times on a few hours' warning so that the military could rehearse. Millions of migrants were rounded up and sent back to their home provinces, and billions of dollars were spent. The country was shut down for a week with just about a week's notice, and the capital was put under martial law. Party members can do all those things in a Maoist state, yet the one thing they cannot do is exercise restraint.

Restraint, however, is the essence of modern governance. A government's self-control permits its people to create, explore, and discover, and that's what allows a nation to progress. In China, however, cadres restrain rather than let go because they're insecure. The biggest birthday bash of the twentieth century was a spectacle not to be forgotten: eleven thousand soldiers and half a million participants on the fiftieth anniversary in Beijing. But there was almost no audience! Hotel guests ejected from rooms overlooking the route for security reasons were given seats for the parade and Party luminaries, of course, had honored spots in Tiananmen Square, but they were the only ones who saw the spectacle live. The people of the People's Republic were not welcome. They watched it, if they watched it at all, on television. "In China it is the leaders who are the centre of everything but abroad we saw ordinary people celebrating," said Zhang Ling, a driver in Beijing, commenting on millennium events around the world. Party members could script the fiftieth anniversary parade down to the last goose step, but they could not duplicate the spontaneity or joy of earlier celebrations in their country. The truth is that the rulers are simply afraid of the ruled.

And their fear is evident when the country mourns. It was February 1997, and Deng Xiaoping had just died after lingering for so long. A single person carried a wreath toward the Martyrs' Monument in Tiananmen Square before twenty to thirty plainclothesmen rushed him into a car. The people were not permitted to mourn in the Chinese capital, or anywhere else in China, except under tight police guard, for there was a nationwide ban on unsupervised expressions of grief. It is in times like these, when great men die, that the Chinese respect the dead and show their anger at those who remain. And the leaders who remained took no chances in 1997, but they should have known that the Chinese would not be denied on such an important occasion. Tens of thousands of mourners spilled into the streets for spontaneous vigils in Deng's home province of Sichuan and other places around China in the days following his death. They even turned a Deng billboard in Shenzhen into a shrine of sorts. It is now the third anniversary of his passing, February 2000, and the Party is reminding the Chinese not to commemorate dead leaders. After all this time the state still feels threatened.

So they're not allowed to celebrate and they're not supposed to mourn, but when the Chinese want to protest, they somehow find a way. They came to show their indignation over centuries of humiliation, and Beijing's leaders had no choice about it. In May 1999, they had to acquiesce and lend their support to protests against the bombing of China's embassy in Belgrade by NATO warplanes. Chinese policemen guarding the American diplomatic compounds in Beijing during the first two days of disturbances came in uniforms for directing traffic, and they were overwhelmed by demonstrators. Only in the later days did they have their riot gear. The emotions poured out, and even a government that is used to scripting events was unprepared for the sentiments of its own people.

A year later, May 2000, and central government officials want no demonstrations on the first anniversary of the bombing. They prevail as students obey and stay on their campuses. Yet success is measured only in weeks this time, because all is not quiet on Beijing's northern front, where China's great universities are located. A mere two weeks after the bombing's anniversary, students in the thousands protest against Beijing University and, indirectly, the Party. Qiu Qingfeng, a first-year student, has been raped and murdered, and the students are angered by their school's suppression of the news, an action apparently taken under instructions from the Party, which has a need to control information of any kind. Word of other campus murders has been suppressed in the past, but this time notice is spread by a bulletin board on the Web, which is subsequently closed down by authorities. Word of mouth and online chat rooms take over, however, and soon everyone knows about their "fallen classmate." At the same time, students put up prodemocracy posters as anger over just about everything erupts. Almost any excuse brings protesters out as frustration simmers. The central government cannot prevent displays of anger and defiance; it can only delay their occurrence. Students, like others in this large land, are seething. They're just waiting for the next opportunity to show how they feel.

The Chinese harbor grievances, but most are still intimidated by their government. So when they protest, they often direct their anger away from the one-party state, which is, in reality, their target. "It could have gone either way," commented Caroline Cooper, an observer of the demonstration. This time the regime was lucky, and young Qiu Qing-feng's classmates did not march on Tiananmen Square. Yet they mourned for her and showed their disrespect for Beijing University, a proxy of their government. The protests sparked by the death of the nineteen-year-old government and administration student occurred just before the eleventh anniversary of the Tiananmen massacre. Beijing University, the place from where the 1989 demonstrations had drawn so much strength, was quiet during the evening as June 3 became June 4 of 2000. Students quietly talked about the past among themselves, but some aired their views more publicly. On that night from the campus you could hear recordings of "Nothing to My Name," the anthem of the spring of 1989 by Cui Jian, China's first, and still most famous, rock star, playing from students' rooms. That's the most protest the state will allow when the subject is as sensitive as Tiananmen.

In its weakened state, the state is intransigent. Today, the regime no longer knows how to speak; it can only shout. And it shouts with conviction, Sharon Narrod thinks, but it's really too early in the morning for this. The uniformed policeman is screaming at Ms. Narrod, a middle-aged teacher from the Chicago suburb of Highland Park. She has no idea what he could possibly be saying—she understands only English and Spanish. The high school band of seventy-eight performers, all dressed in their blue-and-white jackets, and a dozen adult chaperones are as bewildered as she is. There is no mistaking the policeman's mood, however. He is deadly serious about something.

Is this how the modern Chinese state treats its tourists? Narrod and her group just had their picture taken in Tiananmen Square with their high school banner. The group is enjoying a day off from their one-week concert tour of Beijing and Shanghai. Narrod cannot figure out what on earth can be the matter as they sightsee in the center of the Chinese capital.

The local tour guide has a better idea of what's going on, however. He says that they have to take away the banner immediately because it is not allowed. The kids, not used to following orders blindly, want to know why. The adults, having a better grasp of how security forces in a police state think, tell the students to just comply. The banner is put away on this day in March 2000, so no one from Michael Jordan's hometown is detained, but it is a tense moment for Narrod and her group. Who knows why the banner is *verboten,* but the Falun Gong uses banners in its protests and maybe that's the reason. Why is the apparently invincible state so sensitive unless it feels its existence is at stake?

There is no tolerance of dissent these days—at least dissent that is political, religious, or ethnic. Workers and peasants are sometimes allowed to voice their discontent, but that's because the regime can no longer compel their silence. And as the government stiffens in its distress, its weakness becomes evident. The regime can outnumber its enemies now, as the sole mourner for Deng Xiaoping in Tiananmen learned, but what happens when the mourners, or protesters, become too many? And in its zeal to suppress its perceived enemies, it has forgotten how to understand. How can the Highland Park High School Band be perceived as a threat to any nation, especially one as powerful as the People's Republic? Maybe because regimes in decline don't think anymore, they just react.

And they are taken by surprise. The Chinese government is not blind, but often it does not see. In April 1999, senior Party leaders could not believe that any group could, or would, surround their leadership compound of Zhongnanhai, the heart of Communist power in the center of Beijing. The Falun Gong was banned in July of that year as a threat to all of society. Throughout Chinese history strange religious cults have raised armies and endangered imperial power. The Falun Gong commands no divisions, at least none that are armed. Yet it threatens the state in a much more insidious way.

Falun Gong believers are fortified by faith and, unlike most Chinese, are not intimidated by their government. So they hurl themselves against the state, and when it seems as if there could be no more of them, others step forth to protest. The crime of the Falun Gong is not its defiance, although that is in itself a sin from Beijing's point of view. Its true offense is providing inspiration to elements more dangerous to the state. Regimes collapse when people are no longer afraid and think they're no longer alone. Those opposed to the seemingly invincible state are either crushed or remembered. Today we do not know what the fate of the Falun Gong will be, but as the protests continue, the risk for the Party grows. The open defiance of the weak, such as Falun Gong practitioners, can only encourage the actions of the stronger elements of society, who have grievances of their own.

Of course it didn't have to be this way. The Falun Gong's first protest was not the famous incident at Zhongnanhai. If provincial cadres had dealt with the group's minor complaints earlier on, we would not know the name of the sect today. China's regime can build the world's largest radio telescope to listen to the stars, but it cannot hear its own people. The Party has lost so many political skills during its monopoly on power, and now it does not know how to prevail except by intransigence and force. When it uses its force, it often creates new enemies for tomorrow—all the sects and faiths that refuse to accept the meddling of the state, for instance. Today it is clear that the Party's tactics are not working, and Jiang Zemin himself reveals that when he says that the Falun Gong poses a threat like Poland's Solidarity. That assessment seems preposterous, but it reveals that China's leaders have lost their balance. How can they prevail when they no longer understand the people they rule?

Maybe they don't understand because they've failed to confront their past and so can no longer deal with the world as it actually is. It wasn't always this way. "Speaking of our failures, there have really been some," admitted Deng Xiaoping in 1989, as he discussed the Party's shortcomings in general after the Tiananmen massacre. He knew that even China's most powerful political organization would have to examine its past before it could move forward again. Such candor is rarely evident in today's leadership, and that, of course, is the root of the problem. The regime has become haunted because evidence of its history is everywhere.

I WILL SEE MY MOTHER! says a photo caption on the front page of *China Daily* in February 2000. Rural families surrounding the eastern city of Nanjing could not feed their children and had to abandon them in desperation in 1959–61 during "severe drought and famine." Some of the children were exchanged for grain coupons, others were just left in the streets. To this day, a few of the children do not know their real names. Many infants, by order of the Party, were allowed to die where they had been abandoned, but those who were saved were sent north to foster families in Hebei Province, which surrounds Beijing. Now, on Valentine's Day, a roundish woman in peasant clothing arrives in Nanjing with a baby strapped to her back, and soon she will see her mother for the first time in four decades. The joyous smile across her chubby face warms us. What China's official newspaper does not say, however, is that the suffering during that period was directly the result of the Party's utter disregard for human life as its cadres could not report bad news. Peasants starved and died in their fields, but the Party claimed record harvests and taxed them accordingly. That was the Great Leap Forward, a man-made disaster of epic proportions—not a capricious act of nature, as *China Daily* would have us believe. Tens of millions died during that time as the cadres just watched. The Party could not face reality then, and today little has changed in this regard.

It is about one month after the happy woman arrived in Nanjing. Journalists in Hebei are helping to reunite other abandoned children with their families through a newspaper column serving as a bulletin board. Some return south to Nanjing, looking for their relatives. They post notices in a hotel near a temple where some were left by their desperate parents so long ago. They seek nothing but their elder relatives and a part of their past. The Party has come to feel threatened by the reunions, however. The journalists are told by cadres in Hebei that their efforts are criminal. The Civil Affairs Department in Nanjing declares the returned orphans to be an illegal organization that disturbs public order. The Party cannot tolerate even a whisper that reminds people of that period, a half lifetime ago.

It is March 2000, and at the same time as the Party is criminalizing the journalists and the orphans in Hebei and Nanjing, the pope is apologizing to the world and asking for the forgiveness of his institution's sins. If the Catholic Church, another organization dominated by a strong ideology and a sense of its own righteousness, can apologize for twenty centuries of mistakes, why can't the Communist Party do the same for its five decades?

Or maybe those of just one night in 1989 when the People's Liberation Army cleared Tiananmen Square of protesters? And if apologizing for one incident is too difficult, how about a period further back in time, the decade of the Cultural Revolution? Chinese leaders of today can—and do—condemn Mao's campaign of chaos, now a quarter century old, yet they do not allow this time to be studied. American academic Song Yongyi was imprisoned in 1999 for buying publicly available materials from that period. His offense, apparently, was studying the late Premier

Zhou Enlai, thereby endangering his beloved memory. "The whole party made mistakes; they now want to forget about that," he said after his release. Yes, there is much to forget in the past half century, "a parade of rubbish bins that we cannot open," says author and activist Dai Qing. In fact, most of the country's history is off limits to the people of the country.

"Facts do not cease to exist because they are ignored," said Aldous Huxley. The Party can suppress its past, but the people, of course, remember it. In China the sorrow and the tragedy never really go away. And neither do the fear and distrust, passed down from one generation to the next. An actress in her late fifties is playing the role of a great-grandmother in a family of five generations living in one household. She is in Suzhou, in Jiangsu Province, filming a television commercial in early 2000. The director is having a problem with one of the great-grandchildren, who insists, despite persistent prompting, on looking directly into the camera. It has been a long afternoon for the crew, and tempers are a bit short. Finally, great-grandmother takes the toddler aside and says, "Don't look into the camera, these are the Gong An shooting your picture," pointing to the crew and referring to the police. "If you look at them, they will recognize you and then come and get you." That's not too likely, considering that the cameraman is a burly Australian and the crew largely foreign, but that actress acts out the fear that so typically marks those who lived through Mao's decade of upheaval, the Cultural Revolution.

Across China the attitudes of the old are taught to the young as they were on location that day in Suzhou. The state can imprison Song Yongyi and protect its past, but it cannot then win back its people. "Chinese citizens will tell you when they're not on camera that they know of the tragedies of the last fifty years, and many of them are quite cynical about them," says Robert Kapp. Suppression, of course, means that the young are not told the truth about the incidents of the past. Yet when they find out, as they eventually do in this tuned-in, interconnected, and gossipy world, they become, as Kapp mentions, cynical about the regime. Chen Jinzhi is a young, attractive tourist guide at the Stone Forest outside the southwestern city of Kunming. She points to one of the gray limestone pillars in the forest and mentions that a particular inscription about the establishment of this park was defaced during the Cultural Revolution, which ended a year before she was born. "The textbook says it was a mistake of certain individuals using the names of the leaders," she says, referring to what her school taught her about that chaotic period. "But of course that is not the truth." So China lies to its young and compromises its future for failing to acknowledge the past.

And there's another lie that is being told to China's youths. "From our first class in elementary school all through high school we had political study all the time," said Cui Jian, the Chinese rock star, whose songs are a symbol of rebellion in the People's Republic. "The subject was always communism. Our brains were flooded red." That's still true, of course, and is more of a mistake than ever, as experience has conclusively proved that socialism does not work. But that's not the way Beijing's leaders see things. "The Chinese people are convinced socialism can save China," says Jiang Zemin. The senior leaders, by continuing to extol the virtues of outdated ideology, show just how rigid the People's Republic has become. Most of the world thinks China is modern, but that assessment is a mistake.

Forget about "the superior socialist system" and political study. Only realism can save China. And the truth. "The wind may blow from the east, south, west, or north, yet we must take a firm grip on truth and never lose it," says Defense Minister Chi Haotian, who once assured us that not a single protester had died in Tiananmen Square. Senior Communist Party leaders believe they know the truth, which is invariably delivered with the conviction of those who are sure that triumph is inevitable. "China today is enjoying political stability, economic prosperity, social progress, and ethnic unity," says Premier Zhu Rongji in his address at Jing Ulrich's CLSA Forum in May 2000. "And its people, in high spirit and morale, are full of vigor and dynamism."

The truth, if Zhu Rongji would hear it, is that the Chinese care little for the modern Chinese state that rules them. For the most part they are not permitted to say a cross word out loud, and as a result, few dare. But people eventually find a way to manifest dissent in an authoritarian society. Sometimes you just have to skip the lyrics, as the father of rock in China tells us. "The message delivered by the music provides us with a lot of space that allows us to think," says Cui Jian. And some register dissent in ways not so subtle by taking matters into their own hands. About 44 percent of the world's suicides take place in China. That's just a reflection of what has become known as "the death of the spirit." "The children can decide, but I don't believe in anything anymore," says fortysomething Xu Chang, who typifies the feelings of his generation. He's been a banker in Shanghai and now works for a pharmaceutical company in Beijing, but the defining moment of his life was spent in the countryside building the New China during the Cultural Revolution. Today he doesn't care about his daughters' religious upbringing even though they are the most important thing in his life. "I believed in Mao, and he failed me," he says. "I cannot believe in another god."

Many Chinese don't believe in Mao; others don't believe in his successors either. And just a few are direct, making it clear where they stand. "You foreigners have no idea how we Chinese detest this society!" says a taxi driver in Beijing, who has just been shaken down by a traffic policeman. The Chinese seethe, for the Party's cadres visit misery upon them. "Our society is thoroughly rotten," says a father whose son's life was destroyed after he was wrongly imprisoned for disagreeing with his boss. So many have lost their faith due simply to the capriciousness and arbitrariness of officials. Most people know that Communist Party cadres have too much power, and many have no hope that society can be changed as long as the one-party state remains. And that's why more and more Chinese want political reform.

"Taiwan can elect its own leaders—pretty cool," noted a message posted on a Mainland Web site a few days after Taiwan's presidential election in March 2000. Jing Xiuhu, a peasant in inland Shaanxi Province, is more direct: "We want democracy." And Jiang Zemin understands. During his visit to New York in September 2000, the leader of the world's largest dictatorship said, "The Chinese people love democracy and freedom." And because they do, the Party responds by sponsoring village elections. But where sentiment is hostile, the peasants are not allowed to put up their own candidates, such as in Jing Xiuhu's Zizhou County, or even to have elections at all. "Nothing has changed here after the Communists came," says Jing with anger. "The revolution just benefits corrupt leaders."

It also impoverishes the rural poor. In Zizhou the peasants would starve were it not for the handouts of food from their rich neighbors; in 1999, their average annual net income per person was just over US$1. The state provides little to the peasants, yet taxes go up because the Party has spiraling revenue needs in the countryside. The number of rural cadres is increasing to carry out all of Beijing's new campaigns, in favor of family planning one year and against underground Christian churches the next. So in many agricultural areas across China overtaxed peasants are disobeying the Party and threatening its rule, especially when the poor know that their taxes go directly into the pockets of rich officials. Often the cadres withdraw rather than try to govern. "In the past few years, our grassroots organizations have been weak," admitted one county official. "Cadres dare not take action, and they have spoiled the farmers." Spoiled farmers, some twenty thousand of them, rioted against oppressive taxation and corruption in August 2000 near Fengcheng in an area just south of the Jiangxi provincial capital of Nanchang. The disturbances spread from town to town as long-standing grievances ignited. Peasants tore down the houses of corrupt cadres, just as those officials had earlier demolished the homes of peasants who couldn't pay their unjust taxes. And armed with only farm tools, they fought armed police for days.

Jing and his fellow peasants in Zizhou, no longer intimidated by the awesome power of the Chinese state, want the Party to leave. In 1995, cadres in the area began increasing taxation to unbearable levels, and the peasants eventually sought the assistance of the courts. They were turned away, however, and their advocate was beaten and jailed: "Local leaders told us 'Jiang Zemin is corrupt too. All the leaders are corrupt so who are you trying to fight against?' " A group of peasants took matters into their own hands in early 1998, when they detained, for almost a week, a minor official sent to placate them. The Party had only one response to that incident: another cycle of arrests and beatings and jailings.

"The Government keeps talking about development," notes a village Party boss in Sichuan Province. "But the farmers are getting poorer and poorer." In fact, 2000 marked the end of a seven-year campaign to wipe out poverty in the countryside. That goal was achieved before the deadline, at least according to the Party, but this claim would be comical were it not for the continued suffering of the peasantry. Poverty is getting worse, not better, in many parts of China, the World Bank concludes, and there are still 106 million rural poor. So it is no surprise that peasants, angry and desperate, are beginning to band together. "We can only be strong after we unite ourselves," says Zhao Sunan, who organized about twenty-two hundred families in Sichuan Province's Hebian township to sue local Party cadres for collecting illegal taxes. She and her husband were beaten by local officials, and they had to flee their home. She hasn't given up, however. "I am fighting for the right to eat, and I will keep on fighting," she says in Beijing, where she has gone for the fourth time to seek redress from the central government. Central government leaders, in response to increasing rural unrest in 2000, have started to talk about relieving burdens on the peasants, but those in the countryside have heard all these words before.

There's not much high Party officials can actually do until they take back control of the countryside from their own local cadres, who are the source of the instability. And who often call the tune. Perhaps as many as sixty young children and their teachers died when their two-story schoolhouse was demolished in an explosion in March 2001. Parents in the rural village of Fanglin in southern Jiangxi Province complained to local officials for years because students, some of them just eight years old, were forced to make fireworks on the first floor of the school. After the explosion local officials could not admit what had happened, so they said that a mentally ill villager carried firecrackers into the schoolhouse in his pockets and set them off. Premier Zhu Rongji repeated the officials' fabrication on national television. We do not know whether the premier believed the obvious lie or not, but now it's clear that the organization chart has been turned on its head as national leaders are captive to the local ones. Beijing, however, must gather its wits soon, otherwise grieving parents and other peasants will revolt, as they have throughout Chinese history. "If I could, I would shoot all the officials, from the top to the bottom," says Zhu Li, a peasant in Qipan in central Hubei Province. "They are eating our flesh, drinking our blood." And killing their children. As the village Party boss from Sichuan concludes, "The countryside is pretty unstable nowadays."

So the new millennium will look like the old one for China's peasants unless something changes, and that's why Jing Xiuhu and his 900 million colleagues in the countryside are stirring. The Ministry of Public Security says that there were about sixty thousand protests in China in 1998 and about one hundred thousand in 1999. Those figures sound correct from all that is known, but there is no way to verify their accuracy. One thing is clear, however: incidents of disobedience from one end of China to another are on the rise. In the words of one academic in Beijing, today's widespread unrest in the countryside is "the sign of the end of a dynasty." The present dynasty will end when the Party's harsh response to disturbances creates even more enemies, as it already has in Zizhou, Hebian, and Qipan. If the regime is to last, it must come to a new understanding with the people, who are already seizing the initiative from a political party that today can only react. Mao Zedong himself would have realized that the Communist Party has become weak. "All reactionaries are paper tigers," he said. And Mao said something else: repression breeds revolution. "[T]he Chinese," he told us, "never submit to tyrannical rule but invariably use revolutionary means to overthrow or change it."

Current Communist leaders have learned all the wrong lessons from the country's turbulent history. "Historical experience has told us that nothing can be accomplished without stability," says Zhu Rongji. But in their current obsessive pursuit of social order Party members do not listen, and they suppress change that must someday occur. That is why the soldiers marched on 1999's National Day. "They want people to see their power," says one member of the Communist Party in Beijing. "It is that simple." "Very remote villages, desperately poor, dirt poor, are going to see this colorful splash of fireworks, big tanks, roses, magnolias, greenery, and the question they must ask is 'When is it going to trickle down to me?' " Lee Kuan Yew, referring to the 1999 National Day celebrations, tells us that showing off the power of the state has its own risks. "So, the mass media has its pluses, it brings the country together, but it also enables the less advanced parts of China to see how backward they are and to say 'Look, when is my turn?' " Jing Xiuhu wants his turn, of course, but in the meantime he and several hundred thousand peasants in Shaanxi Province simmer as they struggle against corrupt and brutal local cadres. And they do not appear especially impressed by the armed might of the Party. The "great wall of steel," the People's Liberation Army, defends the state against the peasants in Zizhou and all the other peoples of China. But what use is steel when the enemy is an idea? Steel wins the skirmishes, but ultimately it must lose when too many share a thought.

CHINA IS AN UNSTOPPABLE FORCE, says a headline in *China Daily*. No, that is not true. It is the *Chinese people* who are unstoppable. When Deng Xiaoping decided, after Tiananmen, that the Party would have to loosen the mechanisms of social control further, the initiative of the Chinese propelled them forward. The Party, by retreating, gained a few more years of rule at the expense of its long-term future. One day—and that day is not far off—the Party will not be able to control all the people as they make their dash toward tomorrow. The students who surrendered the square on the morning of June 4 could not begin to imagine, in those sad days of 1989, that their ideas would eventually prevail. They set into motion a chain of events that will one day lead to a free and prosperous China, one better than they could, at that time, imagine—perhaps one better than we can imagine today.

To get there, the Chinese people will have to remake their country yet again. The beginning of a new era is the best time to begin, as Reverend Billy Graham suggests. What does "millennium" mean to him? "It means that we have a chance to start some things over again or that we have to start new again," he says. The evangelist's message of renewal is good advice for us all and especially pertinent for a government that believes it's entitled to exist forever.

But the man who leads it has no second thoughts at this special moment in history; in fact, he uses the occasion to reaffirm the past. Seconds after midnight in the first moments of 2000, Jiang Zemin lights Beijing's eternal flame at the China Century Monument. It's the Holy Fire of the Chinese Nation, and it's not supposed to go out. The Communist Party is celebrating five millennia of Chinese history and looking forward to countless more. And at a time when the president could reflect on all that has happened and all that could, he instead speaks of socialism, repeating the same formalized phrases we have heard so many times before.

Only a few miles away from where the leader of the greatest Communist nation on Earth is celebrating, the cadres show that nothing has changed for China's peasants. Party officials are busy helping developers build expatriate housing for all the foreigners who are expected to move to Beijing after China's accession to the World Trade Organization. And the peasants are upset as their land is confiscated. "I'm angry," says a farm woman whose expression reveals more despair than ire. "I used to have farmland. Now I have none." Real estate developers and village officials care nothing for the peasants. "We got no money when they occupied a whole field over there," says a farmer with a straw hat like the type Chico Marx wore. The man is not amusing, however, as he reflects on what has happened. "Our opinions mean nothing," he says bitterly. So the emotions boiled over and villagers who lost their land trashed the clubhouse of a nearby development for foreign families and broke windows in several homes.

The People's Republic looks modern now, with all its new monuments to itself and high-priced new developments for foreigners. It appears more advanced, but will it peacefully evolve to a better society, as we all hope? No, that looks unlikely. China is, in the words of Jonathan Mann of CNN, only just "cosmetically improved." He's right because the essence of Mao's system has changed little over more than two decades of apparent progress. In spite of all the reform since 1978, the cadres still manage to do whatever they want. They continue to believe that their destiny is to lead and still act as if their word were law. They care little for the peasants and the poor, the reason for their revolution in the first place. They say many fine things and build wonderful facades, but often that is the extent of the change. They will make their system appear more up to date, but they won't really change it. And the Party's leaders are still seeking to restrain the people they rule as if the people have an obligation to accept them for all time.

The Chinese today don't believe they have that obligation; they accept the current leaders because they have to. The Party is unpopular but powerful, having built a police state and maintained it for more than five decades. But the people are in motion now, and one day they will want to govern themselves. That is their destiny, despite what Communist Party cadres may think. Observes an American once resident in China, "There's a billion people who don't like following instructions." But there's a government that still insists on issuing them. The people and their government will clash again someday. That's inevitable. For China's one-party state to evolve instead of collapse, it will not only have to change, but it will also have to do so before the people push it aside.

Today, however, there is no consensus in the nation's leadership to undertake fundamental political reform. There is a recognition that small adjustments need to be made, but here too improvement is often more apparent than real and the pace is excruciatingly slow. Unfortunately, the Communist Party believes that the lesson from Taiwan's election in 2000 is that real change must be blocked and absolutely no competition permitted. The cadres still think that they can improve themselves without anyone else's help, but history shows us that their notion is just fantasy. The price the Party pays to maintain its notion of eternal destiny is a loss of realism—no organization, not even one as mighty as the glorious Communist Party of China, can rule for all time.

And there is little realism in the economic realm as well. In 1989, the Party understood that it would have to improve the day-to-day lives of the Chinese people. So it experimented and embraced real change. But those exciting days of flexibility are over. Today the Chinese leadership won't disturb their fundamental ideological precepts and clever theoretical constructs. They may talk about their "socialism with Chinese characteristics," but it is socialism nonetheless. And the government insists on retaining control and ownership of major segments of the economy, making much change impossible. The technocrats still make all their five-year plans as if regimentation were essential to progress.

The leaders speak so loudly of what they have accomplished, and now, believing all that they have told us, have opted for membership in the World Trade Organization. They're unprepared for unforgiving globalization, that's for sure, but they press ahead anyway. It will be just like the Great Leap Forward—disaster brought on by self-deception. As in the Mao era, the leaders today are not self-aware. In the Great Leap, provincial cadres faked grain statistics, and tens of millions of people died. Today the cadres fabricate industrial output numbers, and soon their economy will collapse.

At a time when China needs realism, Jiang Zemin delivers politics. He has fallen back on ideological campaigns, hoping that repetition of Marxist theory will somehow corral the flock. "This is the reaction of leaders who have been sending out orders and directives and finding that everyone is ignoring them," says one longtime foreign resident of China. Jiang's devotion to Marxism shows just a bit of delusion or desperation and tells us that his idea of change is fortifying the defenses.

Senior leaders can resist calls for change, but they should know what will happen next. Any government will fall when its institutions solidify. When they stiffen instead of bend, collapse is near. That's the model for Communist regimes and Chinese ones as well. They don't depart gracefully when they're no longer wanted; they stay until they're pushed. The Chinese leaders of today have only to look at yesterday to see their tomorrow. "Society moved on, and the Party stayed where it was," Alexan-

der Rutskoi, deputy of the Russian Parliament, said, referring to the Soviet Communist Party. And when that happened, the end was inevitable.
"He was trying to dam a river that was in full flood, but the current was
too strong," said Alexander Yakovlev, referring to Mikhail Gorbachev,
the man he served as an aide. "It broke the dam and flooded everything in
its path." Although the parallels between the Soviet Union and China are
not exact, of course, the essentials are the same. The Marxist-Leninist
concepts that gave birth to both republics cannot be reformed; Gorbachev's effort to restructure Soviet society showed us that. The party of
Jiang Zemin, which tries a different route to rejuvenation, will also be
swept away as it too will not, or cannot, bring about the change that has
to occur.

Maybe that's why Jiang Zemin asks, "What legacy do you want to
leave when you are no longer around?" China's schoolchildren can tell us
what his answer is. "Chairman Mao founded China, Deng Xiaoping made
us rich and now Jiang Zemin is leading us into the future," according to
Li Jia, twelve years of age. She's learned her lessons well, yet none of
what she has been taught is true: China existed before Mao, the Chinese
are still not rich, and the Party, if it is going anywhere, is headed for the
past. Jiang Zemin's legacy and that of his predecessors is a squandered
half century. "Forty years later looking back I feel very sad," said Wang
Ruoshui, former deputy editor in chief of *People's Daily,* as he thought
about the People's Republic just after Tiananmen. "I have such an intense
sense of loss. Where is the goal we've been striving for all these years?"
Wang wanted freedom and democracy for his people, and now, more
than a decade later, the Chinese still have neither.

After all those years, China is still backward and poor and its government harsh and oppressive. That's because officials are still responsible to their superiors, not to the people below. So in many ways not
much has changed since the fall of the Qing Dynasty. "The revolution has
not yet succeeded," wrote the founder of modern China, Sun Yat-sen, in
his will. "Comrades, you must carry on." And as the Chinese do so, their
current government trembles. "Communism went against life, against
man's fundamental needs, against the need for freedom, the need to be
enterprising, to associate freely against the will of the nation," Václav
Havel noted. "Something that goes against life may last a long time, but
sooner or later it will collapse."

In the meantime, the cadres should also remember the words of the man whose system they inherited. "The big will be overthrown by the small," Mao Zedong once said. As a matter of fact, he showed how that could be done. Someday the small people will challenge the big state, for over time it has become weak. Today the cadres can rule because few people openly oppose them. Yet just a handful of angry protesters can topple the system because it won't take much for them to prevail. The people only tolerate their government these days; few actively defend it. The Chinese have seen too much of what is wrong in today's China—and how so little has changed.

You can see for yourself what the Chinese see, and it's visible even in the country's backwaters, such as Rugao, that dusty city in eastern Jiangsu Province. Start by looking at the main street—it's the only road wide enough for a power line, which runs down one side carrying electricity to this community in decline. On the other, at a corner of one of the two main intersections, is the grandest building in town, the offices of the city government, set off from the rest of the city by a high fence, a grand lawn, and guards. And on the other side of the city government's majestic compound is the street that has no name—none that the residents know of, anyway.

By day you don't notice them. They are lost in the sea of small storefronts and are hard to spot on the nameless street. At night you can see all of them at once. Bathed in shocking pink light, these shops are about the only thing you can see when the sun goes down and the street darkens. They are made up to look like beauty salons, but no one goes there for a perm. The sliding doors are open, even in the winter's cold, so that you can see inside for yourself. The young girls lounge around with little to do but chat and brush their hair when they are not at work. The signs, visible from the street, advertise the home provinces of the workers, just in case your preferences are geographical. Some of the establishments are within sight of the city offices, and they are all within a ten-minute walk of the seat of government in this poor but sprawling town.

His name, when romanized according to Mainland ways, would be Zhang Jiachen, and what he sees must pain him for he professes not to notice. The pink-light shops are almost as blatant as anything in Amsterdam and more than those in the sordid cities of south China. Zhang has walked this street in his blue Mao suit and cap almost every day after he left his ancestral farm not far outside the city center. Neither he nor his wife, a pleasant woman, will acknowledge what is obviously strange about these establishments. The sign in front of the city's grand compound says something about serving the people, but that is just Party talk. As the sun sets, the pink-light shops come into view and suggest why, when the time comes, the people of Rugao will not stand up and defend the local government from its enemies. Corruption infests their city, and they are ashamed of New China, which to them looks like the old one. The residents will tell you they don't see the pink-light shops, but we all know they do.

12

Roads to Ruin

How the State Will Fall

I am emperor, my descendants will be numerous. From the second generation to the ten thousandth, my line will not end.

—QIN SHIHUANGDI

FROM THE THIRD tallest building in the world, my father looks down over Pudong. A thousand floodlights illuminate the shiny buildings of New China, and the reflections off their glass surfaces streak skyward into another magnificent Shanghai night. A million headlights on the boulevards tell him that even at this late hour, the city is going full tilt. "Foreigners must be surprised and jealous when they see this," he remarks. It is the first time I have heard him praise the People's Republic.

He lives in New Jersey and is American now, but tonight, in September 2000, my father especially feels the pull of his homeland. He was raised just on the other side of the Yangtze River and went to Shanghai's Jiao Tong University. But he left China before the end of the Second World War, and I grew up hearing him say that Mao Zedong's regime would have to fall. He doesn't speak those words this evening because the country he sees on this short visit is apparently thriving.

"What will tomorrow bring?" asks the advertisement for aerospace giant Boeing. My father thinks that the Mainland's future now looks bright. Some of us, however, are not so sure. For the Chinese in China, there is an urgency about finding the answer. Their country stands at so many thresholds, and in a land where there are at least a "million truths" the future is hard to find.

Wang Chuanning thinks about tomorrow and what it may bring. This temporary resident of New York City needs to know; he may be going back to China soon. Whether his future is in the United States or China is not up to him. Some official in Beijing will decide that for him. In the meantime, he and his young family live in one room in lower Manhattan.

The apartment in the Big Apple may be crowded, but life has never been better for the Wangs. At least they are all together now and free to do what they want day to day. Wang Chuanning was sent to California by a Chinese state-owned trading company, China North Industries, in the early 1990s. He had to leave his wife, Yang Yuping, and son, Jason, behind at first, to ensure that he would return to Beijing whenever required. He initially lived in Bellflower, a run-down community in the southern portion of Los Angeles County. Wang never got to know his neighbors. He lived in a gated compound of condominiums bought by China North for its employees, a colony of college-educated Chinese in suits set apart from a working-class neighborhood. Yuping and Jason were finally allowed to follow and arrived in time for Christmas 1996. Jason could not utter a word of English then. Today he speaks that language as if he had lived in the United States from birth and tries to teach his father "to sound like an American." Jason doesn't want to learn more Chinese and resists his mother's efforts to teach him. He dresses in baggy clothes like any other preteen kid and prefers french fries to fried rice. Only his face tells you that he might have been born elsewhere.

If ordered home, patriotic Wang Chuanning will leave New York with his family, even though he has seen the hard edges of modern China and prefers life in America. Following orders from Beijing is what he has to do. He is going to graduate school in New York, just as my father did a half century ago. Wang thinks about continuing his education, for that will allow him to get another visa to extend his stay in a place that's good for his family. That would be just fine with Jason, who does not share his father's ambivalence. The boy knows what he wants, and that is to be with his friends. He's an American now; life in China for him would be hard. Jason might just get his wish because his parents are concerned about all that's happening in China. So what's in store should Wang and his family return to Beijing?

My father was right a long time ago when he predicted that the People's Republic would fall. Despite all the glitter he sees today, the modern Chinese state will not evolve much more. Old and brittle, it will break someday, and that could be soon as the country passes through a critical period. Beginning in 2002 and continuing the following year, power will change hands both in Communist Party senior circles and at the apex of the central government. In the lingo in vogue in today's Beijing, the "Fourth Generation" of leaders will soon take over from the Third.

At the Sixteenth Party Congress in late 2002, the changes will be unprecedented. About 60 percent of the Central Committee, the large body that runs the Party, will retire. Closer to the top, more than half of the twenty-two member Politburo will leave as well. In all, five of the seven members of the Politburo Standing Committee, the most powerful ruling body in the Party and the country, will be replaced. Change will not stop there, however. Slated for retirement are Li Peng and Zhu Rongji, respectively the second- and third-ranked leaders. Finally, the most important job in China will probably see a new holder. According to today's script, Jiang Zemin will relinquish his post as Party general secretary. Jiang has indicated that he wants to stay on as chairman of the Party's Central Military Commission, which oversees the People's Liberation Army. Deng Xiaoping ran the Party and the government as vice chairman of the commission, and Jiang Zemin wants to emulate his predecessor. Yet Jiang will probably have to fight to retain the chairman's post. He is powerful now, but his continued tenure would be unpopular in senior Party councils.

The changes in the Party will be mirrored by changes in the central government. Early 2003 will see all three top government officials of today leaving their posts. There will be a new president, premier, and chairman of the National People's Congress as Jiang Zemin, Zhu Rongji, and Li Peng retire.

When power changes hands, as it will in 2002 and 2003, anything can happen. "No communist country has solved the problem of succession," said Henry Kissinger. And that's true of the People's Republic, where ambition, not law, governs the transfer of power. Recent power struggles have not been as brutish as those of Maoist times, but their fundamental characteristics have not changed. Who knows how far ambitious men will go as they seek to replace Jiang Zemin? Or what Jiang himself might do to remain in power? The changes in the Party and the central government are partially scripted now, but future events could derail today's understandings. Even if everything works according to plan, it will take years for all the transitions to be completed as the new leaders consolidate their positions and seek even more power. It took Deng Xiaoping two years to oust Hua Guofeng, Mao Zedong's chosen successor, and Jiang Zemin needed more time than that to consolidate his position as Deng's.

Beijing can make rational choices if it remains united, but, split at the top, it may take the wrong road—or many roads at the same time. Chinese leaders know that and are trying to ensure stability, but no amount of exhortation can curb the ambition of the already powerful. It is during this uncertain period that the People's Republic, facing challenges that would test the sturdiest of societies, will be especially vulnerable.

Despite all the showy displays of unity, the country's leadership is already split. In January of 2001, a Communist Party cadre under the assumed name of Zhang Liang released *The Tiananmen Papers,* a collection of documents describing how the Party arrived at the decision to use force in 1989 against protesters in Beijing. Zhang says he took this extraordinary step to help the forces of political reform among the leadership. "Even though the end of communism in China seems a foregone conclusion," he writes, "the fall of the Chinese Communist Party will be accomplished not by an outside force but only by its own members." China's Foreign Ministry says that the documents are not genuine, but that's besides the point. The mere fact of their release suggests that old divisions among senior cadres have not yet healed. So as China heads to the next transition of power, its leadership is still split from the last one.

Wang Chuanning and his family will witness the last days of the People's Republic should they go back to their homeland during the upcoming period of change. Here are a few examples of what the Wangs might see.

WAR ACROSS THE WATER

Will Jason have to go to war? Conflict with Taiwan makes no sense for China these days, that's for sure, and hostilities are so hard to imagine when we are dazzled by the bright lights of Pudong. Economic development is, we know, at the very top of the Party's agenda. War surely means international isolation and the end of most trade and investment flows across the country's borders. A government whose basis of legitimacy is economic prosperity is not about to send its troops over the water to Taiwan. "When Jiang Zemin wakes up in the morning, his biggest concern is how he feeds 1.2 billion people," says Terrence Barnett, the head of the China operations of Novartis, the Swiss pharmaceutical giant. Jiang can barely take care of all those souls now. He can feed them or he can go to war, but he cannot do both.

In any event, the Mainland cannot win a conflict with Taiwan, at least by conventional force. China needs years before it can launch a successful invasion across the broad Taiwan Strait. The People's Liberation Army today cannot establish superiority either in the air or on or below the surface of the sea, even with its new Russian-built planes, destroyers, and submarines. Before the first ships set sail from Mainland ports, the Taiwanese will know they're coming. Taiwan's pilots will grab control of the air and then strafe and bomb the ragtag Mainland flotilla of transports, landing craft, and fishing boats traversing more than a hundred miles of water. Many of the vessels will not survive the crossing. Without reliable resupply, those who make it to shore will not be able to push far beyond their beachheads. Staggering Mainland casualties will vindicate Taiwan's military doctrine of winning the war in the strait before the first soldier can reach the island. In the PLA, loyalty to the Communist Party has always been on a par with military capability. So China's armed forces are politically reliable—but militarily inadequate. Add American intelligence and logistical support for Taiwan into the equation, and an attack by the Mainland would be a debacle. "Gentleness beats fortitude," Chen Shui-bian once said, quoting an ancient Taoist philosopher to explain his cross-strait policy. That may be true, but if the Mainland attacks Chen's Taiwan it will be overwhelming firepower that will permit him to beat back the invasion.

So starting a war would be the gravest miscalculation for the People's

Republic. And if all these factors weren't enough, there is one more reason why the Mainland should be able to avoid a conflict now. Jiang Zemin has always been a relative moderate on the Taiwan question. Although he has recognized the possibility of hostilities, he has tended to shy away from taking actions that would lead to them.

At least until now. "History is littered with the wars which everybody knew would never happen," said British politician Enoch Powell. And in Beijing one can hear words of another such war. It is not important that China lacks planes or ships or guided missiles, Premier Zhu Rongji reminded us as Taiwan went to the polls in March 2000. It is not just a matter of hardware, so China will fight whatever the odds, he argued. "The Chinese people will definitely safeguard the Motherland's reunification and national dignity with their own blood and lives." The premier's statements such as this one are often dismissed as bluff because the Mainland has retreated in the past, but his words are clear however we choose to interpret his intentions.

Even if Zhu is not sincere, we should ask why he speaks this way. Years ago Jiang Zemin, his boss, sought and received the support of the leadership of the PLA to consolidate his once shaky position as Deng Xiaoping's successor. In return the bellicose military got the right to shape, and sometimes determine, policy on Taiwan. That's why twice, in 1996 and 2000, China threatened war. Whoever takes over from Jiang in these upcoming transition years of 2002 and 2003 will also need to seek support from the PLA, a major power base in the Party, and he will be equally beholden to the generals, who will name their own price for allegiance. Mao told us that "political power flows from the barrel of a gun," and this will be no more true than when China changes its leaders.

Today, the Mainland's position is clear: taking steps toward independence and even failing to accept the "one-China principle" can only lead to hostilities. That means Jiang Zemin's successor won't have much room to maneuver. Even a strong leader could have trouble avoiding war, but a weak one indebted to the PLA might have no choice. Even if China's new supremo is not beholden to the People's Liberation Army, he might on his own do anything to hold on to power. When China's economy falters after WTO accession, the Party's only remaining basis of legitimacy will be nationalism. As a consequence, war with Taiwan may be considered the only way to retain power in Beijing. And if the leaders in the Chinese capital think they can win without bloodshed, by imposing a blockade or frightening Taiwan by more missile salvos, for instance, the decision to take action will be especially easy to make.

So any provocation may be enough to begin the next confrontation. Another proindependence comment from the feisty, unpredictable Annette Lu, Taiwan's vice president, could be the trigger. Today Chen Shui-bian seeks to restrain his irrepressible partner in governance, but even he may not be successful. That spells trouble. The Mainland says that TAI-WAN LEADER SHOULD FACE REALITY. Here's the reality: although Lu may speak only for a minority, the "vast majority" of people in Taiwan do not want reunification. "This is a reality," says Chen Shui-bian, "and any leader in a democratic country must respect this majority view of the people." Taiwan's leaders, as a practical matter, cannot give what Beijing demands. A showdown, therefore, looks inevitable. Maybe that's why Mainland general Zhang Wannian predicts hostilities by 2005: "During the period of the 10th Five-Year Plan, war is certain to break out in the Taiwan Strait."

The provocation need not relate to independence, of course. War could start with a simple accident. A pattern of aggressive, even reckless, Mainland aerial tactics resulted in the April 2001 collision with an American spy plane, but the consequences could be greater next time if the incident occurs over the Taiwan Strait. Hot-blooded pilots from the People's Republic regularly test the island's air defenses, and one day they will again go too far. Or the trigger for hostilities could relate to Taiwan's domestic politics. Chen Shui-bian's first year in office has been difficult. If his government should falter, the Mainland may deputize itself to restore order on the island. Even normally uncontroversial events could lead to danger in a highly charged atmosphere. Taiwan has traditionally been a refuge of other societies' unsavory elements. Because of its diplomatic isolation, it does not have an extensive network of extradition treaties, and it certainly has no such arrangement with the Mainland. Let's say a Falun Gong leader, a democracy advocate, or even a common criminal is a fugitive from what the Mainland calls "justice." It's easy to enter Taiwan legally on a passport and a Republic of China Multiple Entry and Exit Permit. Taiwanese authorities, especially during one of their many travel promotions, issue these permits in Hong Kong freely and quickly. The specter of some Mainland democracy advocate making vituperative statements about the Politburo while enjoying room service in Taipei may be too much for an overly irritable leadership in the Mainland capital. In the days of Kuomintang rule, any matter involving a fugitive could be solved. The wanted individual could be hustled onto some anonymous fishing boat and, in the middle of the Taiwan Strait, exchanged for someone Taipei wanted. That is not going to happen in a young democracy, however. Taiwan's leaders, these days defiant and proud, will not bend to demands issued from Beijing.

It would be easy for the Communist leaders to punish Taiwan if they should decide to do so. Politicians and generals like fast victories, and Taiwan offers many morsels, "low-hanging fruit" in investment banking jargon. Even the archaic People's Liberation Army can take Kinmen, also known as Quemoy. It's the closest of Taiwan's outlying islands, just a little over a mile to the coast of eastern Fujian Province. Kinmen's civilians are defended by 20,000 soldiers tucked underground in miles of tunnels and hollowed-out mountains. They can put up a good fight, but the island is bound to fall sooner or later. And then there is Matsu, also close to the Mainland shore.

But Kinmen and Matsu would just be appetizers for the PLA. "Like a wolf, the Chinese Communist Party will only be satisfied when it has the sheep in its stomach," said exile Wei Jingsheng, referring to Taiwan. The famous dissident knows that conquering outlying islands will not be enough, especially for military leaders who think they can swallow the entire enchilada. Senior Mainland generals have boasted that they can take the main island of Taiwan in one day. That statement is nonsense, so we assume they don't actually believe what they say. Yet grave miscalculations and undiluted sentiments launch armies. When military leaders lose their sense of reality and political masters have their own selfish agendas, a nation can choose the wrong path.

That's true especially if the survival of the Party is at stake. In the spring of 2000, Jiang Zemin commissioned briefings on the collapse of Communist and authoritarian regimes around the world. He undoubtedly learned the theory that the Second World War deferred the demise of the Soviet Union by dampening corruption and reinforcing the notion of self-sacrifice. Perhaps Beijing talks war these days because China's leaders share the notion that hostilities, even a minor incursion such as China's foray into Vietnam in 1979, are generally beneficial for the People's Republic.

Or perhaps we are hearing those bellicose words because Beijing thinks that it is now or never. Taiwan is drifting away, and someday it will be too late to bring it back into the fold. Some think that if China has to fight, it should do so while there are still serving generals who have seen combat. In a few years' time all experienced officers will have retired, including Defense Minister Chi Haotian and Central Military Commission Vice Chairman Zhang Wannian, both of whom are scheduled to leave their posts in 2002. And the PLA argues that the time for an invasion is now, before Taiwan can rearm with the next generation of American weapons.

So the stars are aligned toward war. Twice Jiang Zemin has threatened conflict, and twice he has backed down. No government, especially one in a country where "face" is critical, can afford to do that a third time. Beijing's leaders think that war will be popular, so it won't take much to start the next crisis. Maybe it will be a mistake or perhaps a deliberate act, but the next crisis looks as if it will be the one that leads to conflict. And if there are hostilities, they will be the last for the People's Republic.

"We need a war, which we will lose," said a Chinese journalist in May 2000. "That will destroy faith in the present dynasty." If there is war, the Mainland will lose. And the losses will be high. "For the Communist leaders, losing ten thousand or one hundred thousand soldiers is nothing," said one Taipei resident recently. "They consider the life of a Chinese worthless." The Party didn't even blink at its horrendous Korean War casualties and probably will not care about those in the future even if they are high. Beijing's leaders will just talk about glory and say that the human sacrifice was worth it. But that's not how our Wang Chuanning will see it if his Jason is needlessly lost in a misconceived military adventure. Wang and grieving relatives may not immediately take to the streets, but the populace will lose its faith that the Communist Party can lead. It will be then that the Chinese demand the right to govern themselves.

Today, in turn-of-the-century China, the forces of dissent are scattered and weak, for there are many grievances but no common one. So the state manages from one incident to the next in one way or another. The People's Republic will be threatened when its enemies organize themselves nationally, linking up one group to another, just as individual Falun Gong practitioners have managed to do.

If the regime loses its war against Taiwan, appalling casualties, or simply the fact of failing to win, will create a common cause. Beijing will not be able to suppress the news, much as it would like to. It strictly controls television, of course, and it can cut off the foreign channels such as CNN for most viewers. But not for all: the regime's ability to suppress foreign television has been eroded by thousands of illegal satellite dishes installed by individual households. And then there is the Internet. China would have to sever the four gateways linking the Internet in China to the outside world if it wanted to suppress foreign news. Think of what television did to the American military effort in Vietnam. Now imagine what the Internet will do to an unsuccessful struggle by China to take Taiwan.

Yet even if Beijing was to completely black out foreign news, there is one situation worse than too much information: not enough of it. When hard news is scarce, rumors arise everywhere. Rumors don't have to be true, they just have to be spread. And these days the Internet is the channel for their communication. So it is not only foreign news that will be subversive—it will be the rumors and gossip and stories that will circulate within China. Even a dictatorial one-party state cannot survive when its people find out the truth and realize they have a common cause. Yugoslavia, the Philippines, and Peru: What do these countries have in common? When the people speak as one, governments fall. It will be China's turn if there is defeat in battle.

Let's say China loses a war with Taiwan. What could happen on the Mainland? It probably will begin with Beijing students marching on Tiananmen Square, as they have so many times since 1919. Seventy years later, in 1989, the protesters had to push their way through ranks of police at each intersection as they headed south toward the square. But after a Taiwan debacle, few would block their progress. Policemen will have been ordered to stop them, but they will be outnumbered. The demonstration will be spontaneous, so the state will be unprepared for confrontation. Besides, many of the police will sympathize with the students. As people move south toward the center of the city, the confidence of the marchers will rise, and they will begin to chant.

"You're either an agent of change, or a victim of it," says an advertisement for Credit Suisse First Boston. The Party throughout much of its history, and especially until 1989, has been the agent, but now it will be a victim. Its consensus style of decision making means that decisions are made slowly, even in emergency situations. In 1989, crowds ruled Tiananmen for weeks as Party leaders watched from the periphery and debated what to do. Post–Taiwan war, the process will be the same, especially because the Party would already have been split during a period of transition in the leadership.

The protesters in Beijing will be change's agents, but it is possible that they will also become its victims. At least some will expect that to happen; apprehension will rise as all expect to see the forces of the state arrive. "We joined hands and waited for the tanks in dead silence," recalled Tatiana Prikhozhan, who, along with other Moscow residents, defended Boris Yeltsin in the streets in 1991 against a coup by hard-line officials. The Chinese will know that their government may use its tanks, and they will wait in silence, too. But the state's military might will not appear. If the central government could simply do something, almost anything, it would prevail as it had a thousand other times in the past. A conciliatory policy would work, as would brutal suppression. Political stalemate will simply freeze the Politburo Standing Committee, however. No one will be able to consolidate his position among the various factions, which include progressive reformers, remnant Maoists, and those who simply want supreme power. The indecision that will follow will result in paralysis of the central government, as no one group will be able to establish its authority. China developed "the world's most sophisticated crowd-control system," but it will not be able to act; it will not know which master to serve.

Within a day, tens of thousands of Beijing residents will join the demonstration, swelling the numbers in the square as word of the protest spreads throughout the capital. In the spring of 1989, the regime did its best to control the flow of information about events in Tiananmen but found its efforts frustrated by fax machines. News traveled across China's borders, primarily between Hong Kong and Beijing, and between points within the country without the sanction of official media. There were, however, only a limited number of fax machines in those days, so information was often sketchy. In the increasingly interconnected China after the Taiwan debacle, word of the Beijing demonstrations will be passed along by messages posted on Web bulletin boards and in chat rooms, and demonstrators will take to the streets around the country. "Chat room mamas," censors employed by China's private portals, will delete subversive messages, but soon there will be too many and the self-censorship system will break down. Dissident groups, although powerless on their own, will provide the organizational platform for otherwise spontaneous demonstrations. In some cases protesters will even use the newly installed Internet connections in state-owned enterprises to coordinate their activities. The power of electronic communication as a tool for dissent, first demonstrated in China by the Falun Gong, will work for others.

"Under no circumstances should we intensify problems by handling them in an oversimplified or crude way," Zhu Rongji said in 1999, referring to protests. "Still less should we use dictatorial means against the people." That was generally good advice, but as the crowd continues to swell the resolution of the situation in Tiananmen will begin to slip beyond the nervous senior cadres. No matter what tactics they use, they will look as if they might not prevail this time. Party leaders will eventually agree to call out the paramilitary People's Armed Police, who will try to clear Tiananmen Square. In the past the state could always handle individual protesters and small groups, but the crowd will be too large and will resist the policemen. It will not tolerate being pushed around by anyone. The armed police will give up after a few hours of halfhearted attempts. They will retreat because there is now a sense shared by most everyone in China that there has been enough bloodshed. As Karl Marx preached, there's no use fighting the inevitable trends of history.

Perhaps the most moving image of the Beijing Spring of 1989 was that of Zhou Yongjun and two other students kneeling on the steps of the Great Hall of the People as they waited to deliver a petition to a government that would not listen. "All kinds of feelings welled up in my heart," Zhou recalled years later. "I stood there and cried silently." They knelt for nearly an hour, alone, and no one came to accept their petition. In 1989, the people did not seek to overthrow their government; they came in supplication. But after the disaster in the Taiwan Strait, the Chinese will not be so subservient. They will see that events are moving beyond the control of the senior leaders and realize that their reign may not last.

The demonstrators will sense that the Party is lost. The official media, without the benefit of direction from the leadership compound of Zhongnanhai, will be able only to issue pleas for people to return to their homes and work for the strengthening of socialism. That, everyone will recognize, is uninspiring. Until some old man or woman can gain the upper hand in the upper reaches of Party councils, however, bland statements will have to do. At this critical moment, the Communist Party, which always tried to look self-assured, will appear incapable of leadership.

The Party will not be able to remove the crowd without the aid of the PLA, but there will be no consensus among the leaders to employ that kind of force. No senior cadre will want to inherit Li Peng's mantle as the "Butcher of Beijing," earned for his role in the 1989 massacre. The more self-aware on the Politburo Standing Committee will realize that brute force just won't work in a China dependent on the outside world to buy its products, make investments, share technology, and provide low-cost loans. Maybe China is not the worst victim of globalization, as *Time* suggests; maybe it is the Party, which has quickly learned that all the benefits of its interconnections with the outside world come at a price. China's economy, some Beijing leaders will realize, is now dependent on the goodwill of foreigners, who cannot do business with a regime that appears barbaric and brutal.

In post-Taiwan Tiananmen Square, the people will wait to be galvanized during the first days of the demonstrations, but no leader will emerge. The crowd will not be able to govern or even agree on what it stands for. It will know only what it is against. Party leaders might prevail by outlasting the formless mob or forcibly removing it from the square with soldiers, but they will not have the chance to decide which way they will go.

Sometimes democracy needs a strongman, and at a crucial moment he or she will appear. In 1989, General Party Secretary Zhao Ziyang went to the square in the middle of May but could not bring himself to renounce the Party and lead a revolt, however much he sympathized with the students and their allies. The next time someone will be bolder. He or she will not have to promise much, perhaps just to hold elections in a year for delegates to a constitutional convention. That will be good enough, however, for a movement without a leader skilled in the art of government. The crowd, a million people behind a single man or woman, will cross Changan Avenue and descend upon Zhongnanhai. During December 1989, but half a world away, a crowd in Bucharest witnessed Nicolae Ceaușescu flee Communist Party headquarters by helicopter. In China, demonstrators will not have to get past the gates of Zhongnanhai before they too will win: the senior cadres will flee any way they can. History repeats itself in dictatorships around the world. And when it does, the people will show that they have what Chinese military thinker Sun-tzu called "the supreme skill"; that is, to be able to win without fighting. It happened in Berlin and Bucharest and will soon occur in Beijing: the people will take back their government.

FROM CORRUPTION TO CHAOS TO CURE

Suppose there is no war with Taiwan. Is there anything else that can topple the Party? "Corruption angers the Chinese people more than anything else and poses the greatest threat to our society," says author and activist Dai Qing, "but the problem is how do you fight corruption without destroying the Communist Party?" Corruption plagues all regimes, and especially Chinese ones, at their end. And this ill has become explosive in the People's Republic of today. "I hate to the marrow crooked officials who take bribes to bend the law and I have no way to resist other than to die to protect state law," wrote Zhu Zhenyuan, who climbed to the top of a building in the center of Beijing and scattered dozens of leaflets onto the crowd below in January 2000. The former soldier, crippled after beatings while in police custody in his home province, threatened to jump to his death before being led away by police. If war does not presage the end of the People's Republic, it may be brought on by the people's revolt against corruption.

Zhu's act was only a protest of one, but sometimes the Chinese march in the hundreds against corruption. Like they did in late December 2000 in Luoyang in inland Henan Province. Poisonous smoke and fire killed 309 people in the Dongdu Commercial Building, most of them in a disco that was operating illegally. For years the authorities knew about the dance hall, one of the worst firetraps in the province.

Nothing was done, however, because its owner was protected by local government officials. So after the blaze about 400 people, watched by bystanders of an equal number, marched in protest against the arrogance and corruption of their government.

Today the Party's internal mechanisms handle thousands of malfeasance cases each year—but evidently not enough of them. From top to bottom, the Party is infested. At the top, senior cadres siphon off millions, even tens of millions, of dollars. Yet it is the petty corruption that especially threatens the Party because that is what the people see day to day. Now local cadres such as Du Mingxiang are able to do whatever they want, even drink themselves to death with public money. Du, the Party boss of Yongshan County in Yunnan Province, went drinking one afternoon and evening in July 2000 in the town of Jingxin with other cadres after finishing a Three Stresses meeting, held to improve internal Party discipline. He and his colleagues spent in one afternoon and evening what the average household of four in his poor rural county earns in a full year. They were using the public's money, not their own. Du died at his favorite nightclub late that evening from too much liquor, and the next morning his relatives demanded that the club owner pay them ¥80,000 (US$9,674) to take his body away. The owner paid a small amount and had to deliver an IOU to the county's deputy police chief for an additional sum to be paid the next day. The owner did not have the money, and his wife, burdened by the pressure, committed suicide by poison. In the countryside the local cadres rule as they please, as do their families. And the peasants, who see all of this in Yongshan County and elsewhere, seethe.

As a consequence, corruption—other than that of his friends—is close to the top of the agenda for Jiang Zemin. That's why he decreed the death penalty for Cheng Kejie, and that is just what the disgraced official got in September 2000 for taking bribes. Cheng, a governor of a province as well as a vice chairman of the Standing Committee of the National People's Congress, was the highest official executed in the history of the People's Republic.

The Party may impose the ultimate penalty and put its own to death, but it is nonetheless losing the war against corruption. There is simply too much official embezzlement, fraud, and theft. Some say that these ills are ingrained in the Chinese soul and blame Confucius. Maybe the sage is at fault for emphasizing family loyalty over the common good, but the problem today belongs to the Communist Party because it has allowed corruption to infest society.

The Party's efforts to rid itself of this evil only make the situation worse by reinforcing cynicism in the population. A couple of years of show trials have confirmed the widespread belief that corruption is widespread, thereby confirming the worst fears of the Party about the effects of publicity. Worse, the show trial campaign has led the people to believe that the Party is not able to control corruption. The execution of Cheng Kejie was apparently intended to show that higher-ups are not above punishment. As a *China Daily* headline noted, HARSH SENTENCE SHOWS STATE'S RESOLUTION TO PUNISH CORRUPTION. But that's not how China's ordinary citizens saw it. "Cheng was caught because he did not have enough supporters in Beijing," said one Beijing taxi driver. "He should have involved Beijing leaders, or their children, in the corruption." So the people know that the nature of prosecution in the People's Republic is still political.

They also know that the Party has yet to confront the reality of corruption. "The perfection of the legal system can help avoid the appearance of the 'second Cheng,' " said a Beijing law professor quoted by official media. There are hundreds of thousands of Chengs in China, some big, some small. If the Party cannot admit the truth, it is lost. That's why the people are beginning to take matters into their own hands. They're not supposed to do that—it's the cadres who are meant to lead. The Communist Party can undertake any initiative as long as it retains control. The one thing it cannot do is let the common people take over. The leaders talk about ridding the state of corruption, but that is not the issue; that's just the subject matter. What most concerns the regime is the stability of the regime. Therefore, Beijing has always prosecuted antigraft activists as vigorously as corrupt cadres. As far as senior leaders are concerned, both threaten public order.

The Party does not want anyone to air grievances, no matter how good the intentions. In 1999, Beijing sent its most famous prosecutor to Xiamen in Fujian Province and by the following year more than a thousand investigators followed her to unravel a smuggling scandal, yet the central government worked hard to keep information about that matter off the Web and out of the news. That was futile, however. Unofficial

Web sites carried stories of the massive corruption case, and the Party, angered by the speed of information dissemination, started a new clamp-down on the Net.

Jiang Zemin can execute another hundred senior cadres—or a thou-sand, for that matter—but he will be no closer to victory until he begins to prosecute his friends. That's because this campaign has become a struggle for the hearts and minds of the Chinese people, who know that imprisoning enemies has little to do with fighting corruption. To them, all the arrests look like just another power struggle. Moreover, the jailing of opponents brings back memories of the Maoist era, a period that most in China would prefer to forget. Unfortunately, the law cannot be im-partially applied under the current leadership because Jiang tolerates fail-ings among cadres personally loyal to him. As he seeks support from Party stalwarts in his attempts to retain power during the transition years of 2002 and 2003, he will not let the fight against corruption impede his personal ambitions. And the prospects beyond those years are not good either, because any successor to Jiang will need to consolidate his posi-tion in Party circles. A new leader will be in no position to imprison supporters for many years, if ever.

As it becomes evident that the Party cannot control corruption, ide-alistic Chinese will demonstrate as they have throughout their country's history. China's Dragon Boat Festival in June honors Qu Yuan, an official who drowned himself in 278 B.C. to protest corruption in the Spring and Autumn Period. Today's protesters may not take their own lives, but the state might do it for them. Should the Party continue to oppose activists fighting this evil, it will put itself at still greater risk. Corruption is the most explosive issue in China today, but fighting those fighting corrup-tion can be even more so. Whenever cadres attempt that, they put them-selves on the wrong side of nationalism.

That's not a place where the Party wants to be. Chiang Kai-shek found himself there and soon had to flee to Taiwan. Cadres don't have that option these days, as that island is already taken. Yet they tempt fate by suppressing all those who seek to clean the stables. Peasants, for in-stance. In August 2000, about twenty thousand Jiangxi Province peasants complained principally about unjust taxation, but they also spoke out against the personal use of government funds by local officials. The Jiangxi rampage spread almost as if all the villages ignited at once, and the state had to use deadly force to quell the outburst. Today resentment smolders in the poorer parts of rural China, and the peasants lack only a leader who can make them into a real movement. From time to time strongmen have emerged in China's past, and one day that will happen again.

Perhaps it will be soon, because China is on the eve of accession to the World Trade Organization. Of all the groups in China, the peasants will be the worst hit by globalization. Although it is difficult to see how things could get worse in the countryside, we know that the peasants of China will not be able to compete with the corporate farmers of, say, the American Midwest or California's San Joaquin Valley. When desperation arising from economic failure mixes with rage over corruption, rebellions will include provinces, not just townships, and hundreds of thousands of people instead of hundreds. The state will be armed and the peasants will not, but this will not necessarily be a contest where might will prevail. Who will want to stand against a genuinely popular movement in the countryside? If a governor loses his nerve or an officer does not want to fire, the forces of the state could melt as rebellion does not spread so much as explode. Mao Zedong used the term "prairie fire," and that's what will occur the next time, except that the countryside will ignite all at once. Nothing, he taught, can stand in the way of a people's movement.

Mao also talked about encircling the cities with peasants, but that's not how the end will come. Next time rebellion in the countryside will merge with unrest in the cities as workers, who have their own grievances against petty officials, join in. There may be no single leader opposing the state, just many opportunists seeking their fifteen minutes of fame. Today the People's Liberation Army and the People's Armed Police are more than a match for any domestic enemy of the state. Yet in the future they could be overwhelmed by all of them at once. And that's exactly what will happen. As order dissolves across China, many groups will seize the moment. Workers will take over their factories, and towns will run themselves as little baronies.

And the splittists will split. The Tibetans and Uighurs will see a chance to slip away, as will the Taiwanese. "All Chinese people have patience," said Chen Shui-bian after his historic election in 2000. He will be rewarded for his. During the turmoil on the Mainland, the island will formally reaffirm its sovereignty as the Republic of Taiwan, effectively declaring its independence. Leaders in Beijing, distracted, will only be able to watch as the world's diplomatic community recognizes the island as a "new" country. The People's Republic may not so much collapse as split apart and then dissolve.

As Wei Jingsheng implied, before the new can grow, it must push aside the old. The Party, eaten away underneath by corruption, still survives. Yet it is only alive, not well. One day the new will push aside the corruption of the old, and China will rebuild itself again.

THE NEW LEFT IN OLD BEIJING

Now that the peasants are simmering, Beijing realizes it has two big problems on its hands instead of just one. That's a real challenge for Party leaders, who used to believe that only the urban proletariat could bring the regime down. Beijing strove hard to keep workers in the cities happy and judged the stability of the Party by their prosperity. To maintain the image of that prosperity, Party leaders, especially during the last half decade, postponed dealing with symptoms, deferring them and their solutions to an indefinite future. As time passed, the sores festered and grew worse. The problems with state-owned enterprises, for instance, were forced not only onto the banks but also into the equity markets, where stock in state-owned enterprises was sold to domestic and foreign investors.

For China, on the eve of accession to the World Trade Organization, the time of deferral is over, both in the countryside and in the city. Bureaucrats and officials have complained too much in the past about possible WTO membership, but as renowned Chinese economist Li Yining tells us, "This time the wolves really are coming." And even before the leadership transition years of 2002 and 2003, the government is split over accession. The dissenters, known as the "New Left," argue that the disadvantages of membership dwarf the benefits. Over the long term that will not be true, but in the short term they will look prophetic. Accession will rock China's economy, and the resulting problems will be apparent before the benefits are felt. As has been predicted, SOEs will fall not by the thousands but by the tens of thousands. A government running out of money and constrained by WTO rules will not be able to save them.

That's too bad, because central government technocrats have pushed ordinary citizens into the equity markets as part of their risky "wealth effect" policy to restart the economy. There are now about 1,100 companies whose shares are listed on the Mainland markets in the emerging financial centers of Shanghai and Shenzhen. But even after a decade of experience, China's regulators are not up to the task of policing the country's securities markets. There are only two dozen investigators dedicated to the enforcement of order in China's stock exchanges. The nation's weak judiciary won't protect investors, and there aren't enough central government auditors. When the cat's away the mice will defraud, and that's what is happening in the markets in a hundred different ways. When personal enrichment is considered patriotic and the forces of law are weak, private investors often become victims of China's new economic order.

China's stock markets are infested to their roots, and they're worse than casinos. "Even casinos have rules and you cannot look at other people's cards," said Wu Jinglian, one of the country's leading economists, in early 2001. Market crimes begin in the steam rooms of Shanghai. There, listening devices taped to a body can't be used, so there are never any recordings of the conspiratorial conversations that hatch the many illegal stock manipulation schemes. And of course there are never any unaccounted-for witnesses. The oldest technique in the dirtiest business is to buy a cheap stock, ramp up its price with unsupportably optimistic forecasts, and then sell out at the top of the market. That's what brokers do in those shiny Pudong buildings my father so admired that September evening.

So what could trigger the fall of the People's Republic? A brokers' stock manipulation scheme could go awry and be discovered. Enraged investors would then demonstrate. Yes, that could happen. After all, at any given time about 30 percent of the stocks on China's markets are being manipulated. Yet the biggest risk is posed by the actions of the biggest stock manipulator of them all: the central government. Beijing wants to continue to sell minority stakes in state-owned enterprises on its public markets in Shanghai and Shenzhen. In order to do that, it must, as a practical matter, keep their stock prices high.

But there's a problem: many of the companies already listed are failing, and they threaten to drag the markets lower. One example, mentioned before, is Zhengzhou Baiwen Group, a department store chain based in Zhengzhou, the capital of inland Henan Province. This enterprise falsified its earnings to obtain a stock market listing in Shanghai in 1996 and then faked them again to report profits afterward. That was futile because the company eventually had to report the largest yearly loss (US$115 million) in the history of China's markets. An overaggressive expansion policy resulted in debts Zhengzhou Baiwen could not repay, and it became the first listed company in China to undergo bankruptcy proceedings, which were started in March 2000. Since then, a bizarre drama has unfolded as the city, provincial, and central governments struggled to keep the dead business alive. Zhengzhou Baiwen's stock even soared after the bankruptcy filing because Mainland officials censored the news of its condition so as to create a boom in the department store's shares. The stock shot up about 31 percent in the space of a month.

"We are resigned to the will of heaven," says Zhang Li, a salesman employed by Zhengzhou Baiwen. It's great that the employees follow the gods, but will 120,000 shareholders, who stand to lose everything, be so passive? After all, they are the victims of an ongoing fraud that should have been detected by central government regulators and local officials. And some stockholders, those who acquired their shares in the boom following the bankruptcy filing, were put at risk by a deliberate stock manipulation campaign orchestrated by their own government. That's undoubtedly one of the reasons why Zhengzhou Baiwen was rescued by a complex arrangement put together at the end of 2000 in which its largest creditor had to write off more than US$180 million, about 75 percent of the debt it held. The plan was intended to restore confidence in the nation's securities markets but was instead a step in the wrong direction. Reformers howled, and the central government retreated by promising in March 2001 to delist the ailing retailer. The nation's securities regulators now say that bad companies must be chased out of the

stock markets, but the reality is that senior leaders in Beijing would prefer to return to "the old style of doing things" to ensure stability. Approximately a third of China's stock traders are laid-off workers, so
there is an "immense risk" inherent in the stock markets. As a senior
securities regulator said, the central government is worried that if it
doesn't save failing companies, "investors will take to the streets and
cause social unrest."

That's already happened, in Shenzhen in 1992, when tens of thousands rioted. In that year the markets were still small. By now, they've
grown, so the potential for disturbances has increased. China's populace
is not yet used to the concept of risk in financial markets. In the Maoist
past people put their savings into state banks, which were as secure as
the state itself. Reform created alternatives, nongovernmental deposit-
taking companies. Whenever savings institutions failed, the state came to
the rescue of the populace to preserve stability. Now that same state is
asking its citizens to invest in the future of the nation by buying, in the
public markets, stock in state-owned enterprises. Up to now, officials
have, one way or another, come to the aid of investors, but they can't rescue all the rotten businesses with stock market listings. Soon the state
will have to delist companies and let them go under. China can withstand
the collapse of a few publicly-held enterprises, but not the failure of a
hundred. Today there are at least that many listed companies that are failing, and accession to the World Trade Organization will kill off even
more. Don't count on the discipline of the public markets to help reform
these enterprises: China's exchanges, despite all the experience gained in
a decade of operation, are still "irregular." The central government,
wishing to sell more shares in state-owned enterprises on the public markets, defers real change. So we will see other corporate failures, many
more of them. And during one of those failures, something will go
wrong and Beijing will not be able to control what happens. The risk will
be especially acute in the next few years when small investors will still
expect the government to save them.

"The revolution will not be televised," says Digital Island, an
e-business company, in one of its advertisements. In fact, when an enterprise fails in a major city in the future, it just may be. If there's a demonstration by employees or shareholders, any person with a small digital

video camera can record the event for a memento—or for a worldwide audience. Today the outside world often *hears* about demonstrations in China days or even months afterward through the reporting of the respected Information Centre for Human Rights and Democracy in Hong Kong. As technology improves, we will *see* these events on our television screens or on the Internet as they occur. And when the world witnesses police clubbing demonstrators and blood in the streets, the reaction will be immediate and emotional. There is no such thing as "brave money" in financial markets, and international investors will flee China stocks at the first signs of brutality. Today's exaggerated swings of the Chinese equity markets will be even more pronounced tomorrow, when we have streaming video brought right to the terminals of stock traders. The reaction will be the same in the financial centers of London, New York, Hong Kong, and Tokyo: professional money managers will bail out of Chinese investments. Television is greater than any state these days, even the Chinese one.

When foreigners dump Chinese stocks, domestic investors will have to follow. When investors in China lose money, they will protest. And when people hear that demonstrators have gotten their money back, others will take to the streets. The rumors will be untrue, but that is unimportant. The Internet will instantaneously carry gossip throughout China, and people will believe what they read. In the past, government officials dampened economic protests by paying demonstrators back wages and pensions or lost deposits. In the future, however, that tactic will not do the trick. There will simply be too many protesters out on the streets: the authorities won't have enough time or money to pay back everyone suffering from the consequences of more than five decades of economic mismanagement.

When it becomes apparent that the central government is not able to save listed companies, ordinary citizens will begin to question the banks. Today experts say that the banks are solid, even though insolvent, because China's citizens supply them with an unending stream of new deposits. The pundits should know better because banks are built on confidence and confidence in insolvent financial institutions can be easily lost. There are already bank runs from time to time as rumors zip across towns and cities. Today a jittery population panics at the first sign of a problem, although up to now the reasons have been trivial. The greatest irony is that the most logical reason for a run—the insolvency of the Big Four banks and therefore of the entire banking system—does not seem to have occurred to hundreds of millions of depositors, who trust their government and its financial institutions implicitly. Without that trust, which can so easily be lost when things go wrong, the populace will stampede to get its savings back. No banking system can withstand massive withdrawals, especially in a time of systemic collapse. The Party will have to close the banks and hope that force will work to keep depositors at bay. In a nationwide panic, however, the government will be swamped by all the people who have lost confidence in their nation.

Across China activists will decide that this is their moment in history. On their own, dissidents are weak, as they are today. Joined with other angry people, they will become powerful. Senior leaders in Beijing will view events with alarm, but they will be divided by personal ambitions and their own ideological perspectives. New Leftists, combined with remnant Maoists, could become as powerful as any other faction in the Party as WTO membership is blamed for the breakdown in order. Especially in the transition years, as power passes from the Third Generation to the Fourth, the Party may not be able to decide just how much force to bring to bear because it does not know which ideological position to adopt. And there will be disagreements over tactics. Some leaders will think that emotions will subside and fear that a harsh crackdown will destroy the Party's remaining popular support. Others will argue for the traditionally tough response. The political party that hesitates is lost, and delay will ultimately be the undoing of the authorities in Beijing.

"We were not bloodthirsty," said Vladimir Kruichkov, head of the Soviet KGB and one of the plotters of the coup in August 1991. "We were not ready to pay any price to hold on to power." By the time the residents of Zhongnanhai decide they are willing to pay that price to defend the central government, it could be too late. PLA units will be called out around the country, but there may not be enough of them. And in conditions like these, ordinary soldiers will not want to kill ordinary citizens. In 1989, the first batch of troops called out by Deng Xiaoping would not move against the students. Those soldiers were relieved to make way for others made of sterner stuff. In the future, however, the regime will be hard pressed to find any troops willing to fight unarmed citizens. A government under siege cannot survive when its soldiers refuse to fire.

Mao Zedong is no longer fashionable, but he predicted what would happen in a nationwide struggle: "small forces linked with the people become strong, while big forces opposed to the people become weak." So the outcome is known even now; there will simply be too many in the country aligned against the cadres in Beijing. Today, for some of us, it might be hard to believe that the People's Republic can fall, but we should listen to Leon Trotsky. "Revolution is impossible until it is inevitable," he told us.

"There are many things which cannot be imagined," the Chinese say, "but there is nothing which may not happen." In a land of a thousand sayings, this one seems especially true. At the end of an era, anything can occur. And the least significant events, happening at the wrong time or place, can cause a government to fall.

It will not take much, as Václav Havel, president of the Czech Republic, tells us. "Society was already pregnant with problems," he said. "In this sort of situation, a snowball can start an avalanche." In Havel's Czechoslovakia of 1989, it was clear that something would happen. In the China of today, many cannot foresee the collapse of the one-party state. Yet, as Havel also knows, facades crack. One moment the state is there and the people cheer; the next moment it is gone and they rejoice. It is the fear of every autocrat. What is Jiang Zemin's biggest concern as he wakes up? We've been told that it's feeding all his country's people. That may be, but it's more probable that his main worry when he rises each morning is whether he will still be the leader of all those souls when he goes to bed that night.

And he has every reason to be concerned, for China's rulers have blinded themselves. "I am emperor, my descendants will be numerous," said Qin Shihuangdi, acknowledged as China's first emperor. "From the second generation to the ten thousandth, my line will not end." But his line did just that, only a little more than two years after his death. Qin teaches us that authoritarian rulers like him can suppress their subjects, but then they can never really know what their subjects think. In China that's still the case, as the model of central leadership has not essentially changed.

There is one truth about leadership that has not changed since then, though it is something that Jiang Zemin and all the other senior cadres in Beijing deny. "A political party, no matter how hard it tries, cannot govern forever," says Chen Shui-bian.

THE TROUBLE THEY MAKE THEMSELVES

For a moment, it looked as if the Japanese would govern China forever. They had already conquered Manchuria in northeast China and had overrun the eastern coast. Now their planes swept low over Kunming in China's interior. My father will always remember the date: December 8, 1941. It was just a few hours after Japanese carrier-based aircraft shattered the calm of a Hawaiian morning over Pearl Harbor and Wheeler Field. On the other side of the International Date Line, Japanese pilots over Kunming went on the attack against the famous Flying Tigers, American and Chinese volunteer pilots. My father jumped into an irrigation ditch as bombs fell on the east side of the city in the evening. China, like so many times in its past, was under attack by foreigners.

The Japanese were eventually forced out of their conquests in China, and to this day my father does not forgive them. They were not the real enemy, however. As soon as the Japanese were defeated, the Chinese continued their struggle against themselves, Communist against Kuomintang. As so many times in the past, the people of China could not live in peace with one another. Today they do, but they know that if they are to have a future, they will need to free themselves of the constraints now binding them together on the Mainland. The current rulers of China are Chinese, but they now stand against the aspirations of their own people.

So what will happen tomorrow in China? There's no hint in western Beijing at the China Century Monument, where 262 bronze slabs tell the tale of the Chinese people. Today the last one has no words; it's reserved for the future. Wang Chuanning cannot predict the future of his homeland either. He has a standard phrase when he cannot answer. "It's hard to say," he always says.

Wang's first name means "spreading peace," and that is what he would like to do. But as we look into the future of the Chinese, there is little that will be peaceful. All the struggle and turmoil of the nineteenth and twentieth centuries are just a prelude to what will come in the twenty-first. So much is unresolved as the Chinese seek to recover what they have lost and try to find their way. Wang does know one thing, though, and that is that the Chinese will have no one else to blame. "The trouble is the trouble we make ourselves," he says as he contemplates the uncertainty ahead. That much he can see. So he worries about his family and especially his son, Jason, if he must return home to Beijing.

There is one thing we know: the Communist Party has failed over its half century of rule, so it will not last. That's what the last tablet at the monument will someday record. When the People's Republic falls, Wang will not be able to say whether the new leaders will be better than the old. Yet there is one thing he will know: Jason will at least have hope.

Epilogue:

The State Begins to Disintegrate

Thinkers prepare the revolution; bandits carry it out.
—MARIANO AZUELA

FOUR NEARLY SIMULTANEOUS blasts ripped through residential build-ings in the heart of Shijiazhuang, the capital of Hebei Province. Hun-dreds were killed in their sleep before dawn in this declining industrial city located about 170 miles southwest of Beijing. Entire families died, especially at the site of the most powerful explosion, a five-story apart-ment building that housed workers from the No. 3 Cotton Mill. Six-year-old Shi Yuanyuan lived there, but now she is in the hospital in critical condition, her body blackened from the blast. She was fortunate, however, to be among the few survivors. Both her parents perished that night.

For the second time in March 2001, state media broadcast the images of soldiers in their shiny green helmets working frantically to save people buried under tons of debris. Ten days earlier young children and their teachers had died in Fanglin, a village in Jiangxi Province. The deaths in Fanglin were an accident; those in Shijiazhuang were not. The series of explosions in the Hebei capital is possibly the worst terrorist act in the history of the People's Republic.

In Fanglin, local authorities blamed a mentally ill man for intentionally destroying the school with two pockets of firecrackers, but few believe that theory. Villagers relate how young children were forced to make fireworks on the ground floor of their schoolhouse, accidentally setting off barrels of explosives stored nearby. In Shijiazhuang, officials quickly blamed a lone deaf man, Jin Ruchao, already wanted for allegedly killing his girlfriend. China declared the case solved a week after the event when the fugitive "confessed all his crimes" within a few hours of his apprehension. But by himself, Jin could not have expertly handled and set the approximately 3,300 pounds of explosives that were used. The blasts were evidently the work of a team of professionals. In Shijiazhuang as in Fanglin, local Party cadres could not admit the truth; they had to find someone to blame. As they invented their stories they also had to censor news and cordon off their communities from the rest of the world.

In Shijiazhuang, people don't have enough to eat, and unemployment is high. Some residents of the city, therefore, think that the jobless were responsible. Others blame the former mayor, Zhang Erchen, who was charged with embezzlement just six days before the detonations. His supporters might have been trying to destabilize the municipal government, many residents believe, in order to derail anticorruption efforts. The people of Shijiazhuang don't yet know who set the explosives, and maybe they will never find out. One thing, however, is certain: the social fabric in their city is fraying. The March blasts were not the first to rock this city. Late in 2000 a young peasant was executed for setting off five bombs in public places, yet apparently the severe penalty didn't do much good, because the disorder in Hebei's capital continues.

As it does across China. The Communist Party has struggled to keep up with great change over the last two decades, but now it is beginning to fail as it often cannot provide the basic needs of its people. Corruption and malfeasance erode the Party's support from small hamlet to great city. Central government leaders do not know what to do as the institutions built over five decades become feeble. Social order in their nation is dissolving. The Chinese are making a break for the future, and the disaffected are beginning to find their voice. The cadres still suppress, but that won't work in the long run. The people are in motion now, and it's just a matter of time before they get what they want.

"Thinkers prepare the revolution; bandits carry it out," wrote Mariano Azuela. That may have been true in the author's Mexico of a hundred years ago but not in the China of today. The Chinese need no thinkers for their next revolution, and the bandits have already started to act.

Notes

Foreword: The Final Chapter

Page

xv   world's largest economy: See Yang Zheng, "Carving Milestones for the Next Century," WorldPaper Online, November 1998 (available at www.worldpaper.com). For an optimistic analysis of China's growth, see Suzanne Harrison, "China Could Be Next to Hit US$10 Trillion," *South China Morning Post,* February 7, 2001, Business Post, p. 2.

xvi   the only nation: Gerald Segal, "Does China Matter?," *Foreign Affairs,* September–October 1999, p. 24.

xvi   "world's sole superpower": "Quest for Dignity," *Asiaweek,* September 24, 1999, p. 40.

xvi   Falun Gong: The name of the group commonly known as the Falun Gong is Falun Dafa; "Falun Gong" is the name of the physical exercises that practitioners engage in. For the sake of convenience, I refer to the group by its common name, Falun Gong.

xviii   "profoundly important": Charlene Barshefsky, "USTR Briefing on the Trade Agreement Reached with China," released by the Office of the USTR, November 15, 1999.

I: The Dinner Party

4   For the Qing: Qing is pronounced "Ching."

8   greatest famine in history: See "China's Chance," *Business China,* January 3, 2000, p. 1.

8   anything but admit: The Party's failure to admit its shortcomings during the Great Leap Forward is generally discussed in Jasper Becker, *Hungry Ghosts: China's Secret Famine* (London: John Murray, 1996).

9   fastest-growing economy in the world: Joseph Stiglitz, "Issues of Reform and Development in China," Workshop on Issues of Reform and Development in China, Tokyo, December 12, 1997.

10   "vanguard production force": See Chapter 5.

11   The Fifth Modernization: See Wei Jingsheng, "The Fifth Modernization: Democracy," in Wei Jingsheng, *The Courage to Stand Alone: Letters from Prison and Other Writings,* ed. and trans. Kristina M. Torgeson (New York: Viking Penguin, 1997), Appendix I.

12   "I didn't really know": *Visions of China, CNN This Morning,* narr. Mike Chinoy, CNN International, September 16, 1999.

12   "not a single person": Simon Beck, "No Protester Died in Tiananmen, Says Chi," *South China Morning Post,* December 12, 1996, p. 8. In other comments Chi admitted that soldiers had died that night. See Tom Rhodes, "General Denies 1989 Tiananmen Square Deaths," *Times* (London), December 11, 1996, p. 10.

13   "Each time I did": Calum MacLeod and Lijia MacLeod, "Boom Times for Female Slave Trade," *South China Morning Post,* May 28, 2000, p. 11.

13–14   "will explode": *Visions of China, CNN This Morning,* narr. Mike Chinoy, CNN International, September 16, 1999.

15   "It is too horrible": *Born Under the Red Flag,* Ambrica Productions and WGBH Educational Foundation, 1997.

16   "shouting the same slogan": *Born Under the Red Flag.*

2: Lake of Gasoline

18   roughly pulls the old man up: "Falun Gong Arrests," *World News,* narr. Lisa Weaver, CNN International, February 5, 2000.

18   Wang Yaoqing: "Hong Kong," *Inside Asia,* narr. Mike Chinoy, CNN International, January 14, 2001.

18   "their bodies aflame": "Beijing," *Asia Tonight,* narr. Rebecca MacKinnon, CNN International, January 23, 2001.

20   "symbol of protest": Willy Wo-Lap Lam, " 'Unprecedented Challenges' to Party," *South China Morning Post,* November 3, 1999, p. 9.

20   "cannot change their hearts": Todd Crowell and David Hsieh, "The Crackdown," *Asiaweek,* August 6, 1999, p. 14.

21   perhaps 30 million: See, e.g., Becker, *Hungry Ghosts,* pp. 266–274.

21   " 'This Li Hongzhi' ": *Inside Asia,* narr. Rebecca MacKinnon, CNN International, January 8, 2000.

22   that party was doomed: Beijing has not relented in its persecution of the China Democracy Party. See "U.S. Legislators Demand Action on China Human Rights,"

Agence France-Presse, February 12, 2001. That party's founder, Xu Wenli, is currently serving a thirteen-year jail sentence for subversion.

22   fewer than 5 million: "Popping the Investment Bubble: There May Be Fewer Than 5 Million Stockholders in China," China Online, May 25, 2000. Domestic media claim that there are about 61 million stock trading accounts. See "New Accounts," *China Daily,* March 23, 2001, p. 7.

22   "more than 100 million": "Nation Respects Religious Freedom, Not Evil Cults," *China Daily,* February 20, 2001, p. 1. Beijing is apparently reluctant to publicize the growth in religious belief. Estimates remain vague, which has the effect of hiding the rising popularity of religion. Despite the apparent growth in believers, official pronouncements have used the 100 million statistic for some time.

23   "believe in dialectical materialism": Jaime A. FlorCruz and Joshua Cooper Ramo, "Inside China's Search for Its Soul," *Time Asia,* October 18, 1999, p. 22.

23   fervently practice Falun Gong: An estimated one third of Falun Gong devotees are members of the Party. Melinda Liu and Katharina Hesse, "Crisis of Faith," *Newsweek,* November 8, 1999, p. 26.

24   "China has achieved a great victory": William Kazer, "Lawmakers Lauded for Smashing Sect," *South China Morning Post,* March 10, 2000, p. 10.

24   "objective discussion": "China Frees Five Detained Christians, Activists," Reuters News Service, January 2, 2000.

24   "They dragged me around": "Perspective," *Asian Edition,* narr. Rebecca MacKinnon, CNN International, January 11, 2000.

24   the Party is not content: See, e.g., Josephine Ma, "Copycat Sects Purged as More Arrests Made," *South China Morning Post,* November 2, 1999, p. 8; Wang Nanfang, "Wuhan Smashes Falun Gong's Mutation, Cibei Gong," *Changjiang Daily* (Wuhan), November 1, 1999, p. 1.

24   even though they are more benign: See "Report: 600 Leaders of Banned Chinese Exercise Group Arrested," Associated Press Newswires, March 4, 2000.

25   Uighurs: Uighurs is pronounced "Wee-gers."

25   the white stick figure: *World News,* narr. Sanjay Singh, CNN International, February 5, 2000.

25   "when the metal bird flies": Tim McGirk, "Just Right for the Part," *Time,* September 8, 1997, p. 39. Padmasambhuva, an eighth-century Indian, had a similar vision: "when the iron bird flies and horses run on wheels, the Tibetan people will be scattered like ants across the earth." Dele Olojede, "The Living God of a Disappearing Land," *Hong Kong Standard,* December 7, 1999, p. 11.

25   "Liberation from whom and what?": Jonathan D. Spence, *The Search for Modern China,* 2nd ed. (New York: W.W. Norton, 1999), p. 500.

26   in the hope: Less than a year after identifying Gyaincain Norbu as the true Panchen Lama, the boy, about seven at the time, was quoted by official Chinese media to have said, "With the help of international anti-China forces, the Dalai Lama has used his religious influence to plot for Tibet's independence, which not only tarnished the Tibetan religion, but also brought disaster to Tibet." "China Says Disputed Boy-Monk Is Free," Reuters News Service, August 16, 1996.

26   from a distance: Charles Hutzler, "China Shows Diplomats Purported Pictures of Missing Panchen Lama Candidate," Associated Press Newswires, October 26, 2000.

27 successor will be democratically elected: Pierre Lesourd and Giles Hewitt, "Tibet's Dalai Lama Searches for Elected Successor," Agence France-Presse, January 28, 2001.

27 is intent on exercising complete control: Beijing's conditions for talks include the Dalai Lama's acknowledging that Taiwan is part of the People's Republic. See "China Restates Terms for Contacts with Dalai Lama," Reuters News Service, December 5, 2000. This condition, completely irrelevant to Tibet, appears designed to avoid discussions of any kind.

27 "The most important tenet": World News, narr. Sanjay Singh, CNN International, February 5, 2000.

28 carry on the struggle: See Marion Lloyd, "Karmapa Seen as Leader," South China Morning Post, February 10, 2000, p. 15.

28 none of the three most important: Although few know where Gedhun Choekyi Nyima, the Dalai Lama's choice of the Panchen Lama, actually lives, it is unlikely to be in Tibet, as Beijing claims. Many have speculated that, assuming that he is alive, he is somewhere near Beijing, if not actually in the capital.

29 "Not the same": Graeme Allen, interview by author, Shanghai, January 28, 2000.

29 "There is not a day": Daniel Kwan, "Xinjiang a Time Bomb Waiting to Explode: Leader," South China Morning Post, May 29, 2000, p. 7.

29 all the weapons and explosives they need: Ibid.

29 "There's a fire burning": Matt Forney, "Suppression in Xinjiang," in China in Transition: Towards the New Millennium, ed. Frank Ching (Hong Kong: Review Publishing, 1997), p. 208.

30 "The two communities live totally apart": Graeme Allen, interview by author, Shanghai, January 28, 2000.

30 prove to be uneconomic: Beijing's massive Tibetan infrastructure project, the railway running between Golmud (in Qinghai Province) and Lhasa, appears to lack economic justification. See Mark O'Neill, "Politically Motivated Tibet Rail Link to Fulfil Mao's Dream," South China Morning Post, February 11, 2001, p. 6.

32 "Totalitarian systems are never forever": "Ignorance Key Worry: Dalai Lama," South China Morning Post, May 18, 2000, p. 10.

33 President Lee Teng-hui's controversial remarks: Former President Lee's thoughts on the "two-states" principle are outlined in his article "Understanding Taiwan: Bridging the Perception Gap," Foreign Affairs, November–December 1999, p. 9.

33 they have little to do at their desks: Christopher S. Shapland Tibbs, interview by author, Shanghai, August 7, 1999.

33 General Zhang Wannian: World News, narr. Rebecca MacKinnon, CNN International, March 7, 2000.

34 "paper missiles": See Josephine Ma, "Cross-Strait Document Dismissed as 'Paper Missile,'" South China Morning Post, February 23, 2000, p. 10.

34 the election had been "a joke": "China's Premier Zhu Says Taiwan Vote a 'Joke,'" Reuters News Service, June 21, 2000. Zhu Rongji said, "If you say the president there was democratically elected, we reckon that's a joke."

34 "The people of Taiwan have spoken!": "Chen Shui Bian," Taiwan Decides, World News, narr. Tim Lister, CNN International, March 18, 2000.

36 "Mao made a big mistake": Ho Ping Hsien, telephone interview by author, March 23, 2000.

37   "to march over a cliff ": Patrick Tyler, interview by Karuna Shinsho, *Visions of China, CNN This Morning,* CNN International, September 29, 1999.

37   once again threatened nuclear war: Jasper Becker, "PLA Newspaper Details Strategies to 'Liberate' Island," *South China Morning Post,* March 20, 2000, p. 3.

38   12.7 percent: John Leicester, "China Increases Military Spending in Budget," Associated Press Newswires, March 5, 2000.

38   17.7 percent rise in 2001: "China to Appropriately Increase Defense Expenditures in 2001," Xinhua News Agency Bulletin, March 6, 2001. For a discussion of this apparently large budget increase, see Jeremy Page, "China Boosts Military Spending with Eye on Taiwan," Reuters News Service, March 6, 2001. Because much, if not most, of China's military budget is kept secret (Fong Tak-ho and Pamela Pun, "Bigger-budget Military Turns Heat on Taiwan," *Hong Kong Standard,* March 7, 2000, p. 1), it is not possible to quantify with assurance the magnitude of any increase or decrease in defense spending.

38   in excess of the economy's rates of growth: China's GDP, according to official statistics, increased by 8.0 percent in 2000. In 2001 it is expected that growth will be somewhat less than that figure. For a discussion of China's slowing economy, see Chapters 3 and 8.

39   shutting the door to compromise: See "China Issues Statement on Taiwan Election," People's Daily Online, March 19, 2000.

39   Destruction of your neighbor: Dalai Lama, interview by Larry King, *CNN 2000, Larry King Live Millennium,* CNN International, January 1, 2000.

40   "I will go to Tiananmen Square": William Kazer, "Internet Sites Full of Patriotic Messages," *South China Morning Post,* March 20, 2000, p. 3.

40   "whole world is just like one entity": Dalai Lama, interview by Larry King, *CNN 2000, Larry King Live Millennium,* CNN International, January 1, 2000.

40   "Have you heard?": Greg Torode, "Protest Anger Turned on China," *South China Morning Post,* December 2, 1999, p. 12.

41   "No one": Robert Kapp, interview by Mike Chinoy, *Visions of China, Insight Special Edition,* CNN International, September 30, 1999.

42   "The Communist Party exploits us anyway": This comment was overheard by Lydia Chang on November 15, 1999.

42   "I want the foreigners to know": Xu Xiaoying, interview by author, Dujiangyan, September 24, 2000.

42   70 to 130 million migrants: See "Country Cousins," *Economist,* April 8, 2000, China Survey, p. 15. Some believe that there are more than 130 million migrants, which is possible because recent statistics from China's Ministry of Labour and Social Security indicate that the number of surplus rural workers is about 150 million. See Bai Tianliang, "Urban and Rural Employment Faces More Pressure This Year," *People's Daily,* February 16, 2001, p. 5. As mentioned in Chapter 9, this surplus could be as high as 200 million.

43   undoubtedly exceeds 200 million: *China Hand: The Complete Guide to Doing Business in China* (Hong Kong: Economist Intelligence Unit, 2001), Chapter 1, p. 41, estimates that unemployment and underemployment in the countryside alone may account for 200 million people. Unemployment is also a problem in the cities, of course. In the larger urban areas, about 23 percent of workers lost a job in the 1999–2000 period.

Vivien Pik-Kwan Chan, "23Pc in Cities Lose Jobs as Reforms Bite," *South China Morning Post,* January 31, 2001, p. 6.

43   one hundred thousand additional unemployed: See "PRC Crackdown on Falungong Said Leaving 100,000 Jobless," Agence France-Presse, August 8, 2000. Another report puts the number of job losses at Zhong Gong businesses at 400,000. See "Report: 600 Leaders of Banned Chinese Exercise Group Arrested," Associated Press Newswires, March 4, 2000.

43   effective labor unions are not permitted: Workers who try to establish real unions are either jailed or committed to psychiatric wards. See, e.g., "China Holding Labor Activist in Mental Hospital," Associated Press Newswires, February 8, 2001 (unionist Cao Maobing). Cao Maobing's imprisonment in a mental institution highlights a disturbing trend in China's treatment of dissenters. See Robin Munro, "China's Judicial Psychiatry," *Asian Wall Street Journal,* February 19, 2001, p. 6.

43   virtually no mechanisms: When China finally ratified the International Covenant on Economic, Social and Cultural Rights in February 2001 it specifically noted that it would implement provisions regarding trade unions only in accordance with Chinese law. Meng Yan and Hu Qihua, "Legislators Approve Covenant on Rights," *China Daily,* March 1, 2001, p. 1. The effect of this reservation is to deny workers the right to organize unions of their own.

43   "the passersby had turned into demonstrators": "Who Deserves the Credit?," *Newsweek,* November 8, 1999, p. 18 (comments of Václav Havel).

44   "I was right": Richard M. Nixon, interview by Larry King, *Larry King Live,* CNN International, December 19, 1999 (replay of January 8, 1992, interview).

44   They fell when fears turned to hope: See "Who Deserves the Credit?," *Newsweek,* November 8, 1999, p. 18 (comments of Joachim Gauck).

44   "The only reason I still support the regime": "China's Long March," *Visions of China, CNN Perspectives,* narr. Rebecca MacKinnon, CNN International, October 1, 1999.

44   the people will follow: Tiananmen protester Han Dongfeng adopts a different view. "When all hope is gone, that is when you can fight for what you believe without fear," he says. Han Dongfeng, " 'When You Lose Hope, You Are Not Afraid of Anything,' " *South China Morning Post,* February 24, 2001, Education, p. 8.

3:   Industrial Theme Parks

46   rate of urban unemployment: China's statistics on "unemployed" do not include SOE workers who are "off duty," those laid off and receiving subsistence stipends while waiting for reemployment.

46   probably six times that or more: See *China Hand,* Chapter 1, p. 41. Some estimate unemployment in rust belt industrial cities is about 30 percent. See, e.g., "Tianjian, China," *Asia Tonight,* narr. Rebecca MacKinnon, CNN International, December 27, 2000. There appear to be no reliable statistics on unemployment and underemployment for China as a whole. All the evidence suggests that the official figure of 3.1 percent is much too low, and the government's assertion that the rate did not increase from 1997 to 2000, a time of increasing layoffs, is unbelievable in light of other central government statistics and all that is known about unemployment.

46   more than 30 percent: "More Than 30% of SOE Employees Still Idle," *Ming Pao* (Hong Kong), August 30, 2000, p. B14.

46   "one of the world's biggest and best collections": Foo Choy Peng, "Communiqué Echoes with Compromise," *South China Morning Post,* September 24, 1999, Business Post, p. 4.

48   Golden Summit: This narrative is based upon Susan V. Lawrence, "Too Many Mothers-in-Law," *Far Eastern Economic Review,* February 18, 1999, p. 12, and the results of Golden Summit's November 3, 2000, shareholders meeting.

49   "The government manages the national economy": "Decision of the CCP Central Committee on Some Issues Concerning the Establishment of a Socialist Market Economic Structure," adopted on November 14, 1993, by the Fourteenth Central Committee of the Party at its Third Plenary Session.

50   prefer to remain unprofitable: "China State Firms Caught in Loss-Making Rut," China Online, March 13, 2000.

50   change the name of the Party: Mark O'Neill, "Party Urged to Drop Communist Tag," *South China Morning Post,* February 28, 1999, p. 5.

51   perhaps two to three percentage points of growth: Gerald Segal, "Does China Matter?," *Foreign Affairs,* September–October 1999, p. 24.

51   about 70 percent of domestic lending: "2000 Crucial for State Firm Reform," *China Daily,* March 1, 2000, p. 4.

52   "If we did": Henny Sender, "Friends in High Places," *Far Eastern Economic Review,* April 29, 1999, p. 68.

53   even more loans for SOEs: See Geng Wei, "How to Improve External Circumstances for Reforming State-Owned Enterprises in the Next Few Years," *People's Daily,* August 21, 2000, p. 12.

53   "rich fruit in SOE reform": "Be Sure of Victory in Decisive Battle," editorial, People's Daily Online, December 23, 1999.

53   an eye-popping 140 percent: "Where the 239.2 Billion SOE Profits Come From," *China Information News* (Beijing), March 2, 2001, p. 1. The 140 percent claim is difficult to reconcile with the 4.5 percent increase announced less than two months earlier by Xinhua News Agency. See "China Confirms Success in SOE Reform," Xinhua News Agency Bulletin, January 9, 2001.

54   the premier declared: See "Premier Zhu Rongji on Economic Issues," People's Daily Online, December 14, 2000.

54   does not take into account: "Deadline for State Firms," *China Daily* (Hong Kong Edition), September 23, 1999, p. 1.

54   to the tune of about ¥1.3 trillion: For analyses of the 2000 figures, see Mark O'Neill, "Data Paints Distorted Picture as State Sector Struggles," *South China Morning Post,* January 20, 2001, Business Post, p. 3. For a discussion of the asset management company program, see Chapter 6.

54   State officials deny: See, e.g., Huang Gang, "Loss-Making State Firms Return to Black," *China Daily,* January 10, 2001, p. 1 (comments of Sheng Huaren, then minister of the State Economic and Trade Commission). Today official media are more candid and acknowledge that profits recently reported by SOEs are mostly the result of state intervention. See "SOEs Reform—Long Way Ahead," Xinhua News Agency Bulletin, March 8, 2001 (comments of economist Wu Shuqing).

54   A study released: See Zhang Dingmin, "SOEs Tainted by Accounts That Don't Add Up: Audit," *China Daily,* December 23, 1999, p. 3.

54   99 percent of SOEs misstated: See Li Jiangxing, "Enterprise Profits Inaccurate up to 33.4%," *People's Daily,* December 22, 2000, p. 2. For another central government study showing falsification of the financial results of state firms, see Zhu Yanyan, "Lots of Problems in Medium to Large State Enterprises," *China Business Times* (Beijing), January 5, 2001, p. 1.

54   profits of China's publicly listed firms: Karby Leggett, "Public Firms Fight to Turn Profit in China," *Asian Wall Street Journal,* May 4, 2000, p. 1.

54   Unsold inventories swelled: See, e.g., Jason Dean, "Industrial Firms in China Report Surge in Profits," *Asian Wall Street Journal,* May 11, 2000, p. 4.

54   valued at more than US$60 billion: Xiao Gong, "Idle Tools Cause Big Concern," *China Daily Business Weekly,* April 30, 2000, p. 1.

54   "preposterous": Mark O'Neill, "Too Good to Be True," *South China Morning Post,* June 29, 2000, Business Post, p. 18 (comments of unnamed Hong Kong merchant banker).

54   SOEs produced: *China Statistical Yearbook 2000,* pp. 118, 168, and 407.

55   "there's actually been a further falloff ": Karby Leggett, "China Posted 8.1% Growth in Quarter on Surge in Spending and Exports," *Asian Wall Street Journal,* April 19, 2000, p. 5 (comments of Hu Biliang of SG Securities).

55   "a great historical leap forward": "Decision of the Central Committee of the Chinese Communist Party (CCP) on Major Issues Concerning the Reform and Development of State-Owned Enterprises," adopted at the Fourth Plenary Session of the Fifteenth Chinese Communist Party Central Committee on September 22, 1999 (hereinafter cited as "Fourth Plenum Decision").

56   "cardiac patients": Cao has written a poem about SOEs, "Farewell, Tonics for Cardiac Patients." The poem is found at the end of his speech "The Unavoidable Question of Privatization," Fortune Global Forum, Shanghai, September 27–28, 1999.

57   approximately 110,000: *China Statistical Yearbook 2000,* p. 407. This number includes enterprises in which the controlling share is held by the state (in other words, it includes partially privatized enterprises). The number of SOEs is subject to great dispute, and estimates vary widely (with foreign estimates generally higher than official ones).

58   Beijing would need: "Efficiency Holds Key to State Firm Reform," *China Daily,* October 7, 1999, p. 4 (estimate of Development Research Centre of the State Council).

59   Growth in 2000 was announced to be 8.0 percent: See Xu Dashan, "Nation's GDP Grew by 8% Last Year," *China Daily,* January 1, 2001, p. 3.

59   the turnaround was more apparent than real: See Chapter 8.

59   "has no clear winners": Edward Steinfeld, interview by Andrew Stevens, *Asia Business Morning,* CNN International, October 1, 1999.

60   "we advance as appropriate": Jiang Zemin, "Strengthen Confidence, Deepen Reform, Create a New Situation in Development of State-Owned Enterprises," Dalian, August 12, 1999 (hereinafter cited as "Dalian Address"). This major speech on SOE reform was published by the Xinhua News Agency.

61   "fundamental guarantee": Fourth Plenum Decision. To similar effect is a more re-

cent pronouncement. "Leaders Call for Enhanced Leadership over State Firms," People's Daily Online, February 28, 2000.

61   "we have gained": Dalian Address.

62   "The core of international economic competition": Ibid.

63   Hualu produced mainly bad debts: See Yasheng Huang, "WTO Entry Is Critical to China's Stability," *Asian Wall Street Journal,* September 28, 1999, p. 10.

63   subsequently canceled: Sun Min, "Company Assumes Debt Loads," *China Daily,* November 3, 1999, p. 5.

63   trying to diversify: Henny Sender, "Friends in High Places," *Far Eastern Economic Review,* April 29, 1999, p. 68.

63   "scientific management": Fourth Plenum Decision.

64   "avert risks": Dalian Address.

64   imposes cost controls: See Kathy Wilhelm, "Out of Business," *Far Eastern Economic Review,* February 18, 1999, p. 10.

66   China's most important issue: Hu Angang, "The Future of China's Economic Development," *China Economic Times* (Beijing), September 3, 1999, p. 5.

66–67   "a new conceptual breakthrough": "A Move to Breakthrough," *China Daily,* September 24, 1999, p. 4.

67   as if it will increase: Fourth Plenum Decision.

68   The grim news: Nicholas R. Lardy, *China's Unfinished Economic Revolution* (Washington, D.C.: Brookings Institution Press, 1998), p. 220.

68   "no one has yet found": Susan V. Lawrence, "Too Many Mothers-in-Law," *Far Eastern Economic Review,* February 18, 1999, p. 12.

68   "its pace of development": William Mellor, "China: The Next 50 Years," *Asia Inc.,* March 1999, p. 14.

4:   future@china.communism

72   "You can use the photograph": Matthew Miller, "Independent Advisers Take Up Baton as Face of Economy Transforms," *South China Morning Post,* November 23, 1999, Business Post, p. 6.

72   China's fourth most popular Web site: "Top 10 Most Popular Sites in 1999," *China Daily Business Weekly,* March 26, 2000, p. 5.

75   about 22.5 million Internet users: "Internet Users up to 22.50Mn in China," People's Daily Online, January 17, 2001. Many analysts challenge the official figures for 2000. See, e.g., Doug Nairne, "Mainland Web Usage Lower Than Estimated, Says Survey," *South China Morning Post,* January 12, 2001, Business Post, p. 3 (usage 25 percent lower than official figures).

75   the number of netizens: Charles Huang, an Internet entrepreneur, estimates that China will surpass the United States by 2003. *Visions of China, CNN This Morning,* narr. Mike Chinoy, CNN International, September 29, 1999.

75   one of China's portals estimates: This prediction was made by King Lai, chief executive of NetEase.com. King Lai, CLSA China Forum 2000, Shanghai, May 10, 2000 (panel discussion comments).

75   Edward Zeng of Sparkice: Edward Q. Zeng, e-mail to author, May 13, 2000.

76 His country cousin needs more than four: State media recently trumpeted the arrival of the New Economy in the countryside by telling the story of Lu Zihan, who sells "black food" online. See "Elderly Villager Makes Money Out of Internet," People's Daily Online, January 10, 2001. In order to enter cyberspace, Lu paid ¥10,000 (about US$1,209) for a computer. Urban per capita income in 1999 was ¥5,854.0, and the corresponding figure for rural areas for that year was ¥2,210.3. China Statistical Yearbook 2000, p. 312.

77 Rutger Palmstierna: interview by author, Shanghai, October 25, 1999.

77 ban on satellite dishes: See, e.g., "Shanghai Seizes Illegal Satellite TV Receivers," Associated Press Newswires, June 14, 2000. The ban is widely flouted. The most popular foreign channel in China is received by almost all of its viewers through illegal dishes. See "Rise of the Phoenix," Business China, October 9, 2000, p. 1.

77 attempting to manage information: Sometimes Beijing's efforts to control the media fail miserably. Protesters in Shandong Province recently prevented authorities from closing an illegal television station carrying foreign films and sex videos. Zhang Hui-jun, "Illegal Television Station Still Broadcasting," Legal Daily (Beijing), February 14, 2001, p. 1.

78 "The truth is, communism exhausted its possibilities": Lech Wałęsa, interview by Chris Burns, Visions of Europe: Ten Years After, World News Europe, CNN International, October 18, 1999.

78 patrolling the Internet: China's provinces and cities are establishing their own Internet police. "China Says Provinces Setting Up Internet Police," Reuters News Service, August 5, 2000.

78 neglects to enforce: The central government is fond of reissuing multiple sets of rules covering the same ground in lieu of enforcing existing provisions. This trend is best illustrated in China's regulation of the Internet. After issuing the January 2000 rules, the central government in September and November 2000 promulgated other sets of prohibitions and requirements. Recently Beijing promised still more Internet rules. See "Internet Regulations to Be Updated," China Daily, January 18, 2001, p. 3.

79 impossible to enforce: The newly-issued encryption requirements were so broad that they had to be cut back. In March 2000 they were clarified to reduce their scope, but they will probably be amended again because important ambiguities remain even after the revision.

79 "Fifty years after China went through a Communist revolution": Visions of China, Q&A in Shanghai, narr. Riz Khan, CNN International, September 28, 1999.

79 "In order to inspect the Internet, we must control it": "Shanghai Tells Corporate Internet Users To Register," Reuters News Service, January 7, 2000.

80 "you could stand with a gun behind a man": Lech Wałęsa, interview by Chris Burns, Visions of Europe: Ten Years After, World News Europe, CNN International, October 18, 1999.

84 The remaining three: Sing Wang, interview by author, Guangzhou, November 14, 1999.

84 "as soon as they hear": Alysha Webb, "China's Expected Entry Draws Venture Capital to Internet," Bridge News, November 25, 1999.

85 "China in this respect is democratic": Cindy Sui, "Chinese Schoolchildren Ignorant of 1989 Tiananmen Massacre," Agence France-Presse, October 1, 1999.

85 "My choice cannot be independent": "Person of the Week," *China Daily Business Weekly,* October 17, 1999, p. 8.

90 "can surpass that of the United States and Japan": "Zhu Pushes Hi-Tech Shenzhen," *South China Morning Post,* October 5, 1999, p. 1.

90 "China needs the Internet": Peter Yip, interview by Marina Kolbe, *Q&A Asia,* CNN International, June 15, 2000. Yip is chief executive officer of China.com.

91 few transactions involving state assets: As Graham Earnshaw, a China Internet analyst, says, "The situation changes, the line moves almost every day." Lydia Zajc, "Lessons in Setting Up Dotcoms in China," review of *The Life and Death of a Dotcom in China,* ed. Graham Earnshaw, *South China Morning Post,* December 5, 2000, Technology Post, p. 10.

91 she did not know what to say: Zhang Jingjun, interview by author, June 15, 2000.

92 "there will be people who are upset": Ibid.

92 still does not have a true Internet: See, e.g., Kristie Lu Stout, interview by Lian Pek, *ebizasia,* CNN International, November 11, 2000. Kristie Lu Stout, a China Internet analyst, says, "Some people say that the Internet in China is not a true Internet. A true Internet is a distributed network where no one is in charge, no one takes control and it's controlled, or, how should I say, managed only by the users or the participants that actually create the communities that generate the Internet. In China it's just the opposite. It's centrally run, there are only four gateways linking the Internet in China to the outside world, and largely running on one single carrier, and that's China Telecom, but that's the way China Internet has always been. Not a real Internet, but an Internet with Chinese characteristics."

92 "China must build": Willy Wo-Lap Lam, "Combatting Web Imperialism," *South China Morning Post,* June 14, 2000, p. 18.

92 "electronic heroin": Ibid.

92 Beijing announced the formation: "China Moving Ahead with Plan for Its Own Internet," Associated Press Newswires, January 6, 2001.

92 "It cannot be stopped": Zhang Jingjun, interview by author, Guangzhou, June 15, 2000.

92 "So that should be the end of it": Ibid.

93 has lost much of its value: In September 2000, Tom.com, a Hong Kong portal controlled by Li Ka-shing, agreed to buy 163.net. The sales price was substantially less than the price agreed upon in the proposed transaction described in the text. Due to Mainland restrictions, Tom.com could not actually acquire ownership of 163.net itself. It could, however, acquire rights to various streams of income from this Guangzhou-based e-mail business.

5: Life Everlasting

94 He could name only: "McEnroe Brands ATP," *USA Today,* November 5, 1999, Sports, p. 1.

94 "gone": Jonathan Alter, "From the Prison of the 'Isms,' " *Newsweek,* December 27, 1999, p. 33.

95 private vendors: Alysha Webb, interview by author, Shanghai, January 7, 2000.

95 "the highest growth potential": "Investing in China," *Visions of China, Asia Business Morning,* narr. Lisa Barron, CNN International, September 29, 1999.

97 "I can't go down in history": "Infatuation's End," *Economist,* September 25, 1999, p. 77.

98 Citic Heavy: See "Luoyang Mining Machinery Factory: A Tragedy of Errors," *Business China,* October 25, 1999, p. 3.

99 the first publicly listed company: Peng Xiaohong, "Will Zhengzhou Baiwen Be Sentenced to Death?," *China Business Times* (Beijing), April 20, 2000, p. 5.

99 only 7,528 bankruptcy filings: Cao Siyuan, telephone interview by Lydia Chang, February 13, 2001. Cao is considered the principal drafter of China's Enterprise Bankruptcy Law.

99 not a system: There were 4,722 bankruptcies in 1999. Cao Siyuan, telephone interview by Lydia Chang, May 18, 2000. The large increase in bankruptcies in 2000 resulted from the central government's postponing bankruptcy filings that would have normally occurred in 1999 (the department in charge of a state-owned enterprise can prevent that enterprise from entering bankruptcy through various means, including invoking the provisions of the bankruptcy law). In 1999, bankruptcies were postponed to avoid alarming foreign lenders and investors who had already expressed concern over the failure of Guangdong International Trust & Investment Corp. in late 1998. Cao Siyuan, telephone interview by Lydia Chang, February 13, 2001.

100 as if cripples: The image of cripples bound to one another is borrowed from General Electric lingo. See "The House That Jack Built," *Economist,* September 18, 1999, p. 21.

100 laying straw and flowers over a minefield: Cao Siyuan, "Evaluation of the 10-Year Implementation of the Bankruptcy Law of the People's Republic of China," Bankruptcy Reform in China: Gitic and Beyond conference in Hong Kong, April 13, 1999.

101 the first borrower in that country's history: Juanito Concepción, "Gitic Default Fuels Concern," *Hong Kong Standard,* October 28, 1998, Business Standard, p. 1.

102 "the world's brashest capitalist economy": "Private Salvation?," *Economist,* April 8, 2000, China Survey, p. 5.

102 they are now regulated: The best example of this trend is the Price Law, which gives the central government virtually unlimited authority to establish prices for tangible goods, nontangible assets, and services.

102 CAAC, acting in its regulatory role: CAAC also acts as a manager to China's newly formed airlines, purchasing aircraft and providing ground support services. Chinese carriers have suffered as a result of CAAC's nonregulatory management functions.

103 80 percent of revenues: Guo Aibing, "Discount Dilemma Lingers," *China Daily Business Weekly,* April 16, 2000, p. 8.

103 "Our purpose is to prevent the airlines": Nora Ying, "Price-Cutting on Airfares Is Under Siege," *Shanghai Daily,* March 29, 2000, p. 1. It evidently has not occurred to CAAC that lower fares mean more passengers, which helps the airlines too.

103 the industry to consolidate: Guo Aibing, "CAAC Pushes Airline Consolidation," *China Daily,* July 22, 2000, p. 1.

103 the third largest alumina producer: Xie Ye, "China Creates Alumina Monolith," *China Daily,* February 24, 2001, p. 3.

104 "We can sit down and talk": "CNPC, Sinopec Sign Pact to Avoid Price Battle," Reuters News Service, March 26, 1999.

104   did not halt the competition: See, e.g., Li Heng, "Grueling Fight by Oil Giants Forecast," People's Daily Online, February 27, 2001; "Cease Gas Station Purchase War," *Ming Pao* (Hong Kong), August 8, 2000, p. B12.

105   using their powers: See, e.g., Hui Yuk-min, "China Unicom Joins Price War," *South China Morning Post,* March 2, 2001, Business Post, p. 4. China Telecom still dominates the telecommunications industry: at the beginning of 2001 it retained a 67 percent share of the overall telecommunications market and 95 percent of the fixed-line business. "One Goliath, Several Davids," *Business China,* January 29, 2001, p. 4.

105   is still trying to stand in the way: See, e.g., Christopher Torrens, "who's in charge.cn: The Orchestration of China's Internet," Economist Intelligence Unit, December 2000, pp. 10–11.

106   "There will be progress only if there is competition": Zhang Jingjun, interview by author, Guangzhou, June 15, 2000.

106   "Practise not doing": Michael Vatikiotis, "Capital Idea," *Far Eastern Economic Review,* June 10, 1999, p. 55.

107   some 120 government-sponsored incubators: Rustam Lalkaka, interview by author, Shanghai, October 25, 2000. The actual number may be slightly lower. See Tao Yungang, "Shanghai Incubators to Hatch High-Tech," *China Daily,* April 19, 2000, p. 2.

107   Only the United States and Germany: Rustam Lalkaka, interview by author, Shanghai, October 25, 2000.

108   "we have a brand name": Quotations in the text attributed to Dinyar Lalkaka were obtained from interviews conducted by the author in Shanghai on April 11, June 19, and September 14, 2000.

108   the Sinofied version of "dot com": The Lalkakas didn't come up with that moniker, but it has somehow stuck through popular demand. Dinyar Lalkaka, interview by author, Shanghai, September 14, 2000.

108   ON-LINE INCUBATOR IMPLEMENTED: Shi Hua, "On-line Incubator Implemented," *China Daily,* April 20, 2000, p. 5.

110   China's "first" incubator: "BCG to Launch E-Commerce Incubator in China," Reuters News Service, March 22, 2000.

110   It has yet to be formed: Dinyar Lalkaka, interviews by author, Shanghai, June 19, 2000, and September 14, 2000.

110   80 percent of the venture capital: Xiao Guo, "Venture Capital Group Established," *China Daily,* February 20, 2001, p. 2.

111   personally attending to the details: Willy Wo-Lap Lam, "Hi-Tech Confucian Future," *South China Morning Post,* October 13, 1999, p. 19.

111   about 99 percent foreign: Antoaneta Bezlova, "Last Chance to Get on IT Train, Global Information Network," IPS Newsfeed, December 3, 1999.

111   "biggest securities fraud": Mark O'Neill, "Light-Rail Project Marks Start of Reluctant Move for Hi-Tech Glory," *South China Morning Post,* August 9, 1999, Business Post, p. 3.

112   "21st century belongs to Zhongguancun": Ibid.

112   "as big as Hong Kong": Willy Wo-Lap Lam, "Hi-Tech Confucian Future," *South China Morning Post,* October 13, 1999, p. 19.

112 "a hot cake for both capital and human talents": "Zhongguancun to Be Built into Leading Science Park," China Business Information Network, December 6, 1999.

112 8,224 in early 2001: "Chinese 'Silicon Valley' Sets New Record," Xinhua News Agency Bulletin, February 5, 2001.

112 up 27 percent in 1999: Mark O'Neill, "Silicon Valley Dream Remote from Reality," South China Morning Post, February 21, 2000, Business Post, p. 3.

112 almost 47 percent: "Chinese 'Silicon Valley' Sets New Record," Xinhua News Agency Bulletin, February 5, 2001.

113 "The single greatest untapped resource": Meredith M. Walker and Richard Alm, "China's Churn," September 2000 (available at www.dallasfed.org).

113 "In Qinghua, 82 per cent of graduates": Mark O'Neill, "Capital Woes at Core of Progress Doubts," South China Morning Post, October 29, 1999, Business Post, p. 4.

113 only about a third of them return: "Debate Arises Over Foreign Study Temptation," People's Daily Online, February 26, 2001. Unofficial sources say that only a quarter of Chinese students have returned. See Mark O'Neill, "Old Heads Rule Roost," South China Morning Post, August 29, 2000, p. 12.

114 "It is more important to create an ideal structure": Wang Chuandong, "Fair Focuses on IT Progress," China Daily Business Weekly, October 17, 1999, p. 5.

115 Marxism is a scientific body of thought: "Learn More Science, Apply It Quickly, President Urges," China Daily, June 6, 2000, p. 1.

115 a rarity: See, e.g., Jennifer Hyman, "Grand Plans Under Threat," South China Morning Post, November 28, 2000, Technology Post, p. 8.

116 becoming a sleazy haven: Karby Leggett, "In the Zone," Asian Wall Street Journal, October 2, 2000, World Business Supplement, p. S8.

117 The three most important inventions: "Hang On Lads, I've Got an Idea," Economist, December 31, 1999, p. 99.

118 "There is no attempt": Rustam Lalkaka, interview by author, Shanghai, October 25, 2000.

118 needed a government bailout: Rustam Lalkaka, interview by author, Shanghai, October 31, 2000.

118 "one of the world's most advanced science parks": "Financial Aid," China Daily, March 3, 2000, p. 2.

118 "the first productive force": Dalian Address.

118 less than 2 percent: Elaine Kurtenbach, "China, Seeking High-Tech Leap Forward, Gets Snagged in Its Past," Associated Press Newswires, February 5, 2001.

119 "it's so vastly different it's unimaginable": Lee Kwan Yew, interview by Riz Khan, Visions of China, Q&A in Shanghai, CNN International, September 29, 1999.

119 "The Communist Party": Vivien Pik-Kwan Chan, "Jiang Tells Party to Embrace Net," South China Morning Post, March 4, 2000, p. 1.

119 his solution to all issues: "Party Building Given Top Priority," China Daily, February 26, 2000, p. 1.

120 "poverty and trouble": Meng Yan, "Textiles Need More Assistance," China Daily, January 28, 2000, p. 5.

120 "virtually doomed": Leslie Chang, "State-Backed Firms Join China's Internet Race," Asian Wall Street Journal, April 26, 2000, p. 1.

121 designed to force private portals to close: See, e.g., Mark O'Neill, "Beijing Closes

Net Around Web Sites," *South China Morning Post,* October 4, 2000, Business Post, p. 10.

6: The Banks That Sank

122   not been one single default: Daniel Kwan, "Junior Banker Hailed as Hero of the System," *South China Morning Post,* October 22, 1998, p. 10.

123   approximately US$720.9 billion: *China Statistical Yearbook 2000,* p. 311. Perhaps a third of the funds in China's household accounts is illegally parked corporate cash. Accordingly, the amount of true private savings in banks is undoubtedly less than the official figures indicate.

124   still comprised 25 percent: Dan Yuqing, "Bad Loans Seen Bottom," *China Economic Times* (Beijing), January 18, 2001, p. 1; "Non-Performing Assets Bottoming Out—Governor," Xinhua News Agency Bulletin, January 17, 2001.

124   mentioned by Standard & Poor's: See Jon Ogden, "S&P Sees Beijing Ratings Steady Despite Potential for Problem Loan Surge," *South China Morning Post,* August 10, 2000, Markets Post, p. 1.

124   "The more I knew": Johannes Schoeter, interview by author, Hong Kong, April 14, 2000.

124   must have reduced: This calculation assumes that, apart from the US$157.0 billion recapitalization, there was no material improvement or deterioration in the portfolios of the state commercial banks in 2000.

124   Beijing's technocrats estimate: See, e.g., Wang Ying, "No Anxiety Needed of Big Debt Burden," *China Daily Business Weekly,* July 9, 2000, p. 1 (estimates of Wang Guogang of the Chinese Academy of Social Sciences).

124   Recent foreign estimates: See, e.g., Bruce Gilley, "Moment of Truth," *Far Eastern Economic Review,* June 15, 2000, p. 58. A recent Merrill Lynch research report assumed, in determining China's fiscal condition, that the country would recover 15 percent of its nonperforming loans. See Merrill Lynch, Pierce, Fenner & Smith, Inc., "China—The New Power," January 12, 2001, p. 24.

124   a figure more consistent: See, e.g., Lardy, *China's Unfinished Economic Revolution,* pp. 142–3 (especially note 51). It is estimated that Gitic creditors will eventually receive about 12 percent of the face value of their claims. Juanito Concepcion, "Banks May Recover Only 12pc from Gitic Unit," *Hong Kong Standard,* April 21, 1999, Business Standard, p. 1.

125   somewhere in the vicinity: A portion of the unrecoverable loans is held by four "asset management companies," which are discussed later in this chapter. The figure in the text includes such loans and loans remaining in the banking system, which is comprised of banks and entities such as rural and urban credit cooperatives. Such figure does not include unrecoverable debt held by the state policy banks, which extend loans as dictated by central government policy.

125   "There is no simple answer": Matt Forney, "China's Economy Slowed in Third Quarter," *Asian Wall Street Journal,* October 20, 1999, p. 1 (comments of He Guangbei of the Bank of China).

125   "According to our audits": Wang Ying, "Banks Pass Audits," *China Daily Business Weekly,* January 23, 2000, p. 1.

125   "seeking truth from facts": "Options for China's Financial System," in *Strengthening the Banking System in China: Issues and Experience,* Bank for International Settlements Policy Paper No. 7, October 1999, p. 321 (hereinafter cited as "BIS Paper No. 7").

125   "For many observers": Rudi Dornbusch and Francesco Giavazzi, "Heading Off China's Financial Crisis," in BIS Paper No. 7, p. 40 (emphasis added).

126   as even central bank statistics admit: See *People's Bank of China Quarterly Statistical Bulletin,* vol. 20 (2000–4), pp. 28–9.

126   even by local units: See, e.g., Matthew Miller and William Kazer, "The Loans That Went Too Far," *South China Morning Post,* March 30, 2000, p. 15 (illegal deposit-taking company run by the local branch of the Party in Zhenjiang in Jiangsu Province).

126   more than its share of unrest: For an example of unrest in Chongqing, see "2,000 Victims of Illegal Chinese Investment Scheme Protest," Agence France-Presse, November 14, 1999.

126   why Beijing is beginning to execute: See Fang Yibo, Wang Xianfu, and Pan Xiande, "Taizhou Tries 'Pagoda Fund' for Fraud and Taking Illegal Deposits," *People's Daily,* November 27, 1999, p. 4.

127   "Isn't slower better?": Bill Savadove, "China Shuts Another Trust in Cleanup," Reuters News Service, August 7, 2000.

127   Big Four: The Big Four are Bank of China, the Industrial and Commercial Bank of China, China Construction Bank, and the Agricultural Bank of China.

127   68.4 percent of the deposits and made some 71.0 percent of the loans: The percentages in the text are derived from preliminary PBOC statistics, which were not adjusted to account for the Big Four's transfer of about ¥1.3 trillion of loans to four asset management companies. The statistics in the text have been adjusted to reflect such transfer.

127   150,000 branches: "Ready or Not," *Business China,* January 3, 2000, p. 12. The number of branches is subject to some dispute, as others believe the number is lower. The disparity in number may be due to how subbranches are counted.

129   "The bad news": Douglas Lee Red, "Outlook for the Chinese Banking System," *Forecasting China to the Year 2002 and Profitability,* Economist Intelligence Unit Business China Group Shanghai, Shanghai, September 17, 1998.

129   "only a portion": Karby Leggett, "China Central Bk Implements New Warning System for Banks," Dow Jones Newswires, May 21, 1999.

129   The run lasted four days: Tian Junrong, "Luan County Relevant Responsible Personnel Seriously Reprimanded," *People's Daily,* November 3, 2000, p. 1.

130   "tiger in a cage": "Run on Chinese Banks Unlikely—Survey," China Online, April 4, 2000.

131   "quite unique": Xu Binglan, "PBOC Says Financial Issues Are Manageable," *China Daily,* April 5, 1999, p. 5.

131   It was a fib: We know that because, only a few years after, the banks began reporting capital adequacy ratios well below 8 percent and today the PBOC is still talking about lifting the ratios to that percentage. See Dan Yuqing, "Bad Loans Seen Bottom," *China Economic Times* (Beijing), January 18, 2001, p. 1.

132   Do it quickly, do it big, and do it just once: See Rudi Dornbusch and Francesco Giavazzi, "Heading Off China's Financial Crisis," in BIS Paper No. 7, p. 40.

132   The aftershocks of a banking crisis: Ibid.

132　"I know some people": Owen Brown, "China to Step Up Reform of Banks as WTO Looms," *Asian Wall Street Journal*, January 21, 2000, p. 3.

133　about ¥1.3 trillion: By the end of 2000, the asset management companies acquired about ¥1.3 trillion of debt (US$157.0 billion) from the Big Four and ¥0.1 trillion (US$12.1 billion) of debt from the policy banks, state banks that make loans as directed by government policy.

133　preventing them from talking: The interference by local officials is discussed in Li Lun, "Seven Difficulties Facing the Restructuring of Financial Institutions," *Economic Daily* (Beijing), January 11, 2000, p. 10.

133　"free lunch": Wu Yan, "Have Debt-Equity Swaps Lost Temperature?," *People's Daily*, March 28, 2000, p. 13.

133　"blackmailing" local governments: Wu Yan, "The Focus Behind the Focus," *People's Daily*, March 30, 2000, p. 13.

134　"Cinda can exert pressure": "Passing the Debt," *Business China*, June 21, 1999, p. 1.

134　will recover less the longer it postpones: Even the official media is coming to this conclusion. See Liu Yuan, "Asset Disposal: The Faster the Better," *People's Daily*, February 7, 2001, p. 5. One of the four AMCs, Huarong Asset Management Corp., is taking an aggressive approach by trying to sell about 5 percent of its portfolio of nonperforming debt to foreign parties. *The Asian Wall Street Journal*, however, suggests that this course of action may be "mission impossible." Peter Wonacott, "Huarong Hires Ernst & Young for Asset Sales," *Asian Wall Street Journal*, February 21, 2001, p. 1.

135　"We hope that": Christine Chan and Renee Lai, "PBOC Vows Radical Financial Overhaul," *South China Morning Post*, November 19, 1998, Business Post, p. 1.

136　"No government agencies or individuals": "China Seen Facing High Bar in Bad Debt Clean-up," Reuters News Service, April 27, 1999.

138　"don't have much retail banking experience": Simon Pritchard and Wang Xiang-wei, "Capitalist Boom and Gloom Predicted," *South China Morning Post*, November 16, 1999, p. 3.

139　all sorts of additional annoying prohibitions: See "Playing Favourites," *Business China*, June 5, 2000, p. 7; "New Hurdles," *Economist*, April 8, 2000, p. 91; "China Weighs Restrictions on Foreign Banks Renminbi Business," China Online, February 4, 2000. The PBOC sought to impose a capital adequacy ratio for the renminbi business of foreign banks. Despite press reports to the contrary, this proposed general restriction was not put in place (although it might have been applied to certain foreign banks on a case-by-case basis). The PBOC then sought to impose the 8 percent Bank for International Settlements capital adequacy standard to the local branches of foreign banks as if those branches were stand-alone banks. At this time it is not known whether the PBOC will continue its efforts to impose such a standard.

139　The country's top think tank: Wang Songqi, "WTO: What Will It Bring to the Chinese Financial Industry?," *China Economic Times* (Beijing), November 16, 1999, p. 4.

141　still paying interest: Johannes Schoeter, interview by author, Hong Kong, April 14, 2000.

141　one third of the homeowners: Gordon Chang, "Big Four Banks Bleeding but Far from Deathbeds," *South China Morning Post*, September 9, 1999, China Business Review, p. 4.

141 "it's better to repay late": Wu Yan, "Have Debt-Equity Swaps Lost Temperature?," *People's Daily*, March 28, 2000, p. 13.

141 "based on the repudiation of debt": "Warning Sounded on Dangers of Converting Bad Loans into Equity," *South China Morning Post,* October 13, 1999, Business Post, p. 6 (comments of Yi Gang, Vice-Director of Beijing University China Economic Research Centre).

142 "deteriorated dramatically in recent years": Nicholas R. Lardy, "The Challenge of Bank Restructuring in China," in BIS Paper No. 7, p. 17.

142 "The Chinese government is not stupid": "Ready or Not," *Business China,* January 3, 2000, p. 12.

143 To ensure greater control: Carsten Holz, "Two Solutions for China's Banks," *Asian Wall Street Journal,* July 29, 1999, p. 10.

143 "no perfect recipe": Liu Mingkang, "Conclusion," in BIS Paper No. 7, p. 341.

143 the same process is at work: Paul Mooney, "An Ancient Wall Street," *Far Eastern Economic Review,* June 17, 1999, p. 47.

7: Biting the Snakes

145 He's possibly the richest: Chen Rong is not the richest person from Shanghai included in *Forbes Global*'s list of richest Chinese entrepreneurs (Rupert Hoogewerf, "China's 50 Richest Entrepreneurs," *Forbes Global,* November 27, 2000, p. 150). The magazine's estimate of his net worth does not include the value of his stock-trading portfolio and other nonbusiness assets because he did not disclose this information to its reporter. Chen Rong, interview by Lydia Chang, Shanghai, December 20, 2000. Some publications have estimated Chen's net worth at about US$100 million. See, e.g., Trish Saywell, "Strike!," *Far Eastern Economic Review,* September 23, 1999, p. 48.

145 "My life seemed like an endless nightmare": Trish Saywell, "Strike!," *Far Eastern Economic Review,* September 23, 1999, p. 48.

145 He multiplied his stake: Chen Rong, discussed his early life with Lydia Chang in interviews conducted in Shanghai on May 25, 2000, October 30, 2000, and December 20, 2000.

146 "they only remember the fun of bowling": Chen Rong, interview by Lydia Chang, Shanghai, May 25, 2000.

146 "a deep impression": Ibid.

146 AMF and Brunswick: Wen Kang, telephone interview by Lydia Chang, October 30, 2000. Kang is the manager of AMF's operations in China.

147 about 45 percent: Anthony Neoh, "The Three Critical Drivers of the Chinese Domestic Capital Markets," CLSA China Forum 2000, Shanghai, May 10, 2000.

147 the range of disagreement is huge: "Private Salvation?," *Economist,* April 8, 2000, China Survey, p. 5. For an explanation of the divergence of these estimates, see "A Private Affair," *Business China,* September 25, 2000, p. 1.

148 "the largest potential for bowling in the world": Gil Klein, "China Trade Divides South," *Richmond Times-Dispatch,* May 1, 2000, p. A1.

150 "I'm going to go put on a bowling shirt": Mark Yost, "AMF Bowling Chief Will Go to Lanes to Learn Business," *Wall Street Journal,* May 4, 1999, Marketplace, p. B9B.

150 Chen Rong studied the technology: Chen Rong, interview by author, Shanghai, June 7, 2000.

152 foreign investment would fall dramatically: As it turned out, actual foreign investment in 1999 declined 11.4 percent from the previous year to US$40.4 billion.

152 "No weapon can wipe out the truth": Wei Jingsheng, "Unorthodox Opinions Are Heard on the Street," *Time Asia,* September 27, 1999, p. 85.

153 "I hope someday that China": *Visions of China, Asia Tonight,* narr. Mike Chinoy, CNN International, September 28, 1999.

153 "It's ironic that Time Warner has not pulled out": Lee Kuan Yew, interview by Riz Khan, *Visions of China, Q&A in Shanghai,* CNN International, September 29, 1999.

155 foreign business often goes to bat: *Visions of China, Asia Tonight,* narr. Mike Chinoy, CNN International, September 28, 1999.

155 "You have no idea": Linda Jakobson, *A Million Truths: A Decade in China* (New York: M. Evans, 1998), p. 143.

156 *Fortune,* contrary to its usual practice, caved in: *Visions of China, Asia Tonight,* narr. Mike Chinoy, CNN International, September 28, 1999.

157 "My childhood can be made into a movie": Chen Rong, interview by author, Shanghai, June 7, 2000.

158 "Making money, that's my goal": *Visions of China, World News,* narr. Mike Chinoy, CNN International, September 22, 1999.

163 Shenyang Micro-electronics: Huo Shiming, "The Saga of an Auction of an Enterprise," *Legal Daily* (Beijing), February 8, 1999, p. 3.

163 five thousand similar disputes: "A Number of Question Marks in the 'Shenyang Micro-Electronics' Situation," *Legal Daily* (Beijing), February 8, 1999, p. 3.

163 "Once it has money": Mark O'Neill, "Ex–State Workers Get Physical over Western-Style Methods," *South China Morning Post,* January 13, 2000, Business Post, p. 4.

163 "What I am positive about": Jack Perkowski, "Creating Globally Competitive Companies in China," CLSA China Forum 2000, Shanghai, May 10, 2000.

164 "The 21st century world belongs to the non-state sector": Willy Wo-Lap Lam, "WTO Strategy Holds Clues to Reform," *South China Morning Post,* September 29, 1999, p. 19.

164 "They do not really believe": Chen Rong, interview by Lydia Chang, Shanghai, May 25, 2000.

164 "He is a Party secretary": Ibid.

164 Deng Liqun: Willy Wo-Lap Lam, "Jiang Walks Tightrope Between Left and Right," *South China Morning Post,* May 6, 2000, p. 7.

164 Conditions approximating slavery: See, e.g., Xu Yue and Yan Hong, "Kunming Police Rescue 19 Abused Workers," *China Youth Daily* (Beijing), March 27, 2000, p. 1.

165 has ordered the media: Willy Wo-Lap Lam, "Jiang Walks Tightrope Between Left and Right," *South China Morning Post,* May 6, 2000, p. 7.

165 "In different situations": Chen Rong, interview by Lydia Chang, Shanghai, May 25, 2000.

165 "should work hard": "Communist Party Must Improve Leadership Skills," People's Daily Online, May 15, 2000.

165 "The Party can do what it will": Chen Rong, interview by author, Shanghai, June 7, 2000.

8: Highway Girls

171 "the retreat of the foreign beer makers": Peng Zuoyi, interview by Yan Zhigang, in Yan Zhigang, "Local Brands vs. Foreign Brands," *Economic Daily* (Beijing), July 7, 2000, p. 6.

171 the fastest in the world: Peter Wonacott, "Tsingtao, Thirsty to Reclaim Its Title, Is on a Buying Blitz," *Asian Wall Street Journal,* July 21, 2000, p. 13.

171 Price competition has wrecked the margins: Matt Pottinger, "Foreigners May Have Introduced Beer to China," Reuters News Service, August 20, 2000. Competition is so fierce in China that beer is now less expensive than bottled water.

172 "a city of superlatives": *Visions of China, CNN This Morning,* narr. Mike Chinoy, CNN International, September 27, 1999.

172 within eight years: See "How Now Hong Kong?," *Economist,* May 9, 1998, Financial Centres Survey, p. 27.

172 more skyscrapers than New York: George Q. Fu (former judge of the Shanghai High People's Court and noted lawyer), interview by author, Shanghai, September 25, 1999.

172 "The culture is tomorrow": Dean T. W. Ho, interview by author, Shanghai, January 22, 2000.

173 "We Shanghainese are shrewd and smart": *Visions of China, CNN This Morning,* narr. Mike Chinoy, CNN International, September 27, 1999.

173 "Manhattan of the East": *China Daily,* November 1, 2000, p. 12.

173 "You make them a little too long": Steven Mufson, "Economy of China Is Cooling," *Washington Post,* November 29, 1997, p. A1.

174 "perfect": "Premier Envisions Perfect Social Welfare," *China Daily,* May 30, 2000, p. 1.

174 taking such a long time: The establishment of a national social welfare system appears years away. See Jasper Becker, "Nationwide Social Security System Stalled by Lack of Will," *South China Morning Post,* December 24, 2000, p. 4.

174 vicious price wars: See, e.g., Dai Yan "Price War Deemed Self-Destructive," *China Daily,* February 22, 2001, p. 5 (air conditioner manufacturers have not learned from the TV price wars).

174 "reward": Zhao Xiaohua, "A Signal for Reduction in Car Prices?," *Beijing Daily,* January 25, 2000, p. 10.

174 the discounts were available to everyone: Chang Weimin, "Tianjin Firm Stages Auto Price War," *China Daily,* January 20, 2000, p. 5.

174 "inevitable": " 'Surplus' an Inevitable Period of Economic Transition," editorial, *China Daily,* December 1, 1999, p. 4.

175 "no need for concrete": Chen Zonglin, interview by author, Dujiangyan, September 24, 2000.

175 biggest ongoing civil engineering project: James Kynge, "Doubt over Three Gorges Power Demand," *Financial Times* (London), March 10, 2000, p. 10.

176 New investment in certain areas is prohibited: China has always restricted foreign investment to specifically-enumerated areas. These days the restrictions have acquired a new purpose: to limit supply.

176 a coordinated price increase: Karby Leggett, "China Sparks Increase in Steel Prices," *Asian Wall Street Journal,* June 1, 2000, p. 1.

176   a similar agreement: Mark O'Neill, "Economic Planners Turn On to Shutdown of TV-Tube Production," *South China Morning Post,* August 16, 1999, Business Post, p. 3.

177   about US$0.73 per day: Du Dengbin, "Peasants' Income Waiting for a 'Turning Point,' " *China Economic Times* (Beijing), January 8, 2001, p. 1.

177   nowhere in sight: Official statistics show that peasants' income increased by 2 percent in 2000. See Zhao Huanxin, "Poor Harvest Not Affecting Supply," *China Daily,* January 8, 2001, p. 1. That statistic does not appear accurate in view of other available evidence about the disappointing harvest in that year.

178   lost her profits (and much more): Zhou Xiaoyi, interview by Lydia Chang, Shanghai, June 1, 2000.

179   Growth picked up: See Xu Dashan, "Nation's GDP Soars 8.2 Per Cent," *China Daily,* July 19, 2000, p. 1; "China's GDP Grows 8.2 Percent," People's Daily Online, July 18, 2000.

179   deflation eased: China claimed that consumer prices rose 0.4 percent in 2000. "China Maintains Stable Market Price in 2000," Xinhua News Agency Bulletin, February 28, 2001.

179   "China's time is now": Kathy Wilhelm, "Starting to Sizzle," *Far Eastern Economic Review,* August 24, 2000, p. 57 (comments of Stephen Roach of Morgan Stanley Dean Witter).

179   "My *qigong* level": Wu Chengwen, "Reveal the True Face of the Falun Gong Cult," *Nanfang Zhoumo* (Guangzhou), March 13, 1998, p. 5.

179   "How can things turn around so quickly?": Jasper Becker, "Guarded Reactions to 'Explosion' of Mainland Economic Growth," *South China Morning Post,* July 21, 2000, p. 18.

179   say whatever is demanded: See Owen Brown, "Chinese Agency Plans Crackdown On Bogus Data," *Asian Wall Street Journal,* December 29, 2000, p. 3.

180   "What's going up?": Matthew Miller, interview by author, Shanghai, September 2, 2000.

180   the central government's 2000 budget deficit: "NPC Session Hears Plan Implementation, Budget Reports," Xinhua News Agency Bulletin, March 6, 2001.

180   US$1.1 trillion: "China's GDP Grows 8 Percent," Xinhua News Agency Bulletin, February 28, 2001.

180   US$246.6 billion: At the end of 2000, China had approximately US$197.6 billion of internal public debt (public debt owed to domestic parties) and US$49.0 billion of external public debt. China does not publish a figure for the total amount of its internal public debt, so this number must be derived from published statistics and is an estimate. The internal debt figure includes US$32.5 billion of bonds issued in the partial recapitalization of the banks in 1998 (as discussed in Chapter 6) but excludes the amount of contingent liabilities. The amount of China's total external debt at the end of 2000, according to official sources, was US$145.7 billion. "China's Foreign Debt Down 4 Percent in 2000," People's Daily Online, April 3, 2001. This amount, larger than the figure used above to calculate total public debt, includes obligations of nonsovereign parties and so is not used for the purposes of analyzing the ability of the central government to service its obligations. As a practical matter, the central government would probably stand behind some of its instrumentalities.

180 Beijing has essentially borrowed: Most of the loans in the commercial banking system were extended to state-owned enterprises and other entities controlled by the state. These loans are, therefore, indirect loans to the state itself and should be considered public debt. See Lawrence J. Lau, "The Macroeconomy and Reform of the Banking Sector in China," in BIS Paper No. 7, p. 59. Loans made by the state-owned policy banks, which extend credit at the behest of the central government for public purposes, can also be considered public debt. See Nicholas R. Lardy, "Fiscal Sustainability: Between a Rock and a Hard Place," *China Economic Quarterly,* vol. 4, No. 2 (2000), p. 36.

180 about US$860.8 billion in 2000: This figure was derived by assuming that 70 percent of the loans in the banking system go to state borrowers. The People's Bank of China these days maintains that only about 40 percent of loans go to state borrowers. This percentage is much too low from all available evidence. In any event, there is no precise figure for the state's share of borrowing and the 70 percent figure is less than the current consensus of 75 percent. The figure in the text includes loans transferred to the asset management companies by the Big Four banks because the central government will, at some point, have to accept financial responsibility for these loans. The US$860.8 billion figure may understate the indirect loan problem because it does not include US$177.5 billion in loans made by China's three policy banks even though all of their loans are extended at the direction of the state.

181 79.4 percent of current GDP: A report from Bank of China International, Bank of China's investment banking operation, says that the Mainland needs US$850 billion to fund its pension system. Bei Hu, "Sick System 'Needs US$850B Lifeline," *South China Morning Post,* February 23, 2001, Business Post, p. 6. A multilateral institution informally puts deferred pension obligations somewhere between 100–125 percent of GDP.

181 issued before the end of that year: *See* "China's GDP Grows 7.1 Percent This Year," Xinhua News Agency Bulletin, December 29, 1999.

181 much more respectful: See Xu Dashan, "Nation's GDP Grew by 8% Last Year," *China Daily,* January 1, 2001, p. 3.

181 Outright fabrication remains a serious problem: See Pan Yuan, "State Statistical Bureau Will Use All Means Against False Statistics," *China Youth Daily* (Beijing), February 28, 2000, p. 2. The discrepancy in GDP statistics is larger than the state admits. See, e.g., Mark O'Neill, "Beijing Has $546B Chasm in Key Data," *South China Morning Post,* February 29, 2000, Business Post, p. 6.

181 may only be a quarter: "Keep Spending," China Online, March 8, 2001 (assessment of the Economist Intelligence Unit).

181 the unrecoverable loans: Most, but not all, of the unrecoverable loans in the banking system were extended to state-owned enterprises and other entities controlled by the state. The central government has to stand behind most of the banks and credit cooperatives by assuming the bad loans they hold because it is not prepared to see these financial institutions collapse. In fact, China's asset management company plan contemplates that the central government will bear financial responsibility for loans made by the Big Four banks (or at least the portion of the loans that ultimately are not recovered). As noted in Chapter 6, the asset management company program is failing. Therefore, the state will, in one way or another, "be forced to pay the bill."

Mark O'Neill, "Despite Asset Management Solution, State Will Foot Debt Bill," *South China Morning Post,* January 22, 2001, Business Post, p. 3 (comment of un-named European banker).

181 about US$490 billion: The assumptions used in deriving this figure are outlined in Chapter 6. By the end of 2000 the Big Four commercial banks had transferred about ¥1.3 trillion (US$157.0 billion) of loans to the four newly-established asset man-agement companies. For purposes of assessing the state's financial strength, it is ir-relevant whether the loans had been transferred because the state owns both the banks and these companies. Accordingly, the US$490 billion figure includes the loans transferred to the asset management companies. This figure does not include the amount of nonrecoverable loans made by China's policy banks.

181 total accumulated debt: This figure is the sum of China's public debt (US$246.6 bil-lion), the unrecoverable loans in the banking system (US$490 billion), and the amount of unfunded pension liabilities (US$850 billion).

181 looks precarious: The central government's condition would look much more pre-carious if all indirect bank lending to the state were included (instead of just nonre-coverable loans). In this case the state's debt would be about 181.4 percent of 2000 GDP.

182 China's spending spree must end soon: For an analysis of Beijing's ability to spend, see Bruce Gilley, "Moment of Truth," *Far Eastern Economic Review,* June 15, 2000, p. 58 (comments of Nicholas Lardy).

182 something even bureaucrats implicitly acknowledge: Although the Ministry of Fi-nance publicly dismisses the concerns of Chinese economists about the govern-ment's ability to service its debt, the finance minister has announced that the fiscal stimulus program should end in 2002. See Andrew Browne, "Chinese Minister Sees Stimulus Spending Winding Down," Reuters News Service, December 19, 2000.

182 "scary": "On a Knife-Edge," *Economist,* May 29, 1999, p. 88. *The Economist*'s estimate of government revenue needed to service debt falls on the high side, but the point remains that China must devote an increasing portion of its budget to servicing its obligations.

182 zoomed up: China's public debt was US$168.9 billion in 1998, US$212.3 billion in 1999, and US$246.6 billion in 2000. The figure for 2000 is an estimate based upon announced government expenditures for that year. The external portion of the debt has increased at a slower pace than the internal portion (due largely to Beijing's fis-cal stimulus program). It is estimated that internal debt increased by 19.8 percent in 2000.

182 will top 2000's record shortfall: The projected budget deficit in 2001 is ¥259.81 bil-lion (US$31.4 billion), which is just a shade under the actual deficit for 2000 of ¥259.82. See "This Year's Deficit Is Equal to Last Year's—Minister," Xinhua News Agency Bulletin, March 6, 2001; "NPC Session Hears Plan Implementation, Budget Reports," Xinhua News Agency Bulletin, March 6, 2001. In 2000 the actual deficit was larger than the ¥229.9 billion first projected, so when history repeats itself, 2001's actual deficit will be higher than the projected one. Therefore, 2001's actual deficit, to be announced in March of 2002, will surely set another record.

182 "a virtuous cycle": Huo Yongzhe, "Boosting Demand a Key Goal," *China Daily,* March 7, 2001, p. 1.

182   and 22.8 percent in 2000: Xu Dashan, "Top Tax Gains Fill Nation's Coffers," *China Daily,* January 5, 2001, p. 1. In 2000 tax revenue hit US$152.9 billion.

182   still behind almost every other nation: Lawrence J. Lau, "The Macroeconomy and Reform of the Banking Sector in China," in BIS Paper No. 7, p. 59. In 1999, revenue was equal to 13.0 percent of gross domestic product (up from 12.4 percent the year before). In 2000, tax revenue hit 14.2 percent of GDP, well below the international average of 30–40 percent. In both 1999 and 2000 China's government revenue as a percentage of GDP was low compared to the corresponding percentage for 1978, the beginning of the reform era, when revenue was 28.5 percent of GDP.

182   as central government officials admit: See, e.g., "Minister Explains Slight Drop in Revenue Growth," Xinhua News Agency Bulletin, March 6, 2001.

182   especially its insolvent banks: John D. Langlois, "Taxing China's Banks," *Asian Wall Street Journal,* October 12, 2000, p. 12. Banks are not the only victims of Beijing's drive for more tax revenue. China's authorities are resorting to unusual taxes that will harm the nation's enterprises. See, e.g., Xin Zhiming, "New Advertising Tax a Dud," *China Daily,* January 4, 2001, p. 4 (tax on advertising expenses).

182   50 percent of the country's fiscal income: Dalian Address.

182   SOEs' profits are illusory: See Chapter 3. Foreign analysts say that SOEs could help the central government out of its revenue squeeze in another way: Beijing could sell them and use the proceeds to pay its ongoing expenses. There is, however, no consensus in senior Party circles to do this, and even if there were, years would be required to dispose of the thousands of state-owned enterprises in an orderly manner. Moreover, there is another consideration: many SOEs are practically worthless.

182   7.0 percent: Sun Shangwu, "GDP Growth to Be Around 7%," *China Daily,* March 6, 2001, p. 1. The premier is not the only person to lower his estimates of GDP growth for 2001: private analysts are also doing the same thing. See "China Economy May Lose Steam, Needs Stimulus," Reuters News Service, February 12, 2001.

182–83   China needs GDP growth: The decline in GDP growth is especially alarming when viewed in the context of China's increasing population. Changes in real GDP per capita growth highlight the trend. This figure measures the per person increase in GDP (minus the effect of inflation or deflation). In 1997, real GDP per capita growth in China was 7.7 percent, in 1998 it fell to 6.7 percent, and in 1999 it ended up at 5.5 percent. *Monthly China Review* (Citibank periodic research report), May 2000, p. 11. The figure for real GDP per capita growth in 2000, when released, will be larger than 1999's, but the increase will be the product of the same magic that produced such a large surge in GDP in 2000. As mentioned in the text, the magnitude of the increase in GDP in 2000 is highly suspect.

183   "The holiday season boom": Zheng Ying, "Holiday Frenzy Shows Up Problems," *China Daily,* May 29, 2000, p. 4 (comments of Huang Guoxiong of Renmin University).

183   consumer spending during the next weeklong holiday: "China Oct Consumer Price Index Flat Vs Consensus +0.3%," Dow Jones International News, November 14, 2000; "Leery Travelers Staying Put," China Online, October 6, 2000.

183   even the official media suggest: See Xin Zhiming, "Consumption Rise Not to Be Pinned on Holidays," *China Daily,* October 21, 2000, p. 4 (rail and air traffic statistics were significantly down from the previous holiday, despite the government's claim that tourism revenue had spurted by 21.5 percent).

183   increasing their level of saving: See, e.g., Bing Lan, "Deposits Up As Income Growth Slows," *China Daily,* February 13, 2001, p. 1.

183   "economic sugar-high": "China's Holiday Economics," *Economist,* May 13, 2000, p. 30.

183   "The answer is no": Peter Wonacott, "Will Forced Holidays Help China?," *Asian Wall Street Journal,* January 26, 2001, p. 1 (comments of Song Guoqing of the China Centre for Economic Research). Holiday economics has changed consumer spending habits (but not necessarily the amount of spending).

183   depends almost entirely: See Kathy Wilhelm, "Starting to Sizzle," *Far Eastern Economic Review,* August 24, 2000, p. 57 (comments of Andy Xie).

183   expensive for the country: See, e.g., "Elusive Inflation," *Business China,* January 1, 2001, p. 6.

184   declined in both 1999: Zhang Yan, "Exports, Imports Boomed Last Year," *China Daily,* January 14, 2000, p. 1.

184   and 2000: "China Reports Increased Foreign Trade," Xinhua News Agency Bulletin, February 28, 2001; Bill Savadove, "China 2000 Trade Surplus Narrows from 1999," Reuters News Service, January 10, 2001. The surplus fell a little more than 17 percent in 2000 as imports rose almost 36 percent.

184   central government officials realize: See, e.g., "Chinese Leaders Raise Alarm on Slowing Exports," Reuters News Service, March 6, 2001.

184   smuggle money offshore: China took drastic steps to stem capital flight in 1998, but the problem continues to plague the nation's finances. See, e.g., "Leaving Home," *Business China,* July 31, 2000, p. 12.

184   "has no parallel in any other country": "Beijing," *Asia Tonight,* narr. Rebecca MacKinnon, CNN International, July 5, 2000.

184   diverting even more: Professors Zhu Xiaodong and Loren Brandt of the University of Toronto argue that China's growth is stagnating "because of a sharp reduction of investment growth in the non-state sector." Zhu Xiaodong and Loren Brandt, "China's Last Frontier in Financial Services Reform," China Online, November 29, 2000. This reduction has occurred because, among other reasons, massive government spending has restricted credit to nonstate businesses.

184   nine of the world's ten most polluted cities: "Younger Chinese Have Stronger Sense of Environment Protection," Xinhua News Agency Bulletin, April 27, 2000.

184   Lanzhou: Mark O'Neill, "Spreading the Word in Gritty Lanzhou," *South China Morning Post,* April 27, 2000, p. 20.

184   Somewhere between 4 to 8 percent: See "China Stresses Overall Ecological Protection," Xinhua News Agency Bulletin, August 23, 2000.

184   About 350 million of China's citizens: Jasper Becker, "Presidential Poser of the Millennium," *South China Morning Post,* December 12, 1999, p. 13.

185   The state does not provide education: See, e.g., Jasper Becker, "At the Back of the Class," *South China Morning Post,* January 1, 2000, Saturday Review, p. 2.

185   China is proud that it can send doctors to Guinea: See "Chinese Doctors Save My Son's Life," People's Daily Online, October 5, 2000.

185   "worse than in Africa": "China's Rural Health Care Crisis: Forward to the Past," *Business China,* November 22, 1999, p. 5 (comments of Marcel Roux of Médécins Sans Frontières). As even the official media admit, "medical treatment is almost impossi-

ble to get" in impoverished areas. Zhang Feng, "Farmers' Medical Services Reformed," *China Daily*, February 16, 2001, p. 1. Beijing is planning comprehensive reforms but has yet to figure out how to pay for better health care. Even optimistic views of the crisis mention the possibility of collapse of the medical care system. See Christine Beasley, "Health Care: The Sick Man of China," China Online, February 7, 2001.

185 corruption cost China: Peter Wonacott, "China's Corruption Costs Estimated at $150 Billion," *Asian Wall Street Journal,* March 8, 2001, p. 4.

185 drop in the bucket: Beijing has already constructed a portion of the Olympic facilities and some of the other infrastructure. "Beijing's Olympic Bid Spurs Massive Infrastructure Investment," Xinhua News Agency Bulletin, February 21, 2001. Xinhua calls these facilities and infrastructure "one of the largest construction projects ever in China since the construction of the Great Wall."

185 National Day: "Can China Change?," *Economist,* October 2, 1999, p. 23.

186 and the economy will stagger: Even official forecasts are becoming more gloomy. See, e.g., "Slowing China Exports Could Dip Growth to 11-Year Low: Report," Agence France-Presse, January 14, 2001 (projections of Qiu Xiaohua of the National Bureau of Statistics).

186 will be ominous: Andy Xie, "China's Debt-Driven Growth Runs Out," *Asian Wall Street Journal,* November 2, 1999, p. 10.

186 Lin Yifu: Lin Yifu, "Six Problems That Need to Be Resolved," *China Business Times Enterprise Weekly* (Beijing), October 11, 1999, p. 1.

186 "will explode within five years": Mark O'Neill, "Maverick Flags Warning of Early Revolt Against Income Gap," *South China Morning Post,* February 12, 2001, Business Post, p. 4.

186 "Until the tide goes out": "Living on Borrowed Time," *Economist,* September 25, 1999, World Economic Survey, p. 23.

9:   Trade Charade

188 "I wouldn't go in there": The events involving Peter Wonacott are derived from telephone interviews by author of February 21, 2000, and November 1, 2000, and e-mails from Wonacott to author of February 22, 2000.

188 glasses fall to the ground: Rebecca MacKinnon, telephone interview by author, February 29, 2000.

189 "The anger and distress": Christian Murck, "Assessing Financial Risk in China" (panel discussion), CLSA China Forum 1999, Beijing, May 12, 1999, in CLSA Global Emerging Markets, *Assessing Financial Risk in China,* 1999.

190 "bears directly on the honour": Bruce Gilley, "Hopping Mad," *Far Eastern Economic Review,* June 15, 2000, p. 32.

191 "Worst Victim of Globalization": *Time Asia,* December 31, 1999, p. 151 (Signs and Portents).

191 "America will be forever young": William J. Clinton, "State of the Union Address," Washington, D.C., January 27, 2000.

192 "We can advance to the future": Geoff Wade, "Facing History," *Far Eastern Economic Review,* December 24, 1998, p. 29.

193 "They evolve or expire, explore or decline": Tim Metcalfe, "Buzz Off into Space," *South China Morning Post,* May 11, 2000, p. 17.

195 staggering foreign exchange reserves: "China's Forex Reserves Hit 165.6 Bln USD," Xinhua News Agency Bulletin, January 17, 2001.

195 China's trade surplus with the United States: Mark Egan, "U.S. Trade Deficit Shrinks Again in December," Reuters News Service, February 21, 2001.

196 "The point about WTO": Robert Kapp, interview by Farland Chang, *Visions of China, Asia Business Morning,* CNN International, September 29, 1999.

196 Those days, however, are over: See, e.g., Long Yongtu, interview by Robert Keatley and Mark O'Neill, "Long March Nears End," *South China Morning Post,* February 28, 2001, Business Post, p. 16 ("future contracts will be decided by the joint venture partners themselves and not by bureaucrats").

196 "about seventy books on WTO": Jasper Becker, "Vested Interests Pit Bureaucrats Against Change," *South China Morning Post,* April 6, 2000, p. 16.

197 "China is fully capable": "Jiang Urges Officials to Fully Understand WTO Entry," Xinhua News Agency Bulletin, January 19, 2000.

198 "Solid and down-to-earth preparatory work": Chang Weimin and Xing Zhigang, "Economic Sector Ill-Prepared," *China Daily,* September 18, 2000, p. 1.

198 have no WTO plans: Jasper Becker, "Vested Interests Pit Bureaucrats Against Change," *South China Morning Post,* April 6, 2000, p. 16.

198 will survive accession: Suzanne Harrison, "Survival of the Fittest as Firms Face Uncertain Future After WTO Entry," *South China Morning Post,* September 8, 2000, Business Post, p. 2.

198 could crumble under the pressure: See, e.g., Matthew Miller, "Lucky Film At Last Concedes Need for Foreign Partner," *South China Morning Post,* March 2, 2001, Business Post, p. 4.

198 The process started first in Beijing: Rachel Morarjee, telephone interview by author, April 2, 2001.

199 "I doubt the time-frame is long enough": Foo Choy Peng, "Dai Outlines Yuan-Trade Plans Before Influx of Foreign Banks," *South China Morning Post,* February 18, 2000, Business Post, p. 4.

199 "dropped to zero": Ian Johnson, "China Continues to Hobble Foreign Firms," *Asian Wall Street Journal,* March 23, 2000, p. 1.

200 "what it means for China": "Jiang Urges Officials to Fully Understand WTO Entry," Xinhua News Agency Bulletin, January 19, 2000. The quotation is Xinhua's paraphrase of President Jiang's remarks.

200 "More unemployment": Jeremy Page, "China's Labourers Lament Life After WTO," Reuters News Service, January 18, 2000.

200 will be taken out of production: Jasper Becker, "WTO Has Mainland Farms in Its Tractor Beam," *South China Morning Post,* November 18, 1999, Business Post, p. 12 (prediction of the State Council's Development Research Centre). Land under cultivation is already decreasing. See, e.g., "China's Acreage Under Grain Plants Hits Record Low," People's Daily Online, January 27, 2001.

200 "irrational": See Zhao Huanxin, "Changes Set to Boost Farming Incomes," *China Daily,* September 4, 2000, p. 6.

200 rural incomes have slumped: Jasper Becker, "Reaping a Harvest of Despair," *South China*

Morning Post, September 24, 2000, p. 11. Beijing maintains that rural incomes are still growing, though it acknowledges that the rate of growth is declining. See Xu Dashan, "Can Our Farmers Compete?," *China Daily Business Weekly,* December 10, 2000, p. 1.

200 unprofitable: For an example of what can go wrong when politics meets crop selection, see Yu Zhenhai and Shuai Zheng, "The Ridiculous 'Scientific Great Leap Forward,' " *Beijing Youth Daily,* February 5, 2001, p. A6.

200 500 million tons of low-grade grain: Zhao Huanxin, "Changes Set to Boost Farming Incomes," *China Daily,* September 4, 2000, p. 6.

200 1.3 billion tons: Jasper Becker, "Reaping a Harvest of Despair," *South China Morning Post,* September 24, 2000, p. 11.

201 has made its agriculture uncompetitive: In order to support peasant incomes, Beijing maintains a system of price supports. The price supports, until the end of 1999, applied to all grain without regard to quality. This system therefore encouraged peasants to grow low-quality crops, about a fifth of which were essentially inedible. The result is that farmers got hooked on producing uncompetitive products.

201 will not be able to compete: Shai Oster, "Farmers Doomed to Grow Poorer," *South China Morning Post,* December 3, 2000, p. 12.

201 150 to 200 million: For an estimate on the high side of the range, see Wu Yunhe, "Agriculture to Face Challenges," *China Daily,* November 26, 1999, p. 6.

201 9.7 million more farmers: "Estimate of Changes in Employment Structure During the Seven Years After China Accedes to the WTO," *Beijing Youth Daily,* November 16, 1999, p. 3.

201 the real number will be four times that: Shai Oster, "Farmers Doomed to Grow Poorer," *South China Morning Post,* December 3, 2000, p. 12.

201 Some have even abandoned their lives: Jasper Becker, "Reaping a Harvest of Despair," *South China Morning Post,* September 24, 2000, p. 11.

201 "they preferred to die early": Huang Guangming and Li Side, "County Party Secretary's Tearful Petition Moved State Council Leaders to Act," *Nanfang Zhoumo* (Guangzhou), August 24, 2000, p. 1.

202 "You cannot just put a farmer in a factory": Paul Eckert, "Experts See China GDP Gains from WTO Entry," Reuters News Service, November 17, 1999.

202 they will source from cheaper foreign suppliers: Mark O'Neill, "Textile City Prepares for Big WTO Windfall," *South China Morning Post,* November 22, 1999, Business Post, p. 5.

202 foreign enterprises may largely own China's economy: Karby Leggett, "China Is Pressured to Bless Private Sector," *Asian Wall Street Journal,* March 14, 2000, p. 1.

203 annual foreign investment more than doubling: "China WTO Entry to Bring FDI Flood—Goldman Sachs," Reuters News Service, April 17, 2000.

203 the phenomenon will accelerate: Contracted (promised) foreign investment increased an impressive 50.8 percent in 2000. The jump in contracted investment indicates that actual foreign investment in 2001 will rise by more than the 0.9 percent increase in 2000. Nonetheless, Beijing is cautious about predicting a boom in foreign investment. The central government's plans indicate that foreign investment will remain at 2000's level during the Tenth Five-Year Plan (2001–2005).

203 "in order to sell products there": William J. Clinton, letter to the Speaker of the House of Representatives and the President of the Senate, January 24, 1999.

203   That's what General Motors plans to do: Gong Zhengzheng, "GM to Sell More Cars in Western Region," *China Daily,* December 5, 2000, p. 5. General Motors also announced that it would import into China car parts for pickup trucks and Chevrolet sedans from its Brazilian subsidiary. Xiao Chen, "Our Country Will Import Cars from Brazil," *Financial News* (Beijing), December 26, 2000, p. 1.

203   Imports surged: "Shanghai Imports Surged Drastically after Tariffs Lowered," *China Securities News* (Beijing), March 16, 2001, p. 14.

203–204   "Once we get into WTO": Mark O'Neill, "Textile City Prepares for Big WTO Windfall," *South China Morning Post,* November 22, 1999, Business Post, p. 5.

204   won't be able to match the prices: The leading foreign car manufacturer in China, Volkswagen, anticipates that its Mainland plants will not be able to keep up with imports after accession due to the scheduled reduction in tariffs. "World Summary," *South China Morning Post,* January 27, 2000, Business Post, p. 12.

204   just two days away by ship: Mark O'Neill, "Industry Faces Day of Reckoning over Entry," *South China Morning Post,* November 16, 1999, Business Post, p. 4.

204   The two German women: *China Daily Business Weekly,* June 11, 2000, p. 2 (photograph).

204   "long-term bonanza": Gil Klein, "China Trade Divides South," *Richmond Times-Dispatch,* May 1, 2000, p. A1.

205   Officials in the provinces want autonomy: Willy Wo-Lap Lam, "Restive Regions Seek More Autonomy," *South China Morning Post,* July 29, 2000, p. 8.

205   will boost China's growth: See, e.g., Ni Xiaolin and Lin Jian, "There Will Be Profits, But Costs Too," *Shanghai Securities News,* November 17, 1999, p. 1.

206   "a rough period": Jason Booth, "China's WTO Membership Could Hurt Some Firms," *Asian Wall Street Journal,* November 11, 1999, p. 15.

206   They will do as they say: As an indication of the trustworthiness of senior leaders, China reduced its tariffs as of the first day of 2001 as it promised the leaders of APEC (Asian-Pacific Economic Cooperation) in 1996. Xiao Xu, "Nation Fulfills Commitment to Cut Tariffs," *China Daily,* December 30, 2000, p. 1.

206   And a thousand new disputes tomorrow: Many of these disputes will involve subsidies. For a detailed discussion in the Chinese media of postaccession subsidies, see Ji Rufeng and Li Zhenzhong, "How Should China Respond to the WTO Countersubsidy Agreement?" *China Economic Times* (Beijing), August 3, 2000, p. 4.

207   fair trade will eventually come: Vice Trade Minister Long Yongtu, Beijing's chief WTO negotiator, points out that China will comply with its WTO commitments because membership in the global organization is in the country's own interests. Referring to the country's WTO obligations, he recently said, "If these commitments weren't beneficial to us, we would never have made these commitments." Owen Brown, "Chinese Official Says WTO Deal Is Imminent," *Asian Wall Street Journal,* February 16, 2001, p. 4.

208   "China finds its own feet and gains world respect": "Good Deal Opens a Promising Future," *China Daily,* November 16, 1999, p. 4.

208   "But if the government betrays us": Sophie Roell, "Who's Afraid of Chinese Nationalism?," *Asian Wall Street Journal,* October 29, 1999, p. 14.

208   "will take the command and control out of communism": Samuel R. Berger, address, East Asian Institute, Columbia University, New York, May 2, 2000.

208 "No communist nation": "China: A Great Leap, and a Big If," editorial, *Business Week,* November 29, 1999, p. 100.

208 boosting its policing capabilities: See Willy Wo-Lap Lam, "Leaders Prepares [*sic*] for WTO Winds of Change," *South China Morning Post,* June 29, 2000, p. 9.

209 "We are the electricity": King Lai (chief executive of NetEase.com), CLSA China Forum 2000, Shanghai, May 10, 2000 (panel discussion comments).

210 "unprecedented pressures": "Wealth and Power," *Economist,* April 8, 2000, China Survey, p. 19.

210 "The reform of the government system": Willy Wo-Lap Lam, "On the Wave of Political Reform," *South China Morning Post,* June 21, 2000, p. 18 (comments from the Forum of 50 Chinese Economists held in Xian). For similar comments, see Tang Daiwang, "Building an Administrative System That Dovetails with the World," *Nanfang Daily* (Guangzhou), June 19, 2000, p. B2.

211 "How do you make sure?": Klaus Schwab, interview by Pranay Gupte, "Neighbors on the Same Planet," *Newsweek,* January 31, 2000, p. 56.

211 "We do not make a liberal by hugging a Nazi": Congressional Record, May 23, 2000, p. H3598.

211 "Everyone must be a winner": Klaus Schwab, interview by Pranay Gupte, "Neighbors on the Same Planet," *Newsweek,* January 31, 2000, p. 56.

211 "they will seek greater say": William J. Clinton, letter to the Speaker of the House of Representatives and the President of the Senate, January 24, 1999.

212 "Snuff out all challenges": Willy Wo-Lap Lam, "On the Wave of Political Reform," *South China Morning Post,* June 21, 2000, p. 18.

10: Sentences Without Verbs

213 "is marching unstoppably": Central Committee of the Communist Party of Peru, "Long Live Maoism," August 1993 (available at www.maoism.org).

214 "various forms of democracy": Shao Zongwei, "Nation Values Human Rights," *China Daily,* November 17, 1999, p. 1.

215 "Chinese-style democracy": Dian Tai, "Complaint? Send Letter or Visit Here," *China Daily,* February 15, 2000, p. 1.

216 missed few opportunities: Perhaps the most flagrant interference up to now has been Vice Premier Qian Qichen's open support of Tung Chee-hwa for a second term as chief executive of the Hong Kong Special Administrative Region. Beijing voiced its backing more than a year ahead of the selection of the chief executive by a select committee. See No Kwai-yan and Kong Lai-fan, "Qian Backs Tung for Second Term in Office," *South China Morning Post,* March 8, 2001, p. 4.

217 "History alone will make a judgment": Mark O'Neill, "A Maverick's Dreams for the Mainland," *South China Morning Post,* February 25, 2000, p. 15.

217 "Look, Tiananmen is behind us": "Ten Years On," *Economist,* June 5, 1999, p. 29.

218 "I don't know anyone": Karby Leggett, interview by author, Shanghai, February 21, 2000. Leggett is a reporter for *The Asian Wall Street Journal.*

218 hounded by security forces: See Chapter 2. The China Democracy Party may be more alive than it appears, as it has apparently been operating from jail. See Willy

Wo-Lap Lam, "Universities Warned over Anniversary," *South China Morning Post,* May 27, 2000, p. 7.

218   "fifteen different political parties": *World News,* narr. Rebecca MacKinnon, CNN International, June 4, 2000.

219   "The Internet tolls": Scott Savitt, "China's Internet Revolution," *Asian Wall Street Journal,* December 21, 1999, p. 10.

219   village elections: See, e.g., "China Says Still Has a Way to Go with Direct Grassroots Elections," Agence France-Presse, February 21, 2001; Tom Mitchell, "The Red Star Stand-off," *South China Morning Post,* September 11, 2000, p. 15.

220   "They said they are only here to talk": "Police Enter House of Chinese Dissident's Mother," Agence France-Presse, October 15, 1999.

220   the bureaucracy of repression: Jasper Becker, "Jiang's Secret Police March On," *South China Morning Post,* February 20, 2000, p. 9.

220   it has stiffened its position: See Willy Wo-Lap Lam, "Beijing to Avoid 'Errors' of KMT," *South China Morning Post,* April 22, 2000, p. 5.

220   levying their own taxes: See, e.g., Jasper Becker, "The Party and the Peasant Uprising," *South China Morning Post,* April 5, 2000, p. 17.

220   dispensing justice: See, e.g., Huang Yong, "Village Cadres Set Up Jails, Imprisoning Two Hundred People," *China Youth Daily* (Beijing), November 24, 2000, p. 7.

220   issuing their own currency: Jasper Becker, "Cadres Caught in Rural Currency Racket," *South China Morning Post,* January 15, 2000, p. 8.

221   "I do not see a clear linkage": Susan V. Lawrence, "Fuelling Fires of a Different Kind," *Far Eastern Economic Review,* March 30, 2000, p. 20.

221   "The higher officials are": Mark O'Neill, "Criminal and Mistress Easy Prey for Press Speculation," *South China Morning Post,* August 2, 2000, p. 18.

221   "Not fighting corruption": Minxin Pei, "The Corruption Conundrum," *South China Morning Post,* September 28, 1999, p. 21.

221   will soon lose its power: Vivien Pik-Kwan Chan, "Graft-busters Preach the Faith," *South China Morning Post,* May 24, 2000, p. 9.

221   "China's biggest corruption scandal": Thom Beal and Peter Wonacott, "Smuggling Case Crosses Border to Hong Kong," *Asian Wall Street Journal,* January 28, 2000, p. 1.

222   "it is equally important": Willy Wo-Lap Lam, "Free-Thinkers Find Little Room to Move," *South China Morning Post,* April 19, 2000, p. 23.

222   the rule of law was already enshrined: Gordon G. Chang, "What Does the Rule of Law Mean in China?," *China Law & Practice,* August 1999, p. 33.

222   Li Peng: "Li Peng on Party's Leadership over NPC's Work," People's Daily Online, March 14, 2000.

222   "the rule of virtue": See, e.g., "Scholars Hail Jiang Zemin's Thinking on Morality," Xinhua News Agency Bulletin, February 21, 2001. Jiang says that the rule of law and the rule of virtue are of equal importance, but in reality he is using virtue to undermine the notion that the Party is subject to law.

222   collectivism over individualism: See Clara Li, "Culture as Vital as Law, Says Jiang Aide," *South China Morning Post,* February 13, 2001, p. 8. For additional views on collectivism, see "Xinhua Stresses Rule of Law, Rule of Virtue," Xinhua News Agency Bulletin, February 13, 2001.

222 In this climate: In view of the trends discussed in the text, it should come as no surprise that there has been little recent progress toward legal reform. See Clara Li, "Legal Reform Too Slow, Says Expert," *South China Morning Post,* March 3, 2001, p. 7 (comments of Jerome Cohen).

223 "suicidal": Su Guiyou, "Focus of State-Owned Enterprise Reform: State-Owned Enterprise Reform Seeks Breakthrough but Will Never Engage in Privatization," Zhongguo Xinwen She News Agency, September 22, 1999.

223 "in the hands of Marxists and Leninists": "Hardliner Slams China's Sell-Off of State Firms," Reuters News Service, December 30, 1998. Another official opposed to privatization is Li Peng. See Charles Hutzler, "China Digs In," Associated Press Newswires, May 23, 2000.

223 "never engage in privatization": Dalian Address.

224 "primary stage of socialism": Dalian Address. Jiang Zemin extensively discussed the primary stage of socialism in Part IV of his work report to the Fifteenth Party Congress, which was held in September 1997.

224 "In China the state took control of too much": Jasper Becker, "How Karl Marx Survived It All," *South China Morning Post,* October 1, 1999, p. 16.

225 "by and large bring about socialist modernization": "China Marks 50th Founding Anniversary," Xinhua News Agency Bulletin, October 1, 1999.

225 "tens of generations": Steven Mufson, "The Real Deal," *Washington Post,* November 21, 1999, p. B1.

225 "the state's control of the economy": Jasper Becker, "How Karl Marx Survived It All," *South China Morning Post,* October 1, 1999, p. 16.

225 "why we still claim to be a socialist country": Ibid.

225 "If you are going to have socialism": Chua Lee Hoong, "Rule of Law Above Democracy, Says SM," *Straits Times* (Singapore), October 29, 1999, p. 3.

225 more people studying Marxism: Jasper Becker, "How Karl Marx Survived It All," *South China Morning Post,* October 1, 1999, p. 16.

226 being sold to corporations and not individuals: Josephine Ma, "Shenyang Woos Foreigners to Manage Firms," *South China Morning Post,* September 27, 1999, p. 10.

226 "socialized public ownership": Jasper Becker, "How Karl Marx Survived It All," *South China Morning Post,* October 1, 1999, p. 16.

227 approximately 55 million: Li Bin, "Zhou Xiaochuan Discusses the Present Situation of the Securities Markets and Their Future," *Shanghai Securities News,* December 4, 2000, p. 1. Since Zhao's estimate there has been a flood of new stock trading accounts. There are now about 61 million such accounts in China today. "New Accounts," *China Daily,* March 23, 2001, p. 7. The percentage in the text is derived from the results of the 2000 census. See "China Issues Communiqué on Major Figures of Population," People's Daily Online, March 28, 2001.

227 "only socialism can save China": This phrase was one of Jiang Zemin's favorite lines during late 1999. See, e.g., "Jiang Stresses Policy on Building Socialism with Chinese Characteristics," Xinhua News Agency Bulletin, October 25, 1999.

227 "Between you and me": Chua Lee Hoong, "Rule of Law Above Democracy, Says SM," *Straits Times* (Singapore), October 29, 1999, p. 3. Lee was referring to Jiang's National Day speech in 1999.

228 a domestic investor filed: See Yan Ming, "A Stockholder Sues Hongguang," *Shanghai Securities News,* December 15, 1998, p. 1.

229 "Or fix it slowly?" Susan V. Lawrence, "Mr. Privatization," *Far Eastern Economic Review,* March 2, 2000, p. 44.

229 "protected by the national constitution": "CPC Meeting to Design Future of State-Owned Sector," Xinhua News Agency Bulletin, September 16, 1999.

229 closer to the mark: Today the central government dismisses talk of large-scale disposals of shares. See, e.g., Li Bin, "Zhou Xiaochuan Discusses the Present Situation of the Securities Markets and Their Future," *Shanghai Securities News,* December 4, 2000, p. 1.

229 "money for nothing": Duncan Clarke, interview by author, Shanghai, October 14, 2000.

231 "The first job is political organization": Susan V. Lawrence, "The Road to Power," *Far Eastern Economic Review,* October 7, 1999, p. 46.

231 "Talk politics": *Jiang Zemin: Discussing "Talk Study, Talk Politics, and Talk Righteousness": Excerpts,* ed. Jian Bian (Beijing: Party Construction Literature Publishing House, 1999). The phrase "talk politics" has its roots in Jiang's "talk more about politics" campaign. For a discussion of Jiang's concept of talking politics, see Willy Wo-Lap Lam, *The Era of Jiang Zemin* (Singapore: Prentice Hall, 1999), pp. 46–49, 159–60.

232 participating in 118 meetings: Wang Mingquan, "Efforts for Democratic Living Meeting in 'Three Stresses' Education," *Qiushi,* Issue 15 (1999), p. 35.

232 "rehearsing for the National Day parade": Susan V. Lawrence, "Stressful Summer," *Far Eastern Economic Review,* August 19, 1999, p. 16.

232 "top priority": "Party Building Given Top Priority," *China Daily,* February 26, 2000, p. 1.

232 "The more complicated": Dalian Address.

232 currently spreading its cells: See, e.g., "New Party Units to Be Established," *Shanghai Daily,* December 7, 1999, p. 2 (Party branches to be established in non-governmental organizations in Shanghai with more than three Party members).

232 "Who do these guys think they are?": John Pomfret, "In 2 Chinese Cities, Celebration and Contradiction," *Washington Post,* September 29, 1999, p. 1.

233 "We swallow our consciences": *Visions of China, World News,* narr. Mike Chinoy, CNN International, September 22, 1999.

233–234 "this great disaster for our country": *Visions of China, Asian Edition,* narr. Stacey Wilkins, CNN International, September 29, 1999.

234 And why today?: Song Yongyi's imprisonment is discussed in Chapter 11.

234 disavow its ideas: The Party's next test of flexibility involves opening its membership to private businessmen. So far, it has resisted doing so. See Daniel Kwan, "Businessmen Still Barred from Party," *South China Morning Post,* March 7, 2001, p. 9.

234 "must not be achieved at the expense of ideology": Willy Wo-Lap Lam, "Beijing to Avoid 'Errors' of KMT," *South China Morning Post,* April 22, 2000, p. 5.

11: Emerging in the East

236 "this is a better China": Lee Kuan Yew, interview by Riz Khan, *Visions of China, Q&A in Shanghai,* CNN International, September 29, 1999.

236   "mesmerized": Robert Kapp, interview by Mike Chinoy, *Visions of China, Insight Special Edition,* CNN International, September 30, 1999.

236   "so that they don't float away": Nicholas D. Kristof and Sheryl WuDunn, *China Wakes: The Struggle for the Soul of a Rising Power* (New York: Vintage Books, 1995), p. 444.

236   "The most likely scenario": Ibid., p. 463.

236   "powerful, democratic and civilized": "Unity, Stability, and Build the Chinese Nation Stronger," *People's Daily,* May 8, 2000, p. 1.

237   "we want to say to the world 'Why not!' ": Hu Qihua, "Exploring into a New Space," *China Daily,* June 5, 2000, p. 10.

237   "has not been realized to the maximum": Lee Kuan Yew, interview by Riz Khan, *Visions of China, Q&A in Shanghai,* CNN International, September 29, 1999.

237   "great, glorious, and correct Communist Party of China": "Zhu Reviews P.R.C.'s Achievements in Past 50 Years," Xinhua News Agency Bulletin, September 30, 1999.

238   the one thing they cannot do: It seems China's leaders are meddling more these days rather than less. Municipal planners in Beijing, proving that restraint is in short supply, now insist that all buildings in the Chinese capital come in gray or shades of that color. See "Beijing Sets Color Style for Buildings," Xinhua News Agency Bulletin, November 4, 2000. A survey showed that most Beijing residents oppose the mandated color scheme, but the bureaucrats are persisting in their efforts to ban offending shades. Jin Baicheng, "Grey Days Coming to Capital," *China Daily,* November 13, 2000, p. 3.

238   biggest birthday bash of the twentieth century: *Visions of China, Asia Tonight,* narr. Michelle Han, CNN International, September 29, 1999.

238   "In China it is the leaders who are the centre of everything": Jasper Becker, "China Says Services Beat Bug," *South China Morning Post,* January 2, 2000, p. 3.

239   not to commemorate dead leaders: "China Prohibits Building Memorials for Late Leaders," Xinhua News Agency Bulletin, February 21, 2000.

239   Only in the later days: Peter Wonacott, telephone interview by author, February 21, 2000.

240   "It could have gone either way": Caroline Cooper, interview by author, Shanghai, February 26, 2001. Cooper was an instructor in the Princeton in Asia program at nearby Qinghua University at the time of the demonstrations.

240   you could hear recordings: Xiao Yu, "Anniversary Passes Quietly at University," *South China Morning Post,* June 5, 2000, p. 8.

241   a tense moment for Narrod: Sharon Narrod, interview by author, Shanghai, March 29, 2000. The incident in Tiananmen Square took place on March 27, 2000.

242   can build the world's largest radio telescope: "China Builds World's Largest Radio Telescope," People's Daily Online, July 10, 2000.

242   like Poland's Solidarity: Willy Wo-Lap Lam, "Jiang Compares Sect's Threat to Solidarity," *South China Morning Post,* February 12, 2000, p. 7.

242   I WILL SEE MY MOTHER!: *China Daily,* February 15, 2000, p. 1.

242   "severe drought and famine": Ibid.

243   returned orphans to be an illegal organization: Jasper Becker, "Nobody's Children," *South China Morning Post,* May 10, 2000, p. 13; Jasper Becker, "Ban on Orphans Hunting Past," *South China Morning Post,* May 10, 2000, p. 1.

244 "The whole party made mistakes": Jasper Becker, "Top Secret Lives," *South China Morning Post,* May 25, 2000, p. 15.

244 "a parade of rubbish bins": Dai Qing, interview by Mark O'Neill, " 'Banned' Voice Will Not Be Silenced," *South China Morning Post,* June 4, 2000, p. 11.

244 "Chinese citizens will tell you": Robert Kapp, interview by Mike Chinoy, *Visions of China, Insight Special Edition,* CNN International, September 30, 1999.

245 "But of course that is not the truth": Chen Jinzhi, interview by author, Stone Forest (Shilin), September 29, 2000.

245 "Our brains were flooded red": *Born Under the Red Flag.*

245 "The Chinese people are convinced": "Communism Remains Supreme Goal: Jiang," *South China Morning Post,* October 26, 1999, p. 9 (comments during his state visit to France).

245 "the superior socialist system": "Zhu Reviews PRC's Achievements in Past 50 Years," Xinhua News Agency Bulletin, September 30, 1999.

245 "yet we must take a firm grip on truth": Huang Huamin, "Xu Chigong Working Report Conference Organized by the Central Military Commission," *Liberation Army Daily* (Beijing), April 26, 2000, p. 1.

245 "are full of vigor and dynamism": Zhu Rongji, address, Asia Society 11th Annual Corporate Conference in Asia and CLSA China Forum 2000, Shanghai, May 10, 2000.

245 "The message delivered by the music": "Nation Builders," *Asiaweek,* September 24, 1999, p. 74.

245 About 44 percent of the world's suicides: Sing Lee and Arthur Kleinman, "Suicide as Resistance in Chinese Society," *Chinese Society: Change, Conflict and Resistance,* eds. Elizabeth J. Perry and Mark Selden (London: Routledge, 2000), p. 221.

246 "I cannot believe in another god": Xu Chang, interview by author, Beijing, January 12, 2001.

246 "You foreigners have no idea": Jakobson, *Million Truths,* p. 144.

246 "Our society is thoroughly rotten": Ibid., p. 146.

246 "Taiwan can elect its own leaders—pretty cool": Matt Forney, "China Worries About Taiwan's Example," *Asian Wall Street Journal,* March 22, 2000, p. 5.

246 "We want democracy": Jasper Becker, "The Party and the Peasant Uprising," *South China Morning Post,* April 5, 2000, p. 17.

246 "The Chinese people love democracy and freedom": Greg Torode, "President Makes an Impression," *South China Morning Post,* September 10, 2000, p. 6.

246 or even to have elections at all: John Pomfret, "China Searches for New Beliefs as Communist Ideology Wanes," *International Herald Tribune,* September 27, 1999, p. 1.

246 "The revolution just benefits corrupt leaders": Jasper Becker, "The Party and the Peasant Uprising," *South China Morning Post,* April 5, 2000, p. 17.

247 The number of rural cadres is increasing: See, e.g., Willy Wo-Lap Lam, "A Matter of Window Dressing," *South China Morning Post,* September 6, 2000, p. 18.

247 "Cadres dare not take action": Liu Chang, "Have Farmers Been Spoiled These Two Years?," *China Youth Daily* (Beijing), July 5, 2000, p. 8.

247 armed with only farm tools: Unarmed Chinese are increasingly willing to fight armed security forces. See, e.g., Zhang Jie, Jing Wei, and Zhou Wu, "Argument Precipitates Problems," *Hefei Evening News,* December 27, 2000, p. 2.

247   " 'Jiang Zemin is corrupt too' ": Jasper Becker, "The Party and the Peasant Uprising," *South China Morning Post,* April 5, 2000, p. 17.

247   "are getting poorer and poorer": Josephine Ma, "Rural Democracy Struggles to Survive," *South China Morning Post,* April 11, 2000, p. 8.

247   at least according to the Party: *See* "Nation Lifts Poor from Rock Bottom," *China Daily,* November 18, 2000, p. 1; "China Declares Elimination of Absolute Poverty," Xinhua News Agency Bulletin, November 17, 2000.

247   Poverty is getting worse: During the two decades of China's reform era the incidence of rural poverty has substantially declined, according to the World Bank, which relied on official statistics. See Leading Group for Poverty Reduction, United Nations Development Program, and the World Bank, "China: Overcoming Rural Poverty," October 18, 2000, p. 1 (hereinafter cited as "World Bank Report"). Nonetheless, the recent drop in rural incomes had undoubtedly aggravated the problem of poverty in the last few years. As this report states (p. 3), the severity of remaining poverty worsened during much of the 1990s.

247   106 million rural poor: World Bank Report, pp. 1–2. As this report notes (pp. 2–3), official Chinese statistics show fewer poor, but the central government employs a low numerical threshold for poverty in order to arrive at the more optimistic numbers.

248   "I am fighting for the right to eat": Calum MacLeod and Lijia MacLeod, "On Grievance Street," *South China Morning Post,* September 25, 2000, p. 17.

248   have heard all these words before: Rural officials call words from central government leaders "conference" or "slogan" agriculture. See Thomas P. Bernstein, "Farmer Discontent and Regime Responses," in *The Paradox of China's Post-Mao Reforms,* eds. Merle Goldman and Roderick MacFarquhar (Cambridge, Massachusetts: Harvard University Press, 1999), p. 197.

248   forced to make fireworks: Many schools across rural China are severely strapped for funds, and this has led to the use of child labor to meet the cost of education. See, e.g., Robert J. Saiget, "Schools Around Rural China Hustling to Make Ends Meet," Agence France-Presse, March 7, 2001.

248   so they said: The official Xinhua News Agency carried the local officials' version of events. Before the central government began propagating the local story, however, the official *China Daily* ran a more credible, although still misleading, account of the tragic explosion. See Wang Ying, "Pupils and Teachers Die in School Explosion," *China Daily,* March 8, 2001, p. 3.

248   "They are eating our flesh, drinking our blood": Jasper Becker, "Reaping a Harvest of Despair," *South China Morning Post,* September 24, 2000, p. 11.

248   "The countryside is pretty unstable nowadays": Josephine Ma, "Rural Democracy Struggles to Survive," *South China Morning Post,* April 11, 2000, p. 8.

248   Ministry of Public Security says: "Workers Hold Protests over Unpaid Wages," *Hong Kong Standard,* January 1, 2000, p. 3.

249   "the sign of the end of a dynasty": Calum MacLeod and Lijia MacLeod, "On Grievance Street," *South China Morning Post,* September 25, 2000, p. 17.

249   "Historical experience": Premier Zhu Rongji, National Day Speech, China Central Television, September 30, 1999.

249   "They want people to see their power": John Pomfret, "In 2 Chinese Cities, Celebration and Contradiction," *Washington Post,* September 29, 1999, p. 1.

249 " 'Look, when is my turn?' ": Lee Kuan Yew, interview by Riz Khan, *Visions of China, Q&A in Shanghai,* CNN International, September 29, 1999.

249 CHINA IS AN UNSTOPPABLE FORCE: Farzam Kamalabadi, "China Is an Unstoppable Force," *China Daily,* March 20, 2000, p. 4.

250 "a chance to start some things over again": Billy Graham, interview by Larry King, *CNN 2000, Larry King Live Millennium,* CNN International, January 1, 2000.

251 "Our opinions mean nothing": "Impact of China WTO," *BizAsia,* narr. Rebecca MacKinnon, CNN International, September 19, 2000.

251 "cosmetically improved": *Visions of China, Insight Special Edition,* narr. Jonathan Mann, CNN International, September 30, 1999.

251 "There's a billion people": Christopher S. Shapland Tibbs, interview by author, Shanghai, June 2, 2000.

252 "This is the reaction": Susan V. Lawrence, "Stressful Summer," *Far Eastern Economic Review,* August 19, 1999, p. 16.

252 "Society moved on": *Cold War: Conclusions 1989–1991,* narr. Kenneth Branagh, CNN, July 2, 2000.

253 "It broke the dam": Ibid.

253 different route to rejuvenation: The Soviet Communist Party under Gorbachev sought to liberalize politics while tightly controlling the economy while the Chinese Communist Party under Deng and Jiang is trying the reverse. The important point is that China is not going far enough to restructure itself, just as the Soviet Union under Gorbachev failed to understand all that had to be done. Incomplete reform did not work in the Soviet Union, and it will fail in China too. That's why the essentials of the reform process in the Soviet Union and China are the same.

253 "What legacy do you want to leave": Daniel Kwan, "Look to Legacy, Urges Jiang," *South China Morning Post,* February 21, 2000, p. 7.

253 "leading us into the future": Erik Eckholm, "Becoming a Young Pioneer Is the Rite of Every Chinese Communist," *International Herald Tribune,* September 28, 1999, p. 6.

253 "Where is the goal?": *Born Under the Red Flag.*

253 "but sooner or later it will collapse": *Cold War: Conclusions 1989–1991,* narr. Kenneth Branagh, CNN, July 2, 2000.

12: Roads to Ruin

257 a "million truths": This phrase comes from the title of Linda Jakobson's book, *A Million Truths.*

257 Jason doesn't want to learn more Chinese: Yang Yuping, telephone interview by Lydia Chang, November 8, 2000.

259 "the fall of the Chinese Communist Party": Preface to Zhang Liang comp., *The Tiananmen Papers,* ed. Andrew J. Nathan and Perry Link (New York: PublicAffairs, 2001), p. xii. Zhang is correct but only in a literal sense. Of course, a united Party can defeat all challengers. Yet the existence of challengers—or even challenges—may split the Party when senior leaders cannot agree, for whatever reason, on what to do.

259 China's Foreign Ministry says: See "US Using Papers to Foment Chaos," *China Daily,*

January 10, 2001, p. 1. Although the central government announced that the documents are not genuine, just a few days after the announcement the Supreme People's Court issued an explanation of penalties for, among other things, leaking documents containing state secrets. See "Supreme People's Court Notice," *Legal Daily* (Beijing), January 22, 2001, p. 2.

260 "his biggest concern": John B. Stuttard, *The New Silk Road: Secrets of Business Success in China Today* (New York: John Wiley & Sons, 2000), p. 75. China's fifth census, conducted at the end of 2000, claims that China has a population of 1.29 billion people. See "China Issues Communique on Major Figures of Population," People's Daily Online, March 28, 2001.

260 China needs years: See, e.g., Greg Torode, "Invasion Would Fail, Says Admiral," *South China Morning Post*, March 9, 2000, p. 6.

260 loyalty to the Communist Party: These days the PLA devotes much of its energies to studying politics. See, e.g., Shi Yongcai, "Seriously Implement the Important 'Three Representatives' Thought, Further Strengthen Party Construction in the Army," *Liberation Army Daily* (Beijing), May 19, 2000, p. 1.

260 "Gentleness beats fortitude": Jason Blatt, "Chen Quotes Tao Sage to Justify Softer Line," *South China Morning Post*, April 17, 2000, p. 7.

261 "with their own blood and lives": Premier Zhu Rongji's annual press conference, China Central Television, March 15, 2000.

262 "Taiwan Leader Should Face Reality": "Taiwan Leader Should Face Reality," People's Daily Online, May 31, 2000.

262 "This is a reality": Chen Shui-bian, interview by Allen T. Cheng, " 'We Don't Want War,' " *Asiaweek*, March 17, 2000, p. 22.

262 "war is certain to break out": "Zhang Wannian: War Over Taiwan Strait Certain Within Next Five Years," *Oriental Daily* (Hong Kong), November 19, 2000, p. A7.

263 "Like a wolf": Alice Hung, "Chinese Dissidents Say Inspired by Taiwan Democracy," Reuters News Service, May 20, 2000.

263 can take the main island: "Jiang Warns Brash Generals," *South China Morning Post*, May 13, 2000, p. 1.

263 Jiang Zemin commissioned briefings: "Jiang Asks What Brings Collapse," *Far Eastern Economic Review*, June 8, 2000, p. 12.

263 the demise of the Soviet Union: See "The Strange Case of Karl and Adolf," *Economist*, September 11, 1999, 20th Century Survey, p. 8.

264 the time for an invasion is now: Willy Wo-Lap Lam, "PLA Main Beneficiary of Taiwan Deadlock," *South China Morning Post*, May 16, 2000, p. 8.

264 leaders think that war will be popular: See, e.g., Jiang Chen, "Poll Backs Stern Stance on Taiwan," *China Daily*, March 17, 2000, p. 2.

264 "We need a war, which we will lose": Christopher Coker, interview by author, Shanghai, May 15, 2000 (the comment in the text was made to Coker in Shanghai in May 2000).

264 "They consider the life of a Chinese worthless": Mark O'Neill, "Ignorance Feeds on Ignorance to Fuel Concern over Military Threat," *South China Morning Post*, March 27, 2000, Business Post, p. 4.

266 "We joined hands and waited for the tanks in dead silence": *Cold War: Conclusions 1989–1991*, narr. Kenneth Branagh, CNN, July 2, 2000.

266 "the world's most sophisticated crowd-control system": Simon Pritchard, "Uncertainty Lies Ahead for Most of Working Class," *South China Morning Post,* November 17, 1999, Business Post, p. 14.

267 "Still less should we use dictatorial means": Vivien Pik-Kwan Chan, "Zhu Warns of Difficult Year Ahead," *South China Morning Post,* March 6, 1999, p. 1.

267 "I stood there and cried silently": *Born Under the Red Flag.*

269 "Corruption angers the Chinese people": "China's Long March," *Visions of China, CNN Perspectives,* narr. Rebecca MacKinnon, CNN International, October 1, 1999.

269 "I hate to the marrow crooked officials": "Chinese Veteran Takes Protest to Beijing Rooftop," Reuters News Service, January 17, 2000.

270 protected by local government officials: See Li Yuxiao, "Questioning the Big Luoyang Fire," *Nanfang Zhoumo* (Guangzhou), January 4, 2001, p. 1.

270 Du died at his favorite nightclub: Chen Hui, "Bureau Chief Drunk Dead in Nightclub, Relatives' Farce Leads to Death," *Beijing Youth Daily,* November 19, 2000, p. 6.

271 HARSH SENTENCE SHOWS STATE'S RESOLUTION: "Death Penalty for Cheng," *China Daily,* August 1, 2000, p. 1.

271 "He should have involved Beijing leaders": Mark O'Neill, "Criminal and Mistress Easy Prey for Press Speculation," *South China Morning Post,* August 2, 2000, p. 18.

271 "can help avoid the appearance": "Cheng Kejie Unlikely to Rid of Death Penalty: Law Expert," People's Daily Online, August 2, 2000.

273 The state will be armed and the peasants will not: With or without arms, peasants fight. In the Jiangxi Province riots of August 2000, peasants fought heavily armed policemen with nothing more than farm tools. See Calum MacLeod and Lijia MacLeod, "On Grievance Street," *South China Morning Post,* September 25, 2000, p. 17. In the future, protesters need not want for arms because China is becoming flooded with them. See Jin Yan, "Guns, Where Are They From?," *Sanlian Weekly* (Shanghai), Issues 3 and 4, January 15, 2001, p. 42.

273 "All Chinese people have patience": Chen Shui-bian, interview by Karen Elliot House, Hugo Restall, and Russell Flannery, *Asian Wall Street Journal,* April 11, 2000, p. 12.

274 "This time the wolves really are coming": James Kynge, "Warning on WTO 'Shock' for China," *Financial Times* (London), November 20, 2000, p. 5.

275 "Even casinos have rules": Tiffany Wu, "Foreigners Welcome China Crackdown as Market Frets," Reuters News Service, February 11, 2001.

275 steam rooms of Shanghai: Li Jing, "Dark Side of Funds," *Caijing (Business & Finance Review),* October 2000, p. 20.

275 about 30 percent of the stocks: "Stocks, Lies and Manipulation," *Business China,* September 11, 2000, p. 4. "Almost every stock in China is manipulated," says Li Yue, a finance professor at People's University in Beijing. Karby Leggett, "Drive Against Manipulation Clouds China's Market Reforms," *Asian Wall Street Journal,* February 2, 2001, Money & Investing, p. M1.

276 the largest yearly loss: Karby Leggett, "Beijing to Save State Retailer with Debt Plan," *Asian Wall Street Journal,* December 4, 2000, p. 1.

276 The stock shot up about 31 percent: Karby Leggett, "Blind Rally: China Pumps Up a Stock Bubble," *Asian Wall Street Journal,* August 1, 2000, p. 1. Zhengzhou Baiwen is

not the only sick company to benefit from stock market boomlets. See Liu Shinan, "Bankruptcy vs Bail Out," *China Daily Business Weekly,* November 17, 2000, p. 10.

276 "We are resigned to the will of heaven": Mark O'Neill, "ZDS Staff Must Wait to See if Heaven Will Fall," *South China Morning Post,* November 20, 2000, Business Post, p. 5.

276 more than US$180 million: Karby Leggett, "Beijing to Save State Retailer with Debt Plan," *Asian Wall Street Journal,* December 4, 2000, p. 1.

276 bad companies must be chased out: On February 22, 2001, the CSRC issued rules for the delisting of loss-making companies. In general, a company posting losses for three straight years is subject to delisting under the new rules (as they were under existing law).

277 "the old style of doing things": William Kazer, "White Knight Saves Baiwen from Threat of Delisting," *South China Morning Post,* December 2, 2000, Business Post, p. 4 (comment of Chen Tiwei, a consultant specializing in corporate reorganizations).

277 "immense risk": Ba Wei, "Financial Risk: Out of the Safety Zone," *China Information News* (Beijing), November 8, 2000, p. 1.

277 "investors will take to the streets": Karby Leggett, "Blind Rally: China Pumps Up a Stock Bubble," *Asian Wall Street Journal,* August 1, 2000, p. 1.

277 they've grown: See, e.g., "China's Stock Market Ranks Sixth in the World in Market Value," People's Daily Online, February 22, 2001.

277 at least that many listed companies that are failing: Liu Shinan, "Bankruptcy vs Bail Out," *China Daily Business Weekly,* November 17, 2000, p. 10.

277 accession to the World Trade Organization: Suzanne Harrison, "Survival of the Fittest as Firms Face Uncertain Future After WTO Entry," *South China Morning Post,* September 8, 2000, Business Post, p. 2.

277 "irregular": Chen Rong, interview by Lydia Chang, Shanghai, May 25, 2000. Chen said that the markets had been "irregular" when they were established and they are "irregular" today. His conclusion is that China itself is "irregular."

277 especially acute: China's markets will fall in a 1929-style crash, according to three prominent economists, because of the lack of institutional safeguards. See Mark O'Neill, "Economists Fear Regulation Void Will Lead to Crash," *South China Morning Post,* March 9, 2001, Business Post, p. 5.

279 "We were not ready": *Cold War: Conclusions 1989–1991,* narr. Kenneth Branagh, CNN, July 2, 2000.

280 "but there is nothing which may not happen": Diana Preston, "A Conspiracy of Triads," review of *The Dragon Syndicates* by Martin Booth, *Asian Wall Street Journal,* August 8, 2000, p. 6.

280 "In this sort of situation": *Cold War: Conclusions 1989–1991,* narr. Kenneth Branagh, CNN, July 2, 2000.

281 "A political party, no matter how hard it tries": Chen Shui-bian, interview by Mark L. Clifford, "China 'Must Learn from [My] Election,'" *Business Week,* August 14, 2000, p. 50.

282 "The trouble is the trouble we make ourselves": Wang Chuanning, interview by author, New York, June 21, 2000.

Epilogue: The State Begins to Disintegrate

283 Shi Yuanyuan: See Clara Li, "Tiny Survivor's Blackened and Battered Body Testifies to Nightmare," *South China Morning Post,* March 18, 2001, p. 1.

283 possibly the worst terrorist act: Xinhua News Agency says that 108 people died, but most assessments indicated that the toll is at least twice that number. The final count will not be known for some time due to efforts by local and central government officials to control the reporting of news.

Index

ABOUT THE AUTHOR

GORDON CHANG has lived and worked in China for almost two decades, most recently in Shanghai as counsel to the American law firm Paul, Weiss, Rifkind, Wharton & Garrison. His articles on China have been published in *The New York Times, The Asian Wall Street Journal,* the *Far Eastern Economic Review,* the *International Herald Tribune,* and the *South China Morning Post.* He lives with his wife, Lydia, in Shanghai. This is his first book.

ABOUT THE TYPE

This book was set in Perpetua, a typeface designed by the English artist Eric Gill, and cut by The Monotype Corporation between 1928 and 1930. Perpetua is a contemporary face of original design, without any direct historical antecedents. The shapes of the roman letters are derived from the techniques of stonecutting. The larger display sizes are extremely elegant and form a most distinguished series of inscriptional letters.